Top-Down Network Design

Third Edition

Priscilla Oppenheimer

Cisco Press

800 East 96th Street

Indianapolis, IN 46240

Top-Down Network Design, Third Edition

Priscilla Oppenheimer

Published by:
Cisco Press
800 East 96th Street
Indianapolis, IN 46240 USA

Printed in the United States of America

First Printing August 2010

Library of Congress Cataloging-in-Publication data is on file.

ISBN-13: 978-1-58720-283-4

ISBN-10: 1-58720-283-2

Warning and Disclaimer

Trademark Acknowledgments

Corporate and Government Sales

The publisher offers excellent discounts on this book when ordered in quantity for bulk purchases or special sales, which may include electronic versions and/or custom covers and content particular to your business, training goals, marketing focus, and branding interests. For more information, please contact:
U.S. Corporate and Government Sales   1-800-382-3419   corpsales@pearsontechgroup.com

For sales outside the United States please contact: International Sales   international@pearsoned.com

Feedback Information

At Cisco Press, our goal is to create in-depth technical books of the highest quality and value. Each book is crafted with care and precision, undergoing rigorous development that involves the unique expertise of members from the professional technical community.

Readers' feedback is a natural continuation of this process. If you have any comments regarding how we could improve the quality of this book, or otherwise alter it to better suit your needs, you can contact us through email at feedback@ciscopress.com. Please make sure to include the book title and ISBN in your message.

We greatly appreciate your assistance.

Publisher: Paul Boger

Associate Publisher: Dave Dusthimer

Executive Editor: Mary Beth Ray

Managing Editor: Sandra Schroeder

Senior Development Editor: Christopher Cleveland

Senior Project Editor: Tonya Simpson

Editorial Assistant: Vanessa Evans

Composition: Mark Shirar

Indexer: Tim Wright

Manager, Global Certification: Erik Ullanderson

Business Operation Manager, Cisco Press: Anand Sundaram

Technical Editors: Keith Nabozny, Joe Wilson

Copy Editor: Bill McManus

Book Designer: Louisa Adair

Proofreader: Apostrophe Editing Services

Americas Headquarters
Cisco Systems, Inc.
San Jose, CA

Asia Pacific Headquarters
Cisco Systems (USA) Pte. Ltd.
Singapore

Europe Headquarters
Cisco Systems International BV
Amsterdam, The Netherlands

Cisco has more than 200 offices worldwide. Addresses, phone numbers, and fax numbers are listed on the Cisco Website at **www.cisco.com/go/offices.**

CCDE, CCENT, Cisco Eos, Cisco HealthPresence, the Cisco logo, Cisco Lumin, Cisco Nexus, Cisco StadiumVision, Cisco TelePresence, Cisco WebEx, DCE, and Welcome to the Human Network are trademarks; Changing the Way We Work, Live, Play, and Learn and Cisco Store are service marks; and Access Registrar, Aironet, AsyncOS, Bringing the Meeting To You, Catalyst, CCDA, CCDP, CCIE, CCIP, CCNA, CCNP, CCSP, CCVP, Cisco, the Cisco Certified Internetwork Expert logo, Cisco IOS, Cisco Press, Cisco Systems, Cisco Systems Capital, the Cisco Systems logo, Cisco Unity, Collaboration Without Limitation, EtherFast, EtherSwitch, Event Center, Fast Step, Follow Me Browsing, FormShare, GigaDrive, HomeLink, Internet Quotient, IOS, iPhone, iQuick Study, IronPort, the IronPort logo, LightStream, Linksys, MediaTone, MeetingPlace, MeetingPlace Chime Sound, MGX, Networkers, Networking Academy, Network Registrar, PCNow, PIX, PowerPanels, ProConnect, ScriptShare, SenderBase, SMARTnet, Spectrum Expert, StackWise, The Fastest Way to Increase Your Internet Quotient, TransPath, WebEx, and the WebEx logo are registered trademarks of Cisco Systems, Inc. and/or its affiliates in the United States and certain other countries.

All other trademarks mentioned in this document or website are the property of their respective owners. The use of the word partner does not imply a partnership relationship between Cisco and any other company. (0812R)

About the Author

Priscilla Oppenheimer has been developing data communications and networking systems since 1980 when she earned her master's degree in information science from the University of Michigan. After many years as a software developer, she became a technical instructor and training developer and has taught more than 3000 network engineers from most of the Fortune 500 companies. Her employment at such companies as Apple Computer, Network General, and Cisco gave her a chance to troubleshoot real-world network design problems and the opportunity to develop a practical methodology for enterprise network design. Priscilla was one of the developers of the Cisco Internetwork Design course and the creator of the Designing Cisco Networks course. Priscilla teaches network design, configuration, and troubleshooting around the world and practices what she preaches in her network consulting business.

About the Technical Reviewers

Keith Nabozny is a technology consultant with HP, an adjunct professor at Macomb Community College, and a graduate of Oakland University in Rochester, Michigan. He has three Cisco professional certifications and is a Certified Information Systems Security Professional (CISSP). Keith has supported large corporate clients for the past 14 years in operations, implementation, and engineering roles. He is currently supporting the firewalls of a major manufacturer with locations around the world. Most recently he taught network design and troubleshooting classes at Macomb Community College. Keith and his family live in Southeast Michigan.

Joe Wilson, MSCS, PMC, CISSP No. 100304, is a senior network design engineer for TelcoCapital Systems, LLC. TelcoCapital is a leading provider of Cisco Unified Communications solutions for small and medium-sized enterprises. Joe is completing his dissertation toward a PhD in information technology at Capella University (Minneapolis, MN), with specializations in college teaching and IT security and assurance. Joe has worked in information technology for the past 20 years and is a retired systems engineer from The Boeing Company in Seattle, Washington, where he designed airborne NMS solutions for commercial aircraft. While working for AT&T Broadband Network Solutions as a broadband systems engineer, Joe designed commercial broadband networks using advanced communications technologies such as ATM, SONET, DWDM, and Gigabit Ethernet. Joe has been a CISSP since 2006 and has distinguished himself as a trusted partner in providing secure communications solutions and services to public and private organizations. Joe teaches courses in the Cisco Networking Academy program at DeVry University in Federal Way, Washington.

Dedication

To my parents, Dr. Stephen T. Worland, PhD, and Mrs. Roberta Worland, MS. They gave me an appreciation for knowledge, logic, and analysis, and taught me that "where there's a will, there's a way."

Acknowledgments

I would like to thank Mary Beth Ray, executive editor at Cisco Press, for giving me the opportunity to update this book and for marshaling the people and resources needed to complete the project. I would especially like to thank Christopher Cleveland, Tonya Simpson, and Bill McManus for their hard work on the book. I am also grateful for the work of the technical editors, Keith Nabozny and Joe Wilson. In many ways, updating a book is even harder than writing it in the first place, and I couldn't have done it without the help of Chris, Tonya, Bill, Keith, and Joe.

I also wish to thank the technical editors for the first two editions, Matthew Birkner, Blair Buchanan, Dr. Peter Welcher, Dr. Alex Cannara, David Jansson, and Hank Mauldin. Their terrific contributions are still evident in the third edition.

I would like to thank other networking professionals who have inspired me over the years, including Joseph Bardwell and Anita Lenk from Connect802, Laura Chappell and her terrific Wireshark University, Howard Berkowitz, Paul Borghese, John Neiberger, Leigh Anne Chisholm, Marty Adkins, Matthias David Moore, Tom Lisa, Scott Vermillion, and many more.

I am grateful for my colleagues and students in Ashland, Oregon, who have inspired and entertained me, including Dr. Lynn Ackler, Jeff McJunkin, Andrew Krug, Brandon Kester, Stephen Perkins, Daniel DeFreeze, Christina Kaiserman, Nicole Colbert, Corey Smith, Stefan Hutchison, Jesse Williamson, Jonathan McCoy, Jennifer Comstock, Linda Sturgeon, Kathleen Marrs, Vinnie Moscaritolo, Louis Kowolowski, and Robert Luaders for his ideas regarding the design scenarios.

I'd like to thank Gary Rubin, Rob Stump, and Kip Peterson from Advanced Network Information for the many opportunities they've given me over the years, in particular the terrific opportunity to work at Cisco. To my colleagues at Cisco, Patrick Stark, our manager, Lisa Bacani, Walt Sacharok, Dax Mickelson, David Daverso, and Paul Azzi; you are terrific!

Finally, I would like to thank Alan Oppenheimer, who throughout this project acted as my technical advisor, therapist, chef, and best friend. I'm glad he doesn't mind that it was finally time to remove AppleTalk.

Contents at a Glance

Contents

Icons Used in This Book

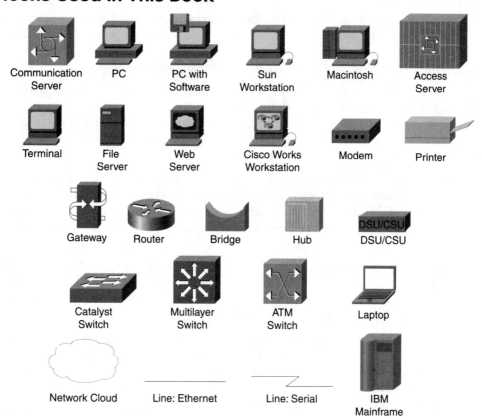

Command Syntax Conventions

The conventions used to present command syntax in this book are the same conventions used in the Cisco IOS Command Reference. The Command Reference describes these conventions as follows:

- **Boldface** indicates commands and keywords that are entered literally as shown. In actual configuration examples and output (not general command syntax), boldface indicates commands that are manually input by the user (such as a **show** command).

- *Italic* indicates arguments for which you supply actual values.

- Vertical bars (|) separate alternative, mutually exclusive elements.

- Square brackets ([ ]) indicate an optional element.

- Braces ({ }) indicate a required choice.

- Braces within brackets ([{ }]) indicate a required choice within an optional element.

Introduction

New business practices are driving changes in enterprise networks. The transition from an industrial to an information economy has changed how employees do their jobs, and the emergence of a global economy of unprecedented competitiveness has accelerated the speed at which companies must adapt to technological and financial changes.

To reduce the time to develop and market products, companies are empowering employees to make strategic decisions that require access to sales, marketing, financial, and engineering data. Employees at corporate headquarters and in worldwide field offices, and telecommuters in home offices, need immediate access to data, regardless of whether the data is on centralized or departmental servers.

To develop, sell, and distribute products into domestic and foreign markets, businesses are forming alliances with local and international partners. Businesses are carefully planning their network designs to meet security goals while also offering network access to resellers, vendors, customers, prospective customers, and contract workers located all over the world.

To accommodate increasing requirements for remote access, security, bandwidth, scalability, and reliability, vendors and standards bodies introduce new protocols and technologies at a rapid rate. Network designers are challenged to develop state-of-the-art networks even though the state of the art is continually changing.

Whether you are a novice network designer or a seasoned network architect, you probably have concerns about how to design a network that can keep pace with the accelerating changes in the internetworking industry. The goal of this book is to teach a systematic design methodology that can help you meet an organization's requirements, regardless of the newness or complexity of applications and technologies.

Objectives

The purpose of *Top-Down Network Design*, Third Edition, is to help you design networks that meet a customer's business and technical goals. Whether your customer is another department within your own company or an external client, this book provides you with tested processes and tools to help you understand traffic flow, protocol behavior, and internetworking technologies. After completing this book, you will be equipped to design enterprise networks that meet a customer's requirements for functionality, capacity, performance, availability, scalability, affordability, security, and manageability.

Audience

This book is for you if you are an internetworking professional responsible for designing and maintaining medium- to large-sized enterprise networks. If you are a network engineer, architect, or technician who has a working knowledge of network protocols and technologies, this book will provide you with practical advice on applying your knowledge to internetwork design.

This book also includes useful information for consultants, systems engineers, and sales engineers who design corporate networks for clients. In the fast-paced presales environment of many systems engineers, it often is difficult to slow down and insist on a top-down, structured systems analysis approach. Wherever possible, this book includes shortcuts and assumptions that can be made to speed up the network design process.

Finally, this book is useful for undergraduate and graduate students in computer science and information technology disciplines. Students who have taken one or two courses in networking theory will find *Top-Down Network Design*, Third Edition, an approachable introduction to the engineering and business issues related to developing real-world networks that solve typical business problems.

Changes for the Third Edition

Networks have changed in many ways since the second edition was published. Many legacy technologies have disappeared and are no longer covered in the book. In addition, modern networks have become multifaceted, providing support for numerous bandwidth-hungry applications and a variety of devices, ranging from smart phones to tablet PCs to high-end servers.

Modern users expect the network to be available all the time, from any device, and to let them securely collaborate with coworkers, friends, and family. Networks today support voice, video, high-definition TV, desktop sharing, virtual meetings, online training, virtual reality, and applications that we can't even imagine that brilliant college students are busily creating in their dorm rooms.

As applications rapidly change and put more demand on networks, the need to teach a systematic approach to network design is even more important than ever. With that need in mind, the third edition has been retooled to make it an ideal textbook for college students. The third edition features review questions and design scenarios at the end of each chapter to help students learn top-down network design.

To address new demands on modern networks, the third edition of *Top-Down Network Design* also has updated material on the following topics:

- Network redundancy

- Modularity in network designs

- The Cisco SAFE security reference architecture

- The Rapid Spanning Tree Protocol (RSTP)

- Internet Protocol version 6 (IPv6)

- Ethernet scalability options, including 10-Gbps Ethernet and Metro Ethernet

- Network design and management tools

Organization

This book is built around the steps for top-down network design. It is organized into four parts that correspond to the major phases of network design.

Part I: Identifying Your Customer's Needs and Goals

Part I covers the requirements-analysis phase. This phase starts with identifying business goals and technical requirements. The task of characterizing the existing network, including the architecture and performance of major network segments and devices, follows. The last step in this phase is to analyze network traffic, including traffic flow and load, protocol behavior, and quality of service (QoS) requirements.

Part II: Logical Network Design

During the logical network design phase, the network designer develops a network topology. Depending on the size of the network and traffic characteristics, the topology can range from simple to complex, requiring hierarchy and modularity. During this phase, the network designer also devises a network layer addressing model and selects switching and routing protocols. Logical design also includes security planning, network management design, and the initial investigation into which service providers can meet WAN and remote-access requirements.

Part III: Physical Network Design

During the physical design phase, specific technologies and products that realize the logical design are selected. Physical network design starts with the selection of technologies and devices for campus networks, including cabling, Ethernet switches, wireless access points, wireless bridges, and routers. Selecting technologies and devices for remote-access and WAN needs follows. Also, the investigation into service providers, which began during the logical design phase, must be completed during this phase.

Part IV: Testing, Optimizing, and Documenting Your Network Design

The final steps in top-down network design are to write and implement a test plan, build a prototype or pilot, optimize the network design, and document your work with a network design proposal. If your test results indicate any performance problems, during this phase you should update your design to include such optimization features as traffic shaping and advanced router queuing and switching mechanisms. A glossary of networking terms concludes the book.

Companion Website

Top-Down Network Design, Third Edition, has a companion website at www.topdownbook.com. The companion website includes updates to the book, links to white papers, and supplemental information about design resources.

Identifying Your Customer's Needs and Goals

Chapter 1

Analyzing Business Goals and Constraints

This chapter serves as an introduction to the rest of the book by describing top-down network design. The first section explains how to use a systematic, top-down process when designing computer networks for your customers. Depending on your job, your customers might consist of other departments within your company, those to whom you are trying to sell products, or clients of your consulting business.

After describing the methodology, this chapter focuses on the first step in top-down network design: analyzing your customer's business goals. Business goals include the capability to run network applications to meet corporate business objectives, and the need to work within business constraints, such as budgets, limited networking personnel, and tight timeframes.

This chapter also covers an important business constraint that some people call the eighth layer of the Open System Interconnection (OSI) reference model: workplace politics. To ensure the success of your network design project, you should gain an understanding of any corporate politics and policies at your customer's site that could affect your project.

The chapter concludes with a checklist to help you determine if you have addressed the business issues in a network design project.

Using a Top-Down Network Design Methodology

According to Albert Einstein:

> "The world we've made as a result of the level of thinking we have done thus far creates problems that we cannot solve at the same level at which we created them."

To paraphrase Einstein, networking professionals have the ability to create networks that are so complex that when problems arise they can't be solved using the same sort of thinking that was used to create the networks. Add to this the fact that each upgrade, patch, and modification to a network can also be created using complex and sometimes convoluted thinking, and you soon realize that the result is a network that is hard to understand and troubleshoot. A network created with this complexity often doesn't perform as well as expected, doesn't scale as the need for growth arises (as it almost always does), and doesn't match a customer's requirements. A solution to this problem is to use a streamlined, systematic methodology in which the network or upgrade is designed in a top-down fashion.

Many network design tools and methodologies in use today resemble the "connect-the-dots" game that some of us played as children. These tools let you place internetworking devices on a palette and connect them with LAN or WAN media. The problem with this methodology is that it skips the steps of analyzing a customer's requirements and selecting devices and media based on those requirements.

Good network design must recognize that a customer's requirements embody many business and technical goals, including requirements for availability, scalability, affordability, security, and manageability. Many customers also want to specify a required level of network performance, often called a *service level*. To meet these needs, difficult network design choices and tradeoffs must be made when designing the logical network before any physical devices or media are selected.

When a customer expects a quick response to a network design request, a bottom-up (connect-the-dots) network design methodology can be used, if the customer's applications and goals are well known. However, network designers often think they understand a customer's applications and requirements only to discover, after a network is installed, that they did not capture the customer's most important needs. Unexpected scalability and performance problems appear as the number of network users increases. These problems can be avoided if the network designer uses top-down methods that perform requirements analysis before technology selection.

Top-down network design is a methodology for designing networks that begins at the upper layers of the OSI reference model before moving to the lower layers. The top-down methodology focuses on applications, sessions, and data transport before the selection of routers, switches, and media that operate at the lower layers.

The top-down network design process includes exploring organizational and group structures to find the people for whom the network will provide services and from whom the designer should get valuable information to make the design succeed.

Top-down network design is also iterative. To avoid getting bogged down in details too quickly, it is important to first get an overall view of a customer's requirements. Later, more detail can be gathered on protocol behavior, scalability requirements, technology preferences, and so on. Top-down network design recognizes that the logical model and the physical design can change as more information is gathered.

Because top-down methodology is iterative, some topics are covered more than once in this book. For example, this chapter discusses network applications. Chapter 4, "Characterizing Network Traffic," covers network applications in detail, with emphasis on network traffic caused by application- and protocol-usage patterns. A top-down approach enables a network designer to get "the big picture" first before spiraling downward into detailed technical requirements and specifications.

Using a Structured Network Design Process

Top-down network design is a discipline that grew out of the success of structured software programming and structured systems analysis. The main goal of structured systems analysis is to more accurately represent users' needs, which unfortunately often are ignored or misrepresented. Another goal is to make the project manageable by dividing it into modules that can be more easily maintained and changed.

Structured systems analysis has the following characteristics:

- The system is designed in a top-down sequence.

- During the design project, several techniques and models can be used to characterize the existing system, determine new user requirements, and propose a structure for the future system.

- A focus is placed on data flow, data types, and processes that access or change the data.

- A focus is placed on understanding the location and needs of user communities that access or change data and processes.

- A logical model is developed before the physical model. The logical model represents the basic building blocks, divided by function, and the structure of the system. The physical model represents devices and specific technologies and implementations.

- Specifications are derived from the requirements gathered at the beginning of the top-down sequence.

With large network design projects, modularity is essential. The design should be split functionally to make the project more manageable. For example, the functions carried out in campus LANs can be analyzed separately from the functions carried out in remote-access networks, virtual private networks (VPN), and WANs.

Cisco recommends a modular approach with its three-layer hierarchical model. This model divides networks into core, distribution, and access layers. The Cisco SAFE architecture, which is discussed in Part II of this book, "Logical Network Design," is another modular approach to network design.

With a structured approach to network design, each module is designed separately, yet in relation to other modules. All the modules are designed using a top-down approach that focuses on requirements, applications, and a logical structure before the selection of physical devices and products to implement the design.

Systems Development Life Cycles

Systems analysis students are familiar with the concept that typical systems are developed and continue to exist over a period of time, often called a systems development life cycle. Many systems analysis books use the acronym SDLC to refer to the system's life cycle, which might sound strange to older networking students who know SDLC as Synchronous Data Link Control, a bit-oriented, full-duplex protocol used on synchronous serial links, often found in a legacy Systems Network Architecture (SNA) environment. Nevertheless, it's important to realize that most systems, including network systems, follow a cyclical set of phases, where the system is planned, created, tested, and optimized.

Feedback from the users of the system causes the system to then be redesigned or modified, tested, and optimized again. New requirements arise as the network opens the door to new uses. As people get used to the new network and take advantage of the services it offers, they soon take it for granted and expect it to do more.

In this book, network design is divided into four major phases that are carried out in a cyclical fashion:

- **Analyze requirements:** In this phase, the network analyst interviews users and technical personnel to gain an understanding of the business and technical goals for a new or enhanced system. The task of characterizing the existing network, including the logical and physical topology and network performance, follows. The last step in this phase is to analyze current and future network traffic, including traffic flow and load, protocol behavior, and quality of service (QoS) requirements.

- **Develop the logical design:** This phase deals with a logical topology for the new or enhanced network, network layer addressing, naming, and switching and routing protocols. Logical design also includes security planning, network management design, and the initial investigation into which service providers can meet WAN and remote access requirements.

- **Develop the physical design:** During the physical design phase, specific technologies and products that realize the logical design are selected. Also, the investigation into service providers, which began during the logical design phase, must be completed during this phase.

- **Test, optimize, and document the design:** The final steps in top-down network design are to write and implement a test plan, build a prototype or pilot, optimize the network design, and document your work with a network design proposal.

These major phases of network design repeat themselves as user feedback and network monitoring suggest enhancements or the need for new applications. Figure 1-1 shows the network design and implementation cycle.

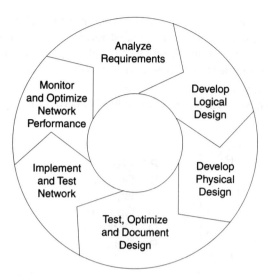

Figure 1-1   *Network Design and Implementation Cycle*

Plan Design Implement Operate Optimize (PDIOO) Network Life Cycle

Cisco documentation refers to the Plan Design Implement Operate Optimize (PDIOO) set of phases for the life cycle of a network. It doesn't matter which life cycle you use, as long as you realize that network design should be accomplished in a structured, planned, modular fashion, and that feedback from the users of the operational network should be fed back into new network projects to enhance or redesign the network. The PDIOO life cycle includes the following steps:

■ **Plan:** Network requirements are identified in this phase. This phase also includes an analysis of areas where the network will be installed and an identification of users who will require network services.

■ **Design:** In this phase, the network designers accomplish the bulk of the logical and physical design, according to requirements gathered during the plan phase.

■ **Implement:** After the design has been approved, implementation begins. The network is built according to the design specifications. Implementation also serves to verify the design.

■ **Operate:** Operation is the final test of the effectiveness of the design. The network is monitored during this phase for performance problems and any faults to provide input into the optimize phase of the network life cycle.

■ **Optimize:** The optimize phase is based on proactive network management that identifies and resolves problems before network disruptions arise. The optimize phase may lead to a network redesign if too many problems arise because of design errors or as network performance degrades over time as actual use and capabilities diverge. Redesign can also be required when requirements change significantly.

■ **Retire:** When the network, or a part of the network, is out-of-date, it might be taken out of production. Although Retire is not incorporated into the name of the life cycle (PDIOO), it is nonetheless an important phase. The retire phase wraps around to the plan phase. The PDIOO life cycle repeats as network requirements evolve.

Figure 1-2 shows a graphical representation of the Cisco PDIOO network life cycle.

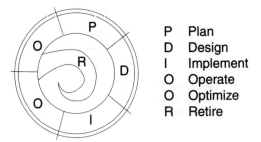

P   Plan
D   Design
I   Implement
O   Operate
O   Optimize
R   Retire

Figure 1-2   *PDIOO Network Life Cycle*

Analyzing Business Goals

Understanding your customer's business goals and constraints is a critical aspect of network design. Armed with a thorough analysis of your customer's business objectives, you can propose a network design that will meet with your customer's approval.

It is tempting to overlook the step of analyzing business goals, because analyzing such technical goals as capacity, performance, security, and so on is more interesting to many network engineers. Chapter 2, "Analyzing Technical Goals and Tradeoffs," covers analyzing technical goals. In this chapter, you learn the importance of analyzing *business* goals, and you pick up some techniques for matching a network design proposal to a customer's business objectives.

Working with Your Client

Before meeting with your customer to discuss business goals for the network design project, it is a good idea to research your client's business. Find out what industry the client is in. Learn something about the client's market, suppliers, products, services, and competitive advantages. With the knowledge of your customer's business and its external relations, you can position technologies and products to help strengthen the customer's status in the customer's own industry.

In your first meeting with your customers, ask them to explain the organizational structure of the company. Your final internetwork design will probably reflect the corporate structure, so it is a good idea to gain an understanding of how the company is structured in departments, lines of business, vendors, partners, and field or remote offices. Understanding the corporate structure can help you locate major user communities and characterize traffic flow. Chapter 4 covers traffic flow in more detail. Understanding the corporate structure can also help you understand the corporate culture, which can affect the network design. For example, a company with a centralized management structure might require that products and vendors be chosen by headquarters management. A decentralized company might let branch offices have more say.

Note   Understanding the corporate structure can also help you recognize the management hierarchy. One of your primary goals in the early stages of a network design project should be to determine who the decision makers are. Who will have the authority to accept or reject your network design proposal? Sometimes, this can be a rather complicated issue, as discussed in the section "Politics and Policies," later in this chapter.

Ask your customer to state an overall goal of the network design project. Explain that you want a short, business-oriented statement that highlights the business purpose of the new network. Why is the customer embarking on this new network design project? For what will the new network be used? How will the new network help the customer be more successful in the customer's business?

After discussing the overall business goals of the network design project, ask your customer to help you understand the customer's criteria for success. What goals must be met for the customer to be satisfied? Sometimes success is based on operational savings because the new network allows employees to be more productive. Sometimes success is based on the ability to increase revenue or build partnerships with other companies. Make sure you know upfront how "success" is defined by executives, managers, end users, network engineers, and any other stakeholders. Also, determine whether the customer's definition of success will change as yearly fiscal goals change.

In addition to determining the criteria for success, you should ascertain the consequences of failure:

- What will happen if the network design project fails or if the network, when installed, does not perform to specification?

- How visible is the project to upper-level management?

- Will the success (or possible failure) of the project be visible to executives?

- To what extent could unforeseen behavior of the new network disrupt business operations?

In general, gather enough information to feel comfortable that you understand the extent and visibility of the network design project.

You should try to get an overall view of whether the new network is critical to the business's mission. Investigate the ramifications of the network failing or experiencing problems. Chapter 2 discusses the details of performance and reliability analysis, but at this point in the design process, you should start addressing these issues. (Remember that top-down network design is iterative. Many network design requirements are addressed more than once.)

Changes in Enterprise Networks

Enterprise networks at many corporations have been undergoing major changes. The value of making vast amounts of data available to employees, customers, and business partners has been recognized. Corporate employees, field employees, contract employees, and telecommuters need access to sales, marketing, engineering, and financial data, regardless of whether the data is stored on centralized or distributed servers or mainframes. Suppliers, vendors, and customers also need access to many types of data.

A network that is used by only internal users is no longer the norm at many companies. Companies are seeking ways to build networks that more closely resemble modern organizations. Many modern organizations are based on an open, collaborative environment that provides access to information and services for many different constituents, including customers, prospective customers, vendors, suppliers, and employees.

To remain competitive, companies need ways to reduce product development time and take advantage of just-in-time manufacturing principles. A lot of companies achieve these goals by partnering with suppliers and by fostering an online, interactive relationship with their suppliers. An example is automobile manufacturing. Instead of producing every automobile component in-house, many manufacturers contract with partners who specialize in specific components and technologies. For example, one partner might produce the engine while another produces the body. If all the partners can access data and services on the manufacturer's network, production costs are reduced, just-in-time manufacturing can be accomplished, and it is easier to plan around component shortages. The ability to share information saves time and money for the automobile manufacturer and for its partners.

A network designer must carefully consider requirements for extending the network to outside users. For security reasons, external access should not mean full network access. Using a modular approach to network design is important here so that a clear boundary exists between the enterprise's private networks and the portions of the internetwork that partners can access.

Networks Must Make Business Sense

Although in the past many companies made "technology for technology's sake" choices, this is no longer the case. Business leaders are more involved in Information Technology (IT) decisions than they once were, and IT managers rely on business managers to help them prioritize and fund IT projects. Network upgrades are made not because some new technology sounds interesting to the engineers, but because it will help an enterprise increase profits, productivity, market share, and cash flow. Network designers must choose solutions that address the business dilemmas faced by business managers.

Network applications have become mission critical. Despite this trend, large budgets for networking and telecommunications operations have been reduced at some companies.

Many companies have gone through difficult reengineering projects to reduce operational costs and are still looking for ways to manage networks with fewer resources and to reduce the recurring costs of WAN circuits.

Companies are researching ways to make their data centers more efficient in their usage of power, cabling, racks, storage, and WAN circuits. Companies seek to reduce data center costs and to make data centers more "green" (whereby energy usage is reduced). Data center managers have discovered that many of their servers' CPUs are underutilized. A major trend in enterprise network design is server virtualization, where one hardware platform supports multiple virtual servers. Instead of many underutilized hardware boxes, there are now just a few hardware boxes, each of which supports multiple virtual servers. Each virtual server looks and acts just like a physical server, including a fully functional operating system and one or more applications.

Streamlining processes and protocols has also led to an increased use of IP telephony and to the continued convergence of voice and data networks. To save money and to reduce the need for specialized data or voice engineers, companies continue to adopt IP telephony technologies. In previous network designs, telecommunications and voice networks were separate. Telecommunications engineers knew little about data networks, and data communications engineers didn't know the difference between a time-division multiplexer (TDM) and a tandem switching system (TSS). In today's environment, voice, data, and video networks are merged.

Networks Offer a Service

Modern IT departments are more service-oriented than they used to be. To meet the needs of their customers, IT departments are spending more time analyzing and documenting their processes for delivering services. A focus on processes helps to ensure effective service delivery and to avoid wasted expenditures on technology that doesn't provide a needed service.

As a network designer, you might find yourself working with IT architects who adhere to the IT Service Management (ITSM) discipline. ITSM defines frameworks and processes that can help an organization match the delivery of IT services with the business needs of the organization. ITSM focuses on processes rather than technology and helps an IT organization think of its users as valued customers rather than problem-generating adversaries. A version of ITSM is documented in the Information Technology Infrastructure Library (ITIL), a series of books published by the United Kingdom Office of Government Commerce (OGC), each of which covers an IT management topic. The details of ITSM and ITIL are outside the scope of this book, but it is worth noting that both ITSM and top-down network design address the need to align the delivery of IT services to the business needs of an organization. This book will help you design networks that comply with ITSM practices.

Other trends in IT management that affect network design are related to governance and compliance. *Governance* refers to a focus on consistent, cohesive decisions, policies, and processes that protect an organization from mismanagement and illegal activities of users of IT services. *Compliance* refers to adherence to regulations that protect against fraud and inadvertent disclosure of private customer data. For example, in the United States, retail organizations must comply with the Payment Card Industry Data Security Standard (PCI DSS) and healthcare organizations must comply with the Health Insurance Portability and Accountability Act (HIPAA).

The Need to Support Mobile Users

Notebook computers have finally become small enough to carry around, and workers now expect to get work done at home, on the train, in hotels, in meeting rooms, at customer sites, and even while having their morning latte at the local coffee shop. Notebook computers ship with wireless networking built in to facilitate users getting work done outside the office.

It shouldn't matter (to the user anyway) where data is and in what format. Network users expect network performance to be uniform, regardless of where the user or data resides. A user should be able to read email on a cell phone, for example, and read voice mail from a web browser while sipping coffee in an Internet cafe. Users should have secure and reliable access to tools and data wherever they are. The challenge for network designers is to build networks that allow data to travel in and out of the enterprise network from various wired and wireless portals without picking up any viruses and without being read by parties for whom it was not intended.

One of the biggest trends in network design is *virtual private networking (VPN)*, where private networks make use of the Internet to reach remote locations or possibly other organizations. Customers getting involved in VPN projects have concerns about security, reliable and predictable performance, and data throughput requirements. Chapter 5, "Designing a Network Topology," covers VPNs in greater detail.

Network architectures are taking on a virtual and ubiquitous form for users, while remaining highly structured and managed from the network engineers' point of view. The designer is challenged to develop secure, resilient, and manageable solutions that enable users to work efficiently and securely wherever they are physically located.

The Importance of Network Security and Resiliency

Network security has filtered to the top of the list of business goals at many companies. Although security was always important, it has become even more important as networks become indispensable and as tools for breaking into networks become ubiquitous. Enterprises must protect their networks from both the unsophisticated "script kiddies" and from more advanced attacks launched by criminals or political enemies. There is also a continued requirement to protect networks from Trojan horses and viruses.

Many enterprise managers now report that the network must be available 99.999 percent of the time. Although this goal might not be achievable without expensive redundancy in staff and equipment, it might be a reasonable goal for companies that would experience a severe loss of revenue or credibility if the network were down for even short periods of time. This goal is linked to goals for security, as the network can't be available if security breaches and viruses are disabling network devices and applications. When security and operational problems occur, networks must recover quickly. Networks must be resilient. More than ever, IT and business managers require high-availability and resiliency features for their network equipment and protocols, as they realize the extent to which network downtime can jeopardize business success.

In addition to security, another goal that has filtered to the top of the list of business goals is the need for business continuity during and after a disaster. Companies that have survived hurricanes, earthquakes, fires, and terrorist attacks have learned the importance of a disaster recovery plan that promotes business continuity despite the loss of critical network devices and services. Many companies have not had the misfortune of learning these lessons the hard way but are nonetheless embarking on network design projects with the goal of developing a network that will recover quickly if a natural or unnatural disaster occurs.

One aspect of analyzing a customer's business goals is the process of analyzing vulnerabilities related to disasters and the impact on business operations. Help your customer determine which network capabilities are critical and which facilities provide them. Consider how much of the network could be damaged without completely disrupting the company's mission. Determine whether other locations in the company are prepared to take on mission-critical functions.

In the past few years, networks have become more interconnected and complex, which can make meeting goals for business continuity and network resiliency more difficult. Many enterprise networks are linked to telecommuter home networks, branch-office networks, extranets that offer access to business partners and customers, and the Internet. The diversity and quantity of portals into the enterprise network pose many security and stability risks. On the other hand, geographical diversity of mission-critical capabilities has turned out to be a lifesaver for some companies hit with disaster. One reason that *The Wall Street Journal* was able to publish its newspaper the day after the 9/11 attacks was because it had learned from 1990s power outages about the need to disperse critical functions across many different sites.

In the current business environment, security and disaster recovery should be considered with every network design choice, and the network designer must propose solutions that provide resiliency and stability. A systematic and modular design process, as taught in this book, is even more important than it once was, as networks become increasingly more complex and vital to an organization's success.

Typical Network Design Business Goals

After considering the changes in business strategies and enterprise networking discussed in the previous sections, it is possible to list some typical network design business goals:

- Increase revenue and profit
- Increase market share

- Expand into new markets

- Increase competitive advantages over companies in the same market

- Reduce costs

- Increase employee productivity

- Shorten product-development cycles

- Use just-in-time manufacturing

- Plan around component shortages

- Offer new customer services

- Offer better customer support

- Open the network to key constituents (prospects, investors, customers, business partners, suppliers, and employees)

- Avoid business disruption caused by network security problems

- Avoid business disruption caused by natural and unnatural disasters

- Modernize outdated technologies

- Reduce telecommunications and network costs, including overhead associated with separate networks for voice, data, and video

- Make data centers more efficient in their usage of power, cabling, racks, storage, and WAN circuits

- Comply with IT architecture design and governance goals

Identifying the Scope of a Network Design Project

One of the first steps in starting a network design project is to determine its scope. Some of the most common network design projects these days are small in scope—for example, projects to allow a few people in a sales office to access the enterprise network via a VPN. On the other hand, some design projects are large in scope. Ask your customer to help you understand if the design is for a single network segment, a set of LANs, a set of WANs or remote-access networks, or the entire enterprise network. Also ask your customer if the design is for a new network or a modification to an existing one.

Explain to your customer any concerns you have about the scope of the project, including technical and business concerns. Subsequent sections in this chapter discuss politics and scheduling, which are tightly linked to the scope of a network design project. (Many network designers have learned the hard way what happens when you don't help your customers match the schedules of their projects to the scope.)

Make sure your customers tell you everything they can about the network and the design project. You might want to poke around outside the stated scope of the project, just to make sure nothing essential has been omitted. Double-check that you have gathered all the requirements and that you have accurate information about sites, links, and devices. If the project addresses network security, make sure you know about all external links, including any legacy dial-in access.

Note Designers rarely get a chance to design a network from scratch. Usually a network design project involves an upgrade to an existing network. However, this is not always the case. Some senior network designers have developed completely new next-generation networks to replace old networks. Other designers have designed networks for a new building or new campus. Even in these cases, however, the new network usually has to fit into an existing infrastructure—for example, a new campus network that has to communicate with an existing WAN. Where there is an existing network, the design project must include plans for migrating to the new design with minimal disruption and risk.

When analyzing the scope of a network design, you can refer to the seven layers of the OSI reference model to specify the types of functionality the new network design must address. For example, you might decide that the design project is concerned only with network layer matters such as routing and IP addressing. Or you might decide that the design also concerns the application layer because the focus is on voice applications, such as Interactive Voice Response (IVR), which directs customers to the correct location in a call center, or unified messaging, where email can be retrieved via voice mail and text messages can be converted into speech. Figure 1-3 shows the OSI reference model.

Layer 7	Application
Layer 6	Presentation
Layer 5	Session
Layer 4	Transport
Layer 3	Network
Layer 2	Data Link
Layer 1	Physical

Figure 1-3 *Open System Interconnection (OSI) Reference Model*

In addition to using the OSI reference model, this book also uses the following terms to define the scope of a network and the scope of a network design project:

- **Segment:** A single network bounded by a switch or router and based on a particular Layer 1 and Layer 2 protocol such as Fast Ethernet.

- **LAN:** A set of switched segments based on a particular Layer 2 protocol such as Fast Ethernet and an interswitch trunking protocol such as the IEEE 802.1Q standard.

- **Building network:** Multiple LANs within a building, usually connected to a building-backbone network.

- **Campus network:** Multiple buildings within a local geographical area (within a few miles), usually connected to a campus-backbone network.

- **Remote access:** Networking solutions that support individual remote users or small remote branch offices accessing the network.

- **WAN:** A geographically dispersed network including point-to-point, Frame Relay, ATM, and other long-distance connections.

- **Wireless network:** A LAN or WAN that uses the air (rather than a cable) for its medium.

- **Enterprise network:** A large and diverse network, consisting of campuses, remote-access services, and one or more WANs or long-range LANs. An enterprise network is also called an *internetwork*.

Identifying a Customer's Network Applications

At this point in the design process, you have identified your customer's business goals and the scope of the project. It is now time to focus on the real reason networks exist: applications. The identification of your customer's applications should include both current applications and new applications. Ask your customer to help you fill out a chart, such as the one in Table 1-1.

> **Note**   Table 1-1 identifies network applications. In Chapters 2 and 4, it will be enhanced to include technical requirements and network-traffic characteristics. At this point, your goal is simply to identify network applications.

Table 1-1   *Network Applications*

Name of Application	Type of Application	New Application? (Yes or No)	Criticality	Comments

For Name of Application, simply use a name that your customer gives you. This could be an industry-standard name, such as Lotus Notes, or it could be an application name that means something only to the customer (especially for a home-grown application). For new applications, the name might be a code name for a software-development project.

For Type of Application, you can use any appropriate text that describes the type of application, or you can classify the application as one of the following standard network applications:

- Email

- File transfer, sharing, and access

- Database access and updating

- Web browsing

- Network game

- Remote terminal

- Calendar

- Medical imaging

- Videoconferencing

- Video on demand (VoD)

- Scheduled multicast video

- Surveillance and security camera video

- Internet or intranet voice (IP telephony)

- Internet or intranet fax

- Sales order entry

- Management reporting

- Sales tracking

- Computer-aided design

- Document imaging

- Inventory control and shipping

- Telemetry

- Interactive Voice Response (IVR)

- Unified messaging

- Desktop publishing

- Web publishing

- Electronic whiteboard

- Terminal emulation

- Online directory (phone book)

- Distance learning

- Point of sales (retail store)

- Electronic commerce

- Financial modeling

- Human resources management

- Computer-aided manufacturing

- Process control and factory floor

The preceding list includes user applications. The chart in Table 1-1 should also include *system* applications. (Or if you prefer, you can do a separate chart for system applications.) System applications include the following types of network services:

- User authentication and authorization

- Host naming and name resolution

- Dynamic host addressing

- Remote booting

- Remote configuration download

- Directory services

- Network backup

- Network management

- Software distribution

In the Criticality column of the Network Applications chart, you can give each application a ranking from 1 to 3 with the following meanings:

1. Extremely critical

2. Somewhat critical

3. Not critical

Later, you can gather more specific information on mission criticality, including precisely how much downtime is acceptable (if the customer can quantify availability requirements).

In the Comments column, add any observations relevant to the network design. For example, include any information you have about corporate directions, such as plans to stop using an application in the future or specific rollout schedules and regional-use plans.

Analyzing Business Constraints

In addition to analyzing business goals and determining your customer's need to support new and existing applications, it is important to analyze any business constraints that will affect your network design.

Politics and Policies

It has been said that there are two things not to talk about with friends: politics and religion. It would be nice if you could escape discussing office politics and technological religion (technology preferences) with a network design customer, but avoiding these topics puts your project at risk.

In the case of office politics, your best bet is to listen rather than talk. Your goal is to learn about any hidden agendas, turf wars, biases, group relations, or history behind the project that could cause it to fail. In some cases, a similar project was already tried and didn't work. You should determine if this has happened in your case and, if it has, the reasons why the project failed or never had a chance to come to fruition.

Pay attention to personnel issues that could affect the project. Which manager or managers started the project and how much do they have at stake? Are there any managers, network engineers, or users who want the project to fail for any reason? Find out who your advocates and opponents are. In some cases, no matter how technically sound your network design is, there will be people who have a negative reaction to it.

Be sure to find out if your project will cause any jobs to be eliminated. Some network design projects involve automating tasks that were once done by highly paid workers. These workers obviously will have reasons to want the project to fail.

Find out if there is a strategic business or IT plan. Does your network design need to fit into an overall architecture that is based on strategic planning? Are there external regulatory or governmental pressures on the planning process or on the architecture? These sorts of pressures can often lead to messy political battles that can affect your network design.

Be prepared for the possibility of formidable office politics if your network design project involves the merging of voice and data networks. Voice experts and data experts have traditionally lived in their own worlds. They might face each other with some mistrust and fear for the future. You can often reduce the uncertainty by running short IP telephony seminars for voice technicians and traditional telephony seminars for the data network administrators.

While working with a client, you will gain a feeling for the client's business style. One aspect of style that is important to understand is tolerance to risk. Is risk taking rewarded in the company, or are most people afraid of change? Knowing the employment history of the decision makers will help you select appropriate technologies. The employment history of the decision makers affects their tolerance to risk and their biases toward certain technologies. Understanding these issues will help you determine whether your network design should be conservative or if it can include new, state-of-the art technologies and processes.

Another aspect of the client's business style has to do with testing the design. At some companies, the testers might claim they have carefully tested a new Voice over IP (VoIP) implementation, for example, when what they actually did was get a VoIP call to complete. Your idea of testing, on the other hand, might be to make numerous calls under various load conditions. See Chapter 12, "Testing Your Network Design," for more information on testing.

You need to discuss with your customer any policies about protocols, standards, and vendors. Try to learn of any "forbidden technologies" where the users or network engineers have decided, possibly for the wrong reasons, that a particular protocol is slow or unstable.

Find out whether the company has standardized on any transport, routing, desktop, or other protocols. Determine whether there is any doctrine regarding open versus proprietary solutions. Find out if there are any policies on approved vendors or platforms. In many cases, a company has already chosen technologies and products for the new network, and your design must fit into the plans. Ask your customer if there are any policies regarding distributed authority for network design and implementation. For example, are there departments that control their own internetworking purchases? Find out if departments and end users are involved in choosing their own applications. Make sure you know who the decision makers are for your network design project.

A lot of organizations need to implement policies in response to legal, regulatory, or contractual requirements. In the United States, Generally Accepted Accounting Principles (GAAP) drive many accounting policies. In the medical profession, network designs might be affected by security and privacy policies that are regulated by HIPAA. In other parts of the world, network equipment choices may be regulated by governmental Postal, Telegraph, and Telephone (PTT) organizations.

In the rush to get to technical requirements, network designers sometimes ignore nontechnical issues, which is a mistake. Many brilliant network designs have been rejected by a customer because the designer focused on the lower layers of the OSI reference model and forgot about company politics and technical biases.

Budgetary and Staffing Constraints

Your network design must fit the customer's budget. The budget should include allocations for equipment purchases, software licenses, maintenance and support agreements, testing, training, and staffing. The budget might also include consulting fees (including your fees) and outsourcing expenses.

Throughout the project, work with your customer to identify requirements for new personnel, such as additional network managers. Point out the need for personnel training, which will affect the budget for the project.

In general, it is a good idea to analyze the abilities of the networking staff. How much in-house expertise is there? Should you recommend any training or outsourcing for network operations and management? The technologies and protocols that you recommend will depend on the abilities of internal staff. It is not a good idea to recommend a complex routing protocol, such as Open Shortest Path First (OSPF), for example, if the engineering staff is just starting to learn internetworking concepts (unless you also recommend a comprehensive training plan).

Analyzing in-house expertise is especially important and challenging for companies that merge their voice and data networks. Consider the need to train the traditional voice experts on data technologies and the data experts on voice technologies. Also, implementing voice and video often requires advanced QoS knowledge that may necessitate training.

To ensure the success of your project, determine who controls the network budget—the Information Systems (IS) department, network managers, or users' departments? How much control do users and groups have over network expenditures? Are there any departmental charge-back schemes?

Regardless of who controls the budget, one common network design goal is to contain costs. Reduced budgets or limited resources often force network designers to select the most affordable solution instead of the best solution. It is useful to know the areas in which the network design can be changed with the least effect on performance to meet budget requirements. Chapter 2 discusses typical tradeoffs that must be made to meet the goal of affordability while achieving good performance and reliability.

If possible, work with your customer to develop a return on investment (ROI) analysis for the network design. Make a business case to the customer that explains how quickly the new network will pay for itself, due to reduced operational costs, improved employee productivity, or the enabling of higher revenue potential and market expansion.

Project Scheduling

An additional business-oriented topic that you should review with your customer is the timeframe for the network design project. When is the final due date and what are the intermediate and major milestones? In most cases, management of the project schedule is the customer's obligation, not yours, but you should ask the customer to give you a copy of the schedule and to keep you informed about any slips in the schedule.

Note   It's important to include intermediate milestones in the project schedule. They give you and your client a way to detect slips in the schedule.

Consider the state of building wiring, which might be poor quality and not support new applications. If the wiring needs to be replaced, this will have a major impact on the schedule. Also, be sure to include circuit disconnect or circuit capacity changes in the project schedule. There is often a long lead time for these changes. Plan to document when the circuit changes and other major changes take place so that if problems occur, you can analyze what has changed to help you troubleshoot.

Many tools exist for developing a schedule that includes milestones, resource assignments, critical-path analysis, and so on. Take a look at these aspects of the schedule and voice your view on whether the schedule is practical, considering what you have learned about the scope of the project. An aggressive implementation schedule might require a reduction in the scope of the project or a reduction in the quality of the planning and testing that will be conducted. During the technical-analysis stage and the logical- and physical-design phases of the project, be sure to keep the schedule in mind. As you iteratively develop a concrete understanding of the technical scope of the network design project, point out any concerns you have about the schedule.

Business Goals Checklist

You can use the following checklist to determine if you have addressed your client's business-oriented objectives and concerns. If you can't gather every piece of data mentioned in the checklist, make sure you document what is missing in case it becomes critical, but don't stall the project to gather every last detail. This book teaches an ideal network design methodology that you should try to follow, but if real-world constraints, such as uncooperative network design customers, budget cuts, and time constraints, hamper your ability to follow the methodology precisely, just follow it as much as you can. In general, the methodology still works even if some data is missing after you do your analysis.

❑   I have researched the customer's industry and competition.

❑   I understand the customer's corporate structure.

❑   I have compiled a list of the customer's business goals, starting with one overall business goal that explains the primary purpose of the network design project.

❑   The customer has identified any mission-critical operations.

❑   I understand the customer's criteria for success and the ramifications of failure.

❑   I understand the scope of the network design project.

❑   I have identified the customer's network applications (using the Network Applications chart).

❑   The customer has explained policies regarding approved vendors, protocols, or platforms.

❑   The customer has explained any policies regarding open versus proprietary solutions.

❑   The customer has explained any policies regarding distributed authority for network design and implementation.

❑   I know the budget for this project.

❑   I know the schedule for this project, including the final due date and major milestones, and I believe it is practical.

❑   I have a good understanding of the technical expertise of my clients and any relevant internal or external staff.

❑   I have discussed a staff-education plan with the customer.

❑   I am aware of any office politics that might affect the network design.

Summary

This chapter covered typical network design business goals and constraints. It also talked about the top-down process for gathering information on goals, and the importance of using systematic methods for network design. Using systematic methods will help you keep pace with changing technologies and customer requirements. The next chapter covers analyzing technical goals and constraints.

This chapter also talked about the importance of analyzing your customer's business style, tolerance to risk, biases, and technical expertise. You should also work with your customer to understand the budget and schedule for the network design project to make sure the deadlines and milestones are practical.

Finally, you need to start gaining an understanding of your client's corporate structure. Understanding the corporate structure will help you analyze data flow and develop a network topology, which usually parallels the corporate structure. It will also help you identify the managers who will have the authority to accept or reject your network design, which will help you prepare and present your network design appropriately.

Review Questions

1.   Why is it important to use a structured, systematic method for designing networks? What problems can occur if such methods are not used?

2.   Compare and contrast the top-down network design method shown in Figure 1-1 with the PDIOO method shown in Figure 1-2.

3.   Why is it important to explore divisional and group structures of an organization when starting a network design project?

4.   The "Networks Offer a Service" section mentioned ITSM and ITIL. Research these topics in more detail. What are ITSM and ITIL? How can a network design project benefit from the principles of ITSM? How might ITSM impede a network design project?

Design Scenario

You are a network consultant who has been asked to attend an initial meeting with the executive management team of ElectroMyCycle, LLC. ElectroMyCycle manufactures motorcycles. Its new electric motorcycle was just picked up by a large retail chain. ElectroMyCycle is upgrading its manufacturing capacity and hiring new employees.

Recently, ElectroMyCycle employees have started saying, "The Internet is slow." They are also experiencing problems sending email, accessing web-based applications, and printing. In the past, when the company was small, it didn't have these problems. The operations manager outsourced computer services to a local business called Network Rogues, which installed new workstations and servers as needed, provided desktop support, and managed the switches, router, and firewall. ElectroMyCycle is now considering bringing computer services in-house and is wondering how its network should evolve as it increases production of its electric motorcycle.

1.   What research will you do before your initial meeting with the executive management team?

2.   What general problems does ElectroMyCycle seem to be experiencing? What network design principles may have been ignored when Network Rogues designed and operated the existing network?

3.   List four major stakeholders for a new network design for ElectroMyCycle. For each stakeholder, list some design goals, constraints, and biases.

4.   List five questions you will pose to the executive management team. Why will you pose those questions?

Chapter 2

Analyzing Technical Goals and Tradeoffs

This chapter provides techniques for analyzing a customer's technical goals for a new network design or network upgrade. Analyzing your customer's technical goals can help you confidently recommend technologies that will perform to your customer's expectations.

Typical technical goals include scalability, availability, network performance, security, manageability, usability, adaptability, and affordability. Of course, there are tradeoffs associated with these goals. For example, meeting strict requirements for performance can make it hard to meet a goal of affordability. The section "Making Network Design Tradeoffs" later in this chapter discusses tradeoffs in more detail.

One of the objectives of this chapter is to give you terminology that will help you discuss technical goals with your customer. Network designers and users have many terms for technical goals, and, unfortunately, many different meanings for the terms. This chapter can help you choose terminology that has technical merit and is understandable by business and IT customers.

This chapter concludes with a checklist to help you determine whether you have addressed all your customer's technical goals and constraints.

Scalability

Scalability refers to how much growth a network design must support. For many enterprise network design customers, scalability is a primary goal. Many large companies add users, applications, additional sites, and external network connections at a rapid rate. The network design you propose to a customer should be able to adapt to increases in network usage and scope.

Planning for Expansion

Your customer should help you understand how much the network will expand in the next year and in the next 2 years. (Ask your customer to analyze goals for growth in the next 5 years also, but be aware that not many companies have a clear 5-year vision.)

You can use the following list of questions to analyze your customer's short-term goals for expansion:

- How many more sites will be added in the next year? The next 2 years?

- How extensive will the networks be at each new site?

- How many more users will access the corporate internetwork in the next year? The next 2 years?

- How many more servers will be added to the internetwork in the next year? The next 2 years?

Expanding Access to Data

Chapter 1, "Analyzing Business Goals and Constraints," talked about a common business goal of expanding access to data for employees who use enterprise networks. Managers empower employees to make strategic decisions that require access to sales, marketing, engineering, and financial data. In the 1970s and early 1980s, this data was stored on mainframes. In the late 1980s and the 1990s, this data was stored on servers in departmental LANs. Today, this data is again stored on centralized mainframes and servers.

In the 1990s, networking books and training classes taught the 80/20 rule for capacity planning: 80 percent of traffic stays local in departmental LANs, and 20 percent of traffic is destined for other departments or external networks. This rule is no longer universal and is rapidly moving to the other side of the scale. Many companies have centralized servers residing in data centers. In addition, corporations increasingly implement intranets that enable employees to access centralized web servers using Internet Protocol (IP) technologies.

At some companies, employees can access intranet web servers to arrange business travel, search online phone directories, order equipment, and attend distance-learning training classes. The web servers are centrally located, which breaks the classic 80/20 rule.

As Chapter 1 also mentioned, there has been a trend of companies connecting internetworks with other companies to collaborate with partners, resellers, suppliers, and strategic customers. The term *extranet* is sometimes used to describe an internal internetwork that is accessible by outside parties. If your customer has plans to implement an extranet, you should document this in your list of technical goals so that you can design a topology and provision bandwidth appropriately.

In the 1980s and 1990s, mainframes running Systems Network Architecture (SNA) protocols stored most of a company's financial and sales data. In recent years, the value of making this data available to more than just financial analysts has been recognized. The business goal of making data available to more departments often results in a technical goal of using the mainframe as an incredibly powerful database server.

The business goal of making more data available to users results in the following technical goals for scaling and upgrading corporate enterprise networks:

- Connect separated departmental LANs into the corporate internetwork.

- Solve LAN/WAN bottleneck problems caused by large increases in internetwork traffic.

- Provide centralized servers that reside in a data center.

- Make mainframe data accessible to the enterprise IP network.

- Add new sites to support field offices and telecommuters.

- Add new sites and services to support secure communication with customers, suppliers, resellers, and other business partners.

Constraints on Scalability

When analyzing a customer's scalability goals, it is important to keep in mind that there are impediments to scalability inherent in networking technologies. Selecting technologies that can meet a customer's scalability goals is a complex process with significant ramifications if not done correctly. For example, selecting a flat network topology with Layer 2 switches can cause problems as the number of users scales, especially if the users' applications or network protocols send numerous broadcast frames. (Switches forward broadcast frames to all connected segments.)

Subsequent chapters in this book consider scalability again. Chapter 4, "Characterizing Network Traffic," discusses the fact that network traffic (for example, broadcast traffic) affects the scalability of a network. Part II, "Logical Network Design," provides details on the scalability of routing and switching protocols. Part III, "Physical Network Design," provides information on the scalability of LAN and WAN technologies and internetworking devices. Remember that top-down network design is an iterative process. Scalability goals and solutions are revisited during many phases of the network design process.

Availability

Availability refers to the amount of time a network is available to users and is often a critical goal for network design customers. Availability can be expressed as a percent uptime per year, month, week, day, or hour, compared to the total time in that period. For example, in a network that offers 24-hour, 7-days-a-week service, if the network is up 165 hours in the 168-hour week, availability is 98.21 percent.

Network design customers don't use the word *availability* in everyday English and have a tendency to think it means more than it does. In general, availability means how much time the network is operational. Availability is linked to reliability but has a more specific meaning (percent uptime) than reliability. Reliability refers to a variety of issues, including accuracy, error rates, stability, and the amount of time between failures.

Note   Sometimes network engineers classify *capacity* as part of availability. The thinking is that even if a network is available at Layer 1 (the physical layer), it is not available from a user's point of view if there is not enough capacity to send the user's traffic.

For example, Asynchronous Transfer Mode (ATM) has a connection admission control function that regulates the number of cells allowed into an ATM network. If the capacity and quality of service (QoS) requested for a connection are not available, cells for the connection are not allowed to enter the network. This problem could be considered an availability issue. However, this book classifies capacity with performance goals. Availability is considered simply a goal for percent uptime.

Availability is also linked to redundancy, but redundancy is not a network goal. Redundancy is a solution to a goal of high availability. Redundancy means adding duplicate links or devices to a network to avoid downtime. Redundant network topologies are becoming increasingly important for many network design customers who want to ensure business continuity after a major fault or disaster. Chapter 5, "Designing a Network Topology," covers designing redundant network topologies in more detail.

Availability is also associated with *resiliency*, which is a word that is becoming more popular in the networking field. Resiliency means how much stress a network can handle and how quickly the network can rebound from problems including security breaches, natural and unnatural disasters, human error, and catastrophic software or hardware failures. A network that has good resiliency usually has good availability.

Disaster Recovery

Most large institutions have recognized the need for a plan to sustain business and technical operations after natural disasters, such as floods, fires, hurricanes, and earthquakes. Also, some large enterprises (especially service providers) must plan how to recover from satellite outages. Satellite outages can be caused by meteorite storms, collisions with space debris, solar flares, or system failures. Unfortunately, institutions have also found the need to specify a recovery plan for unnatural disasters, such as bombs, terrorist attacks, riots, or hostage situations. A disaster recovery plan includes a process for keeping data backed up in one or more places that are unlikely to be hit by disaster, and a process for switching to backup technologies if the main technologies are affected by a disaster.

Although this book doesn't cover the details of disaster recovery planning, the concepts in this book can be applied to the process of planning for a disaster. Not surprisingly, a top-down approach is recommended, with an emphasis on planning before implementing. One goal of the planning process should be to recognize which parts of the network are critical and must be backed up. A good understanding of the organization's business purpose is needed to understand which devices, network links, applications, and people are critical. As is the case with top-down network design, business goals must be analyzed before selecting technologies and devices that will be one component of the implementation.

Note   Don't underestimate the importance of having enough staff to activate a disaster recovery plan. Have you figured out what to do if the disaster involves a serious disease where the server and network administrators need to be quarantined? This could be a justification for providing high-speed VPN access from workers' homes and testing that capability before a disaster strikes.

One of the most important steps in disaster recovery planning is testing. Not only must the technology be tested, but employees must be drilled on the actions they should take in a disaster. If the people don't survive, the technology won't help much. Also, people should practice working with the network in the configuration it will likely have after a disaster when redundant servers or sites are in use. Although employees might object to emergency drills, especially if they are too frequent, periodic practice is a necessary part of achieving business continuity when a real disaster hits. The drills should be taken seriously and should be designed to include time and stress pressures to simulate the real thing.

Specifying Availability Requirements

You should encourage your customers to specify availability requirements with precision. Consider the difference between an uptime of 99.70 percent and an uptime of 99.95 percent. An uptime of 99.70 percent means the network is down 30 minutes per week, which is not acceptable to many customers. An uptime of 99.95 percent means the network is down 5 minutes per week, which might be acceptable, depending on the type of business. Availability requirements should be specified with at least two digits following the decimal point.

It is also important to specify a timeframe with percent uptime requirements. Go back to the example of 99.70 percent uptime, which equated to 30 minutes of downtime per week. A downtime of 30 minutes in the middle of a working day is probably not acceptable. But a downtime of 30 minutes every Saturday evening for regularly scheduled maintenance might be fine.

Not only should your customers specify a timeframe with percent uptime requirements, they should also specify a time unit. Availability requirements should be specified as uptime per year, month, week, day, or hour. Consider an uptime of 99.70 percent again. This uptime means 30 minutes of downtime during a week. The downtime could be all at once, which could be a problem if it's not during a regularly scheduled maintenance window, or it could be spread out over the week. An uptime of 99.70 percent could mean that approximately every hour the network is down for 10.70 seconds. Will users notice a downtime of 10.70 seconds? Certainly some users will, but for some applications, a downtime of 10.70 seconds every hour is tolerable. Availability goals must be based on output from the first network design step of analyzing business goals, where you gained an understanding of the customer's applications.

Five Nines Availability

Although the examples cited so far use numbers in the 99.70 to 99.95 percent range, many companies require higher availability, especially during critical time periods. Some customers might insist on a network uptime of 99.999 percent, which is sometimes referred to as *five nines availability*. For some customers, this requirement might be linked to a particular business process or timeframe. For example, the requirement might refer to the monthly closing of financial records or to the holiday season for a company that sells holiday gifts via catalog and web orders. On the other hand, some design customers might need, or think they need, five nines availability all the time.

Five nines availability is extremely hard to achieve. You should explain to a network design customer that to achieve such a level, redundant equipment and links will be necessary, as will extra staffing possibly, and extremely reliable hardware and software. Some managers will back down from such a requirement when they hear the cost, but, for others, the goal might be appropriate. If a company would experience a severe loss of revenue or reputation if the network were not operational for even short periods of time, five nines availability is a reasonable goal.

Many hardware manufacturers specify 99.999 percent uptime for their devices and operating systems and have real customer examples where this level of uptime was achieved. This might lead a naive network design customer to assume that a complex internetwork can also have 99.999 percent uptime without too much extra effort or cost. Achieving such a high level on a complex internetwork, however, is much more difficult than achieving it for particular components of the internetwork. Potential failures include carrier outages, faulty software in routers and switches, an unexpected and sudden increase in bandwidth or server usage, configuration problems, human errors, power failures, security breaches, and software glitches in network applications.

Note   Some networking experts say that 80 to 90 percent of failures are due to human errors, either errors made by local administrators or errors made by service provider employees (or the infamous backhoe operator). Avoiding and recovering from human errors requires skill and good processes. You need smart people thinking about availability all the time and processes that are precise without stifling thought. Good network management and troubleshooting play a role. Network management tools should provide immediate alerts upon failures and enough information for a network administrator to make a quick fix.

Consider a network that is used 24 hours a day for 365 days per year. This equates to 8760 hours. If the network can be down only 0.001 percent of the time, it can be down for only 0.0876th of an hour or about 5 minutes per year. If the customer says the network must be available 99.999 percent of the time, you better make it clear that this doesn't include regularly scheduled maintenance time, or you better make sure that the network will have the capability to support in-service upgrades. In-service upgrades refer to mechanisms for upgrading network equipment and services without disrupting operations. Most internetworking vendors sell high-end internetworking devices that include hot-swappable components for in-service upgrading.

For situations where hot-swapping is not practical, it might be necessary to have extra equipment so there's never a need to disable services for maintenance. In some networks, each critical component has triple redundancy, with one being active, one in hot standby ready to be used immediately, and one in standby or maintenance. With triple redundancy, you can bring a standby router down to upgrade or reconfigure it. After it is upgraded, you can then designate it as the hot standby, and take the previous hot standby down and upgrade it. You can then switch from the active to the hot standby and upgrade the active.

Depending on the network design, you might load share among the redundant components during normal operations. The key design decision is whether your users can accept degraded performance when some of the components are unusable. If all this sounds too complicated or expensive, another possibility is not to do it all yourself but put resources at collocation centers that can amortize the highly redundant equipment over many customers.

The Cost of Downtime

In general, a customer's goal for availability is to keep mission-critical applications running smoothly, with little or no downtime. A method to help you, the network designer, and your customer understand availability requirements is to specify a cost of downtime. For each critical application, document how much money the company loses per hour of downtime. (For some applications, such as order processing, specifying money lost per minute might have more impact.) If network operations will be outsourced to a third-party network management firm, explaining the cost of downtime can help the firm understand the criticality of applications to a business's mission. Specifying the cost of downtime can also help clarify whether in-service upgrades or triple redundancy must be supported.

Mean Time Between Failure and Mean Time to Repair

In addition to expressing availability as the percent of uptime, you can define availability as a mean time between failure (MTBF) and mean time to repair (MTTR). You can use MTBF and MTTR to calculate availability goals when the customer wants to specify explicit periods of uptime and downtime, rather than a simple percent uptime value.

MTBF is a term that comes from the computer industry and is best suited to specifying how long a computer or computer component will last before it fails. When specifying availability requirements in the networking field, MTBF is sometimes designated with the more cumbersome phrase *mean time between service outage* (MTBSO), to account for the fact that a network is a service, not a component. Similarly, MTTR can be replaced with the phrase *mean time to service repair (MTTSR)*. This book uses the simpler and better-known terms MTBF and MTTR.

A typical MTBF goal for a network that is highly relied upon is 4000 hours. In other words, the network should not fail more often than once every 4000 hours or 166.67 days. A typical MTTR goal is 1 hour. In other words, the network failure should be fixed within 1 hour. In this case, the mean availability goal is as follows:

4000 / 4001 = 99.98 percent

A goal of 99.98 percent is typical for many companies.

When specifying availability using MTBF and MTTR, the equation to use is as follows:

Availability = MTBF / (MTBF + MTTR)

Using this availability equation allows a customer to clearly state the acceptable frequency and length of network outages.

Remember that what is calculated is the mean. The variation in failure and repair times can be high and must be considered as well. It is not enough to just consider mean rates, especially if you depend on external service agents (vendors or contractors) who are not under your tight control. Also, be aware that customers might need to specify different MTBF and MTTR goals for different parts of a network. For example, the goals for the core of the enterprise network are probably much more stringent than the goals for a switch port that affects only one user.

Although not all customers can specify detailed application requirements, it is a good idea to identify availability goals for specific applications, in addition to the network as a whole. Application availability goals can vary widely depending on the cost of downtime. For each application that has a high cost of downtime, you should document the acceptable MTBF and MTTR.

For MTBF values for specific networking components, you can generally use data supplied by the vendor of the component. Most router, switch, and hub manufacturers can provide MTBF and MTTR figures for their products. You should also investigate other sources of information, such as trade publications, to avoid any credibility problems with figures published by manufacturers. Search for variability figures and mean figures. Also, try to get written commitments for MTBF, MTTR, and variability values from the providers of equipment and services.

Network Performance

When analyzing technical requirements for a network design, you should isolate your customer's criteria for accepting the performance of a network, including throughput, accuracy, efficiency, delay, and response time.

Many mathematical treatises have been written on network performance. This book approaches network performance in a practical and mostly nonmathematical way, avoiding the daunting equations that appear in mathematical treatments of performance. Although the equations are much simpler than they seem, they are usually not necessary for understanding a customer's goals. The objective of this section is to offer an uncomplicated view of network performance, including real-world conclusions you can draw when there is no time to do a mathematical analysis.

Analyzing a customer's network performance goals is tightly tied to analyzing the existing network, which is covered in Chapter 3, "Characterizing the Existing Internetwork." Analyzing the existing network can help you determine what changes need to be made to meet performance goals. Network performance goals are also tightly linked to scalability goals. You should gain an understanding of plans for network growth before analyzing performance goals.

Network Performance Definitions

Many network design customers cannot quantify their performance goals beyond, "It has to work with no complaints from users." If this is the case, you can make assumptions about throughput, response time, and so on. On the other hand, some customers have specific performance requirements, based on a service level that has been agreed upon with network users.

The following list provides definitions for network performance goals that you can use when analyzing precise requirements:

- **Capacity (bandwidth):** The data-carrying capability of a circuit or network, usually measured in bits per second (bps)

- **Utilization:** The percent of total available capacity in use

- **Optimum utilization:** Maximum average utilization before the network is considered saturated

- **Throughput:** Quantity of error-free data successfully transferred between nodes per unit of time, usually seconds

- **Offered load:** Sum of all the data all network nodes have ready to send at a particular time

- **Accuracy:** The amount of useful traffic that is correctly transmitted, relative to total traffic

- **Efficiency:** An analysis of how much effort is required to produce a certain amount of data throughput

- **Delay (latency):** Time between a frame being ready for transmission from a node and delivery of the frame elsewhere in the network

- **Delay variation:** The amount of time average delay varies

- **Response time:** The amount of time between a request for some network service and a response to the request

Optimum Network Utilization

Network utilization is a measurement of how much bandwidth is used during a specific time period. Utilization is commonly specified as a percentage of capacity. For example, a network-monitoring tool might state that network utilization on an Ethernet segment is 30 percent, meaning that 30 percent of the capacity is in use.

Network-analysis tools use varying methods for measuring bandwidth usage and averaging the usage over elapsed time. Usage can be averaged every millisecond, every second, every minute, every hour, and so on. Some tools use a weighted average whereby more recent values are weighted more prominently than older values. Chapter 3 discusses measuring network utilization in more depth.

Your customer might have a network design goal for the maximum average network utilization allowed on a segment. Actually, this is a design constraint more than a design goal. The design constraint states that if utilization on a segment is more than a predefined threshold, the segment should be divided into multiple segments or bandwidth must be added.

Optimum average network utilization is about 70 percent. A 70 percent threshold for average utilization means that peaks in network traffic can probably be handled without obvious performance degradation. Most WANs have less capacity than LANs, so more care is needed in selecting WAN bandwidth that can cover actual and reasonable variations. Customers have many options for technologies that can reduce bandwidth utilization on WANs, including advanced routing-protocol features and compression. Chapter 13, "Optimizing Your Network Design," covers optimizing bandwidth utilization in more detail.

With LANs, less attention is paid to monitoring network utilization because many LANs are already overbuilt with full-duplex Gigabit Ethernet links to servers and 100-Mbps or Gigabit Ethernet links to clients. If configured for full-duplex operations, which is typical these days, a Fast or Gigabit Ethernet link supports simultaneous transmitting and receiving. So, in theory, a 100-Mbps Fast Ethernet segment could support 100 percent utilization of the transmit channel and 100 percent utilization of the receive channel, using 200 Mbps. However, total bandwidth in both directions isn't used all the time in most cases. Consider the case of a client system communicating with a server. The client sends requests and the server responds, in lock step. The client doesn't try to send at the same time as the server, so the bandwidth usage does not double on the client's link to the Ethernet switch.

A point-to-point full-duplex link that connects a switch to a server or to another switch, on the other hand, could use all the bandwidth, depending on traffic patterns. Full-duplex Ethernet has become the standard method for connecting servers, switches, and end users' machines. It's an essential performance boost for servers, in particular. With full-duplex Ethernet, a switch can transmit the next client's request at the same time the server is sending a response to a previous request. If the utilization exceeds about 70 percent of the full-duplex bandwidth, however, it's probably time to upgrade to more bandwidth. Network traffic is bursty. You should provision both LAN and WAN capacity with the assumption that the average utilization will be exceeded during bursts.

Throughput

Throughput is defined as the quantity of error-free data that is transmitted per unit of time. Throughput is often defined for a specific connection or session, but in some cases the total throughput of a network is specified. Network novices consistently misuse the words *throughput* and *bandwidth*. Remember, bandwidth means capacity and is generally fixed. Throughput is an assessment of the amount of data that can be transmitted per unit of time. You measure throughput, which can vary depending on network performance characteristics and how you make the measurement. Bandwidth is a given.

Note   To understand bandwidth and throughput, think of a steel pipe that has a capacity of 100 gallons per minute. The pipe has fixed capacity (bandwidth). If just a trickle is coming through, throughput is low. If throughput is at 70 percent, you may have a flood.

Ideally, throughput should be the same as capacity. However, this is not the case on real networks. Capacity depends on the physical layer technologies in use. The capacity of a network should be adequate to handle the offered load, even when there are peaks in network traffic. (Offered load is the data that all nodes have to send at a particular moment in time.) Theoretically, throughput should increase as offered load increases, up to a maximum of the full capacity of the network. However, network throughput depends on the access method (for example, token passing or carrier sensing), the load on the network, and the error rate.

Figure 2-1 shows the ideal situation, where throughput increases linearly with the offered load, and the real world, where actual throughput tapers off as the offered load reaches a certain maximum.

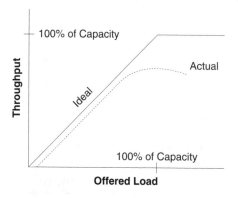

Figure 2-1   *Offered Load and Throughput*

Throughput of Internetworking Devices

Some customers specify throughput goals in terms of the number of packets per second (pps) an internetworking device must process. (In the case of an ATM device, the goal is cells per second, or [cps].) The throughput for an internetworking device is the maximum rate at which the device can forward packets without dropping any packets.

Most internetworking vendors publish pps ratings for their products, based on their own tests and independent tests. To test an internetworking device, engineers place the device between traffic generators and a traffic checker. The traffic generators send packets ranging in size from 64 bytes to 1518 bytes for Ethernet. By running multiple generators, the investigation can test devices with multiple ports.

The generators send bursts of traffic through the device at an initial rate that is half of what is theoretically possible for test conditions. If all packets are received, the rate is increased. If all packets are not received, the rate is decreased. This process is repeated until the highest rate at which packets can be forwarded without loss is determined. Pps values for small frames are much higher than pps values for large frames, so be sure you understand which value you are looking at when reading vendor test results for an internetworking device.

Many internetworking devices can forward packets at the theoretical maximum, which is also called *wire speed* . The theoretical maximum is calculated by dividing bandwidth by packet size, including any headers, preambles, and interframe gaps. Table 2-1 shows the theoretical maximum pps for one 100-Mbps Ethernet stream, based on frame size.

To rate the pps value for a multiport device, testers send multiple streams of data through the device to multiple output ports. The extreme numbers that you sometimes see in vendor marketing material (for example, 400 million pps for the Cisco Catalyst 6500 switch) come from measurements made with multiple Gigabit Ethernet data flows, each using 64-byte packets.

Table 2-1   *Theoretical Maximum Packets per Second (pps)*

Frame Size (in Bytes)	100-Mbps Ethernet Maximum pps	1-Gbps Ethernet Maximum pps
64	148,800	1,488,000
128	84,450	844,500
256	45,280	452,800
512	23,490	234,900
768	15,860	158,600
1024	11,970	119,700
1280	9610	96,100
1518	8120	81,200

Application Layer Throughput

Most end users are concerned about the throughput for applications. Marketing materials from some networking vendors refer to application layer throughput as *goodput* . Calling it goodput sheds light on the fact that it is a measurement of good and relevant application layer data transmitted per unit of time.

It is possible to improve throughput, such that more data per second is transmitted, but not increase goodput, because the extra data transmitted is overhead or retransmissions. Keep in mind what throughput means (bytes per second). Are these good (useful) application layer bytes or simply bytes used by the protocol to get its job done? It is also possible to increase throughput by not using compression. More data is transmitted per unit of time, but the user sees worse performance.

A simple goal for throughput based on data-per-second rates between stations does not identify the requirements for specific applications. When specifying throughput goals for applications, make it clear that the goal specifies good (error-free) application layer data per unit of time. Application layer throughput is usually measured in kilobytes per second (KBps) or megabytes per second (MBps).

Work with your customer to identify throughput requirements for all applications that can benefit from maximized application layer throughput, such as file transfer and database applications. (Throughput is not important for all applications; for example, some interactive character-based applications don't need large screen updates.) Explain to your customer the factors that constrain application layer throughput, which include the following:

- End-to-end error rates

- Protocol functions, such as handshaking, windows, and acknowledgments

- Protocol parameters, such as frame size and retransmission timers

- The pps or cps rate of internetworking devices

- Lost packets or cells at internetworking devices

- Workstation and server performance factors:

    - Disk-access speed

    - Disk-caching size

    - Device driver performance

    - Computer bus performance (capacity and arbitration methods)

    - Processor (CPU) performance

    - Memory performance (access time for real and virtual memory)

    - Operating system inefficiencies

    - Application inefficiencies or bugs

If necessary, work with your customer to identify application throughput problems caused by errors or inefficiencies in protocols, operating systems, and applications. Protocol analyzers are important tools for this. Chapter 3 discusses isolating performance problems in more detail.

Accuracy

The overall goal for accuracy is that the data received at the destination must be the same as the data sent by the source. Typical causes of data errors include power surges or spikes, impedance mismatch problems, poor physical connections, failing devices, and noise caused by electrical machinery. Sometimes software bugs can cause data errors also, although software problems are a less common cause of errors than physical layer problems. Frames that have an error must be retransmitted, which has a negative effect on throughput. In the case of IP networks, Transmission Control Protocol (TCP) provides retransmission of data.

For WAN links, accuracy goals can be specified as a bit error rate (BER) threshold. If the error rate goes above the specified BER, the accuracy is considered unacceptable. Analog links have a typical BER threshold of about 1 in 10^5. Digital circuits have a much lower error rate than analog circuits, especially if fiber-optic cable is used. Fiber-optic links have an error rate of about 1 in 10^{11}. Copper links have an error rate of about 1 in 10^6.

For LANs, a BER is not usually specified, mainly because measuring tools such as protocol analyzers focus on frames, not bits; however, you can approximate a BER by comparing the number of frames with errors in them to the total number of bytes seen by the measuring tool. A good threshold to use is that there should not be more than one bad frame per 10^6 bytes of data.

On shared Ethernet, errors are often the result of collisions. Two stations try to send a frame at the same time and the resulting collision damages the frames, causing cyclic redundancy check (CRC) errors. Depending on the size of the Ethernet network, many of these collisions happen in the 8-byte preamble of the frames and are not registered by troubleshooting tools. If the collision happens past the preamble and somewhere in the first 64 bytes of the data frame, this is registered as a legal collision, and the frame is called a *runt frame*. A general goal for Ethernet collisions is that less than 0.1 percent of the frames should be affected by a legal collision (not counting the collisions that happen in the preamble).

A collision that happens beyond the first 64 bytes of a frame is a *late collision*. Late collisions are illegal and should never happen. Ethernet networks that are too large experience late collisions because stations sending minimum-sized frames cannot hear other stations within the allowed timeframe. The extra propagation delay caused by the excessive size of the network causes late collisions between the most widely separated nodes. Faulty repeaters and network interface cards (NIC) can also cause late collisions.

Collisions should never occur on full-duplex Ethernet links. If they do, there's probably a duplex mismatch. Collisions on a properly configured full-duplex link have no meaning. Both stations sending at the same time is normal. Receiving while sending is normal. So, there is no need for collision detection and collisions shouldn't occur. Chapter 3 has more to say about duplex mismatch problems and how to recognize if they cause errors on your networks.

Collisions also never occur on WAN links. Unfortunately, the output of the **show interface serial** command on Cisco routers includes a collision count. It should be ignored. Cisco programmers used a template for this part of the output. The template is based on the output from the **show interface ethernet** command. There are no collisions on a serial interface, regardless of the encapsulation or technology. Collisions occur only on carrier sense multiple access (CSMA) networks including Ethernet, 802.3, LocalTalk, Aloha, and 802.11 networks. Collisions are a normal part of the "management-by-contention" approach that defines CSMA. (And although LocalTalk and 802.11 use CSMA with collision avoidance, collisions can still occur.)

Accuracy usually refers to the number of error-free frames transmitted relative to the total number of frames transmitted. Accuracy can also characterize how often the network reorders sequences of packets. Packet reordering occurs in many situations, including the use of parallel switching fabrics within a single network device and the use of parallel links between routers. Although upper-layer protocols, such as TCP and Real-Time Transport Protocol (RTP), correct for the reordering of packets, the problem can cause minor performance degradation. Some applications don't use a protocol that corrects the problem and thus might be more severely affected. Because the problem is often corrected, it can be hard to detect. IP routers are not designed to detect, let alone correct, packet reordering, and because they do not detect this condition, they cannot report the problem to network management software. Measurements must be made at end hosts. For example, you could use a protocol analyzer on an end-station host to detect the reordering of packets.

Efficiency

Efficiency is a term borrowed from engineering and scientific fields. It is a measurement of how effective an operation is in comparison to the cost in effort, energy, time, or money. Efficiency specifies how much overhead is required to produce a required outcome. For example, you could measure the efficiency of a method for boiling water. Does most of the energy go to actually boiling the water or does a lot of the energy get wasted heating the electrical wiring, the pot the water is in, and the air around it? How much overhead is required to produce the desired outcome?

Efficiency also provides a useful way to talk about network performance. For example, shared Ethernet is inefficient when the collision rate is high. (The amount of effort to successfully send a frame becomes considerable because so many frames experience collisions.) Network efficiency specifies how much overhead is required to send traffic, whether that overhead is caused by collisions, token passing, error reporting, rerouting, acknowledgments, large frame headers, a bad network design, and so on.

Large frame headers are one cause for inefficiency. We worry a lot less about frame headers than we used to when bandwidth was scarcer. Nonetheless, for networks where bandwidth is still (or may become) scarce, a good network performance goal is for applications that send bulk data to minimize the amount of bandwidth used by headers by using the largest possible frame the MAC layer allows. Using a large frame maximizes the amount of useful application data compared to header data and improves application layer throughput.

Figure 2-2 shows a bandwidth pipe used by small frames and the same pipe used by large frames. The header of each frame is shaded. Note that there is an interframe gap between each frame in addition to the headers. From the graphic, you can see that large frames use bandwidth more efficiently than small frames.

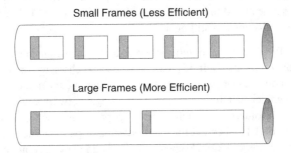

Figure 2-2 *Bandwidth Utilization Efficiency for Small Versus Large Frames*

The maximum frame size is a tradeoff with the BER discussed in the previous section. Bigger frames have more bits and hence are more likely to be hit by an error. If there were no errors, an infinitely big frame would be the most efficient (although not the most fair to other senders). If a frame is hit by an error, it must be retransmitted, which wastes time and effort and reduces efficiency. The bigger the frame, the more bandwidth is wasted retransmitting. So, because networks experience errors, frame sizes are limited to maximize efficiency and fairness. The maximum frame size for Ethernet, for example, is 1522 bytes, including the header, CRC, and an 802.1Q VLAN tag.

As is the case with many network design goals, there are tradeoffs associated with a goal of improving efficiency by using large frame sizes. On slow WAN links, the time to output a large frame is significant. The time to output a frame is called *serialization delay*. Serialization delay becomes an issue when applications that send large frames, such as file transfer, share a WAN link with applications that are delay-sensitive, such as voice and video. One solution is to use ATM, which divides frames into cells. Other solutions include the use of link-layer fragmentation and interleaving options, such as Frame Relay FRF.12, Multilink Frame Relay (FRF.16), and Multilink PPP.

Delay and Delay Variation

Users of interactive applications expect minimal delay in receiving feedback from the network. Voice and video applications also require minimal delay. In addition, voice and video applications require a minimal variation in the amount of delay that packets experience. Variations in delay, called *jitter*, cause disruptions in voice quality and jumpiness in video streams.

Applications that use the Telnet protocol are also sensitive to delay because the user expects quick feedback when typing characters. Telnet is becoming obsolete, but it hasn't disappeared yet. With the Telnet remote echo option, the character typed by a user doesn't appear on the screen until it has been acknowledged and echoed by the far end, and the near end has sent an acknowledgment for the echo. To help you recognize the need to design a network with low delay, you should determine if your customer plans to run any delay-sensitive applications, such as voice or video, or applications based on delay-sensitive protocols such as Telnet.

Causes of Delay

Any goals regarding delay must take into account fundamental physics. Despite science fiction stories that say differently, any signal experiences a *propagation delay* resulting from the finite speed of light, which is about 300,000 kilometers per second (186,000 miles per second). Network designers can also remember 1 nanosecond per foot. These values are for light traveling in a vacuum. A signal in a cable or optical fiber travels approximately two-thirds the speed of light in a vacuum.

Delay is relevant for all data transmission technologies but especially for satellite links and long terrestrial cables. Geostationary satellites are in orbit above the earth at a height of about 36,000 kilometers, or 24,000 miles. This long distance leads to a propagation delay of about 270 milliseconds (ms) for an intercontinental satellite hop. In the case of terrestrial cable connections, propagation delay is about 1 ms for every 200 kilometers (120 miles).

Another fundamental cause for delay is *serialization delay*, the time to put digital data onto a transmission line, which depends on the data volume and the speed of the line. For example, to transmit a 1024-byte packet on a 1.544-Mbps T1 line takes about 5 ms.

An additional fundamental delay is packet-switching delay. *Packet-switching delay* refers to the latency accrued when switches and routers forward data. The latency depends on the speed of the internal circuitry and CPU, and the switching architecture of the internetworking device. Latency also depends on the type of RAM that the device uses. Dynamic RAM (DRAM) needs to be refreshed thousands of times per second. Static RAM (SRAM) doesn't need to be refreshed, which makes it faster, but it is also more expensive than DRAM. Low-end internetworking devices often use DRAM to keep the cost low.

Packet-switching delay can be quite small on high-end switches, in the 5- to 20-microsecond range for 64-byte Ethernet frames. Routers tend to introduce more latency than switches. The amount of latency that a router causes for packet switching depends on many variables, including the router architecture, configuration, and software features that optimize the forwarding of packets. Despite marketing claims by switch salespeople, you should not assume that a router has higher latency than a switch. A high-end router with a fast CPU, SRAM, optimized software, and a highly evolved switching fabric can outperform many low-end or medium-end switches.

Of course, a router has a more complicated job than a Layer 2 switch. In general terms, when a packet comes into a router, the router checks its routing table, decides which interface should send the packet, and encapsulates the packet with the correct data link layer header and trailer. Routing vendors, such as Cisco, have advanced caching mechanisms so that a frame destined for a known destination can receive its new encapsulation quickly without requiring the CPU to do any table lookup or other processing. These mechanisms minimize packet-switching delay.

Packet-switching speed depends on the type and number of advanced features that are enabled on a packet-switching device. When designing an internetwork fabric, consider the power that you will need to incorporate into the design to implement quality of service (QoS), Network Address Translation (NAT), IPsec, filtering, and so on. Consider the policies that your design customer wants to enforce and the effect they will have on packet-switching delay.

Packet-switching delay can also include *queuing delay* . The average number of packets in a queue on a packet-switching device increases exponentially as utilization increases, as you can see from Figure 2-3. If utilization is 50 percent, the average queue depth is one packet. If utilization is 90 percent, the average queue depth is nine packets. Without going into mathematical queuing theory, the general rule of thumb for queue depth is as follows:

Queue depth = Utilization / (1 − Utilization)

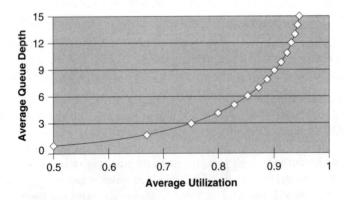

Figure 2-3   *Queue Depth and Bandwidth Utilization*

Consider the following example. A packet switch has five users, each offering packets at a rate of 10 pps. The average length of the packets is 1024 bits. The packet switch needs to transmit this data over a 56-kbps WAN circuit. Putting all this together, you have the following equations:

Load = 5 × 10 × 1024 = 51,200 bps

Utilization = 51,200 / 56,000 = 91.4 percent

Average number of packets in the queue = (0.914) / (1 − 0.914) = 10.63 packets

By increasing bandwidth on a WAN circuit, you can decrease queue depth and hence decrease delay. Alternatively, to improve performance, you can use an advanced queuing algorithm that outputs certain types of packets first—for example, voice or video packets. Chapter 13 covers advanced router queuing techniques in more detail.

Delay Variation

As customers implement new digital voice and video applications, they are becoming concerned about delay and delay variation. Additionally, customers are becoming more aware of the issues associated with supporting bursty traffic on the same network that carries delay-sensitive traffic. If bursts in traffic cause jitter, audio and video streams experience problems that disrupt communications.

Desktop audio/video applications can minimize jitter by providing a jitter buffer. Display software or hardware pulls data from the buffer. The insulating buffer reduces the effect of jitter because variations on the input side are smaller than the total buffer size and therefore not obvious on the output side. The data is smoothed in the output, and the user experiences no ill effects from the input jitter.

If possible, you should gather exact requirements for delay variation from a customer. For customers who cannot provide exact goals, a good rule of thumb is that the variation should be less than 1 or 2 percent of the delay. For example, for a goal of an average delay of 40 ms, the variation should not be more than 400 or 800 microseconds.

Short fixed-length cells, such as ATM 53-byte cells, are inherently better than frames for meeting delay and delay-variance goals. To help understand this concept, consider the analogy of people trying to get onto an escalator. The escalator is like a bandwidth pipe. At first, each person gets onto the escalator in an orderly fashion and the delay is predictable. Then a school class arrives and the children are all holding hands, expecting to get onto the escalator all at once! What happens to your delay if you happen to be behind the children?

A gaggle of school children holding hands is analogous to a large frame causing extra delay for small frames. Consider the case of a user starting a file transfer using 1518-byte frames. This user's data affects bandwidth usage and queuing mechanisms at internetworking devices, causing unexpected delay for other traffic. Good throughput for one application causes delay problems for another application.

Cell-relay technologies (ATM, for example) were designed to support traffic that is sensitive to delay and jitter. Depending on the class of service, ATM lets a session specify a maximum cell transfer delay (MCTD) and maximum cell delay variation (MCDV). Chapter 4 describes ATM service classes in more detail.

Response Time

Response time is the network performance goal that users care about most. Users don't know about propagation delay and jitter. They don't understand throughput in pps or in MBps. They aren't concerned about BERs, although perhaps they should be! Users recognize the amount of time to receive a response from the network system. They also recognize small changes in the expected response time and become frustrated when the response time is long.

Users begin to get frustrated when response time is more than about 100 ms or 1/10th of a second. Beyond 100 ms, users notice they are waiting for the network to display a web page, echo a typed character, start downloading email, and so on. If the response happens within 100 ms, most users do not notice any delay.

The 100-ms threshold is often used as a timer value for protocols that offer reliable transport of data. For example, many TCP implementations retransmit unacknowledged data after 100 ms by default.

Note Good TCP implementations also adjust the retransmit timer based on network conditions. TCP should keep track of the average amount of time to receive a response and dynamically adjust the retransmit timer based on the expected delay.

The 100-ms response time threshold applies to interactive applications. For bulk applications, such as transferring large files or graphical web pages, users are willing to wait at least 10 to 20 seconds. Technically savvy users expect to wait even longer if they know the file is large and the transmission medium is slow. If your network users are not technically savvy, you should provide some guidelines on how long to wait, depending on the size of files and the technologies in use (modems, high-speed digital networks, geostationary satellites, and so on).

Security

Security is a key technical goal, and security design is one of the most important aspects of enterprise network design. Increased threats from both inside and outside the enterprise network require the most up-to-date security rules and technologies. An overall goal that most companies have is that security problems should not disrupt the company's ability to conduct business. Network design customers need assurances that a design offers protection against business data and other assets getting damaged or accessed inappropriately. Every company has trade secrets, business operations, and equipment to protect.

The first task in security design is planning. Planning involves identifying network assets that must be protected, analyzing risks, and developing requirements. This chapter briefly discusses security planning. Chapter 8, "Developing Network Security Strategies," covers planning for secure networks in more detail.

As is the case with most technical design requirements, achieving security goals means making tradeoffs. Security implementations can add to the cost of deploying and operating a network. Strict security policies can also affect the productivity of users, especially if some ease of use must be sacrificed to protect resources and data. Poor security implementations can annoy users, causing them to think of ways to get around security policies. Security can also affect the redundancy of a network design if all traffic must pass through encryption devices, for example.

It is common practice to build systems with just enough security to bring potential losses from a security breach down to a desired level. A practical goal is to ensure that the cost to implement security does not exceed the cost to recover from security incidents. Alternatively, some organizations might want to implement stronger measures to mitigate unforeseen risks. As you work with your customer, you should analyze the cost associated with security incidents disrupting business and determine whether the customer wants to try to address unexpected problems.

Identifying Network Assets

The first step in security design is identifying the assets that must be protected, the value of the assets, and the expected cost associated with losing these assets if a security breach occurs. Network assets include hardware, software, applications, and data. Assets also include intellectual property, trade secrets, and a company's reputation.

Consider the possibility of a hacker damaging an enterprise's reputation by changing the enterprise's public web pages. You may have read about some of the cases of hackers changing U.S. government web pages. These security breaches affected the government's reputation in two ways: The changed web pages had silly graphics and text, and the government lost credibility because it appeared that it was easy to hack into government networks.

The data that a company uses to achieve its mission is an often-overlooked asset. Data can include engineering blueprints, financial planning documents, customer relations information, competitive analysis documents, configuration information for hardware and software, employee Social Security numbers, employee badge information, and so on. The integrity and confidentiality of this data must be protected from intentional or unintentional damage.

Some of the most important network assets are the networking devices themselves, including servers, switches and routers, and especially the firewalls and intrusion detection systems (IDS) that provide security services to network users. These devices are attractive targets to hackers and must be hardened (strengthened) against intrusions. As Chapter 8 discusses in more detail, hardening network devices involves running only the minimal necessary services, establishing trust only with authenticated partners, using secure device-management channels, and patching the device software to install fixes for known security problems.

You should consider more than just data and devices when identifying assets. The network user's time can be considered an asset. Whenever a virus attacks a system, it takes time to get rid of it, even if it's innocuous. The fact that this time is wasted is similar to a denial-of-service (DOS) attack. An asset might also be the capability to offer services to customers. This is especially true for Internet service providers (ISP), but also true for many other companies that offer medical, educational, financial, and other types of services.

Every design customer has different business assets and varying needs regarding the importance of assets. As a network designer, you should work with technical and business managers to identify which assets are critical to a business's mission. A financial services business, for example, has different assets than a health organization or a biomedical research company. As part of the first step of network design, analyzing business requirements, you should have developed a good understanding of your network design customer's overall business mission (which might be different from the corporate mission statement, by the way, which is often written in a lofty manner to motivate employees and impress shareholders).

Analyzing Security Risks

In addition to identifying assets, an important step in security planning is analyzing potential threats and gaining an understanding of their likelihood and business impact. Risk analysis and the consequent building of a security policy and secure network design is a continuous process, as risks change in their severity and probability on a regular basis. For example, a company's encryption algorithm and the length of the encryption key might need to be reconsidered if a relatively inexpensive and exceptionally fast code-cracking computer becomes available, which allows easier decryption of valuable secrets.

Risk assessment includes an analysis of the danger of not taking any action. Ask your customer to help you understand the risks associated with not implementing a secure network. How sensitive is the customer's data? What would be the financial cost of someone accessing the data and stealing trade secrets? What would be the financial cost of someone changing the data? What would be the financial cost associated with the network being down because of a security breach, causing employees to be unable to do their jobs?

As mentioned previously, one of the biggest risks that must be managed is the risk that a hacker can undermine the security of a network device, such as a switch, router, server, firewall, or IDS. When a network device is compromised, the following threats arise:

- Data flowing through the network can be intercepted, analyzed, altered, or deleted, compromising integrity and confidentiality.

- Additional, related network services, which rely on trust among network devices, can be compromised. For example, bad routing data or incorrect authentication information could be injected into the network.

- User passwords can be compromised and used for further intrusions and perhaps to reach out and attack other networks.

- The configuration of the device can be altered to allow connections that shouldn't be allowed or to disallow connections that should be allowed.

Some customers worry about hackers using protocol analyzers to sniff packets to see passwords, credit cards numbers, or other private data. This is not as big a risk as it appears. Credit card numbers are almost always sent encrypted, using technologies such as the Secure Sockets Layer (SSL) protocol. Passwords are also sent encrypted and are often good for only one use anyway, if one-time passwords (OTP) are used. Even when passwords or credit cards are not encrypted, it is extremely difficult to find these minute pieces of data in the midst of millions of sniffed packets. Also, to sniff relevant packets, a hacker needs physical access to a link that carries relevant traffic or needs to have compromised a switch that supports port monitoring.

Hackers are getting more creative, though. Hackers disguised as customers, repair technicians, and contractors have been known to walk into organizations and gain network access via a network connection in an empty cubicle or a conference room. Sometimes companies have demo rooms, where they showcase their products. For ease of use of the people who configure the products, these rooms sometimes have access to the company's intranet and to the Internet. Hackers love that sort of setup. Hackers who are less brazen, and don't want to walk into an organization's building, often sit outside in the parking lot with a wireless 802.11-enabled notebook computer or wireless handheld device and access corporate networks where the security was not well planned.

In addition to considering outside hackers as a security risk, companies should heed problems caused by inept or malicious internal network users. Attacks might come from inadvertent user errors, including the downloading of software from untrusted sites that introduce malware. Attacks might also come from malicious acts by internal users, including employees disgruntled by cost cuts, employees who become greedy during tough economic times, and employees with a political agenda. Organizations should have information security training and awareness programs to mitigate the risk of internal user attacks.

Reconnaissance Attacks

A set of security risks falls into the category of a *reconnaissance attack* . A reconnaissance attack provides information about potential targets and their weaknesses and is usually carried out in preparation for a more focused attack against a particular target. Reconnaissance attackers use tools to discover the reachability of hosts, subnets, services, and applications. In some cases the tools are relatively sophisticated and can break through firewalls. A less-sophisticated hacker could convince users to download a file from an alleged music, video, pornographic, or game website. The file could actually be a Trojan horse that gathers reconnaissance data.

During a reconnaissance attack, the attacker might make the following attempts to learn more about the network:

- Gather information about the network's configuration and management from Domain Name System (DNS) registries.

- Discover access possibilities using "war dialing" (attempts to discover and connect to dialup access points) and "war driving" (attempts to discover and connect to misconfigured wireless access points).

- Gather information about a network's topology and addressing using network mapping tools. Some tools, such as traceroute and Simple Network Management Protocol (SNMP) queries, are primitive. Others are sophisticated and can send seemingly legitimate packets to map a network.

- Discover the reachability of hosts, services, and applications using ping scans and port scans.

- Discover operating system and application versions and probe for well-known security holes in the software.

- Discover temporary holes created while systems, configurations, and software releases are being upgraded.

Denial-of-Service Attacks

Denial-of-service (DoS) attacks target the availability of a network, host, or application, making it impossible for legitimate users to gain access. DoS attacks are a major risk because they can easily interrupt business processes and are relatively simple to conduct, even by an unskilled attacker. DoS attacks include the flooding of public servers with enormous numbers of connection requests, rendering the server unresponsive to legitimate users, and the flooding of network connections with random traffic, in an attempt to consume as much bandwidth as possible. Distributed denial-of-service (DDoS) attacks are even worse than DoS attacks because the attacker marshals multiple hosts, from various networks, to attack the target.

DoS attacks are usually the consequence of a network's, host's, or application's inability to handle an enormous quantity of data, which crashes the system or halts services on the system. DoS attacks also take advantage of a host's or application's failure to handle unexpected conditions, such as maliciously formatted input data or a buffer overflow. DoS attacks are one of the most significant risks that a company must recognize and manage, because they have the capability to cause significant downtime.

Developing Security Requirements

Security problems should not disrupt an organization's capability to conduct business. That's the most basic security requirement that every organization has. A secondary security requirement is to protect assets from being incapacitated, stolen, altered, or harmed. Although every design customer has different detailed security requirements, basic requirements boil down to the need to develop and select procedures and technologies that ensure the following:

- Confidentiality of data so that only authorized users can view sensitive information

- Integrity of data so that only authorized users can change sensitive information and so that authorized users of data can depend on its authenticity

- System and data availability, which should provide uninterrupted access to important computing resources

Other, more specific requirements could include one or more of the following goals:

- Let outsiders (customers, vendors, suppliers) access data on public web or File Transfer Protocol (FTP) servers but not access internal data.

- Authorize and authenticate branch-office users, mobile users, and telecommuters.

- Detect intruders and isolate the amount of damage they do.

- Authenticate routing-table updates received from internal or external routers.

- Protect data transmitted to remote sites across a VPN.

- Physically secure hosts and internetworking devices (for example, keep devices in a locked room).

- Logically secure hosts and internetworking devices with user accounts and access rights for directories and files.

- Protect applications and data from software viruses.

- Train network users and network managers on security risks and how to avoid security problems.

- Implement copyright or other legal methods of protecting products and intellectual property.

- Meet compliance and regulatory requirements.

Manageability

Every customer has different objectives regarding the manageability of a network. Some customers have precise goals, such as a plan to use SNMP to record the number of bytes each router receives and sends. Other clients have less-specific goals. If your client has definite plans, be sure to document them, because you will need to refer to the plans when selecting equipment. In some cases, equipment has to be ruled out because it does not support the management functions a customer requires.

Network management is discussed in more detail in Chapter 9, "Developing Network Management Strategies," but it's also important to consider management at the onset of a design project. During the initial gathering of technical requirements for a new network design or upgrade, you can use International Organization for Standardization (ISO) terminology to simplify the discussion of network management goals with your design customer. ISO uses the FCAPS acronym to help you remember the following network management functions:

- **Fault management:** Detecting, isolating, and correcting problems; reporting problems to end users and managers; tracking trends related to problems

- **Configuration management:** Controlling, operating, identifying, and collecting data from managed devices

■ **Accounting management:** Accounting of network usage to allocate costs to network users and/or plan for changes in capacity requirements

■ **Performance management:** Analyzing traffic and application behavior to optimize a network, meet service-level agreements, and plan for expansion

■ **Security management:** Monitoring and testing security and protection policies, maintaining and distributing passwords and other authentication and authorization information, managing encryption keys, and auditing adherence to security policies

Usability

A goal that is related to manageability, but is not exactly the same as manageability, is usability. Usability refers to the ease of use with which network users can access the network and services. Whereas manageability focuses on making network managers' jobs easier, usability focuses on making network users' jobs easier.

It is important to gain an understanding of how important usability is to your network design customer, because some network design components can have a negative effect on usability. For example, strict security policies can have a negative effect on usability (which is a tradeoff that most customers are willing to make, but not all customers). You can plan to maximize usability by deploying user-friendly, host-naming schemes and easy-to-use configuration methods that make use of dynamic protocols, such as the Dynamic Host Configuration Protocol (DHCP).

Usability might also include a need for mobility. As mentioned in Chapter 1, users expect to get their jobs done regardless of their physical location. They expect to have network access in conference rooms, at home, at a customer's site, and so on. Documenting this requirement as part of the technical requirements will help you recognize the need to select wireless and VPN solutions during the logical and physical design phases of the network design project. It will also help you recognize the need to conduct a site survey to prepare for a wireless infrastructure, as discussed in greater detail in the "Checking Architectural and Environmental Constraints" section of Chapter 3.

Adaptability

When designing a network, you should try to avoid incorporating any elements that would make it hard to implement new technologies in the future. A good network design can adapt to new technologies and changes. Changes can come in the form of new protocols, new business practices, new fiscal goals, new legislation, and a myriad of other possibilities. For example, some states have enacted environmental laws that require a reduction in the number of employees driving to work. To meet the legal requirement to reduce automobile emissions, companies need their remote-access designs to be flexible enough to adapt to increasing numbers of employees working at home. The adaptability of a network affects its availability. For example, some networks must operate in environments that change drastically from day to night or from winter to summer. Extreme changes in temperature can affect the behavior of electronic components of a network. A network that cannot adapt cannot offer good availability.

A flexible network design can also adapt to changing traffic patterns and QoS requirements. For some customers, the selected WAN or LAN technology must adapt to new users randomly joining the network to use applications that require a constant-bit-rate service. Chapter 4 discusses QoS requirements in more detail.

One other aspect of adaptability is how quickly internetworking devices must adapt to problems and to upgrades. For example, how quickly do switches and bridges adapt to another switch failing, causing a change in the spanning-tree topology? How quickly do routers adapt to new networks joining the topology? How quickly do routing protocols adapt to link failures? Chapter 7, "Selecting Switching and Routing Protocols," discusses these issues in more detail.

Affordability

The final technical goal this chapter covers is *affordability* which is sometimes called *cost-effectiveness*. Most customers have a goal for affordability, although sometimes other goals such as performance and availability are more important. Affordability is partly a business goal and was discussed in Chapter 1. It is covered again in this chapter because of the technical issues involved.

For a network design to be affordable, it should carry the maximum amount of traffic for a given financial cost. Financial costs include nonrecurring equipment costs and recurring network operation costs. As mentioned in Chapter 1, you should learn about your customer's budget so that you can recommend solutions that are affordable.

In campus networks, low cost is often a primary goal. Customers expect to be able to purchase affordable switches that have numerous ports and a low cost per port. They expect cabling costs to be minimal and service provider charges to be minimal or nonexistent. They also expect NICs for end systems and servers to be inexpensive. Depending on the applications running on end systems, low cost is often more important than availability and performance in campus network designs. For enterprise networks, availability is usually more important than low cost. Nonetheless, customers are looking for ways to contain costs for enterprise networks. Recurring monthly charges for WAN circuits are the most expensive aspect of running a large network.

To reduce the cost of operating a WAN, customers often have one or more of the following technical goals to achieve affordability:

- Use a routing protocol that minimizes WAN traffic.

- Consolidate parallel leased lines carrying voice and data into fewer WAN trunks.

- Select technologies that dynamically allocate WAN bandwidth—for example, ATM rather than time-division multiplexing (TDM).

- Improve efficiency on WAN circuits by using such features as compression.

- Eliminate underutilized trunks from the internetwork and save money by eliminating both circuit costs and trunk hardware.

- Use technologies that support oversubscription.

With old-style TDM networks, the core backbone capacity had to be at least the sum of the speeds of the incoming access networks. With cell and frame switching, oversubscription is common. Because of the bursty nature of frame-based traffic, access port speeds can add up to more than the speed of a backbone network, within reason. Enterprise network managers who have a goal of reducing operational costs are especially interested in solutions that will let them oversubscribe their trunks, while still maintaining service guarantees they have offered their users.

The second most expensive aspect of running a network, following the cost of WAN circuits, is the cost of hiring, training, and maintaining personnel to operate and manage the network. To reduce this aspect of operational costs, customers may require you to do the following as you develop the network design:

- Select internetworking equipment that is easy to configure, operate, maintain, and manage.

- Select a network design that is easy to understand and troubleshoot.

- Develop good network documentation that can help reduce troubleshooting time.

- Select network applications and protocols that are easy to use so that users can support themselves to some extent.

Making Network Design Tradeoffs

Despite what politicians tell us about state and federal budgets during an election year, in the real world meeting goals requires making tradeoffs. This section describes some typical network design tradeoffs.

To meet high expectations for availability, redundant components are often necessary, which raises the cost of a network implementation. To meet rigorous performance requirements, high-cost circuits and equipment are required. To enforce strict security policies, expensive monitoring might be required and users must forgo some ease of use. To implement a scalable network, availability might suffer, because a scalable network is always in flux as new users and sites are added. Implementing good throughput for one application might cause delay problems for another application. Lack of qualified personnel might suggest the need for expensive training or the need to drop certain features. The network design that you develop must take these tradeoffs into consideration.

One cause of network problems can be inadequate staffing and reduced training due to overzealous cost cutting. The tradeoff with cutting costs might be a network that isn't robust or has substandard performance until the problem is recognized, which often takes a year or two. If the in-house network staff was cut, outsourcing might become a necessity, which could end up being more costly than it would have been to keep the in-house staff.

The network design process is usually progressive. This means that legacy equipment must coexist with new equipment. Your design might not be as elegant as you would like because you might need for it to support old devices and old applications. If the new network is not being introduced at the same time as new applications, the design must provide compatibility with old applications. Also, be aware that insufficient bandwidth in parts of the network, where the bandwidth cannot be increased due to technical or business constraints, must be resolved by other means.

To help you analyze tradeoffs, ask your customer to identify a single driving network design goal. This goal can be the same overall business goal for the network design project that was identified in Chapter 1, or it can be a rephrasing of that goal to include technical issues. In addition, ask your customer to prioritize the rest of the goals. Prioritizing will help the customer get through the process of making tradeoffs.

One analogy that helps with prioritizing goals is the "kid in the candy store with a dollar bill" analogy. Using the dollar bill analogy, explain to the customers that they are like children in a candy store who have exactly one dollar to spend. The dollar can be spent on different types of candy: chocolates, licorice, jelly beans, and so on. But each time more money is spent on one type of candy, less money is available to spend on other types. Ask customers to add up how much they want to spend on scalability, availability, network performance, security, manageability, usability, adaptability, and affordability. For example, a customer could make the following selections:

Scalability: 20

Availability: 30

Network performance: 15

Security: 5

Manageability: 5

Usability: 5

Adaptability: 5

Affordability: 15

Total (must add up to 100): 100

Keep in mind that, sometimes, making tradeoffs is more complex than what has been described because goals can differ for various parts of an internetwork. One group of users might value availability more than affordability. Another group might deploy state-of-the-art applications and value performance more than availability. In addition, sometimes a particular group's goals are different from the overall goals for the internetwork as a whole. If this is the case, document individual group goals and goals for the network as a whole. Later, when selecting network technologies, you might see some opportunities to meet both types of goals—for example, choosing LAN technologies that meet individual group goals and WAN technologies that meet overall goals.

Technical Goals Checklist

You can use the following checklist to determine if you have addressed all your client's technical objectives and concerns:

❑ I have documented the customer's plans for expanding the number of sites, users, and servers for the next 1 year and the next 2 years.

❑ The customer has told me about any plans to migrate departmental servers to a centralized data center.

❑ The customer has told me about any plans to integrate data stored on a legacy mainframe with the enterprise network.

❑ The customer has told me about any plans to implement an extranet to communicate with partners or other companies.

❑ I have documented a goal for network availability in percent uptime and/or MTBF and MTTR.

❑ I have documented any goals for maximum average network utilization.

❑ I have documented goals for network throughput.

❑ I have documented goals for pps throughput of internetworking devices.

❑ I have documented goals for accuracy and acceptable BERs.

❑ I have discussed with the customer the importance of using large frame sizes to maximize efficiency.

❑ I have discussed with the customer the tradeoffs associated with large frame sizes and serialization delay.

❑ I have identified any applications that have a more restrictive response-time requirement than the industry standard of less than 100 ms.

❑ I have discussed network security risks and requirements with the customer.

❑ I have gathered manageability requirements, including goals for performance, fault, configuration, security, and accounting management.

❑ I have updated the Network Applications chart to include the technical application goals shown in Table 2-2.

Table 2-2   *Network Applications Technical Requirements*

Name of Application	Type of Application	New Application? (Yes or No)	Criticality	Cost of Downtime	Acceptable MTBF

❑   Working with my customer, I have developed a list of network design goals, including both business and technical goals. The list starts with one overall goal and includes the rest of the goals in priority order. Critical goals are marked as such.

Chapter 1 provided a Network Applications chart. At this point in the design process, you can expand the chart to include technical application requirements, such as MTBF, MTTR, and throughput and delay goals, as shown in Table 2-2.

Summary

This chapter covered technical requirements for a network design, including scalability, availability, network performance, security, manageability, usability, adaptability, and affordability. It also covered typical tradeoffs that must be made to meet these goals.

Analyzing your customer's technical and business goals prepares you to carry out the next steps in the top-down network design process, including making decisions about network technologies to recommend to a customer. Researchers who study decision models say that one of the most important aspects of making a sound decision is having a good list of goals.

At this point in the network design process, you have gathered both business and technical goals. You should make a list of your customer's most important technical goals and merge this list with the list of business goals you made in Chapter 1. You should put the goals in the list in priority order, starting with the overall most important business and technical goal, and following with critical goals and then less critical goals. Later, you can make a list of options and correlate options with goals. Any options that do not meet critical goals can be eliminated. Other options can be ranked by how well they meet a goal. This process can help you select network components that meet a customer's requirements.

Acceptable MTTR	Throughput Goal	Delay Must Be Less Than	Delay Variation Must Be Less Than	Comments

Review Questions

1. Discuss the term "scalability." What does it mean? Why is it an important network design goal? What are some challenges designers face when designing for scalability?

2. A network design customer has a goal of 99.80 percent uptime. How much downtime will be permitted in hours per week? How much downtime will be permitted in minutes per day and seconds per hour? Which values are acceptable in which circumstances?

3. Assume you are in New York City in the United States and you are downloading a 100-KB web page from a server in Cape Town, South Africa. Assume that the bandwidth between the two cities is 1 Gbps. Which type of delay will be more significant, propagation delay or transmission delay? Defend your answer.

4. The chapter mentioned reconnaissance attacks. Do some research to learn more about the tools that attackers use when on a reconnaissance mission. In your own words, describe two tools that you researched.

Design Scenario

Harriet's Fruit and Chocolate Company was established in 1935 in the Pacific Northwest of the United States to ship gift baskets of locally grown peaches and pears to customers in the United States. The company also makes chocolates and baked goods to include in the gift baskets. It has grown extensively over the years and is currently one of the biggest companies in the Pacific Northwest.

Recently, Harriet's descendants, who still run the company, have identified a need to immediately report when fruit is starting to ripen and should be picked and placed in cold storage. Employees in the marketing department have identified a need to access inventory data for the fruit in the orchards and in cold storage. With this data, they can design and sell gift-basket products that take advantage of the ripe fruit. This data must also be fed into e-commerce applications so that web orders can correctly specify product availability.

In addition, the company recently hired an ambitious programmer who is anxious to use her knowledge of SAS programming, SQL, and DB2 to design reporting applications for senior management. She calls you every day with new ideas on what she could accomplish if the network were upgraded so that she could reach up-to-date data from the orchards and cold storage buildings.

As the network designer for this company, you have been charged with selecting network technologies to reach the orchards and cold storage buildings. Each of the six orchards has a shack with one or two standalone PCs and a printer. The three cold storage buildings are huge warehouses that include a few standalone PCs and printers. The local telephone company has suggested that you lease fractional T1 links, but these links are expensive and possibly beyond your budget. Wireless technologies are also possible, but you have heard that fruit trees, especially full-grown trees that are tall and leafy, can absorb a wireless radio frequency (RF) signal. You have also heard that the cold storage buildings have ice hazards, making it hard to install equipment. But you will not let these challenges faze you.

1. What investigation will you do with regard to the physical infrastructure of the orchards, the orchard shacks, and the cold storage buildings?

2. Make a list of business goals for Harriet's Fruit and Chocolate Company. What are some constraints that will affect these goals?

3. Make a list of technical goals for Harriet's Fruit and Chocolate Company. What tradeoffs might you need to make to meet these goals?

4. Will a wireless solution support the low delay that will be needed to meet the needs of the applications? Defend your answer.

5. What security concerns should you bring up as you design the network upgrade?

Chapter 3

Characterizing the Existing Internetwork

According to Abraham Lincoln:

> "If we could first know where we are and whither we are tending, we could better judge what to do and how to do it."

An important step in top-down network design is to examine a customer's existing network to better judge how to meet expectations for network scalability, performance, and availability. Examining the existing network includes learning about the topology and physical structure and assessing the network's performance.

By developing an understanding of the existing network's structure, uses, and behavior, you can determine whether a customer's design goals are realistic. You can document any bottlenecks or network performance problems, and identify internetworking devices and links that will need to be replaced because the number of ports or capacity is insufficient for the new design. Identifying performance problems can help you select solutions to solve problems and develop a baseline for future measurements of performance.

Most network designers do not design networks from scratch. Instead, they design enhancements to existing networks. Developing a successful network design requires that you develop skills in characterizing an incumbent network to ensure interoperability between the existing and anticipated networks. This chapter describes techniques and tools to help you develop those skills. This chapter concludes with a Network Health checklist that documents typical thresholds for diagnosing a network as "healthy."

Characterizing the Network Infrastructure

Characterizing the infrastructure of a network means developing a set of network maps and learning the location of major internetworking devices and network segments. It also includes documenting the names and addresses of major devices and segments, and identifying any standard methods for addressing and naming. Documenting the types and lengths of physical cabling and investigating architectural and environmental constraints are also important aspects of characterizing the network infrastructure. Architectural and environmental constraints are becoming increasingly important in modern network designs that must accommodate wireless networking, which may not work if the signal is blocked by cement walls, for example.

Developing a Network Map

Learning the location of major hosts, interconnection devices, and network segments is a good way to start developing an understanding of traffic flow. Coupled with data on the performance characteristics of network segments, location information gives you insight into where users are concentrated and the level of traffic that a network design must support.

At this point in the network design process, your goal is to obtain a map (or set of maps) of the existing network. Some design customers might have maps for the new network design as well. If that is the case, you might be one step ahead, but be careful of any assumptions that are not based on your detailed analysis of business and technical requirements.

To develop a network drawing, you should invest in a good network-diagramming tool. Tools include IBM's Tivoli products, WhatsUp Gold from Ipswitch, and LANsurveyor from SolarWinds. The Microsoft Visio Professional product is also highly recommended for network diagramming. For large enterprises and service providers, Visionael Corporation offers client/server network documentation products.

Note   Tools that automatically diagram a network can be helpful, but the generated maps might require a lot of cleanup to make them useful.

Characterizing Large Internetworks

Developing a single network map might not be possible for large internetworks. There are many approaches to solving this problem, including simply developing many maps, one for each location. Another approach is to apply a top-down method. Start with a map or set of maps that shows the following high-level information:

- Geographical information, such as countries, states or provinces, cities, and campuses

- WAN connections between countries, states, and cities

- WAN and LAN connections between buildings and between campuses

For each campus network, you can develop more precise maps that show the following more detailed information:

- Buildings and floors, and possibly rooms or cubicles

- The location of major servers or server farms

- The location of routers and switches

- The location of firewalls, Network Address Translation (NAT) devices, intrusion detection systems (IDS), and intrusion prevention systems (IPS)

- The location of mainframes

- The location of major network-management stations

- The location and reach of virtual LANs (VLAN)

- Some indication of where workstations reside, although not necessarily the explicit location of each workstation

Another method for characterizing large, complex networks is to use a top-down approach that is influenced by the OSI reference model. First, develop a logical map that shows applications and services used by network users. This map can call out internal web, email, FTP, and print and file-sharing servers. It can also include external web, email, and FTP servers.

Note   Be sure to show web caching servers on your network maps because they can affect traffic flow. Documenting the location of web caching servers will make it easier to troubleshoot any problems reaching web servers during the implementation and operation phases of the network design cycle.

Next develop a map that shows network services. This map might depict the location of security servers; for example, Terminal Access Controller Access Control System (TACACS) and Remote Authentication Dial-In User Service (RADIUS) servers. Other network services include Dynamic Host Configuration Protocol (DHCP), Domain Name System (DNS), and Simple Network Management Protocol (SNMP) and other management services. The location and reach of any virtual private networks (VPN) that connect corporate sites via a service provider's WAN or the Internet can be depicted, including major VPN devices, such as VPN concentrators. Dial-in and dial-out servers can be shown on this map as well.

You may also want to develop a map that depicts the Layer 3 topology of the internetwork. This map can leave out switches and hubs, but should depict routers, logical links between the routers, and high-level routing protocol configuration information (for example, the location of the desired designated router [DR] if Open Shortest Path First [OSPF] is being used).

Layer 3 drawings should also include router interface names in Cisco shorthand nomenclature (such as s0/0) if Cisco routers are used. Other useful information includes Hot Standby Router Protocol (HSRP) router groupings, redistribution points between routing protocols, and demarcation points where route filters occur. The Layer 3 drawing should also include the location and high-level configuration of firewalls and NAT, IDS, and IPS devices.

A map or set of maps that shows detailed information about data link layer links and devices is often extremely helpful. This map reveals LAN devices and interfaces connected to public or private WANs. This map may hide the logical Layer 3 routing topology, which is shown in the previous map(s), but it should provide a good characterization of the physical topology. A data link layer map includes the following information:

- An indication of the data link layer technology for WANs and LANs (Frame Relay, Point-to-Point Protocol [PPP], VPN, 100-Mbps or 1000-Mbps Ethernet, and so on)

- The name of the service provider for WANs

- WAN circuit IDs

- The location and high-level configuration information for LAN switches (for example, the location of the desired root bridge if the Spanning Tree Protocol [STP] is used)

- The location and reach of any VLANs and VLAN Trunking Protocol (VTP) configurations

- The location and high-level configuration of trunks between LAN switches

- The location and high-level configuration of any Layer 2 firewalls

Characterizing the Logical Architecture

While documenting the network infrastructure, take a step back from the diagrams you develop and try to characterize the logical topology of the network and the physical components. The logical topology illustrates the architecture of the network, which can be hierarchical or flat, structured or unstructured, layered or not, and other possibilities. The logical topology also describes methods for connecting devices in a geometric shape (for example, a star, ring, bus, hub and spoke, or mesh).

When characterizing the logical topology, look for "ticking time bombs" or implementations that might hinder scalability. Ticking time bombs include large Layer 2 STP domains that will take a long time to converge and overly complex or oversized networks that might lead to Enhanced Interior Gateway Routing Protocol (EIGRP) stuck-in-active (SIA) problems and other routing problems. If the customer has fully redundant network equipment and cabling but the servers are all single-homed (attached to a single switch), keep this in mind as you plan your redesign of the network. This could be another ticking time bomb that can be fixed with a redesign.

The logical topology can affect your ability to upgrade a network. For example, a flat topology does not scale as well as a hierarchical topology. A typical hierarchical topology that does scale is a core layer of high-end routers and switches that are optimized for availability and performance, a distribution layer of routers and switches that implement policies, and an access layer that connects users via hubs, switches, and other devices. Logical topologies are discussed in more detail in Chapter 5, "Designing a Network Topology."

Figure 3-1 shows a high-level network diagram for an electronics manufacturing company. The drawing shows a physical topology, but it is not hard to step back and visualize that the logical topology is a hub-and-spoke shape with three layers. The core layer of the network is a Gigabit Ethernet network. The distribution layer includes routers and switches, and Frame Relay and T1 links. The access layer is composed of 10-Mbps and 100-Mbps Ethernet networks. An Ethernet network hosts the company's web server. As you can see from the figure, the network included some rather old design components. The company required design consultation to select new technologies and to meet new goals for high availability and security.

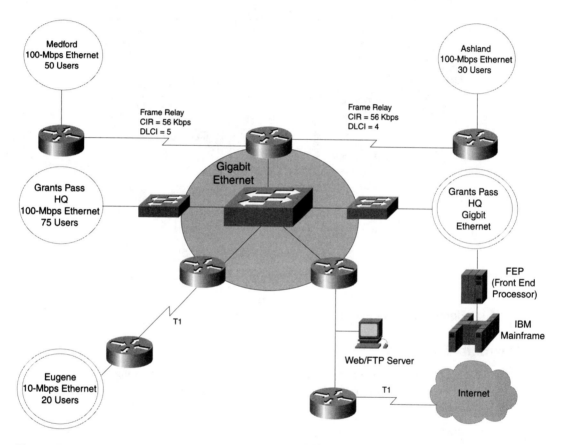

Figure 3-1 *Network Diagram for an Electronics Manufacturing Company*

Developing a Modular Block Diagram

In addition to developing a set of detailed maps, it is often helpful to draw a simplified block diagram of the network or parts of the network. The diagram can depict the major functions of the network in a modular fashion. Figure 3-2 shows a block, modularized network topology map that is based on the Cisco Enterprise Composite Network Model.

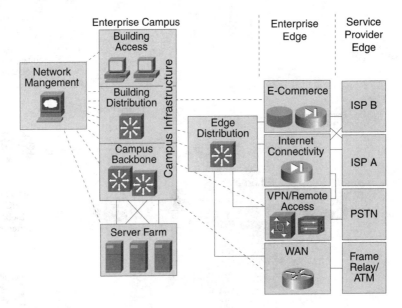

Figure 3-2   *Modularized Network Topology Example*

Characterizing Network Addressing and Naming

Characterizing the logical infrastructure of a network involves documenting any strategies your customer has for network addressing and naming. Addressing and naming are discussed in greater detail in Part II of this book, "Logical Network Design."

When drawing detailed network maps, include the names of major sites, routers, network segments, and servers. Also document any standard strategies your customer uses for naming network elements. For example, some customers name sites using airport codes (San Francisco = SFO, Oakland = OAK, and so on). You might find that a customer suffixes names with an alias that describes the type of device (for example, *RTR* for router). Some customers use a standard naming system, such as DNS, for IP networks, or NetBIOS Windows Internet Naming Service (WINS) on Windows networks. In such cases, you should document the location of the DNS and WINS servers and relevant high-level configuration information.

You should also investigate the network layer addresses your customer uses. Your customer's addressing scheme (or lack of any scheme) can influence your ability to adapt the network to new design goals. For example, your customer might use unregistered IP addresses that will need to be changed or translated before connecting to the Internet.

As another example, current IP subnet masking might limit the number of nodes in a LAN or VLAN.

Your customer might have a goal of using route summarization, which is also called *route aggregation* or *supernetting*. *Route summarization* reduces routes in a routing table, routing-table update traffic, and overall router overhead. Route summarization also improves network stability and availability, because problems in one part of a network are less likely to affect the whole internetwork. Summarization is most effective when address prefixes have been assigned in a consistent and contiguous manner, which is often not the case.

Your customer's existing addressing scheme might affect the routing protocols you can select. Some routing protocols do not support classless addressing, variable-length subnet masking (VLSM), or discontiguous subnets. A *discontiguous subnet* is a subnet that is divided, as shown in Figure 3-3. Subnet 108 of network 10 is divided into two areas that are separated by network 192.168.49.0.

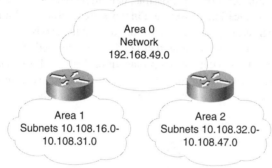

Figure 3-3   *Example of a Discontiguous Subnet*

Characterizing Wiring and Media

To help you meet scalability and availability goals for your new network design, it is important to understand the cabling design and wiring of the existing network. Documenting the existing cabling design can help you plan for enhancements and identify any potential problems. If possible, you should document the types of cabling in use as well as cable distances. Distance information is useful when selecting data link layer technologies based on distance restrictions.

While exploring the cabling design, assess how well equipment and cables are labeled in the current network. The extent and accuracy of labeling will affect your ability to implement and test enhancements to the network.

Your network diagram should document the connections between buildings. The diagram should include information on the number of pairs of wires and the type of wiring (or wireless technology) in use. The diagram should also indicate how far buildings are from one another. Distance information can help you select new cabling. For example, if you plan to upgrade from copper to fiber cabling, the distance between buildings can be much longer.

Probably the wiring (or wireless technology) between buildings is one of the following:

- Single-mode fiber
- Multimode fiber
- Shielded twisted-pair (STP) copper
- Unshielded twisted-pair (UTP) copper
- Coaxial cable
- Microwave
- Laser
- Radio
- Infrared

Within buildings, try to locate telecommunications wiring closets, cross-connect rooms, and any laboratories or computer rooms. If possible, determine the type of cabling that is installed between telecommunications closets and in work areas. (Some technologies, such as 100BASE-TX Ethernet, require Category 5 or later cabling, so be sure to document the existence of any Category 3 cabling that needs to be replaced.) Gather information about both vertical and horizontal wiring. As shown in Figure 3-4, *vertical wiring* runs between floors. *Horizontal wiring* runs from telecommunications closets to wallplates in cubicles or offices. *Work-area wiring* runs from the wallplate to a workstation in a cubicle or office.

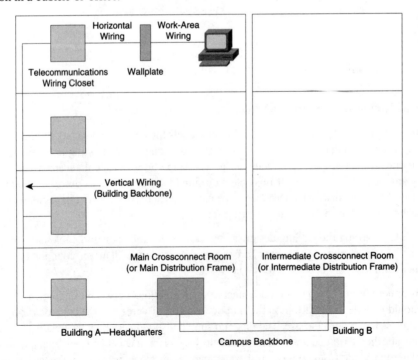

Figure 3-4 *Example of Campus Network Wiring*

In most buildings, the cabling from a telecommunications closet to a workstation is approximately 100 meters (about 300 feet), including the work-area wiring, which is usually just a few meters. If you have any indication that the cabling might be longer than 100 meters, you should use a time-domain reflectometer (TDR) to verify your suspicions. (TDR functionality is included in most cable testers.) Many network designs are based on the assumption that workstations are no more than 100 meters from the telecommunications closet.

Ask the client for a copy of the copper or fiber certification tests that were completed when the cabling was first installed. Test results will help you learn the type of cabling that was installed, its certification, and the warranty period for the installation work. Many modern network designers do just that one step of verifying that the cable was tested and certified rather than going through a detailed analysis of the cabling infrastructure. On the other hand, many network designers still focus on cabling because they have learned the hard way that meeting availability goals can be difficult when the cabling was not installed properly.

For each building, you can fill out the chart shown in Table 3-1. The data that you fill in depends on how much time you have to gather information and how important you think cabling details will be to your network design. If you do not have a lot of information, just put an X for each type of cabling present and document any assumptions (for example, an assumption that workstations are no more than 100 meters from the telecommunications closet). If you have time to gather more details, include information on the length and number of pairs of cables. If you prefer, you can document building wiring information in a network diagram instead of in a table.

Table 3-1   *Building Wiring*

Building name
Location of telecommunications closets
Location of cross-connect rooms and demarcations to external networks
Logical wiring topology (structured, star, bus, ring, centralized, distributed, mesh, tree, or whatever fits)

Vertical Wiring

	Coaxial	Fiber	STP	Category 3 UTP	Category 5 or 6 UTP	Other
Vertical shaft 1						
Vertical shaft 2						
Vertical shaft *n*						

Horizontal Wiring

	Coaxial	Fiber	STP	Category 3 UTP	Category 5 or 6 UTP	Other
Floor 1						
Floor 2						
Floor 3						
Floor *n*						

Work-Area Wiring

	Coaxial	Fiber	STP	Category 3 UTP	Category 5 or 6 UTP	Other
Floor 1						
Floor 2						
Floor 3						
Floor *n*						

Checking Architectural and Environmental Constraints

When investigating cabling, pay attention to such environmental issues as the possibility that cabling will run near creeks that could flood, railroad tracks or highways where traffic could jostle cables, or construction or manufacturing areas where heavy equipment or digging could break cables.

Be sure to determine if there are any legal right-of-way issues that must be dealt with before cabling can be put into place. For example, will cabling need to cross a public street? Will it be necessary to run cables through property owned by other companies? For line-of-sight technologies, such as laser or infrared, make sure there aren't any obstacles blocking the line of sight.

Within buildings, pay attention to architectural issues that could affect the feasibility of implementing your network design. Make sure the following architectural elements are sufficient to support your design:

- Air conditioning
- Heating
- Ventilation
- Power
- Protection from electromagnetic interference
- Doors that can lock

- Space for:

    - Cabling conduits

    - Patch panels

    - Equipment racks

    - Work areas for technicians installing and troubleshooting equipment

Note   Keep in mind that cabling and power are highly influenced by human factors. Installing new cabling might require working with labor unions, for example. Maintaining the reliability of cabling might require monitoring the infamous backhoe operator or the janitor who knocks cables around. It's also not unheard of for security guards to lean against a wall late at night and accidentally activate emergency power off (EPO) or discharge fire suppressant. To avoid problems, make sure EPO and fire suppressant buttons have safety covers and are out of the way.

Checking a Site for a Wireless Installation

A common goal for modern campus network designs is to install a wireless LAN (WLAN) based on IEEE 802.11 standards. An important aspect of inspecting the architectural and environmental constraints of a site is determining the feasibility of using wireless transmission. The term *wireless site survey* is often used to describe the process of analyzing a site to see if it will be appropriate for wireless transmission.

In some ways, doing a wireless site survey is no different from checking an architecture for wired capabilities, where you might need to document obstructions or areas that have water leaks, for example. But in many ways, a wireless site survey is quite different from a wired site survey because the transmission isn't going through guided wires; it's being sent in radio frequency (RF) waves through air. Learning RF transmission theory in depth requires a lot of time and a good background in physics. For complex RF designs and concerns, it often makes sense to hire an RF expert. To do a basic site survey, you might not need help, though.

A site survey starts with a draft WLAN design. Using a floor plan or blueprint for the site, the designer decides on the initial placement of the wireless access points. An access point is a station that transmits and receives data for users of the WLAN. It usually serves also as the point of interconnection between the WLAN and the wired Ethernet network. A network designer can decide where to place access points for initial testing based on some knowledge of where the users will be located, characteristics of the access points' antennas, and the location of major obstructions.

The initial placement of an access point is based on an estimate of the signal loss that will occur between the access point and the users of the access point. The starting point for an estimate depends on how much loss in power a signal would experience in the vacuum of space, without any obstructions or other interference. This is called the *free space path loss* and is specified in decibels (dB). The estimate is tuned with an understanding that the actual expected signal loss depends on the medium through which the signal will travel, which is undoubtedly not a vacuum. An RF signal traveling through objects of various sorts can be affected by many different problems, including the following:

■ **Reflection:** Reflection causes the signal to bounce back on itself. The signal can interfere with itself in the air and affect the receiver's capability to discriminate between the signal and noise in the environment. Reflection is caused by metal surfaces such as steel girders, scaffolding, shelving units, steel pillars, and metal doors. As an example, implementing a WLAN across a parking lot can be tricky because of metal cars (sources of reflection) that come and go.

■ **Absorption:** Some of the electromagnetic energy of the signal can be absorbed by the material in objects through which it passes, resulting in a reduced signal level. Water has significant absorption properties, and objects such as trees or thick wooden structures can have a high water content. Implementing a WLAN in a coffee shop can be tricky if there are large canisters of liquid coffee. Coffee shop WLAN users have also noticed that people coming and going can affect the signal level. (On *Star Trek*, a nonhuman character once called a human "an ugly giant bag of mostly water"!)

■ **Refraction:** When an RF signal passes from a medium with one density into a medium with another density, the signal can be bent, much like light passing through a prism. The signal changes direction and might interfere with the nonrefracted signal. It can take a different path and encounter other, unexpected obstructions and arrive at recipients damaged or later than expected. As an example, a water tank not only introduces absorption, but also the difference in density between the atmosphere and the water can bend the RF signal.

■ **Diffraction:** Diffraction, which is similar to refraction, results when a region through which the RF signal can pass easily is adjacent to a region in which reflective obstructions exist. Like refraction, the RF signal is bent around the edge of the diffractive region and can then interfere with that part of the RF signal that is not bent.

The designers of 802.11 transmitting devices attempt to compensate for variable environmental factors that might cause reflection, absorption, refraction, or diffraction by boosting the power level above what would be required if free space path were the only consideration. The additional power added to a transmission is called the *fade margin*.

Performing a Wireless Site Survey

A site survey confirms signal propagation, strength, and accuracy in different locations. Many wireless network interface cards (NIC) ship with utilities that enable you to measure signal strength. Cisco 802.11 NICs ship with the Cisco Aironet Client Utility (ACU), which is a graphical tool for configuring, monitoring, and managing the NIC and its wireless environment. A site survey can be as simple as walking around with a wireless notebook computer and using the utility to measure signal strength.

Signal strength can also be determined with a protocol analyzer. The WildPackets AiroPeek analyzer, for example, presents the signal strength for each frame received.

An access point typically sends a beacon frame every 100 milliseconds (ms). You can divide the area being surveyed into a grid, and then move your protocol analyzer from gridpoint to gridpoint and plot on a diagram the signal strength of the beacon frames.

When evaluating the various metrics that are provided by wireless utilities, be sure to measure frame corruption and not just signal strength. With a protocol analyzer, capture frames and check for cyclic redundancy check (CRC) errors. CRC errors are the result of corruption from environmental noise or collisions between frames.

You can also indirectly measure signal quality by determining if frames are being lost in transmission. If your protocol analyzer is capturing relatively close to an access point and a mobile client is pinging a server, through the access point, onto the wired Ethernet, you can determine whether ping packets are getting lost.

As part of your site survey, you can also look at acknowledgments (ACK) and frame retries after a missing ACK. With 802.11 WLANs, both the client and the access point send ACKs to each other. An ACK frame is one of six special frames called *control frames*. All directed traffic (frames addressed to any nonbroadcast, nonmulticast destination) are positively acknowledged with an ACK. Clients and access points use ACKs to implement a retransmission mechanism not unlike the Ethernet retry process that occurs after a collision.

In a wired Ethernet, the transmitting station detects collisions through the rules of carrier sense multiple access with collision detection (CSMA/CD). 802.11 uses carrier sense multiple access with collision avoidance (CSMA/CA) as the access method and does not depend on collision detection to operate. Instead, an ACK control frame is returned to a sender for each directed packet received. If a directed frame does not receive an ACK, the frame is retransmitted.

Wireless networking is covered again in later chapters, but remember to consider it early in your design planning. Using a wireless utility, such as the Cisco ACU, WildPackets OmniPeek, or NetStumbler, check signal strength and accuracy with potential access point placements to determine if the architecture of the physical site will be a problem. Performing a basic wireless site survey is an important part of the top-down network design process of checking for architectural and environmental constraints.

Checking the Health of the Existing Internetwork

Studying the performance of the existing internetwork gives you a baseline measurement from which to measure new network performance. Armed with measurements of the present internetwork, you can demonstrate to your customer how much better the new internetwork performs once your design is implemented.

Many of the network-performance goals discussed in Chapter 2, "Analyzing Technical Goals and Tradeoffs," are overall goals for an internetwork. Because the performance of existing network segments will affect overall performance, you need to study the performance of existing segments to determine how to meet overall network performance goals.

If an internetwork is too large to study all segments, you should analyze the segments that will interoperate the most with the new network design. Pay particular attention to backbone networks and networks that connect old and new areas.

In some cases, a customer's goals might be at odds with improving network performance. The customer might want to reduce costs, for example, and not worry about performance. In this case, you will be glad that you documented the original performance so that you can prove that the network was not optimized to start with and your new design has not made performance worse.

By analyzing existing networks, you can also recognize legacy systems that must be incorporated into the new design. Sometimes customers are not aware that older protocols are still running on their internetworks. By capturing network traffic with a protocol analyzer as part of your baseline analysis, you can identify which protocols are actually running on the network and not rely on customers' beliefs.

Developing a Baseline of Network Performance

Developing an accurate baseline of a network's performance is not an easy task. One challenging aspect is selecting a time to do the analysis. It is important that you allocate a lot of time (multiple days) if you want the baseline to be accurate. If measurements are made over too short a timeframe, temporary errors appear more significant than they are.

In addition to allocating sufficient time for a baseline analysis, it is also important to find a typical time period to do the analysis. A baseline of normal performance should not include atypical problems caused by exceptionally large traffic loads. For example, at some companies, end-of-the-quarter sales processing puts an abnormal load on the network. In a retail environment, network traffic can increase fivefold around Christmas time. Network traffic to a web server can unexpectedly increase tenfold if the website gets linked to other popular sites or listed in search engines.

In general, errors, packet/cell loss, and latency increase with load. To get a meaningful measurement of typical accuracy and delay, try to do your baseline analysis during periods of normal traffic load. On the other hand, if your customer's main goal is to improve performance during peak load, be sure to study performance during peak load. The decision whether to measure normal performance, performance during peak load, or both, depends on the goals of the network design.

Some customers do not recognize the value of studying the existing network before designing and implementing enhancements. Your customer's expectations for a speedy design proposal might make it difficult for you to take a step back and insist on time to develop a baseline of performance on the existing network. Also, your other job tasks and goals, especially if you are a sales engineer, might make it impractical to spend days developing a precise baseline.

The work you do before the baseline step in the top-down network design methodology can increase your efficiency in developing a baseline. A good understanding of your customer's technical and business goals can help you decide how thorough to make your study. Your discussions with your customer on business goals can help you identify segments that are important to study because they carry critical and/or backbone traffic. You can also ask your customer to help you identify typical segments from which you can extrapolate other segments.

Analyzing Network Availability

To document availability characteristics of the existing network, gather any statistics that the customer has on the mean time between failure (MTBF) and mean time to repair (MTTR) for the internetwork as a whole and major network segments. Compare these statistics with information you have gathered on MTBF and MTTR goals, as discussed in Chapter 2. Does the customer expect your new design to increase MTBF and decrease MTTR? Are the customer's goals realistic considering the current state of the network?

Talk to the network engineers and technicians about the root causes of the most recent and most disruptive periods of downtime. Assuming the role of a forensic investigator, try to get many sides to the story. Sometimes myths develop about what caused a network outage. (You can usually get a more accurate view of problem causes from engineers and technicians than from users and managers.)

You can use Table 3-2 to document availability characteristics of the current network.

Table 3-2 *Availability Characteristics of the Current Network*

	MTBF	MTTR	Date and Duration of Last Major Downtime	Cause of Last Major Downtime	Fix for Last Major Downtime
Enterprise (as a whole)					
Segment 1					
Segment 2					
Segment 3					
Segment *n*					

Analyzing Network Utilization

Network utilization is a measurement of the amount of bandwidth that is in use during a specific time interval. Utilization is commonly specified as a percentage of capacity. If a network-monitoring tool says that network utilization on a Fast Ethernet segment is 70 percent, for example, this means that 70 percent of the 100-Mbps capacity is in use, averaged over a specified timeframe or window.

Different tools use different averaging windows for computing network utilization. Some tools let the user change the window. Using a long interval can be useful for reducing the amount of statistical data that must be analyzed, but granularity is sacrificed. As Figure 3-5 shows, it can be informative (though tedious) to look at a chart that shows network utilization averaged every minute.

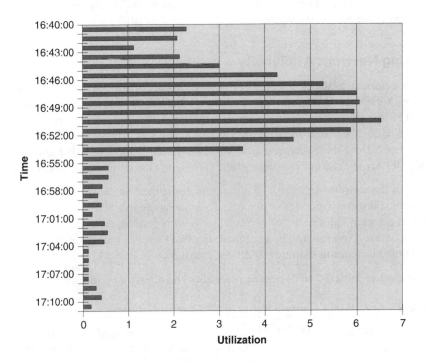

Figure 3-5   *Network Utilization in Minute Intervals*

Figure 3-6 shows the same data averaged over 1-hour intervals. Note that the network was not very busy, so neither chart goes above 7 percent utilization. Note also that changing to a long interval can be misleading because peaks in traffic get averaged out (the detail is lost). In Figure 3-5, you can see that the network was relatively busy around 4:50 p.m. You cannot see this in Figure 3-6, when the data was averaged on an hourly basis.

In general, you should record network utilization with sufficient granularity in time to see short-term peaks in network traffic so that you can accurately assess the capacity requirements of devices and segments. Changing the interval to a small amount of time, say a fraction of a second, can be misleading also, however. To understand the concern, consider a small time interval. In a packet-sized window, at a time when a station is sending traffic, the utilization is 100 percent, which is what is wanted.

The size of the averaging window for network utilization measurements depends on your goals. When troubleshooting network problems, keep the interval small, either minutes or seconds. A small interval helps you recognize peaks caused by problems such as broadcast storms or stations retransmitting quickly due to a misconfigured timer. For performance analysis and baselining purposes, use an interval of 1 to 5 minutes. For long-term load analysis, to determine peak hours, days, or months, set the interval to 10 minutes.

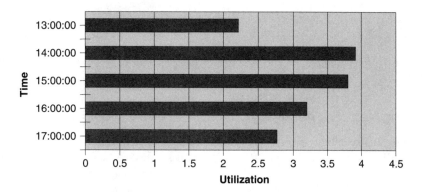

Figure 3-6   *Network Utilization in Hour Intervals*

When developing a baseline, it is usually a good idea to err on the side of gathering too much data. You can always summarize the data later. When characterizing network utilization, use protocol analyzers or other monitoring tools to measure utilization in 1- to 5-minute intervals on each major network segment. If practical, leave the monitoring tools running for at least 1 or 2 typical days. If the customer's goals include improving performance during peak times, measure utilization during peak times and typical times. To determine if the measured utilization is healthy, use the Network Health checklist that appears at the end of this chapter.

Measuring Bandwidth Utilization by Protocol

Developing a baseline of network performance should also include measuring utilization from broadcast traffic versus unicast traffic, and by each major protocol. As discussed in Chapter 4, "Characterizing Network Traffic," some protocols send excessive broadcast traffic, which can seriously degrade performance, especially on switched networks.

To measure bandwidth utilization by protocol, place a protocol analyzer or remote monitoring (RMON) probe on each major network segment and fill out a chart such as the one shown in Table 3-3. If the analyzer supports relative and absolute percentages, specify the bandwidth used by protocols as relative and absolute. Relative *usage* specifies how much bandwidth is used by the protocol in comparison to the total bandwidth currently in use on the segment. *Absolute usage* specifies how much bandwidth is used by the protocol in comparison to the total capacity of the segment (for example, in comparison to 100 Mbps on Fast Ethernet).

Table 3-3   *Bandwidth Utilization by Protocol*

	Relative Network Utilization	**Absolute Network Utilization**	**Broadcast/Multicast Rate**
Protocol 1			
Protocol 2			
Protocol 3			
Protocol *n*			

Analyzing Network Accuracy

Chapter 2 talked about specifying network accuracy as a bit error rate (BER). You can use a BER tester (also called a *BERT*) on serial lines to test the number of damaged bits compared to total bits. As discussed in the "Checking the Status of Major Routers, Switches, and Firewalls" section later in this chapter, you can also use Cisco **show** commands to gain an understanding of errors on a serial interface, which is a more common practice on modern networks than using a BERT.

With packet-switched networks, it makes more sense to measure frame (packet) errors because a whole frame is considered bad if a single bit is changed or dropped. In packet-switched networks, a sending station calculates a CRC based on the bits in a frame. The sending station places the value of the CRC in the frame. A receiving station determines if a bit has been changed or dropped by calculating the CRC again and comparing the result to the CRC in the frame. A frame with a bad CRC is dropped and must be retransmitted by the sender. Usually an upper-layer protocol has the job of retransmitting frames that do not get acknowledged.

A protocol analyzer can check the CRC on received frames. As part of your baseline analysis, you should track the number of frames received with a bad CRC every hour for 1 or 2 days. Because it is normal for errors to increase with utilization, document errors as a function of the number of bytes seen by the monitoring tool. A good rule-of-thumb threshold for considering errors unhealthy is that a network should not have more than one bad frame per megabyte of data. (Calculating errors this way lets you simulate a serial BERT. Simply calculating a percentage of bad frames compared to good frames does not account for the size of frames and hence does not give a good indication of how many bits are actually getting damaged.)

In addition to tracking data link layer errors, such as CRC errors, a baseline analysis should include information on upper-layer problems. A protocol analyzer that includes an expert system, such as CACE Technologies' Wireshark analyzer or WildPackets' OmniPeek analyzer, speeds the identification of upper-layer problems by automatically generating diagnoses and symptoms for network conversations and applications.

Accuracy should also include a measurement of lost packets. You can measure lost packets while measuring response time, which is covered later in this chapter in the "Analyzing

Delay and Response Time" section. When sending packets to measure how long it takes to receive a response, document any packets that do not receive a response, presumably because either the request or the response got lost. Correlate the information about lost packets with other performance measurements to determine if the lost packets indicate a need to increase bandwidth, decrease CRC errors, or upgrade internetworking devices. You can also measure lost packets by looking at statistics kept by routers on the number of packets dropped from input or output queues.

Analyzing Errors on Switched Ethernet Networks

Switches have replaced hubs in most campus networks. A switch port that is in half-duplex mode follows the normal rules of CSMA/CD. The port checks the medium for any traffic by watching the carrier sense signal, defers to traffic if necessary, detects collisions, backs off, and retransmits. Whether a collision can occur depends on what is connected to the switched port. If a shared medium is connected to the switch, collisions can occur. A good rule of thumb is that fewer than 0.1 percent of frames should encounter collisions. There should be no late collisions. Late collisions are collisions that happen after a port or interface has sent the first 64 bytes of a frame. Late collisions indicate bad cabling, cabling that is longer than the 100-meter standard, a bad NIC, or a duplex mismatch.

If the switch port connects a single device, such as another switch, a server, or a single workstation, both ends of this point-to-point link should be configured for full duplex. In this case, collisions should never occur. Full-duplex Ethernet isn't CSMA/CD. There are only two stations that can send because full duplex requires a point-to-point link, and each station has its own private transmit channel. So full duplex isn't multiple access (MA). There's no need for a station to check the medium to see if someone else is sending on its transmit channel. There isn't anyone else. So full duplex doesn't use carrier sense (CS). There are no collisions. Both stations sending at the same time is normal. Receiving while sending is normal. So, there is no collision detection (CD) either.

Unfortunately, the autonegotiation of half versus full duplex has been fraught with problems over the years, resulting in one end of a point-to-point link being set to half duplex and the other being set to full duplex. This is a misconfiguration and must be fixed. Autonegotiation problems can result from hardware incompatibilities and old or defective Ethernet software drivers. Some vendors' NICs or switches do not conform exactly to the IEEE 802.3u specification, which results in incompatibilities. Hardware incompatibility can also occur when vendors add advanced features, such as autopolarity, that are not in the IEEE 802.3u specification. (Autopolarity corrects reversed polarity on the transmit and receive twisted pairs.)

The autonegotiation of speed isn't usually a problem. If the speed doesn't negotiate correctly, the interface doesn't work, and the administrator hopefully notices and corrects the problem immediately. Manually configuring the speed for 10 Mbps, 100 Mbps, or 1000 Mbps usually isn't necessary (except for cases where the user interface requires this before it will allow manual configuration of duplex mode). If a LAN still has Category 3 cabling, manually configuring the speed to 10 Mbps is recommended, however. Errors can increase on a LAN that has autonegotiated for 100 Mbps or 1000 Mbps if there is Category 3 cabling that does not support the high-frequency signal used on 100- or 1000-Mbps Ethernet.

Duplex negotiation happens after the speed is negotiated. Problems with duplex negotiation are harder to detect because any performance impact is dependent on the link partners transmitting at the same time. A workstation user who doesn't send much traffic might not notice a problem, whereas a server could be severely impacted by a duplex mismatch. As part of analyzing the performance of the existing network, be sure to check for duplex mismatch problems. A surprisingly high number of networks have been hobbling along for years with performance problems related to a duplex mismatch.

To detect a duplex mismatch, look at the number and type of errors on either end of the link. You can view errors with the **show interface** or **show port** command on Cisco routers and switches. Look for CRC and runt errors on one side and collisions on the other side of the link. The side that is set for full duplex can send whenever it wants. It doesn't need to check for traffic. The side that is set for half duplex does check for traffic and will stop transmitting if it detects a simultaneous transmission from the other side. It will back off, retransmit, and report a collision. The result of the half-duplex station's stopping transmission is usually a runt frame (shorter than 64 bytes) and is always a CRC-errored frame.

The full-duplex side receives runts and CRC-errored frames and reports these errors. The half-duplex station reports collisions. Most of these will be legal collisions; some might be illegal late collisions. When checking the health of Ethernet LANs, check for these errors. Notice the asymmetry of the errors when there is a duplex mismatch. If you see collisions and CRC errors on both sides of the link, the problem is probably something other than a duplex mismatch, perhaps a wiring problem or bad NIC.

Until recently, most engineers recommended avoiding autonegotiation, but that is changing. Improvements in the interoperability of autonegotiation and the maturity of the technology mean that it is generally safer to rely on autonegotiation than to not rely on it.

There are numerous problems with not using autonegotiation. The most obvious one is human error. The network engineer sets one end of the link and forgets to set the other end. Another problem is that some NICs and switch ports don't participate in autonegotiation if manually set. This means they don't send the link pulses to report their setting.

How should the partner react to such a situation? The answer is undefined. Some NICs and switch ports assume the other side is too old to understand full duplex and must be using half. This causes the NIC or switch port to set itself to half. This is a serious problem if the other side is manually configured to full. On the other hand, there are cases where autonegotiation simply does not work, and you might need to carefully configure the mode manually.

Analyzing Network Efficiency

Chapter 2 talked about the importance of using maximum frame sizes to increase network efficiency. Bandwidth utilization is optimized for efficiency when applications and protocols are configured to send large amounts of data per frame, thus minimizing the number of frames and round-trip delays required for a transaction. The number of frames per transaction can also be minimized if the receiver is configured with a large receive window allowing it to accept multiple frames before it must send an acknowledgment. The goal is to maximize the number of data bytes compared to the number of bytes in headers and in acknowledgment packets sent by the other end of a conversation.

Changing frame and receive window sizes on clients and servers can result in improved efficiency. Increasing the maximum transmission unit (MTU) on router interfaces can also improve efficiency, although doing this is not appropriate on low-bandwidth links that are used for voice or other real-time traffic. (As Chapter 2 mentioned, you don't want to increase serialization delay.)

On the other hand, increasing the MTU is sometimes necessary on router interfaces that use tunnels. Problems can occur when the extra header added by the tunnel causes frames to be larger than the default MTU, especially in cases where an application sets the IP Don't Fragment (DF) bit and a firewall is blocking the Internet Control Message Protocol (ICMP) packets that notify the sender of the need to fragment. A typical symptom of this problem is that users can ping and telnet but not use HTTP, FTP, and other protocols that use large frames. A solution is to increase the MTU on the router interface.

To determine if your customer's goals for network efficiency are realistic, you should use a protocol analyzer to examine the current frame sizes on the network. Many protocol analyzers let you output a chart, such as the one in Figure 3-7, that documents how many frames fall into standard categories for frame sizes. Figure 3-7 shows packet sizes at an Internet service provider (ISP). Many of the frames were 64-byte acknowledgments. A lot of the traffic was HTTP, which used 1500-byte packets in most cases, but also sent 500- and 600-byte packets. If many web-hosting customers had been transferring pages to a web server using a file-transfer or file-sharing protocol, there would have been many more 1500-byte frames. The other traffic consisted of DNS lookups and replies and Simple Mail Transfer Protocol (SMTP), Post Office Protocol (POP), and Address Resolution Protocol (ARP) packets.

A simple way to determine an *average* frame size is to divide the total number of megabytes seen on a segment by the total number of frames in a specified timeframe. Unfortunately, this is a case in which a simple statistical technique does not result in useful data. The average frame size is not a meaningful piece of information. On most networks, there are many small frames, many large frames, but few average-sized frames. Small frames consist of acknowledgments and control information. Data frames fall into the large frame-size categories. Frame sizes typically fall into what is called a *bimodal distribution*, also known as a *camel-back distribution*. A "hump" is on either side of the average but not many values are near the average.

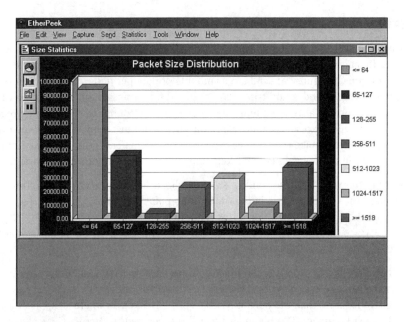

Figure 3-7   *Graph of Packet Sizes on an Internet Service Provider's Ethernet Backbone*

Note   Network performance data is often bimodal, multimodal, or skewed from the mean. (*Mean* is another word for average.) Frame size is often bimodal. Response times from a server can also be bimodal, if sometimes the data is quickly available from RAM cache and sometimes the data is retrieved from a slow mechanical disk drive.

When network-performance data is bimodal, multimodal, or skewed from the mean, you should document a standard deviation with any measurements of the mean. *Standard deviation* is a measurement of how widely data disperses from the mean.

Analyzing frame sizes can help you understand the health of a network, not just the efficiency. For example, an excessive number of Ethernet runt frames (less than 64 bytes) can indicate too many collisions on a shared Ethernet segment. It is normal for collisions to increase with utilization that results from access contention. If collisions increase even when utilization does not increase or even when only a few nodes are transmitting, there could be a more serious problem, such as a bad NIC or a duplex mismatch problem.

Analyzing Delay and Response Time

To verify that performance of a new network design meets a customer's requirements, you need to measure response time between significant network devices before and after a new network design is implemented. Response time can be measured many ways. Using a protocol analyzer, you can look at the amount of time between frames and get a rough estimate of response time at the data link layer, transport layer, and application layer.

(This is a rough estimate because packet arrival times on an analyzer can only approximate packet arrival times on end stations.)

A more common way to measure response time is to send ping packets and measure the round-trip time (RTT) to send a request and receive a response. While measuring RTT, you can also measure an RTT variance. *Variance measurements* are important for applications that cannot tolerate much jitter (for example, voice and video applications). You can also document any loss of packets.

You can use Table 3-4 to document response time measurements. The table uses the term *node* to mean *router*, *server*, *client*, or *mainframe*.

Table 3-4   *Response-Time Measurements*

	Node A	Node B	Node C	Node D
Node A	X			
Node B		X		
Node C			X	
Node D				X

Depending on the amount of time you have for your analysis and depending on your customer's network design goals, you should also measure response time from a user's point of view. On a typical workstation, run some representative applications and measure how long it takes to get a response for typical operations, such as checking email, sending a file to a server, downloading a web page, updating a sales order, printing a report, and so on.

Sometimes applications or protocol implementations are notoriously slow or poorly written. Some peripherals are known to cause extra delay because of incompatibilities with operating systems or hardware. By joining mailing lists and newsgroups and reading information in journals and on the World Wide Web, you can learn about causes of response-time problems. Be sure to do some testing on your own also, though, because every environment is different.

In addition to testing user applications, test the response time for network-services protocols (for example, DNS queries, DHCP requests for an IP address, RADIUS authentication requests, and so on). Chapter 4 covers protocol issues in more detail.

You should also measure how much time a workstation takes to boot. Some workstation operating systems take a long time to boot due to the amount of network traffic that they send and receive while booting. You can include boot time measurements in your analysis of the existing network so that you have a baseline. When the new network design is implemented, you can compare the amount of time a workstation takes to boot with the baseline time. Hopefully you can use this data to prove that your design is an improvement.

Although your customer might not give you permission to simulate network problems, it makes sense to do some testing of response times when the network is experiencing problems or change. For example, if possible, measure response times while routing protocols are converging after a link has gone down. Measure response times during convergence again, after your new design is implemented, to see if the results have improved. As covered in Chapter 12, "Testing Your Network Design," you can test network problems on a pilot implementation.

Checking the Status of Major Routers, Switches, and Firewalls

The final step in characterizing the existing internetwork is to check the behavior of the internetworking devices in the internetwork. This includes routers and switches that connect layers of a hierarchical topology, and devices that will have the most significant roles in your new network design. It's not necessary to check every LAN switch, just the major switches, routers, and firewalls.

Checking the behavior and health of an internetworking device includes determining how busy the device is (CPU utilization), how many packets it has processed, how many packets it has dropped, and the status of buffers and queues. Your method for assessing the health of an internetworking device depends on the vendor and architecture of the device. In the case of Cisco routers, switches, and firewalls, you can use the following Cisco IOS commands:

- **show buffers:** Displays information on buffer sizes, buffer creation and deletion, buffer usage, and a count of successful and unsuccessful attempts to get buffers when needed.

- **show cdp neighbors detail:** Displays information about neighbor devices, including which protocols are enabled, network addresses for enabled protocols, the number and type of interfaces, the type of platform and its capabilities, and the version of Cisco IOS Software.

- **show environment:** Displays temperature, voltage, and blower information on the Cisco 7000 series, Cisco 7200 series, and Cisco 7500 series routers, and the Cisco 12000 series Gigabit Switch Router.

- **show interfaces:** Displays statistics for interfaces, including the input and output rate of packets, a count of packets dropped from input and output queues, the size and usage of queues, a count of packets ignored due to lack of I/O buffer space on a card, CRC errors, collision counts, and how often interfaces have restarted.

- **show ip cache flow:** Displays information about NetFlow, a Cisco technology that collects and measures data as it enters router and switch interfaces, including source and destination IP addresses, source and destination TCP or UDP port numbers, differentiated services codepoint (DSCP) values, packet and byte counts, start and end time stamps, input and output interface numbers, and routing information (next-hop address, source and destination autonomous system numbers, and source and destination prefix masks).

- **show memory:** Displays statistics about system memory, including total bytes, used bytes, and free bytes. Also shows detailed information about memory blocks.

- **show processes:** Displays CPU utilization for the last 5 seconds, 1 minute, and 5 minutes, and the percentage of CPU used by various processes, including routing protocol processes, buffer management, and user-interface processes. (The **show processes cpu** and **show processes cpu history** commands are both useful variations of the **show processes** command.)

- **show running-config:** Displays the router's configuration stored in memory and currently in use.

- **show startup-config:** Displays the configuration the router will use upon the next reboot.

- **show version:** Displays software version and features, the names and sources of configuration files, the boot images, the configuration register, router uptime, and the reason for the last reboot.

Network Health Checklist

You can use the following Network Health checklist to assist you in verifying the health of an existing internetwork. The Network Health checklist is generic in nature and documents a best-case scenario. The thresholds might not apply to all networks.

- ❏ The network topology and physical infrastructure are well documented.

- ❏ Network addresses and names are assigned in a structured manner and are well documented.

- ❏ Network wiring is installed in a structured manner and is well labeled.

- ❏ Network wiring has been tested and certified.

- ❏ Network wiring between telecommunications closets and end stations is no more than 100 meters.

- ❏ Network availability meets current customer goals.

- ❏ Network security meets current customer goals.

- ❏ No LAN or WAN segments are becoming saturated (70 percent average network utilization in a 10-minute window).

- ❏ There are no collisions on Ethernet full-duplex links.

- ❏ Broadcast traffic is less than 20 percent of all traffic on each network segment. (Some networks are more sensitive to broadcast traffic and should use a 10 percent threshold.)

- ❏ Wherever possible and appropriate, frame sizes have been optimized to be as large as possible for the data link layer in use.

❑   No routers are overused (5-minute CPU utilization is under 75 percent).

❑   On average, routers are not dropping more than 1 percent of packets. (For networks that are intentionally oversubscribed to keep costs low, a higher threshold can be used.)

❑   Up-to-date router, switch, and other device configurations have been collected, archived, and analyzed as part of the design study.

❑   The response time between clients and hosts is generally less than 100 ms (1/10th of a second).

Summary

This chapter covered techniques and tools for characterizing a network before designing enhancements to the network. Characterizing an existing network is an important step in top-down network design because it helps you verify that a customer's technical design goals are realistic. It also helps you understand the current topology and locate existing network segments and equipment, which will be useful information when the time comes to install new equipment.

As part of the task of characterizing the existing network, you should develop a baseline of current performance. Baseline performance measurements can be compared to new measurements once your design is implemented to demonstrate to your customer that your new design (hopefully) improves performance.

Review Questions

1.   What is a discontiguous network? Why does it pose challenges for a network designer?

2.   Why is it important to characterize a network's logical topology and not just its physical topology? What information does a logical topology illustrate that might be missed with just a physical topology?

3.   The Cooperative Association for Internet Data Analysis (CAIDA) collects information on network measurement and visualization resources. How could CAIDA's work help a network designer characterize an existing network?

4.   The IETF Internet Protocol Performance Metrics (IPPM) working group develops standard metrics that can be applied to the quality, performance, and reliability of a network. How could this group's work help a network designer characterize an existing network?

Hands-On Project

The chapter mentioned using a protocol analyzer to characterize a network. Download and install the Wireshark protocol analyzer from www.wireshark.org. Unless you signed an Acceptable Use Policy (AUP) document that disallows this, capture traffic from your live business or school network. (If you have signed an AUP that disallows capturing network traffic, capture from your home network instead.) Answer the following questions.

1. In Wireshark, go to **Statistics > Summary**. What is the Average Mbps?

2. Go to **Statistics > Protocol Hierarchy**. Which protocols use most of the bandwidth?

3. Go to **Statistics > Packet Lengths > Create Stat**. What percentage of packets are less than 80 bytes? What percentage of packets are 80–1279 bytes? What percentage of packets are larger than 1279 bytes?

4. Capture network traffic while accessing a website with your web browser. In Wireshark, go to **Statistics > HTTP > Packet Counter >Create Stat**. How many Response Packets did you capture? What types of Response Packets and how many of each type did you capture?

Design Scenario

The city of Mapleland, Oregon, which owns and operates its own power utility, built a fiber-optic network to monitor power meters at residents' homes. The network is called Mapleland Fiber Network (MFN). Because MFN had more capacity than was needed to monitor meters, the city expanded its services to offer access to the network for city businesses. The businesses use the network to communicate with each other and to access the Internet. At the MFN headend, which is located with the city government offices, three routers and WAN links connect to the Internet for use by the city. The businesses on MFN also use these routers to reach the Internet.

In addition to the business service, MFN also offers cable modem service to homes. A cable modem router at the MFN headend connects to the fiber-optic network. In the city neighborhoods, hybrid fiber-coax nodes bring coax cabling to each street and into the homes for cable modem Internet access.

The MFN backbone consists of a fiber-optic Gigabit Ethernet network that runs through the city in a ring topology. The fiber-optic ring connects the hybrid fiber-coax nodes that bring coax cabling to each neighborhood. Also connected to the ring are six data routers. Each router links one or more Mapleland businesses to MFN via simple point-to-point connections. At the business, the fiber-optic network enters the building and connects to a media converter. A UTP cable connects to the media converter and typically to a 100-Mbps Ethernet switch. The switch links the business's computers and servers in a star topology via UTP cabling.

1. Draw a network map that shows the topology of the MFN and how the main components are connected.

2. What other information would you gather to improve your map and add more detail?

3. Mapleland is considering expanding the MFN to include wireless access for its residences. What additional investigation will you do to prepare for a citywide wireless network?

4. What security concerns do you have for the wireless network?

Chapter 4

Characterizing Network Traffic

This chapter describes techniques for characterizing traffic flow, traffic volume, and protocol behavior. The techniques include recognizing traffic sources and data stores, documenting application and protocol usage, and evaluating network traffic caused by common protocols. Upon completion of this chapter, you will be able to analyze network traffic patterns to help you select appropriate logical and physical network design solutions to meet a customer's goals.

The previous chapter talked about characterizing the existing network in terms of its structure and performance. Because analyzing the existing situation is an important step in a systems analysis approach to design, this chapter discusses characterizing the existing network in terms of traffic flow. The chapter also covers new network design requirements, building on the first two chapters that covered business and technical design goals. This chapter refocuses on design requirements and describes requirements in terms of traffic flow, traffic load, protocol behavior, and quality of service (QoS) requirements.

Characterizing Traffic Flow

Characterizing traffic flow involves identifying sources and destinations of network traffic and analyzing the direction and symmetry of data traveling between sources and destinations. In some applications, the flow is bidirectional and symmetric. (Both ends of the flow send traffic at about the same rate.) In other applications, the flow is bidirectional and asymmetric. (Clients send small queries and servers send large streams of data.) In a broadcast application, the flow is unidirectional and asymmetric. This section talks about characterizing the direction and symmetry of traffic flow on an existing network and analyzing flow for new network applications.

Identifying Major Traffic Sources and Stores

To understand network traffic flow, you should first identify user communities and data stores for existing and new applications.

> **Note**   Chapter 3, "Characterizing the Existing Internetwork," talked about locating major hosts, interconnect devices, and network segments on a customer's network. The tasks discussed in Chapter 3 facilitate the tasks discussed in this chapter of identifying major user communities and data stores.

A *user community* is a set of workers who use a particular application or set of applications. A user community can be a corporate department or set of departments. In many environments, however, application usage crosses departmental boundaries. As more corporations use matrix management and form virtual teams to complete ad hoc projects, it becomes increasingly necessary to characterize user communities by application and protocol usage rather than by departmental boundary.

To document user communities, ask your customer to help you fill out the User Communities chart shown in Table 4-1. For the Locations of Community column in Table 4-1, use location names that you already documented on a network map. For the Applications Used by Community column, use application names that you already documented in the Network Applications charts in Chapter 1, "Analyzing Business Goals and Constraints," and Chapter 2, "Analyzing Technical Goals and Tradeoffs." The case study in Chapter 10, "Selecting Technologies and Devices for Campus Networks," provides an example of a filled-in chart.

Table 4-1   *User Communities*

User Community Name	Size of Community (Number of Users)	Locations of Community	Applications Used by Community

In addition to documenting user communities, characterizing traffic flow also requires that you document major data stores. A *data store* (sometimes called a *data sink*) is an area in a network where application layer data resides. A data store can be a server, a server farm, a storage-area network (SAN), a mainframe, a tape backup unit, a digital video library, or any device or component of an internetwork where large quantities of data are stored. To help you document major data stores, ask your customer to help you fill out Table 4-2. For the Location, Applications, and Used by User Community columns, use names that you already documented on a network map and other charts.

Table 4-2   *Data Stores*

Data Store	Location	Applications	Used by User Community (or Communities)

Documenting Traffic Flow on the Existing Network

Documenting traffic flow involves identifying and characterizing individual traffic flows between traffic sources and stores. Traffic flows have recently become a hot topic for discussion in the Internet community. A lot of progress is being made on defining flows, measuring flow behavior, and allowing an end station to specify performance requirements for flows.

To understand traffic flow behavior better, you can read Request For Comments (RFC) 2722, "Traffic Flow Measurement: Architecture." RFC 2722 describes an architecture for the measurement and reporting of network traffic flows and discusses how the architecture relates to an overall traffic flow architecture for intranets and the Internet.

Note   You can find all RFCs online at http://www.ietf.org/rfc/rfcxxxx.txt, where xxxx is the number of the RFC.

Measuring traffic flow behavior can help a network designer determine which routers should be peers in routing protocols that use a peering system, such as the Border Gateway Protocol (BGP). Measuring traffic flow behavior can also help network designers do the following:

■   Characterize the behavior of existing networks.

■   Plan for network development and expansion.

■   Quantify network performance.

■   Verify the quality of network service.

■   Ascribe network usage to users and applications.

An *individual network traffic flow* can be defined as protocol and application information transmitted between communicating entities during a single session. A flow has attributes such as direction, symmetry, routing path and routing options, number of packets, number of bytes, and addresses for each end of the flow. A communicating entity can be an end system (host), a network, or an autonomous system (AS).

The simplest method for characterizing the size of a flow is to measure the number of megabytes per second (MBps) between communicating entities. To characterize the size of a flow, use a protocol analyzer or network management system to record load between important sources and destinations. You can also use Cisco NetFlow, which collects and measures data as it enters router and switch interfaces, including source and destination IP addresses, source and destination TCP or UDP port numbers, packet and byte counts, and so on.

You can use Table 4-3 to document information about the direction and volume of traffic flows. The objective is to document the megabytes per second between pairs of autonomous systems, networks, hosts, and applications. To get the information to fill out the charts, place a monitoring device in the core of the network and let it collect data for one or two days. To get the information to fill out the Path column, you can turn on the record-route option in an IP network. The record-route option has some disadvantages, however. It doesn't support large internetworks and is often disabled for security reasons. You can also estimate the path by looking at routing tables and analyzing network traffic on multiple segments.

Table 4-3   *Network Traffic Flow on the Existing Network*

	Destination 1		**Destination 2**		**Destination 3**		**Destination *n***	
	MBps	**Path**	**MBps**	**Path**	**MBps**	**Path**	**MBps**	**Path**
Source 1								
Source 2								
Source 3								
Source n								

Characterizing Types of Traffic Flow for New Network Applications

As mentioned, a network flow can be characterized by its direction and symmetry. Direction specifies whether data travels in both directions or in just one direction. Direction also specifies the path that a flow takes as it travels from source to destination through an internetwork. Symmetry describes whether the flow tends to have higher performance or QoS requirements in one direction than the other direction. Many network applications have different requirements in each direction. Some data link layer transmission technologies, such as Asymmetric Digital Subscriber Line (ADSL), are fundamentally asymmetric. A good technique for characterizing network traffic flow is to classify applications as supporting one of a few well-known flow types:

■   Terminal/host traffic flow

■   Client/server traffic flow

- Peer-to-peer traffic flow

- Server/server traffic flow

- Distributed computing traffic flow

In his book *Network Analysis, Architecture, and Design*, Third Edition, James D. McCabe does an excellent job of characterizing and distinguishing flow models. The descriptions of flow types in the sections that follow are partially based on McCabe's work.

Terminal/Host Traffic Flow

Terminal/host traffic is usually asymmetric. The terminal sends a few characters and the host sends many characters. Telnet is an example of an application that generates terminal/host traffic. The default behavior for Telnet is that the terminal sends each character a user types in a single packet. The host returns multiple characters, depending on what the user typed. As an illustration, consider the beginning of a Telnet session that starts with the user typing a username. When the host receives each packet for the characters in the name, the host sends back a message (such as Password Required) in one packet.

Note   Default Telnet behavior can be changed so that instead of sending one character at a time, the terminal sends characters after a timeout or after the user types a carriage return. This behavior uses network bandwidth more efficiently but can cause problems for some applications. For example, the *vi editor* on UNIX systems must see each character immediately to recognize whether the user has pressed a special character for moving up a line, down a line, to the end of a line, and so on.

Terminal/host traffic flows are less prevalent on networks than they once were, but they have not disappeared. In fact, so-called thin clients, which have become quite popular, can behave like terminal/host applications. Thin clients are covered following the next section on client/server traffic flow.

Client/Server Traffic Flow

Client/server traffic is the best-known and most widely used flow type. Servers are generally powerful computers dedicated to managing disk storage, printers, or other network resources. Clients are PCs or workstations on which users run applications. Clients rely on servers for access to resources, such as storage, peripherals, application software, and processing power.

Clients send queries and requests to a server. The server responds with data or permission for the client to send data. The flow is usually bidirectional and asymmetric. Requests from the client are typically small frames, except when writing data to the server, in which case they are larger. Responses from the server range from 64 bytes to 1500 bytes or more, depending on the maximum frame size allowed for the data link layer in use.

Client/server protocols include Server Message Block (SMB), Network File System (NFS), Apple Filing Protocol (AFP), and NetWare Core Protocol (NCP). In a TCP/IP environment, many applications are implemented in a client/server fashion, although the applications were invented before the client/server model was invented. For example, FTP has a client and server side. FTP clients use FTP applications to talk to FTP servers. X Window System is an example of a server (the screen manager) that actually runs on the user's machine. This can lead to a great deal of traffic in both directions, such as when the user enables a blinking cursor or ticking clock that needs continual updating across the network, even when the user isn't present.

These days, HTTP is the most widely used client/server protocol. Clients use a web browser application, such as Firefox, to talk to web servers. The flow is bidirectional and asymmetric. Each session often lasts just a few seconds because users tend to jump from one website to another.

The flow for HTTP traffic is not always between the web browser and the web server because of caching. When users access data that has been cached to their own systems, there is no network traffic. Another possibility is that a network administrator has set up a cache engine. A cache engine is software or hardware that makes recently accessed web pages available locally, which can speed the delivery of the pages and reduce WAN bandwidth utilization. A cache engine can also be used to control the type of content that users are allowed to view.

A content delivery network (CDN) can also affect the flow of HTTP traffic. A CDN is a network of servers that delivers web pages to users based on their geographic location. A CDN copies the pages of a website to a network of servers that can be dispersed at different locations. When a user requests a web page that is part of a CDN, the CDN redirects the request to a server that is closest to the user and delivers the cached content. The CDN can also communicate with the originating server to deliver any content that has not been previously cached. CDNs speed the delivery of content and can protect a website from large surges in traffic.

Thin Client Traffic Flow

A special case of the client/server architecture is a *thin client*, which is software or hardware that is designed to be particularly simple and to work in an environment where the bulk of data processing occurs on a server. With thin client technology (also known as *server-based computing*), user applications originate on a central server. In some cases, the application runs on the central server, and in other cases, the software is installed on the server and is downloaded into the client machine for execution.

An information appliance or computing appliance is a thin client designed to perform a particular set of dedicated tasks. A computing appliance could be a cash register, a dedicated email machine, or a database-retrieval device. Computing appliances often run the Linux operating system and a Java-enhanced Internet browser.

The main advantage of thin client technology is lower support costs. Network managers can have a centralized base of applications that are managed, configured, and upgraded only once. There is no need to individually configure each user's machine. In addition, because applications are controlled from the central server, security can be better managed. Thin clients provide a lower total cost of ownership (TCO) and a scalable TCO for large enterprises. Thin client technology is not applicable to every computing application, however, because users might need computers capable of operating without constant connection to a central server.

A downside of thin client technology is that the amount of data flowing from the server to the client can be substantial, especially when many computers start up at the same time every day. Networks that include thin clients should be carefully designed with sufficient capacity and an appropriate topology. Switched networking (rather than shared media) is recommended, and to avoid problems caused by too much broadcast traffic, each switched network should be limited to a few hundred thin clients and their servers. The switched networks can be connected via routers for communications between departments and accessing outside networks such as the Internet.

Peer-to-Peer Traffic Flow

With peer-to-peer traffic, the flow is usually bidirectional and symmetric. Communicating entities transmit approximately equal amounts of information. There is no hierarchy. Each device is considered as important as each other device, and no device stores substantially more data than any other device. In small LAN environments, network administrators often set up PCs in a peer-to-peer configuration so that everyone can access each other's data and printers. There is no central file or print server. Another example of a peer-to-peer environment is a set of multiuser UNIX hosts where users set up FTP, Telnet, HTTP, and NFS sessions between hosts. Each host acts as both a client and server. There are many flows in both directions.

Recently, peer-to-peer applications for downloading music, videos, and software have gained popularity. Each user publishes music or other material and allows other users on the Internet to download the data. This is considered peer-to-peer traffic because every user acts as both a distributor and consumer of data. Traffic flow is bidirectional and symmetric. Most enterprises and many university networks disallow this type of peer-to-peer traffic for two reasons:

- It can cause an inordinate amount of traffic.

- The published material is often copyrighted by someone other than the person publishing it.

One other example of a peer-to-peer application is a meeting between business people at remote sites using videoconferencing equipment. In a meeting, every attendee can communicate as much data as needed at any time. All sites have the same QoS requirements. A meeting is different from a situation where videoconferencing is used to disseminate information. With information dissemination, such as a training class or a speech by a corporate president to employees, most of the data flows from the central site. A few questions are permitted from the remote sites. Information dissemination is usually implemented using a client/server model.

Server/Server Traffic Flow

Server/server traffic includes transmissions between servers and transmissions between servers and management applications. Servers talk to other servers to implement directory services, to cache heavily used data, to mirror data for load balancing and redundancy, to back up data, and to broadcast service availability. Servers talk to management applications for some of the same reasons but also to enforce security policies and to update network management data.

With server/server network traffic, the flow is generally bidirectional. The symmetry of the flow depends on the application. With most server/server applications, the flow is symmetrical, but in some cases there is a hierarchy of servers, with some servers sending and storing more data than others.

Distributed Computing Traffic Flow

Distributed computing refers to applications that require multiple computing nodes working together to complete a job. Some complex modeling and rendering tasks cannot be accomplished in a reasonable timeframe unless multiple computers process data and run algorithms simultaneously. The visual effects for movies are often developed in a distributed computing environment. Distributed computing is also used in the semiconductor industry to serve the extreme computing needs of microchip design and verification, and in the defense industry to provide engineering and military simulations.

With distributed computing, data travels between a task manager and computing nodes and between computing nodes. In his book *Network Analysis, Architecture, and Design*, Third Edition, McCabe distinguishes between tightly coupled and loosely coupled computing nodes. Nodes that are tightly coupled transfer information to each other frequently. Nodes that are loosely coupled transfer little or no information.

With some distributed computing applications, the task manager tells the computing nodes what to do on an infrequent basis, resulting in little traffic flow. With other applications, there is frequent communication between the task manager and the computing nodes. In some cases, the task manager allocates tasks based on resource availability, which makes predicting flow somewhat difficult.

Characterizing traffic flow for distributed computing applications might require you to study the traffic with a protocol analyzer or model potential traffic with a network simulator.

Traffic Flow in Voice over IP Networks

The most important concept to understand when considering traffic flow in VoIP networks is that there are two flows. The flow associated with transmitting the audio voice is separate from the flow associated with call setup and teardown. The flow for transmitting the digital voice is peer-to-peer, between two phones or between two PCs running software such as Skype or Cisco IP Communicator (CIPC). Call setup and teardown, on the other hand, can be characterized as a client/server flow because a phone needs to talk to a more complicated device, such as a server or traditional phone switch, that understands phone numbers, addresses, capabilities negotiation, and so on.

The audio voice flow between two IP endpoints is carried by the Real-Time Transport Protocol (RTP), which is a connectionless protocol that runs on top of UDP. The main call setup, teardown, and control protocols in an IP network are H.323, the Cisco Skinny Client Control Protocol (SCCP), Simple Gateway Control Protocol (SGCP), Media Gateway Control Protocol (MGCP), and Session Initiation Protocol (SIP). These signaling protocols run between an IP endpoint and a voice-enabled server and follow the client/server paradigm.

Both traditional voice networks, which are based on private branch exchanges (PBX) and circuit switching, and modern VoIP networks, which use packet switching, must handle two fundamental functions: call control and call switching. Call control handles call <$Icharacterizing;traffic flow;VoIP networks>**Error! Bookmark not defined.** setup and teardown, addressing and routing, and informational and supplementary services. A fundamental job of call control is to compare the digits dialed by the user making a call to configured number patterns to determine how to route a call. In a VoIP network, call control maps a telephone number or username to an IP destination address, which is understood by the packet infrastructure layer. In a Cisco environment, an IP phone talks to the Cisco Unified Communications Manager software to get an IP destination address to use.

Call switching handles the actual switching of calls. In traditional voice networks, when a call is placed, a PBX connects the calling phone via a so-called *line-side interface* to another phone's line-side interface. If the call is destined for the public switched telephone network (PSTN), the call switching function connects the line-side interface with the trunk-side interface. In a VoIP network, switching of voice packets is handled by the packet infrastructure layer, which provides Ethernet switches and IP routers. The line-side devices are IP phones and PCs running VoIP software such as Cisco IP Communicator (CIPC). The trunk-side interface is handled by a PSTN gateway such as a voice-enabled router.

The audio voice packets, which are encapsulated in RTP, UDP, and IP and a data link layer header, might be switched through the internetwork using a different path from that used by the call control packets. The audio packets represent a distinct traffic flow that should be analyzed differently from the call control flow when considering bandwidth and QoS requirements.

Documenting Traffic Flow for New and Existing Network Applications

To document traffic flow for new (and existing) network applications, characterize the flow type for each application and list the user communities and data stores that are associated with applications. You can use Table 4-4 to enhance the Network Applications charts already discussed in Chapters 1 and 2. When filling out Table 4-4, use the same application names you used in the other charts. (The Protocols Used by Application, Approximate Bandwidth Requirement for the Application, and QoS Requirements columns are described later in this chapter.)

Table 4-4   *Network Applications Traffic Characteristics*

Name of Application	Type of Traffic Flow	Protocols Used by Application	User Communities That Use the Application	Data Stores (Servers, Hosts, and So On)	Approximate Bandwidth Requirement for the Application	QoS Requirements

When identifying the type of traffic flow for an application, select one of the well-known types:

- Terminal/host

- Client/server

- Peer-to-peer

- Server/server

- Distributed computing

If necessary, add a comment to qualify the type of flow. For example, if the type is terminal/host and full screen, make sure to say this, because in a full-screen application, the host sends more data than in a so-called dumb-terminal application. If the flow type is distributed computing, add some text to specify whether the computing nodes are tightly or loosely coupled. If the flow is peer-to-peer and used for voice, include a comment to that effect because voice traffic needs different QoS characteristics than most peer-to-peer applications need.

Characterizing Traffic Load

To select appropriate topologies and technologies to meet a customer's goals, it is important to characterize traffic load with traffic flow. Characterizing traffic load can help you design networks with sufficient capacity for local usage and internetwork flows.

Because of the many factors involved in characterizing network traffic, traffic load estimates are unlikely to be precise. The goal is simply to avoid a design that has any critical bottlenecks. To avoid bottlenecks, you can research application-usage patterns, idle times between packets and sessions, frame sizes, and other traffic behavioral patterns for application and system protocols. For customers with numerous applications, this level of analysis might not be practical, however. For these customers, you could limit the analysis to the top five or ten applications.

Another approach to avoiding bottlenecks is simply to throw large amounts of bandwidth at the problem (also known as *overprovisioning*). A strict interpretation of systems analysis principles wouldn't approve of such an approach, but bandwidth is cheap these days. LAN bandwidth is extremely cheap. There's no excuse for not using Fast Ethernet (or better) on all new workstations and switches, and most organizations can also afford to use Gigabit Ethernet on switch-to-switch and switch-to-server links. WAN bandwidth is still expensive in some parts of the world, including rural areas of the United States. But in many parts of the United States and the rest of the world, bandwidth has been overprovisioned and isn't overutilized. If you know that bandwidth will not be a constraint in your network designs, you can skip the next few sections and jump to "Characterizing Traffic Behavior."

Calculating Theoretical Traffic Load

As described in Chapter 2, *traffic load* (sometimes called *offered load*) is the sum of all the data all network nodes have ready to send at a particular time. A general goal for most network designs is that the network capacity should be more than adequate to handle the traffic load. The challenge is to determine if the capacity proposed for a new network design is sufficient to handle the potential load.

In his book *Local and Metropolitan Area Networks*, Sixth Edition, William Stallings provides some back-of-the-envelope computations for calculating traffic load. Stallings points out that you can make an elementary calculation based simply on the number of stations transmitting, how quickly each station generates messages, and the size of messages. For example, for a network with a proposed capacity of 1 Mbps, if 1000 stations send 1000-bit frames every second, the offered load equals the capacity. Although Stallings was referring to the capacity of a LAN, *capacity* could refer to the capacity of a WAN link, an entire internetwork or parts of an internetwork, or the backplane of a switch or router.

In general, to calculate whether capacity is sufficient, only a few parameters are necessary:

- The number of stations

- The average time that a station is idle between sending frames

- The time required to transmit a message once medium access is gained

By studying idle times and frame sizes with a protocol analyzer, and estimating the number of stations, you can determine if the proposed capacity is sufficient.

If you research traffic flow types, as discussed earlier in this chapter, you can develop more precise estimates of load. Instead of assuming that all stations have similar load-generating qualities, you can assume that stations using a particular application have similar load-generating qualities. Assumptions can be made about frame size and idle time for an application after you have classified the type of flow and identified the protocols (discussed later in this chapter) used by the application.

For a client/server application, idle time for the server depends on the number of clients using the server, and the architecture and performance characteristics of the server (disk access speed, RAM access speed, caching mechanisms, and so on). By studying network traffic from servers with a protocol analyzer, you can estimate an average idle time. In general, servers should have little idle time. If a server is underutilized, you should consider moving it to a shared server platform using server virtualization technology.

Idle time on the client side depends partly on user action, which means it is impossible to precisely predict idle time. However, you can make estimates of idle time by studying traffic with a protocol analyzer and using scripts to simulate worst-case user actions, or by using a network-modeling tool. A good network-modeling tool knows what assumptions to make about idle time, MAC-layer delays, the distribution of packet arrival at servers and internetworking devices, and queuing and buffering behavior at internetworking devices.

After you have identified the approximate traffic load for an application flow, you can estimate total load for an application by multiplying the load for the flow by the number of devices that use the application. The research you do on the size of user communities and the number of data stores (servers) can help you calculate an approximate aggregated bandwidth requirement for each application.

Documenting the location of user communities and data stores, which you did in Tables 4-1 and 4-2, can help you understand the amount of traffic that will flow from one segment to another. This can aid in the selection of backbone technologies and internetworking devices.

When estimating traffic load, in addition to investigating idle times between packets, frames sizes, and flow behavior, you should also investigate application-usage patterns and QoS requirements. Some applications are used infrequently, but require a large amount of bandwidth when they are used. For example, perhaps workers normally access an Ethernet LAN to read email, store small files on servers, and print small documents on network printers. But once every three months, they use real-time multimedia software on their PCs to watch the corporate president's speech on quarterly sales figures. This means that once a quarter traffic characteristics and QoS requirements are different than normal.

In general, to accurately characterize traffic load, you need to understand application-usage patterns and QoS requirements in addition to idle times and frame sizes. Some applications expect the network to simply make a best effort to meet load (bandwidth) requirements. Other applications, such as video applications, have inflexible requirements for a constant amount of bandwidth.

The next section covers characterizing usage patterns in more detail. The section "Characterizing Quality of Service Requirements" later in this chapter discusses characterizing QoS requirements.

Documenting Application-Usage Patterns

The first step in documenting application-usage patterns is to identify user communities, the number of users in the communities, and the applications the users employ. This step, which was already covered in the "Identifying Major Traffic Sources and Stores" section in this chapter, can help you identify the total number of users for each application.

In addition to identifying the total number of users for each application, you should also document the following information:

- The frequency of application sessions (number of sessions per day, week, month, or whatever time period is appropriate)

- The length of an average application session

- The number of *simultaneous* users of an application

Armed with information on the frequency and length of sessions and the number of simultaneous sessions, you can more accurately predict the aggregate bandwidth requirement for all users of an application. If it is not practical to research these details, you can make some assumptions:

- The number of users of an application equals the number of simultaneous users.

- All applications are used all the time, so that your bandwidth calculation is a worst-case (peak) estimate.

- Each user opens just one session, and that session lasts all day until the user shuts down the application at the end of the day.

Refining Estimates of Traffic Load Caused by Applications

To refine your estimate of application bandwidth requirements, you need to research the size of data objects sent by applications, the overhead caused by protocol layers, and any additional load caused by application initialization. (Some applications send much more traffic during initialization than during steady-state operation.)

Because applications and users vary widely in behavior, it is hard to accurately estimate the average size of data objects that users transfer to each other and to servers. (The true engineering answer to most questions related to network traffic is "it depends.") In the past, some networking books specified the average size of an email message, web page, multimedia object, database record, and so on. These days, with email messages that include video attachments, web pages that offer video on demand, and databases that might be used for voicemail, it's difficult to make any generalizations about the average size of objects sent on a network. A thorough analysis of actual application behavior is required if you want to get a precise answer as you provision your networks to handle the offered load.

To completely characterize application behavior, you should investigate which protocols an application uses. When you know the protocols, you can calculate traffic load more precisely by adding the size of protocol headers to the size of data objects. Table 4-5 shows some typical protocol header sizes.

Table 4-5   *Traffic Overhead for Various Protocols*

Protocol	Overhead Details	Total Bytes
Ethernet Version II	Preamble = 8 bytes, header = 14 bytes, CRC = 4 bytes, interframe gap (IFG) = 12 bytes	38
IEEE 802.3 with 802.2	Preamble = 8 bytes, header = 14 bytes, LLC = 3 or 4 bytes, SNAP (if present) = 5 bytes, CRC = 4 bytes, IFG = 12 bytes	46
HDLC	Flags = 2 bytes, addresses = 2 bytes, control = 1 or 2 bytes, CRC = 4 bytes	10
IP	Header size with no options	20
TCP	Header size with no options	20
UDP	Header size	8

Depending on the applications and protocols that a workstation uses, workstation initialization can cause a load on networks due to the number of packets and, in some cases, the number of broadcast packets. Although this is becoming less of a problem as network bandwidth has become so inexpensive, and extremely fast CPUs in workstations are readily available so that broadcast processing isn't a concern, it is still worthy of note for networks that are bound by bandwidth and processing concerns, especially networks at schools and nonprofit organizations. In addition to applications that are set to start upon bootup, the following system-level protocols send packets as a workstation initializes:

- Address Resolution Protocol (ARP)

- Dynamic Host Configuration Protocol (DHCP)

- Internet Control Message Protocol (ICMP), version 4 and 6

- Internet Group Management Protocol (IGMP), version 4 and 6

- Domain Name System (DNS)

- Multicast DNS (mDNS)

- NetBIOS name queries

- Network Time Protocol (NTP)

- Simple Service Discovery Protocol (SSDP)

- Service Location Protocol (SLP)

- Simple Network Management Protocol (SNMP)

Estimating Traffic Load Caused by Routing Protocols

At this point in the network design process, you might not have selected routing protocols for the new network design, but you should have identified routing protocols running on the existing network.

Estimating traffic load caused by legacy routing protocols is important in a topology that includes many networks on one side of a slow WAN link. A router sending a large distance-vector routing table every half minute can use a significant percentage of WAN bandwidth. Because routing protocols limit the number of routes per packet, on large networks, a router sends multiple packets to send the entire table. Routing Information Protocol (RIP), for example, sends a routing packet every 30 seconds. Each route in the packet uses 20 bytes, and there are 25 routes per packet. When headers are added, this means that a router running RIP sends one or more 532-byte packets every 30 seconds, depending on the size of the routing table.

Newer routing protocols, such as Open Shortest Path First (OSPF) and Enhanced Interior Gateway Routing Protocol (EIGRP), use little bandwidth. In the case of OSPF, your main concern should be the amount of bandwidth consumed by the database-synchronization packets that routers send every 30 minutes. By subdividing an OSPF network into areas and using route summarization, this traffic can be minimized. Other than the database-synchronization traffic, the only traffic OSPF sends after initialization is small Hello packets every 10 seconds.

EIGRP also sends Hello packets but more frequently than OSPF (every 5 seconds). On the other hand, EIGRP doesn't send any periodic route updates or database-synchronization packets. It sends route updates only when there are changes.

Characterizing Traffic Behavior

To select appropriate network design solutions, you need to understand protocol and application behavior in addition to traffic flows and load. For example, to select appropriate LAN topologies, you need to investigate the level of broadcast traffic on the LANs. To provision adequate capacity for LANs and WANs, you need to check for extra bandwidth utilization caused by protocol inefficiencies and suboptimal frame sizes or retransmission timers.

Broadcast/Multicast Behavior

A broadcast frame is a frame that goes to all network stations on a LAN. At the data link layer, the destination address of a broadcast frame is FF:FF:FF:FF:FF:FF (all 1s in binary). A multicast frame is a frame that goes to a subset of stations. For example, a frame destined to 01:00:0C:CC:CC:CC goes to Cisco routers and switches that are running the Cisco Discovery Protocol (CDP) on a LAN.

Layer 2 internetworking devices, such as switches and bridges, forward broadcast and multicast frames out all ports. The forwarding of broadcast and multicast frames can be a scalability problem for large flat (switched or bridged) networks. A router does not forward broadcasts or multicasts. All devices on one side of a router are considered part of a single *broadcast domain*.

In addition to including routers in a network design to decrease broadcast forwarding, you can also limit the size of a broadcast domain by implementing virtual LANs (VLAN). VLAN technology, which Chapter 5, "Designing a Network Topology," discusses in more detail, allows a network administrator to subdivide users into subnets by associating switch ports with one or more VLANs. Although a VLAN can span many switches, broadcast traffic within a VLAN is not transmitted outside the VLAN.

Too many broadcast frames can overwhelm end stations, switches, and routers. It is important that you research the level of broadcast traffic in your proposed design and limit the number of stations in a single broadcast domain. The term *broadcast radiation* is often used to describe the effect of broadcasts spreading from the sender to all other devices in a broadcast domain. Broadcast radiation can degrade performance at network endpoints.

The network interface card (NIC) in a network station passes broadcasts and relevant multicasts to the CPU of the station. Some NICs pass all multicasts to the CPU, even when the multicasts are not relevant, because the NICs do not have driver software that is more selective. Intelligent driver software can tell a NIC which multicasts to pass to the CPU. Unfortunately, not all drivers have this intelligence. The CPUs on network stations become overwhelmed when processing high levels of broadcasts and multicasts. If more than 20 percent of the network traffic is broadcasts or multicasts, the network needs to be segmented using routers or VLANs.

Another possible cause of heavy broadcast traffic is intermittent broadcast storms caused by misconfigured or misbehaving network stations. For example, a misconfigured subnet mask can cause a station to send ARP frames unnecessarily because the station does not correctly distinguish between station and broadcast addresses, causing it to send ARPs for broadcast addresses.

In general, however, broadcast traffic is necessary and unavoidable. Routing and switching protocols use broadcasts and multicasts to share information about the internetwork topology. Servers send broadcasts and multicasts to advertise their services. Clients send broadcasts and multicasts to find services and check for uniqueness of addresses and names.

Network Efficiency

Characterizing network traffic behavior requires gaining an understanding of the efficiency of new network applications. *Efficiency* refers to whether applications and protocols use bandwidth effectively. Efficiency is affected by frame size, the interaction of protocols used by an application, windowing and flow control, and error-recovery mechanisms.

Frame Size

Using a frame size that is the maximum supported for the medium in use has a positive impact on network performance for bulk applications. For file-transfer applications, in particular, you should use the largest possible maximum transmission unit (MTU). Depending on the protocol stacks that your customer will use in the new network design, the MTU can be configured for some applications.

In an IP environment, you should avoid increasing the MTU to larger than the maximum supported for the media traversed by the frames, to avoid fragmentation and reassembly of frames. When devices such as end nodes or routers need to fragment and reassemble frames, performance degrades.

Modern operating systems support MTU discovery. With MTU discovery, the software can dynamically discover and use the largest frame size that will traverse the network without requiring fragmentation. MTU discovery generally works, but there are some problems with it as mentioned in the "Analyzing Network Efficiency" section in Chapter 3.

Windowing and Flow Control

To really understand network traffic, you need to understand windowing and flow control. A TCP/IP device, for example, sends segments (packets) of data in quick sequence, without waiting for an acknowledgment, until its *send window* has been exhausted. A station's send window is based on the recipient's *receive window*. The recipient states in every TCP packet how much data it is ready to receive. This total can vary from a few bytes up to 65,535 bytes. The recipient's receive window is based on how much memory the receiver has and how quickly it can process received data. You can optimize network efficiency by increasing memory and CPU power on end stations, which can result in a larger receive window.

Note Theoretically, the optimal window size is the bandwidth of a link multiplied by delay on the link. To maximize throughput and use bandwidth efficiently, the send window should be large enough for the sender to completely fill the bandwidth pipe with data before stopping transmission and waiting for an acknowledgment.

RFC 1323 illustrates the need for a larger window than the standard maximum TCP window size of 65,535 bytes. The product of bandwidth times delay is larger than 65,535 bytes on links of high speeds but long delay, such as high-capacity satellite channels and terrestrial fiber-optic links that go a long distance (for example, across the United States). RFC 1323 refers to a path operating in this region as a *long, fat pipe* and a network containing this path as a *long, fat network* or *LFN* (pronounced "elephant"). If your customer's network includes any LFNs, you should recommend implementations of TCP that are based on RFC 1323. The Window field in the TCP header is 16 bits. RFC 1323 defines a window-scale extension that expands the definition of the TCP window to 32 bits and uses a scale factor to carry this 32-bit value in the 16-bit Window field. During the TCP three-way handshake, hosts can include a TCP option that indicates their support for the window-scale extension.

Some IP-based applications run on top of UDP, not TCP. In this case, there is either no flow control or the flow control is handled at the session or application layer. The following list shows which protocols are based on TCP and which protocols are based on UDP:

- **File Transfer Protocol (FTP):** TCP port 20 (data) and TCP port 21 (control)

- **Telnet:** TCP port 23

- **Simple Mail Transfer Protocol (SMTP):** TCP port 25

- **Hypertext Transfer Protocol (HTTP):** TCP port 80

- **Simple Network Management Protocol (SNMP):** UDP ports 161 and 162

- **Domain Name System (DNS):** UDP port 53

- **Trivial File Transfer Protocol (TFTP):** UDP port 69

- **DHCP server:** UDP port 67

- **DHCP client:** UDP port 68

- **Remote Procedure Call (RPC):** UDP port 111

Protocols that run on UNIX systems, such as NFS and Network Information Services (NIS), often use RPC, although newer versions support TCP.

Protocols that send a reply to each request are often called *Ping-Pong protocols*. Ping-Pong protocols do not use bandwidth efficiently. As an example, consider SMB, the file-sharing protocol used on Windows platforms. Although SMB uses non-Ping-Pong protocols at the lower layers, it behaves like a Ping-Pong protocol at the application layer. The client sends a Read request to receive data. A typical SMB server can send 32 KB of data at a time, divided into TCP segments. The client waits until this data is received before requesting more data. This greatly limits throughput.

Do the calculation for an IPsec VPN, for example, that connects a user in New York City with a server in Washington, DC. The one-way delay is about 50 ms. Ignoring client and server delays for disk I/O and serialization delay, the client receives at most 32 KB every 100 ms or 320 KBps. This means that the maximum throughput is 2.56 Mbps. With packet losses and consequent retransmissions, actual throughput might be even lower. This problem suggests that you should advise your network design customers not to plan on launching programs or copying large directories off a remote SMB file server.

Error-Recovery Mechanisms

Poorly designed error-recovery mechanisms can waste bandwidth. For example, if a protocol retransmits data quickly without waiting a long enough time to receive an acknowledgment, this can cause performance degradation for the rest of the network due to the bandwidth used. Acknowledgments at multiple layers can also waste bandwidth.

Connectionless protocols usually do not implement error recovery. Most data link layer and network layer protocols are connectionless. Some transport layer protocols, such as UDP, are connectionless.

Error-recovery mechanisms for connection-oriented protocols vary. TCP implements an adaptive retransmission algorithm, which means that the rate of retransmissions slows when the network is congested, which optimizes the use of bandwidth.

Newer TCP implementations also implement Selective ACK (SACK), as described in RFC 2018. Without SACK, error-prone, high-delay paths can experience low throughput due to the way that TCP acknowledges data. TCP acknowledgments (ACK) are cumulative up to the point where a problem occurs. If segments get lost, the ACK number is one more than the number of the last byte that was received before the loss, even if more segments arrived after the loss. There's no way for the receiver to report a hole in the received data. This causes the sender either to wait a round-trip time to find out about each lost segment or to unnecessarily retransmit segments that the recipient may have correctly received.

With the SACK mechanism, the TCP recipient fills in the SACK option field in the TCP header to inform the sender of the noncontiguous blocks of data that have been received. The sender can then retransmit only the missing segments. RFC 2018 defines a TCP option for filling in the sequence numbers for received blocks and another TCP option for informing the recipient during the three-way handshake that the host supports SACK.

Using a protocol analyzer, you can determine whether your customer's protocols implement effective error recovery. In some cases you can configure retransmission and time-out timers or upgrade to a better protocol implementation.

Characterizing Quality of Service Requirements

Analyzing network traffic requirements isn't quite as simple as identifying flows, measuring the load for flows, and characterizing traffic behavior such as broadcast and error-recovery behavior. You need to also characterize the QoS requirements for applications.

Just knowing the load (bandwidth) requirement for an application is not sufficient. You also need to know if the requirement is flexible or inflexible. Some applications continue to work (although slowly) when bandwidth is not sufficient. Other applications, such as voice and video applications, are rendered useless if a certain level of bandwidth is not available. In addition, if you have a mix of flexible and inflexible applications on a network, you need to determine if it is practical to borrow bandwidth from the flexible application to keep the inflexible application working.

As discussed in Chapter 2, voice is also inflexible with regard to delay. Voice is also sensitive to packet loss, which results in voice clipping and skips. Without proper network-wide QoS configuration, loss can occur because of congested links and poor packet-buffer and queue management on routers.

The sections that follow cover analyzing QoS requirements using ATM and Internet Engineering Task Force (IETF) techniques. The goal of these sections is to introduce you to terminology that ATM and IETF engineers use for classifying traffic and specifying QoS requirements for classes of traffic. Although the material is highly technical and detailed, it should give you some fundamental ideas about classifying the types of applications that will play a part in your network design, and it should prepare you for future chapters that cover strategies for designing and optimizing networks that can meet the needs of various applications.

ATM QoS Specifications

In their document "Traffic Management Specification Version 4.1," the ATM Forum does an excellent job of categorizing the types of service that a network can offer to support different sorts of applications. In 2004, the ATM Forum joined forces with the MPLS and Frame Relay Alliance to form the MFA Forum. The MFA Forum later merged with the IP/MPLS Forum and in 2008 with the Broadband Forum. Nonetheless, network engineers still refer to the work of the ATM Forum.

Even if your customer has no plans to use Asynchronous Transfer Mode (ATM) technology, the ATM Forum terminology is still helpful because it identifies the parameters that different sorts of applications must specify to request a certain type of network service. These parameters include delay and delay variation, data-burst sizes, data loss, and peak, sustainable, and minimum traffic rates. Although you might have to replace the word *cell* with *packet* in some cases, the ATM Forum definitions can help you classify applications on any network, even non-ATM networks.

The ATM Forum defines six service categories, each of which is described in more detail later in this section:

- Constant bit rate (CBR)

- Real-time variable bit rate (rt-VBR)

- Non-real-time variable bit rate (nrt-VBR)

- Unspecified bit rate (UBR)

- Available bit rate (ABR)

- Guaranteed frame rate (GFR)

For each service category, the ATM Forum specifies a set of parameters to describe both the traffic presented to the network and the QoS required of the network. The ATM Forum also defines traffic control mechanisms that the network can use to meet QoS objectives. The network can implement such mechanisms as connection admission control and resource allocation differently for each service category.

Service categories are distinguished as being either real-time or non-real-time. CBR and rtVBR are real-time service categories. Real-time applications, such as voice and video applications, require tightly constrained delay and delay variation. Non-real-time applications, such as client/server and terminal/host data applications, do not require tightly constrained delay and delay variation. Nrt-VBR, UBR, ABR, and GFR are non-real-time service categories.

It is important to work with your customer to correctly map applications and protocols to the correct service category to meet network performance objectives. A brief overview of ATM service categories is provided here. You can learn more about ATM service categories and traffic management by reading the document "Traffic Management Specification Version 4.1." This document is available from the ATM Forum at http://broadband-forum.org/ftp/pub/approved-specs/af-tm-0121.000.pdf.

Constant Bit Rate Service Category

When CBR is used, a source end system reserves network resources in advance and asks for a guarantee that the negotiated QoS be assured to all cells as long as the cells conform to the relevant conformance specifications. The source can emit cells at the peak cell rate (PCR) at any time and for any duration and the QoS commitments should pertain. CBR is used by applications that need the capability to request a static amount of bandwidth to be continuously available during a connection lifetime. The amount of bandwidth that a connection requires is specified by the PCR value.

CBR service is intended to support real-time applications requiring tightly constrained delay variation (for example, voice, video, and circuit emulation) but is not restricted to these applications. The source may emit cells at or below the negotiated PCR or be silent for periods of time. Cells that are delayed beyond the value specified by the maximum cell transfer delay (maxCTD) parameter are assumed to be of significantly reduced value to the application.

Real-time Variable Bit Rate Service Category

rt-VBR connections are characterized in terms of a PCR, sustainable cell rate (SCR), and maximum burst size (MBS). Sources are expected to transmit in a bursty fashion at a rate that varies with time. Cells that are delayed beyond the value specified by maxCTD are assumed to be of significantly reduced value to the application. rt-VBR service may support statistical multiplexing of real-time data sources.

Non-real-time Variable Bit Rate Service Category

The nrt-VBR service category is intended for non-real-time applications that have bursty traffic characteristics. No delay bounds are associated with this service category. The service is characterized in terms of a PCR, SCR, and MBS. For cells that are transferred within the traffic contract, the application expects a low cell loss ratio (CLR). nrt-VBR service may support statistical multiplexing of connections.

Unspecified Bit Rate Service Category

UBR service does not specify any traffic-related service guarantees. No numeric commitments are made regarding the cell loss ratio or cell transfer delay (CTD) experienced by a UBR connection. A network might or might not apply PCR to the connection admission control and usage parameter control (UPC) functions. (UPC is defined as the set of actions taken by the network to monitor and control traffic at the end-system access point.)

Where the network does not enforce PCR, the value of PCR is informational only. (It is still useful to negotiate PCR to allow the source to discover the smallest bandwidth limitation along the path of the connection.)

The UBR service category is intended for nonreal-time applications, including traditional computer communications applications such as file transfer and email. With UBR, congestion control can be performed at a higher layer on an end-to-end basis.

Available Bit Rate Service Category

With ABR, the transfer characteristics provided by the network can change subsequent to connection establishment. A flow-control mechanism offers several types of feedback to control the source rate in response to changing ATM-layer conditions. This feedback is conveyed to the source through control cells called *resource management (RM) cells*. An end system that adapts its traffic in accordance with the feedback should experience a low CLR and obtain a fair share of the available bandwidth according to a network-specific allocation policy. The ABR service does not require bounding the delay or the delay variation experienced by a given connection. ABR service is not intended to support real-time applications.

On the establishment of an ABR connection, an end system specifies to the network both a maximum required bandwidth and a minimum usable bandwidth. These are designated as the peak cell rate (PCR) and the minimum cell rate (MCR), respectively. The MCR can be specified as zero. The bandwidth available from the network can vary, but not become less than the MCR.

Guaranteed Frame Rate Service Category

The GFR service category was added to the Traffic Management Specification in 1999, after the other categories, which were defined in 1996. GFR is designed for applications that require a minimum rate guarantee and can benefit from dynamically accessing additional bandwidth available in the network. Devices connecting LANs to an ATM network can use GFR to transport multiple TCP/IP connections over a single GFR virtual circuit (VC). GFR does not require adherence to a flow-control protocol. Under congestion conditions, the network attempts to discard complete frames instead of discarding cells without reference to frame boundaries.

On establishment of a GFR connection, an end system specifies a PCR, MCR, MBS, and maximum frame size (MFS). The MCR can be zero. The end system can send cells up to the PCR, but the network only commits to sending cells (in complete unmarked frames) at the MCR. Traffic beyond the MCR and MBS is delivered within the limits of available resources.

IETF Integrated Services Working Group QoS Specifications

In an IP environment, you can use the work that the IETF Integrated Services working group is doing on QoS requirements. In RFC 2205, the working group describes the Resource Reservation Protocol (RSVP). In RFC 2208, the working group provides information on the applicability of RSVP and some guidelines for deploying it. RFCs 2209 through 2216 are also related to supporting QoS on the Internet and intranets.

RSVP is a setup protocol used by a host to request specific qualities of service from the network for particular application flows. RSVP is also used by routers to deliver QoS requests to other routers (or other types of nodes) along the paths of a flow. RSVP requests generally result in resources being reserved in each node along the path.

RSVP implements QoS for a particular data flow using mechanisms collectively called *traffic control*. These mechanisms include the following:

- A packet classifier that determines the QoS class (and perhaps the route) for each packet

- An admission control function that determines whether the node has sufficient available resources to supply the requested QoS

- A packet scheduler that determines when particular packets are forwarded to meet QoS requirements of a flow

RSVP works with mechanisms at end systems to request services. To ensure that QoS conditions are met, RSVP clients provide the intermediate network nodes with an estimate of the data traffic they will generate. This is done with a traffic specification (TSpec) and a service-request specification (RSpec), as described in RFC 2216.

Note   A *TSpec* is a description of the traffic pattern for which service is being requested. The TSpec forms one side of a "contract" between the data flow and the service "provider." After a service request is accepted, the service provider agrees to provide a specific QoS as long as the flow's traffic continues to conform to the TSpec.

An *RSpec* is a specification of the QoS that a flow wants to request from a network element. The contents of an RSpec are specific to a particular service. The RSpec might contain information about bandwidth required for the flow, maximum delay, or packet-loss rates.

RSVP provides a general facility for reserving resources. RSVP does not define the different types of services that applications can request. The Integrated Services working group describes services in RFCs 2210 through 2216. For a complete understanding of the working group's view of how integrated services should be handled on the Internet or an intranet, you should read the RFCs. The sections that follow provide an overview of the two major types of service: controlled-load service and guaranteed service.

Controlled-Load Service

Controlled-load service is defined in RFC 2211 and provides a client data flow with a QoS closely approximating the QoS that same flow would receive on an unloaded network. Admission control is applied to requests to ensure that the requested service is received even when the network is overloaded.

The controlled-load service is intended for applications that are highly sensitive to overloaded conditions, such as real-time applications. These applications work well on unloaded networks but degrade quickly on overloaded networks. A service, such as the controlled-load service, that mimics unloaded networks serves these types of applications well.

Assuming the network is functioning correctly, an application requesting controlled-load service can assume the following:

- A high percentage of transmitted packets will be successfully delivered by the network to the receiving end nodes. (The percentage of packets not successfully delivered must closely approximate the basic packet-error rate of the transmission medium.)

- The transit delay experienced by a high percentage of the delivered packets will not greatly exceed the minimum transmit delay experienced by any successfully delivered packet. (This minimum transit delay includes speed-of-light delay plus the fixed processing time in routers and other communications devices along the path.)

The controlled-load service does not accept or make use of specific target values for parameters such as delay or loss. Instead, acceptance of a request for controlled-load service implies a commitment by the network node to provide the requester with service closely equivalent to that provided to uncontrolled (best-effort) traffic under lightly loaded conditions.

A network node that accepts a request for controlled-load service must use admission control functions to ensure that adequate resources are available to handle the requested level of traffic, as defined by the requester's TSpec. Resources include link bandwidth, router or switch port-buffer space, and computational capacity of the packet-forwarding engine.

Guaranteed Service

RFC 2212 describes the network node behavior required to deliver a service called *guaranteed service* that guarantees both bandwidth and delay characteristics. Guaranteed service provides a firm limit on end-to-end packet-queuing delays. (By *firm*, the RFC means that the limit can be proven mathematically.) It does not attempt to minimize jitter and is not concerned about fixed delay, such as transmission delay. (Fixed delay is a property of the chosen path, which is determined by the setup mechanism, such as RSVP.)

Guaranteed service guarantees that packets will arrive within the guaranteed delivery time and will not be discarded due to queue overflows, provided the flow's traffic conforms to its TSpec. A series of network nodes that implement RFC 2212 ensures a level of bandwidth that, when used by a regulated flow, produces a delay-bounded service with no queuing loss (assuming no failure of network components or changes in routing during the life of the flow).

Guaranteed service is intended for applications that need a guarantee that a packet will arrive no later than a certain time after it was transmitted by its source. For example, some audio and video playback applications are intolerant of a packet arriving after its expected playback time. Applications that have real-time requirements can also use guaranteed service.

In RFC 2212, a flow is described using a *token bucket*. A token bucket has a *bucket rate* and a *bucket size*. The rate specifies the continually sustainable data rate, and the size specifies the extent to which the data rate can exceed the sustainable level for short periods of time.

The rate is measured in bytes of IP datagrams per second and can range from 1 byte per second to as large as 40 TB per second (the maximum theoretical bandwidth of a single strand of fiber). The bucket size can range from 1 byte to 250 GB. The range of values is intentionally large to allow for future bandwidths. The range is not intended to imply that a network node has to support the entire range.

The expectation of the Integrated Services working group is that a software developer can use the relevant RFCs to develop intelligent applications that can accurately set the bucket rate and size. An application usually can accurately estimate the expected queuing delay the guaranteed service will provide. If the delay is larger than expected, the application can modify its token bucket to achieve a lower delay.

As a network designer, you won't generally be called upon to estimate token-bucket rates and sizes. On the other hand, you should recognize which applications need guaranteed service, and you should have some idea of their default behavior and whether a reconfiguration of the default behavior is possible. If an application can request terabytes-per-second bandwidth, you need to know this because of the negative effect it could have on other applications.

IETF Differentiated Services Working Group QoS Specifications

The IETF also has a Differentiated Services working group that works on QoS-related specifications. RFC 2475, "An Architecture for Differentiated Services," defines an architecture for implementing scalable service differentiation in an internetwork or the Internet. As Chapter 13, "Optimizing Your Network Design," covers in more detail, IP packets can be marked with a differentiated services codepoint (DSCP) to influence queuing and packet-dropping decisions for IP datagrams on an output interface of a router. RFC 2475 refers to these decisions as per-hop behaviors (PHB). The DSCP can have 1 of 64 possible values, each of which outlines a PHB, although on a real network you would only use at most 6 to 8 DSCP values.

Although the integrated services (RSVP) model, described in the previous section, offers finer granularity, it is less scalable than the differentiated service model. The integrated services model allows sources and receivers to exchange signaling messages that establish packet classification and forwarding state on each router along the path between them. State information at each router can be potentially large. The amount of information grows in proportion to the number of concurrent reservations, which can be a high number on high-capacity backbone links. Differentiated services doesn't require RSVP and can be utilized to aggregate integrated services/RSVP state in the core of a network.

RFC 2475 compares its approach to the relative priority-marking model used by such QoS solutions as the IPv4 precedence marking defined in RFC 791, IEEE 802.5 Token Ring priority, and IEEE 802.1p traffic classes. Compared to those solutions, the differentiated services architecture more clearly specifies the role and importance of boundary nodes and traffic conditioners, and uses a per-hop behavior model that permits more general forwarding behaviors than a relative priority. An example of relative priority is IPv4 precedence, which can range from routine (the bits are set to 000) to high (the bits are set to 111).

RFC 2475 also compares its approach to the service-marking model in the IPv4 Type of Service (ToS) bits. As defined in RFC 1349, applications can use the ToS bits to mark each packet with a request for a type of service (for example, a request to minimize delay, maximize throughput, maximize reliability, or minimize cost). The intent of those bits, which were never used, was to allow a router to select routing paths or forwarding behaviors that were suitably engineered to satisfy the service request. The differentiated services model, on the other hand, does not describe the use of the DSCP field as an input to route selection.

The ToS markings defined in RFC 1349 are generic and do not match the actual services that routers and service providers offer. Furthermore, the service request is associated with each individual packet, whereas some service semantics may depend on the aggregate forwarding behavior of a sequence of packets. The ToS marking model does not easily accommodate growth in the number and range of future services (because the code-point space is small) and involves configuration of the forwarding behavior for each ToS in each core network node. The differentiated services model does not have these problems.

Grade of Service Requirements for Voice Applications

In a voice network, in addition to the need for QoS to ensure low and nonvariable delay and low packet loss, there is also a need for what voice experts call *a high grade of service (GoS)*. GoS refers to the fraction of calls that are successfully completed in a timely fashion. Call completion rate (CCR) is another name for the requirement.

A network must have high availability to support a high GoS. In an unreliable network, GoS is adversely affected when call setup and teardown messages are lost. A lost signal for call setup can result in an unsuccessful call attempt. A lost signal for call teardown can cause voice resources to be unavailable for other calls. Call setup and teardown messages aren't as delay-sensitive as the audio sent during the actual call, so retransmission of these messages is permitted but should generally be avoided to avoid impacting users. (The voice packets themselves are not retransmitted because there's no point. The voice wouldn't sound right if the packets arrived later than they were supposed to arrive.)

To achieve high GoS, you should follow the recommendations that will be presented in subsequent chapters to use reliable components (cables, patch panels, switches, routers, and so on) and to build redundancy and failover into the network using such techniques as dynamic routing, the Spanning Tree Protocol (STP) for switched networks, Hot Standby Router Protocol (HSRP), and so on. As discussed in Chapter 9, "Developing Network Management Strategies," achieving a high GoS also requires implementing a network management strategy that will quickly alert you to network outages and degraded service.

Documenting QoS Requirements

You should work with your customer to classify each network application in a service category. When you have classified the application, you should fill in the QoS Requirements column in Table 4-4.

If your customer has applications that can be characterized as needing controlled-load or guaranteed service, you can use those terms when filling in the QoS Requirements column. If your customer plans to use ATM, you can use the ATM Forum's terminology for service categories. Even if your customer does not plan to use ATM or IETF QoS, you can still use the ATM Forum or Integrated Services working group terminology. Another alternative is to simply use the following terms:

- **Inflexible:** A generic term to describe any application that has specific requirements for constant bandwidth, delay, delay variation, accuracy, and throughput.

- **Flexible:** A generic term to describe any application that simply expects the network to make a best effort to meet requirements. Many nonmultimedia applications have flexible QoS requirements.

For voice applications, you should make more than one entry in Table 4-4 due to the different requirements for the call control flow and the audio stream. The call control flow, used for setting up and tearing down calls, doesn't have strict delay constraints, but it does require high network availability and there may be a GoS requirement that should be specified. For the voice stream, the QoS classification should be listed using the ATM term *CBR* or the IETF term *guaranteed service*.

When documenting QoS requirements for applications, it's also a good idea to let your clients know that QoS is an end-to-end proposition. Such issues as mapping LAN-based QoS (for example, the 802.1p bits) to IP DSCP and Multiprotocol Label Switching (MPLS) experimental (EXP) bits should be part of the QoS requirements analysis discussion. The detailed discussion of QoS solutions will happen later in the design cycle as covered in Chapter 13.

Network Traffic Checklist

You can use the following Network Traffic checklist to determine if you have completed all the steps for characterizing network traffic:

❑   I have identified major traffic sources and stores and documented traffic flow between them.

❑   I have categorized the traffic flow for each application as being terminal/host, client/server, peer-to-peer, server/server, or distributed computing.

❑   I have estimated the bandwidth requirements for each application.

❑   I have estimated the bandwidth requirements for routing protocols.

❑   I have characterized network traffic in terms of broadcast/multicast rates, efficiency, frame sizes, windowing and flow control, and error-recovery mechanisms.

❑   I have categorized the QoS requirements of each application.

❑   I have discussed the challenges associated with implementing end-to-end QoS and the need for devices across the network to do their part in implementing QoS strategies.

Summary

This chapter provided techniques for analyzing network traffic caused by applications and protocols. The chapter discussed methods for identifying traffic sources and data stores, measuring traffic flow and load, documenting application and protocol usage, and evaluating QoS requirements.

Review Questions

1.   Why is it important to explore traffic behavior when designing a network? What problems could arise if you don't understand traffic behavior when you build a new network or upgrade a network?

2.   Do some research regarding TCP selective ACK (SACK). Find out if the operating system (OS) on your computer uses it by default and, if not, if there's a mechanism for configuring the OS to use it.

3.   Do some research regarding TCP window scaling. Find out if the OS on your computer uses it by default and, if not, if there's a mechanism for configuring the OS to use it.

4.   Do some research on distributed computing. Find an application that uses distributed computing and write a paragraph about the application.

5.   Do some research regarding cloud computing. Does cloud computing fit into the types of traffic flow discussed in this book (terminal/host, client/server, peer-to-peer, server/server, and distributed computing) or is it a new type of traffic flow? Defend your answer.

Design Scenario

Genome4U is a scientific research project at a large university in the United States. Genome4U has recently started a large-scale project to sequence the genomes of 100,000 volunteers with a goal of creating a set of publicly accessible databases with human genomic, trait, and medical data.

The project's founder, a brilliant man with many talents and interests, tells you that the public databases will provide information to the world's scientific community in general, not just those interested in medical research. Genome4U is trying not to prejudge how the data will be used because there may be opportunities for interconnections and correlations that computers can find that people might have missed. The founder envisions clusters of servers that will be accessible by researchers all over the world. The databases will be used by end users to study their own genetic heritage, with the help of their doctors and genetic counselors. In addition, the data will be used by computer scientists, mathematicians, physicists, social scientists, and other researchers.

The genome for a single human consists of complementary DNA strands wound together in a double helix. The strands hold 6 billion base pairs of nucleotides connected by hydrogen bonds. To store the research data, 1 byte of capacity is used for each base pair. As a result, 6 GB of data capacity is needed to store the genetic information of just one person. The project plans to use network-attached storage (NAS) clusters.

In addition to genetic information, the project will ask volunteers to provide detailed information about their traits so that researchers can find correlations between traits and genes. Volunteers will also provide their medical records. Storage will be required for these data sets and the raw nucleotide data.

You have been brought in as a network design consultant to help the Genome4U project.

1. List the major user communities.

2. List the major data stores and the user communities for each data store.

3. Characterize the network traffic in terms of flow, load, behavior, and QoS requirements. You will not be able to precisely characterize the traffic but provide some theories about it and document the types of tests you would conduct to prove your theories right or wrong.

4. What additional questions would you ask Genome4U's founder about this project? Who besides the founder would you talk to and what questions would you ask them?

Summary for Part I

At this point in the network design process, you have identified a customer's network applications and the technical requirements for a network design that can support the applications. You should take another look at Table 4-4, "Network Applications Traffic Characteristics," and Table 2-2, "Network Applications Technical Requirements," to make sure you understand your customer's application requirements. If you want, you can merge these two tables so that there is one row for each application.

A top-down methodology for network design focuses on applications. Chapter 1 covered identifying applications and business goals. Chapter 2 analyzed technical goals for applications and the network as a whole, such as availability, performance, and manageability. Chapter 3 concentrated on techniques for characterizing the existing network, and Chapter 4 refocused on technical requirements in terms of the network traffic characteristics of applications and protocols.

This summary wraps up Part I, "Identifying Your Customer's Needs and Goals," which presented the requirements-analysis phase of network design. The requirements-analysis phase is the most important phase in top-down network design. Gaining a solid understanding of your customer's requirements helps you select technologies that meet a customer's criteria for success.

You should now be able to analyze a customer's business and technical goals and be ready to start developing a logical and physical network design. Part II, "Logical Network Design," covers designing a logical network topology, developing a network layer addressing and naming model, selecting switching and routing protocols, and planning network security and management strategies.

Part II

Logical Network Design

Chapter 5

Designing a Network Topology

In this chapter, you will learn techniques for developing a network topology. A *topology* is a map of an internetwork that indicates network segments, interconnection points, and user communities. Although geographical sites can appear on the map, the purpose of the map is to show the geometry of the network, not the physical geography or technical implementation. The map is a high-level blueprint of the network, analogous to an architectural drawing that shows the location and size of rooms for a building, but not the construction materials for fabricating the rooms.

Designing a network topology is the first step in the logical design phase of the top-down network design methodology. To meet a customer's goals for scalability and adaptability, it is important to architect a logical topology before selecting physical products or technologies. During the topology design phase, you identify networks and interconnection points, the size and scope of networks, and the types of internetworking devices that will be required, but not the actual devices.

This chapter provides tips for both campus and enterprise WAN network design and focuses on hierarchical network design, which is a technique for designing scalable campus and WAN networks using a layered, modular model. In addition to covering hierarchical network design, the chapter also covers redundant network design topologies and topologies that meet security goals. (Security is covered in more detail in Chapter 8, "Developing Network Security Strategies.") This chapter also discusses the Cisco SAFE security reference architecture.

Upon completion of this chapter, you will know more about designing secure, redundant, hierarchical, and modularized topologies. A topology diagram is a useful tool to help you and your customer begin the process of moving from a logical design to a physical implementation of the customer's network environment.

Hierarchical Network Design

To meet a customer's business and technical goals for a corporate network design, you might need to recommend a network topology consisting of many interrelated components. This task is made easier if you can "divide and conquer" the job and develop the design in layers.

Network design experts have developed the hierarchical network design model to help you develop a topology in discrete layers. Each layer can be focused on specific functions, allowing you to choose the right systems and features for the layer. For example, in Figure 5-1, high-speed WAN routers can carry traffic across the enterprise WAN backbone, medium-speed routers can connect buildings at each campus, and switches can connect user devices and servers within buildings.

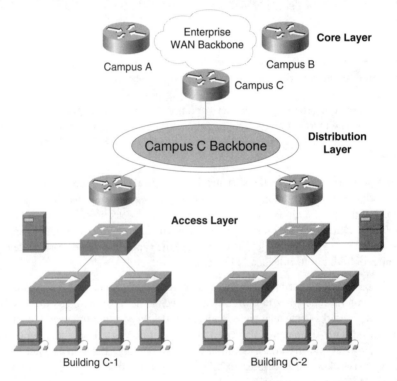

Figure 5-1 *Hierarchical Topology*

A typical hierarchical topology is

- A *core* layer of high-end routers and switches that are optimized for availability and performance.

- A *distribution* layer of routers and switches that implement policies. In small and medium-sized organizations, the core and distribution layers can be combined.

- An *access* layer that connects users via lower-end switches and wireless access points.

Why Use a Hierarchical Network Design Model?

Networks that grow unheeded without any plan in place tend to develop in an unstructured format. Dr. Peter Welcher, the author of network design and technology articles for *Cisco World* and other publications, refers to unplanned networks as *fur-ball networks*.

Welcher explains the disadvantages of a fur-ball topology by pointing out the problems that too many CPU adjacencies cause. When network devices communicate with many other devices, the workload required of the CPUs on the devices can be burdensome. For example, in a large flat (switched) network, broadcast packets are burdensome. A broadcast packet interrupts the CPU on each device within the broadcast domain and demands processing time on every device (including routers, workstations, and servers) for which a protocol understanding for that broadcast is installed.

Another potential problem with nonhierarchical networks, besides broadcast packets, is the CPU workload required for routers to communicate with many other routers and process numerous route advertisements. A hierarchical network design methodology enables you to design a modular topology that limits the number of communicating routers.

Using a hierarchical model can help you minimize costs. You can purchase the appropriate internetworking devices for each layer of the hierarchy, thus avoiding spending money on unnecessary features for a layer. Also, the modular nature of the hierarchical design model enables accurate capacity planning within each layer of the hierarchy, thus reducing wasted bandwidth. Network management responsibility and network management systems can be distributed to the different layers of a modular network architecture to control management costs.

Modularity enables you to keep each design element simple and easy to understand. Simplicity minimizes the need for extensive training for network operations personnel and expedites the implementation of a design. Testing a network design is made easy because there is clear functionality at each layer. Fault isolation is improved because network technicians can easily recognize the transition points in the network to help them isolate possible failure points.

Hierarchical design facilitates changes. As elements in a network require change, the cost of making an upgrade is contained to a small subset of the overall network. In large flat or meshed network architectures, changes tend to impact a large number of systems. Replacing one device can affect numerous networks because of the complex interconnections.

How Can You Tell When You Have a Good Design?

Here are some wise answers from Peter Welcher that are based on the tenets of hierarchical, modular network design:

- When you already know how to add a new building, floor, WAN link, remote site, e-commerce service, and so on

- When new additions cause only local change to the directly connected devices

- When your network can double or triple in size without major design changes

- When troubleshooting is easy because there are no complex protocol interactions to wrap your brain around

When scalability is a major goal, a hierarchical topology is recommended because modularity in a design enables creating design elements that can be replicated as the network grows. Because each instance of a module is consistent, expansion is easy to plan and implement. For example, planning a campus network for a new site might simply be a matter of replicating an existing campus network design.

Today's fast-converging routing protocols were designed for hierarchical topologies. Route summarization, which Chapter 6, "Designing Models for Addressing and Naming," covers in more detail, is facilitated by hierarchical network design. To control routing CPU overhead and bandwidth consumption, modular hierarchical topologies should be used with such protocols as Open Shortest Path First (OSPF), Intermediate System-to-Intermediate System (IS-IS), Border Gateway Protocol (BGP), and Enhanced Interior Gateway Routing Protocol (Enhanced IGRP).

Flat Versus Hierarchical Topologies

A flat network topology is adequate for small networks. With a flat network design, there is no hierarchy. Each network device has essentially the same job, and the network is not divided into layers or modules. A flat network topology is easy to design and implement, and it is easy to maintain, as long as the network stays small. When the network grows, however, a flat network is undesirable. The lack of hierarchy makes troubleshooting difficult. Rather than being able to concentrate troubleshooting efforts in just one area of the network, you might need to inspect the entire network.

Flat WAN Topologies

A WAN for a small company can consist of a few sites connected in a loop. Each site has a WAN router that connects to two other adjacent sites via point-to-point links, as shown at the top of Figure 5-2. As long as the WAN is small (a few sites), routing protocols can converge quickly, and communication with any other site can recover when a link fails. As long as only one link fails, communication recovers. When more than one link fails, some sites are isolated from others.

A flat loop topology is generally not recommended for networks with many sites, however. A loop topology can mean that there are many hops between routers on opposite sides of the loop, resulting in significant delay and a higher probability of failure. If your analysis of traffic flow indicates that routers on opposite sides of a loop topology exchange a lot of traffic, you should recommend a hierarchical topology instead of a loop. To avoid any single point of failure, you can place redundant routers or switches at upper layers of the hierarchy, as shown at the bottom of Figure 5-2.

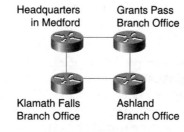

Flat Loop Topology

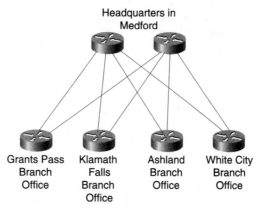

Hierarchical Redundant Topology

Figure 5-2 *Flat Loop Topology (Top) and Hierarchical Redundant Topology (Bottom)*

The flat loop topology shown at the top of Figure 5-2 meets goals for low cost and reasonably good availability. The hierarchical redundant topology shown at the bottom of Figure 5-2 meets goals for scalability, high availability, and low delay.

Flat LAN Topologies

In the early and mid-1990s, a typical design for a LAN was PCs and servers attached to one or more hubs in a flat topology. The PCs and servers implemented a media-access control process, such as token passing or carrier sense multiple access with collision detection (CSMA/CD) to control access to the shared bandwidth. The devices were all part of the same bandwidth domain and had the capability to negatively affect delay and throughput for other devices.

These days, network designers recommend attaching the PCs and servers to data link layer (Layer 2) switches instead of hubs. In this case, the network is segmented into small bandwidth domains so that a limited number of devices compete for bandwidth at any one time. The devices do compete for service by the switching hardware and software, however, so it is important to understand the performance characteristics of candidate switches, as discussed in Chapter 10, "Selecting Technologies and Devices for Campus Networks."

As discussed in Chapter 4, "Characterizing Network Traffic," devices connected in a switched or bridged network are part of the same broadcast domain. Switches forward broadcast frames out all ports. Routers, on the other hand, segment networks into separate broadcast domains. A single broadcast domain should be limited to a few hundred devices so that devices are not overwhelmed by the task of processing broadcast traffic. Introducing hierarchy into a network design by adding routers curtails broadcast radiation.

With a hierarchical design, you can deploy internetworking devices to do the job they do best. You can add routers to a campus network design to isolate broadcast traffic. You can deploy high-end switches to maximize bandwidth for high-traffic applications, and use low-end switches when simple, inexpensive access is required. Maximizing overall performance by modularizing the tasks required of internetworking devices is one of the many benefits of using a hierarchical design model.

Mesh Versus Hierarchical-Mesh Topologies

Network designers often recommend a mesh topology to meet availability requirements. In a *full-mesh topology*, every router or switch connects to every other router or switch. A full-mesh network provides complete redundancy and offers good performance because there is just a single-link delay between any two sites. A *partial-mesh network* has fewer connections. To reach another router or switch in a partial-mesh network might require traversing intermediate links, as shown in Figure 5-3.

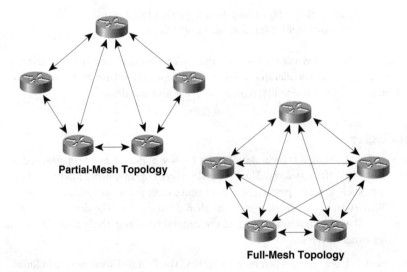

Partial-Mesh Topology

Full-Mesh Topology

Figure 5-3 *Partial-Mesh Topology (Left) and Full-Mesh Topology (Right)*

> **Note** In a full-mesh topology, every router or switch is connected to every other router or switch. The number of links in a full-mesh topology is as follows:
>
> `(N * (N - 1)) / 2`
>
> N is the number of routers or switches. (Divide the result by 2 to avoid counting Router X to Router Y and Router Y to Router X as two different links.)

Although mesh networks feature good reliability, they have many disadvantages if they are not designed carefully. Mesh networks can be expensive to deploy and maintain. (A full-mesh network is expensive.) Mesh networks can also be hard to optimize, troubleshoot, and upgrade, unless they are designed using a simple, hierarchical model. In a nonhierarchical mesh topology, internetworking devices are not optimized for specific functions. Containing network problems is difficult because of the lack of modularity. Network upgrades are problematic because it is difficult to upgrade just one part of a network.

Mesh networks have scalability limits for groups of routers that broadcast routing updates or service advertisements. As the number of router CPU adjacencies increases, the amount of bandwidth and CPU resources devoted to processing updates increases.

A good rule of thumb is that you should keep broadcast traffic at less than 20 percent of the traffic on each link. This rule limits the number of adjacent routers that can exchange routing tables and service advertisements. This limitation is not a problem, however, if you follow guidelines for simple, hierarchical design. A hierarchical design, by its very nature, limits the number of router adjacencies.

With routing protocols, such as OSPF and EIGRP, the problem is not with the broadcast/multicast traffic and CPU resources used for day-to-day routing. The problem is the amount of work and bandwidth required to reestablish routing after an outage. Be careful not to let your network grow into a complicated mesh just because it's still working. There will probably be an outage someday, and then you might learn the hard way the downfalls associated with a complex mesh of routers.

Figure 5-4 shows a classic hierarchical and redundant enterprise design. The design uses a partial-mesh hierarchy rather than a full mesh. The figure shows an enterprise routed network, but the topology could also be used for a switched campus network.

For small and medium-sized companies, the hierarchical model is often implemented as a *hub-and-spoke topology* with little or no meshing. Corporate headquarters or a data center form the hub. Links to remote offices and telecommuters' homes form the spokes, as shown in Figure 5-5.

Classic Three-Layer Hierarchical Model

Literature published by Cisco and other networking vendors talks about a classic three-layer hierarchical model for network design topologies. The three-layer model permits traffic aggregation and filtering at three successive routing or switching levels. This makes the three-layer hierarchical model scalable to large international internetworks.

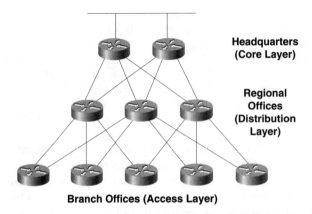

Figure 5-4 *Partial-Mesh Hierarchical Design*

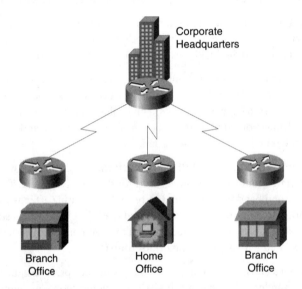

Figure 5-5 *Hub-and-Spoke Hierarchical Topology for a Medium-Sized Business*

Although the model was developed at a time when routers delineated layers, the model can be used for switched networks and routed networks. Figure 5-1 and Figure 5-4 show three-layer hierarchical topologies.

Each layer of the hierarchical model has a specific role:

■ The core layer provides optimal transport between sites.

■ The distribution layer connects network services to the access layer and implements policies regarding security, traffic loading, and routing.

- In a WAN design, the access layer consists of the routers at the edge of the campus networks. In a campus network, the access layer provides switches or hubs for end-user access.

The sections that follow discuss the core, distribution, and access layers in greater detail.

Core Layer

The *core layer* of a three-layer hierarchical topology is the high-speed backbone of the internetwork. Because the core layer is critical for interconnectivity, you should design the core layer with redundant components. The core layer should be highly reliable and should adapt to changes quickly.

When configuring routers in the core layer, you should use routing features that optimize packet throughput. You should avoid using packet filters or other features that slow down the manipulation of packets. You should optimize the core for low latency and good manageability.

The core should have a limited and consistent diameter. Distribution layer routers (or switches) and client LANs can be added to the model without increasing the diameter of the core. Limiting the diameter of the core provides predictable performance and ease of troubleshooting.

For customers who need to connect to other enterprises via an extranet or the Internet, the core topology should include one or more links to external networks. Corporate network administrators should discourage regional and branch-office administrators from planning their own extranets or connections to the Internet. Centralizing these functions in the core layer reduces complexity and the potential for routing problems, and is essential to minimizing security concerns.

Bringing business-partner links into the branch office where collaboration is taking place might seem logical, but it means you have to allow the partner's traffic into the branch office but not beyond. Over time, you'll end up with a hodgepodge of distributed access control lists (ACL) and firewalls, which complicates policy enforcement. It also greatly raises costs if you want to use intrusion detection systems (IDS) and other security technologies.

Similarly, some remote offices with IPsec VPN connectivity are shifting away from split access at the remote sites where users have local access to the Internet in addition to remote IPsec access to corporate headquarters. Despite bandwidth costs, forcing all external access to go through the core of the network means having only one security structure to administer, which is a good way to avoid security problems.

Distribution Layer

The *distribution layer* of the network is the demarcation point between the access and core layers of the network. The distribution layer has many roles, including controlling access to resources for security reasons and controlling network traffic that traverses the core for performance reasons. The distribution layer is often the layer that delineates broadcast domains. (Although this can be done at the access layer as well.) In network designs that include virtual LANs (VLAN), the distribution layer can be configured to route between VLANs.

The distribution layer allows the core layer to connect sites that run different protocols while maintaining high performance. To maintain good performance in the core, the distribution layer can redistribute between bandwidth-intensive access layer routing protocols and optimized core routing protocols. For example, perhaps one site in the access layer is still running an older protocol, such as IGRP. The distribution layer can redistribute between IGRP at the access layer and EIGRP in the core layer.

To improve routing-protocol performance, the distribution layer can summarize routes from the access layer. For some networks, the distribution layer offers a default route to access layer routers and runs only dynamic routing protocols when communicating with core routers.

To maximize hierarchy, modularity, and performance, the distribution layer should hide detailed topology information about the access layer from core routers. The distribution layer should summarize numerous access layer destinations into a few advertisements into the core. Likewise, the distribution layer should hide detailed topology information about the core layer from the access layer by summarizing to a small set of advertisements or just one default route, if possible. The distribution layer can provide the access layer with a route to the closest distribution layer router that has access to the core.

Access Layer

The *access layer* provides users on local segments with access to the internetwork. The access layer can include routers, switches, bridges, shared-media hubs, and wireless access points. As mentioned, switches are often implemented at the access layer in campus networks to divide up bandwidth domains to meet the demands of applications that need a lot of bandwidth or cannot withstand the variable delay characterized by shared bandwidth.

For internetworks that include small branch offices and telecommuter home offices, the access layer can provide access into the corporate internetwork using wide-area technologies such as ISDN, Frame Relay, leased digital lines, and analog modem lines. You can implement routing features, such as dial-on-demand routing (DDR) and static routing, to control bandwidth utilization and minimize cost on access layer remote links. (DDR keeps a link inactive except when specified traffic needs to be sent.)

Guidelines for Hierarchical Network Design

This section briefly describes some guidelines for hierarchical network design. Following these simple guidelines will help you design networks that take advantage of the benefits of hierarchical design.

The first guideline is that you should control the diameter of a hierarchical enterprise network topology. In most cases, three major layers are sufficient (as shown in Figure 5-4):

■ The core layer

■ The distribution layer

■ The access layer

Controlling the network diameter provides low and predictable latency. It also helps you predict routing paths, traffic flows, and capacity requirements. A controlled network diameter also makes troubleshooting and network documentation easier.

Strict control of the network topology at the access layer should be maintained. The access layer is most susceptible to violations of hierarchical network design guidelines. Users at the access layer have a tendency to add networks to the internetwork inappropriately. For example, a network administrator at a branch office might connect the branch network to another branch, adding a fourth layer. This is a common network design mistake known as *adding a chain*. Figure 5-6 shows a chain.

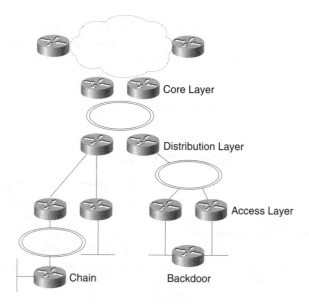

Figure 5-6 *Chain and Backdoor at the Access Layer*

In addition to avoiding chains, you should avoid backdoors. A *backdoor* is a connection between devices in the same layer, as shown in Figure 5-6. A backdoor can be an extra router, bridge, or switch added to connect two networks. A backdoor can also be a hub; for example, someone might install a minihub in a conference room and accidentally connect the hub to two jacks instead of just one. Backdoors should be avoided because they cause unexpected routing and switching problems and make network documentation and troubleshooting more difficult.

> **Note**   Sometimes there are valid reasons for adding a chain or a backdoor. For example, international network topologies sometimes get skewed by the availability of fiber-optic links, the ease and cost of provisioning new networks, and the availability of competent carriers. An international network might require a chain to add another country. A backdoor is sometimes added to increase performance and redundancy between two parallel devices in a layer. In general, however, other design options can usually be found that let the design retain its hierarchical structure. To maximize the benefits of a hierarchical model, you should usually avoid chains and backdoors.

Finally, one other guideline for hierarchical network design is that you should design the access layer first, followed by the distribution layer, and then finally the core layer. By starting with the access layer, you can more accurately perform capacity planning for the distribution and core layers. You can also recognize the optimization techniques you will need for the distribution and core layers.

You should design each layer using modular and hierarchical techniques and then plan the interconnections between layers based on your analysis of traffic load, flow, and behavior. To better understand network traffic characteristics, you can review the concepts covered in Chapter 4. As you select technologies for each layer, as discussed in Part III, "Physical Network Design," you might need to go back and tweak the design for other layers. Remember that network design is an iterative process.

Redundant Network Design Topologies

Redundant network designs enable you to meet requirements for network availability by duplicating elements in a network. Redundancy attempts to eliminate any single point of failure on the network. The goal is to duplicate any required component whose failure could disable critical applications. The component could be a core router, a switch, a link between two switches, a channel service unit (CSU), a power supply, a WAN trunk, Internet connectivity, and so on. To enable business survivability after a disaster and offer performance benefits from load sharing, some organizations have completely redundant data centers. Other organizations try to constrain network operational expenses by using a less-comprehensive level of redundancy.

You can implement redundancy inside individual campus networks and between layers of the hierarchical model. Implementing redundancy on campus networks can help you meet availability goals for users accessing local services. You can also implement redundancy on the edge of the enterprise network to ensure high availability for Internet, extranet, and virtual private network (VPN) access.

Note Because redundancy is expensive to deploy and maintain, you should implement redundant topologies with care. Be sure to select a level of redundancy that matches your customer's requirements for availability and affordability.

Before you select redundant design solutions, you should first analyze the business and technical goals of your customer, as discussed in Part I, "Identifying Your Customer's Needs and Goals." Make sure you can identify critical applications, systems, internet-working devices, and links. Analyze your customer's tolerance for risk and the consequences of not implementing redundancy. Make sure to discuss with your customer the tradeoffs of redundancy versus low cost, and simplicity versus complexity. Redundancy adds complexity to the network topology and to network addressing and routing.

Backup Paths

To maintain interconnectivity even when one or more links are down, redundant network designs include a backup path for packets to travel when there are problems on the primary path. A backup path consists of routers and switches and individual backup links between routers and switches, which duplicate devices and links on the primary path.

When estimating network performance for a redundant network design, you should take into consideration two aspects of the backup path:

- How much capacity the backup path supports
- How quickly the network will begin to use the backup path

You can use a network-modeling tool to predict network performance when the backup path is in use. Sometimes the performance is worse than the primary path, but still acceptable.

It is quite common for a backup path to have less capacity than a primary path. Individual backup links within the backup path often use different technologies. For example, a leased line can be in parallel with a backup dialup line or ISDN circuit. Designing a backup path that has the same capacity as the primary path can be expensive and is appropriate only if the customer's business requirements dictate a backup path with the same performance characteristics as the primary path.

If switching to the backup path requires manual reconfiguration of any components, users will notice disruption. For mission-critical applications, disruption is probably not acceptable. An automatic failover is necessary for mission-critical applications. By using redundant, partial-mesh network designs, you can speed automatic recovery time when a link fails.

One other important consideration with backup paths is that they must be tested. Sometimes network designers develop backup solutions that are never tested until a catastrophe happens. When the catastrophe occurs, the backup links do not work. In some network designs, the backup links are used for load sharing and redundancy. This has the advantage that the backup path is a tested solution that is regularly used and monitored as a part of day to day operations. Load sharing is discussed in more detail in the next section.

Load Sharing

The primary purpose of redundancy is to meet availability requirements. A secondary goal is to improve performance by supporting load sharing across parallel links. Load sharing, sometimes called load balancing, allows two or more interfaces or paths to share traffic load.

Note   Purists use the term load sharing instead of load balancing because the load is usually not precisely balanced across multiple links. Because routers can cache the interface that they use for a destination host or even an entire destination network, all traffic to that destination tends to take the same path. This results in the load not being balanced across multiple links, although the load should be shared across the links if there are many different destinations.

In WAN environments, you can facilitate load sharing by configuring channel aggregation. Channel aggregation means that a router can automatically bring up multiple channels as bandwidth requirements increase. The Multilink Point-to-Point Protocol (MPPP) is an Internet Engineering Task Force (IETF) standard for channel aggregation. MPPP ensures that packets arrive in sequence at the receiving router. To accomplish this, data is encapsulated within the Point-to-Point Protocol (PPP), and datagrams are given a sequence number. At the receiving router, PPP uses the sequence number to re-create the original data stream. Multiple channels appear as one logical link to upper-layer protocols.

Most vendors' implementations of IP routing protocols support load sharing across parallel links that have equal cost. (Cost values are used by routing protocols to determine the most favorable path to a destination. Depending on the routing protocol, cost can be based on hop count, bandwidth, delay, or other factors.) With EIGRP, Cisco supports load sharing even when the paths do not have the same cost. Using a feature called variance, EIGRP can load share across paths that do not have the same cost. Cisco supports load sharing across six parallel paths.

Some routing protocols base cost on the number of hops to a particular destination. These routing protocols load balance over unequal bandwidth paths as long as the hop count is equal. When a slow link becomes saturated, however, higher-capacity links cannot be filled. This is called pinhole congestion, which can be avoided by designing equal bandwidth links within one layer of the hierarchy, or by using a routing protocol that bases cost on bandwidth and has the variance feature.

Modular Network Design

Top-down network design lets you drill down to the components of the network design and apply fundamental design principles to the components and the overall design. Hierarchy and redundancy, as mentioned in the previous sections, are fundamental network design concepts. Another fundamental concept related to hierarchy is modularity.

Large network design projects and large networks in general consist of different areas or modules. Each area should be designed using a systematic, top-down approach, applying hierarchy and redundancy where appropriate. Network solutions and services can be selected on a per-module basis but validated as part of the overall network design. Cisco developed the SAFE security reference architecture to depict the components or modules of a typical enterprise network. The next section describes the architecture.

Cisco SAFE Security Reference Architecture

SAFE is a reference architecture that network designers can use to simplify the complexity of a large internetwork. The architecture lets you apply a modular approach to network design. With SAFE, you can analyze the functional, logical, and physical components of a network and thus simplify the process of designing an overall enterprise network.

Cisco SAFE architecture is especially concerned with security. SAFE takes a defense-in-depth approach, in which multiple layers of protection are strategically located throughout the network. The layers are under a unified strategy for protecting the entire network and the various components of the network, including individual network segments, infrastructure devices, network services, endpoints, and applications. Figure 5-7 shows the main modules in the SAFE architecture.

High-Level View

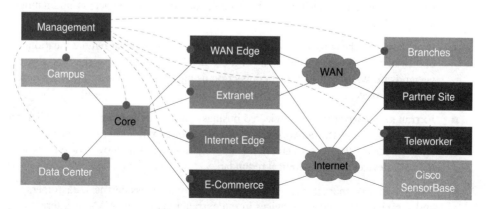

Figure 5-7 *High-Level View of Cisco SAFE Architecture*

SAFE architecture comprises the following major modules:

- **Core:** The core stitches together all the other modules. The core is a high-speed infrastructure that provides reliable and scalable Layer 2 and Layer 3 transport. The core is typically implemented with redundant switches that aggregate the connections to the campus, data center, WAN edge, and Internet edge.

- **Data center:** The data center hosts servers, applications, and storage devices for use by internal users. The data center also connects the network infrastructure that these devices require, including routers, switches, load balancers, content delivery devices, and application acceleration devices. The data center is not directly accessible from the Internet to the general public.

- **Campus:** The campus network provides network access to end users and devices located in a single geographical location. The campus may span several floors in a single building or multiple buildings for larger enterprises. The campus hosts local data, voice, and video services. The campus design should allow campus users to securely access data center and Internet resources from the campus infrastructure.

- **Management:** The management network provides monitoring, analysis, authentication, and logging services. Management servers support RADIUS, Kerberos, Network Time Protocol (NTP), Simple Network Management Protocol (SNMP), and syslog traffic. The management network combines out-of-band (OOB) management and in-band (IB) management, spanning all the building blocks of the SAFE architecture. The OOB management network can be implemented as a collection of dedicated switches or through the use of isolated VLANs.

- **WAN edge:** The WAN edge is the portion of the network that aggregates WAN links that connect geographically distant branch offices to a central site or regional hub. The WAN can be owned by the enterprise or by a service provider, the latter being the more common option.

- **Internet edge:** The Internet edge is the infrastructure that provides connectivity to the Internet and that acts as a gateway for the enterprise to the rest of the world. Internet edge services include a public DMZ, corporate Internet access, and remote-access VPN.

- **Branches:** Branches provide connectivity to users and devices at remote locations. A branch office typically includes one or more LANs and connects to the central site via a private WAN or an Internet connection using VPN technology. Branches host local data, voice, and video services.

- **Extranet:** An extranet allows selected business partners, customers, and suppliers to access a portion of the network via secure protocols. Extranet services include remote-access VPN, threat detection and mitigation, stateful failover for servers and network devices, and topological redundancy.

- **Partner site:** Partner sites are networks owned by business partners, customers, and suppliers. They access services in the extranet via secure WAN or Internet connectivity.

- **E-Commerce:** The e-commerce module hosts applications, servers, and data used in the selling and buying of products. Services include Layer 2 through 7 security, server farms with traffic filtering, and server load balancing. Virtual contexts provide segmentation and policy enforcement for server-to-server communication.

- **Teleworker:** The teleworker module is the home office of a full-time or part-time employee. Services in the teleworker module include remote-access VPN, desktop security, secure wireless networking, IP telephony, and IP video.

- **Cisco SensorBase:** Cisco SensorBase consists of threat collection servers that receive daily updates from globally deployed sensors regarding threats such as botnets, dark nets, malware, and serial attackers. Sensors include intrusion prevention systems, email servers, and web security appliances.

Designing a Campus Network Design Topology

Campus network design topologies should meet a customer's goals for availability and performance by featuring small bandwidth domains, small broadcast domains, redundancy, mirrored servers, and multiple ways for a workstation to reach a router for off-net communications. Campus networks should be designed using a hierarchical, modular approach so that the network offers good performance, maintainability, and scalability.

A campus network can consist of access, distribution, and core layers:

- **Campus access layer:** This module contains end-user workstations and IP phones connected to switches or wireless access points. Higher-end switches provide uplinks to the distribution layer. Services offered by this module include network access, broadcast control, protocol filtering, and the marking of packets for quality of service (QoS) features.

- **Campus distribution layer:** The job of this module is to aggregate wiring closets within a building and provide connectivity to the campus core via routers (or switches with routing modules). This module provides routing, QoS, and access control methods for meeting security and performance requirements. Redundancy and load sharing are recommended for this module. For example, each building should have two equal-cost paths to the campus core.

- **Campus core layer:** The campus core interconnects the access and distribution modules with the data center, network management, and edge modules. The campus core provides redundant and fast-converging connectivity. It routes and switches traffic as quickly as possible from one module to another. This module usually uses high-speed routers (or switches with routing capability) and provides QoS and security features.

Spanning Tree Protocol

The topology of a campus network design is often determined by the Spanning Tree Protocol (STP), which is a protocol and algorithm, documented in IEEE 802.1D, for dynamically "pruning" an arbitrary topology of connected Layer 2 switches into a spanning tree. The topology that results spans the entire switched domain and is shaped like a mathematical tree, with branches that spread out from a stem without forming loops or polygons. The network designer physically connects switches in a meshed, redundant topology, but STP creates a logical tree with no redundancy.

> **Note**   Because STP was first developed when bridges were used instead of switches, STP discussions use the word *bridge* for the Layer 2 device that today we call a *switch*.

The spanning tree has one root bridge and a set of ports on other bridges that forward traffic toward the root bridge. Bridges send bridge protocol data unit (BPDU) frames to each other to build and maintain the spanning tree. BPDUs identify the root bridge and help the other bridges compute their lowest-cost path to the root. Bridges send *topology change notification BPDUs* when bridge ports change state. Bridges send *configuration BPDUs* every 2 seconds to maintain the spanning tree. BPDUs are sent to the Bridge Group Address 01:80:C2:00:00:00.

Spanning Tree Cost Values

As already mentioned, bridges compute their lowest-cost path to the root bridge. The lowest-cost path is usually the highest-bandwidth path, although the cost is configurable. The original IEEE 802.1D specification used a 16-bit field for the cost of links of different speeds. The 2004 version uses a 32-bit field. Cisco switches by default use a 16-bit field with the default values shown in Table 5-1. Cisco switches can also be configured for 32-bit values. Table 5-1 shows the default Cisco 16-bit values and the default 32-bit values for the 2004 version of IEEE 802.1D.

Table 5-1   *IEEE 802.1D and Cisco 16-Bit Cost Values*

Link Speed	Cisco 16-Bit Cost	IEEE 802.1D 2004 32-Bit Cost
100 kbps	Not applicable	200,000,000
1 Mbps	Not applicable	20,000,000
10 Mbps	100	2,000,000
100 Mbps	10	200,000
1 Gbps	4	20,000
10 Gbps	2	2000
100 Gbps	Not applicable	200
1 Tbps	Not applicable	20
10 Tbps	Not applicable	2

Rapid Spanning Tree Protocol

In 2004, the IEEE incorporated its 802.1w standard, "Rapid Reconfiguration of Spanning Tree," into the IEEE 802.1D standard. The goal of the 802.1w committee was to standardize an improved mode of switch operation that reduces the time STP takes to converge to a least-cost spanning tree and to restore service after link failures. With the original 802.1D standard, networks took almost a minute to converge. In a properly configured network, the new 802.1D Rapid Spanning Tree Protocol (RSTP) can achieve convergence or reconvergence in a few hundred milliseconds.

With RSTP, bridge ports can be in one of three states:

■ **Discarding:** A port that is neither learning MAC addresses nor forwarding users' frames

■ **Learning:** A port that is learning MAC addresses to populate the MAC-address table but is not yet forwarding user frames

■ **Forwarding:** A port that is learning MAC addresses and forwarding user frames

The original STP passively waited for the network to converge before it transitioned a port into the forwarding state. To achieve quick convergence, a network administrator had to carefully tune the conservative default values for the Maximum Age and Forward Delay timers, which put the stability of the network at stake. RSTP, on the other hand, can actively confirm that a port can safely transition to the forwarding state without having to rely on any timer configuration. There is now a synchronization mechanism that takes place between RSTP-compliant bridges so that they actively build the topology as quickly as possible.

As was the case with STP, RSTP elects the bridge with the lowest bridge ID as the root bridge. Every bridge has a root path cost associated with it. For the root bridge this is zero. For all other bridges, it is the sum of the port path costs on the least-cost path to the root bridge.

When the switched network has converged, each bridge port has one of the following roles:

■ **Root:** Assigned to the one port on a nonroot bridge that provides the lowest-cost path to the root bridge. If a bridge has two or more ports with the same cost, the port with the lowest port ID is selected as the root port. A root port is a forwarding port.

■ **Designated:** Assigned to the one port attached to a LAN that provides the lowest-cost path from that LAN to the root bridge. All ports on the root bridge are designated ports. If there are two or more bridges with the same cost, the bridge with the lowest bridge ID is the *designated bridge*. The bridge port on the designated bridge that is connected to the LAN is assigned the role of designated port for that LAN. If the designated bridge has two or more ports connected to the LAN, the bridge port with the lowest port ID is selected as the designated port. A designated port is a forwarding port.

- **Alternate:** Assigned to a port that offers an alternative path in the direction of the root bridge to that provided by the bridge's root port. An alternative port is a discarding port.

- **Backup:** Assigned to a port on a designated bridge that acts as a backup for the path provided by a designated port in the direction of the leaves of the spanning tree. Backup ports exist only where two ports on a bridge are connected together in loopback by a point-to-point link, or where the bridge has two or more connections to a shared-media LAN. A backup port is a discarding port.

- **Disabled:** Assigned to a port that is not operational or is excluded from the active topology by network management. A disabled port is a discarding port.

The 2004 version of 802.1D also supports the concept of an *edge port*. A network manager can configure a port as an edge port if it is attached to a LAN that has no other bridges attached. (RSTP can also automatically detect edge ports.) Edge ports transition directly to the forwarding state, which is a major benefit for access layer ports that connect end-user systems. RSTP still continues to monitor the port for BPDUs in case a bridge is connected. As soon as the bridge detects a BPDU arriving at an edge port, the port becomes a nonedge port. An edge port corresponds to the Cisco PortFast feature (and is configured with the Cisco **spanning-tree portfast** command).

In a stable network where RSTP has communicated consistent information throughout the network, every LAN has one and only one designated port, and every bridge with the exception of the root bridge has a single root port connected to a LAN. Because each bridge provides connectivity between its root port and its designated ports, the resulting active topology connects all LANs and has no loops. In other words, it is a spanning tree.

RSTP Convergence and Reconvergence

RSTP can converge quickly to a tree topology where the lowest-cost paths are forwarding frames. RSTP achieves rapid transition to the forwarding state on edge ports, root ports, and point-to-point links. Edge and root ports can transition to forwarding without transmitting or receiving messages from other bridges.

A designated port attached to a point-to-point link can transition to the forwarding state when it receives an explicit role agreement transmitted by the other bridge attached to the link. In the case of a shared LAN, the forwarding transition delay used by a designated port is long enough for other bridges attached to the LAN to receive and act on transmitted messages but is independent of the overall network size. If all the LANs in a network are point-to-point links, RSTP timers define worst-case delays that occur only if protocol messages are lost or rate transmission limits are exceeded.

The link type for a LAN is automatically derived from the duplex mode of a port. A port that operates in full-duplex mode is assumed to be point-to-point, whereas a half-duplex port is considered to be a shared port by default. (The automatic link type setting can also be overridden by explicit configuration.) In modern switched networks, most links operate in full-duplex mode and RSTP treats them as point-to-point links. This makes them candidates for rapid transition to the forwarding state.

If the physical connectivity of the network changes or management parameters change, new spanning-tree information propagates rapidly. Each bridge accepts better information from any bridge on a LAN or revised information from the prior designated bridge for the LAN. Updated configuration BPDUs are transmitted through designated ports until the leaves of the spanning tree are reached. The transmission of information ceases as new configuration BPDUs reach designated ports that have already received the new information through redundant paths in the network, or reach LANs that are not redundantly connected.

In the original 802.1D specification, a bridge that detected a topology change generated a topology change notification up to the root. The root then flooded the change until the Maximum Age and Forward Delay timers expired. In the newer 802.1D specification, which includes the 802.1w enhancements, the change propagation is a one-step process. The initiator of the topology change floods the information throughout the network. There is no need to wait for the root bridge to be notified or for bridges to maintain a topology change state until the timers expire.

RSTP includes another form of immediate transition to the forwarding state that is similar to the Cisco proprietary UplinkFast extension to STP. When a bridge loses its root port, it can immediately transition an alternative port into the forwarding state. The selection of an alternative port as the new root port generates a topology change. The RSTP topology change mechanism clears the appropriate entries in the MAC address tables of the affected bridges, a necessary step to ensure that the table accurately reflects the new topology and the path to destination MAC addresses.

Selecting the Root Bridge

It is good practice to control which switch becomes the root bridge. The root bridge should be a reliable, high-speed switch in the center of the switched topology. If you let switches elect the root on their own, you have little control over the direction that traffic flows and the amount of frame-forwarding delay in your network. If you aren't careful, a slow bridge can become the root bridge. Also, high-speed ports can accidentally be removed from the spanning tree in deference to low-speed ports that are closer to the root bridge.

The root bridge is the switch with the lowest bridge ID. The bridge ID has two parts, a priority field and the MAC address of the switch. If all priorities are left at their default value, the switch or bridge with the lowest MAC address becomes the root. This could easily be one of the earliest products from Cisco, because Cisco had such a low vendor ID. (The vendor ID makes up the first 3 bytes of a MAC address, and the original vendor ID for Cisco was 00:00:0C.)

Manual control of the root bridge selection process is critical to maintaining high throughput on switched networks. This can be accomplished by ensuring that a particular switch has the lowest bridge ID. It is not recommended (or even possible on some switches) to change the MAC address portion of a bridge ID. Instead, to control the bridge ID, set the bridge priority. On Cisco switches, you can use the **spanning-tree vlan** *vlan-id* **priority** command. You should give a single, high-speed, centrally located switch the lowest priority so that it becomes the root bridge. You should also lower the priority on another high-speed, centrally located switch so that it becomes the root if the primary root fails. Generally these two switches are distribution layer switches.

Note   Cisco also supports a Root Guard feature that protects your network from a low-speed switch hijacking the job of root bridge. A switch port configured for Root Guard cannot become a root port. Instead the port becomes a designated port for its LAN segment. If there is a better BPDU received on the port, Root Guard disables the port, rather than taking the BPDU into account and restarting election of the root bridge. Root Guard needs to be enabled on all ports on all switches that should not become the root bridge.

Scaling the Spanning Tree Protocol

STP works best when the switched network is kept relatively small and the switches have sufficient CPU power and RAM to do their jobs effectively. On an oversized network with switches that have too little CPU power, BPDUs might not be sent and received properly, resulting in loops. A switch with insufficient RAM or a software problem could also drop BPDUs. In addition, a congested network could cause problems for the transmission of BPDUs.

To ensure that old information does not endlessly circulate through redundant paths in a network, thus preventing the propagation of new information, each BPDU includes a Message Age and a Maximum Age. When the Message Age exceeds the Maximum Age, the BPDU is discarded. On large, slow switched networks, BPDUs can get discarded before they reach all the switches. This problem causes STP to reconverge much more frequently than it should.

STP relies on the timely reception of BPDUs. Cisco has a *BPDU skew detection* feature that enables a switch to keep track of late-arriving BPDUs and notify the administrator by means of syslog messages. This feature is more of a workaround than a solution. A better plan is to design a switched network with care. Keep the switched network small with a root bridge selected for its high performance and central placement in the network.

It is also common to develop campus networks that rely on STP only for inadvertent loops. In other words, the Layer 2 topology is intentionally designed to be a tree topology by default, so there's no need for STP to remove loops to create a tree. STP is still enabled in case a novice network engineer (or a user) places a switch into the network in a looped fashion, but STP is relegated to a protection role instead of its legacy operational role. Routers and routing protocols are added to the design at the distribution and core layers. Routers have advantages compared to switches in their capability to implement fast-converging routing protocols and security policies, load sharing, and QoS features.

Note Cisco also supports a *BPDU Guard* feature that protects your network from a low-speed switch joining a network and sending BPDUs. A switch port configured for BPDU Guard goes into errdisable mode.

Virtual LANs

A campus network should be designed using small bandwidth and small broadcast domains. A *bandwidth domain* is a set of devices that share bandwidth and compete for access to the bandwidth. A traditional bus topology or hub-based Ethernet, for example, is a single bandwidth domain. A switch divides up bandwidth domains and is often used to connect each device so that the network consists of many, extremely small bandwidth domains. With switches, as opposed to hubs, the bandwidth domain consists of the switch port and the device that connects it. If full-duplex transmission mode is used, a bandwidth domain becomes even smaller and consists of just the port or the device.

Note On networks that experience collisions, including traditional Ethernet, a bandwidth domain is also called a *collision domain*.

A *broadcast domain* is a set of devices that can all hear each other's broadcast frames. A broadcast frame is a frame that is sent to the MAC address FF:FF:FF:FF:FF:FF. By default, switches do not divide broadcast domains. The campus access layer should use switches and provide broadcast control, however. To accomplish this, virtual LANs are necessary.

A *virtual LAN (VLAN)* is an emulation of a standard LAN that allows data transfer to take place without the traditional physical restraints placed on a network. A VLAN is a set of LAN devices that belong to an administrative group. Group membership is based on configuration parameters and administrative policies rather than physical location. Members of a VLAN communicate with each other as if they were on the same wire or hub, when they might be located on different physical LAN segments. Members of a VLAN communicate with members in a different VLAN as if they were on different LAN segments, even when they are located in the same switch. Because VLANs are based on logical instead of physical connections, they are extremely flexible.

In the early days of VLANs in the mid-1990s, there was a lot of talk about using VLANs to group users working on a project together, even though they weren't physically located together. With VLANs, the physical location of a user doesn't matter. A network administrator can assign a user to a VLAN regardless of the user's location. In theory, VLAN assignment can be based on applications, protocols, performance requirements, security requirements, traffic-loading characteristics, or other factors.

There was also a lot of talk about VLANs simplifying moves, adds, and changes in a campus network. The theory was that with VLANs, network administrators can stay seated in their offices or in the wiring closet when an end user moves into a new office or cubicle. If a user in the marketing department, for example, moves to a new office that is physically located among engineers, the marketing person might not have the skills to configure IP addressing for compatibility with the new location. Asking the engineers for help might not work because engineers don't like marketers, and asking the network administrator to come to the office and make the change might take a long time because administrators are so busy. Instead, the network administrator can configure the switch port for the moved device to be part of the marketing VLAN. Additional changes might be necessary to make sure the other switches learn that the marketing VLAN has expanded into a new area; however, no change is required on the marketer's computer.

In modern networks, VLANs aren't often used this way. Manually configuring IP addresses isn't common because DHCP has become so popular. Also, when a VLAN is dispersed across many physical networks, traffic must flow to each of those networks, which affects the performance of the networks and adds to the capacity requirements of links that connect VLANs. Networks with VLANs that migrate all over the campus topology are hard to manage and optimize.

In modern networks, instead of allowing for the spread of a logical LAN or administrative group across many physical LANs, a VLAN has become a method to subdivide physical switch-based LANs into many logical LANs. VLANs allow a large, flat, switch-based network to be divided into separate broadcast domains. Instead of flooding all broadcasts out every port, a VLAN-enabled switch floods a broadcast out only the ports that are part of the same VLAN as the sending station.

When switches first became popular in the mid-1990s, many companies implemented large, switched campus networks with few routers. The goals were to keep costs down by using switches instead of routers, and to provide good performance because presumably switches were faster than routers. Without the router capability of containing broadcast traffic, however, the companies needed VLANs, which enable the large flat network to be divided into broadcast domains. A router (or a routing module within a switch) is still needed for inter-VLAN communication.

In IP-based campus networks, a VLAN is usually its own IP subnet, due to the way the Address Resolution Protocol (ARP) works. When an IP host in a subnet needs to reach another host in the same subnet, it sends an ARP message to determine the Media Access Control (MAC) address of the host it is trying to reach. The ARP message is sent as a broadcast. All devices that find each other this way need to be in the same VLAN. Thus, in an IP network, VLANs are implemented as separate IP subnets. A router (or a routing module within a switch) provides intersubnet communication just as it would for a set of interconnected real (not virtual) LANs.

Fundamental VLAN Designs

To understand VLANs, it helps to think about real (nonvirtual) LANs first. Imagine two switches that are not connected to each other in any way. Switch A connects stations in Network A, and Switch B connects stations in Network B, as shown in Figure 5-8.

When Station A1 in Figure 5-8 sends a broadcast, Station A2 and Station A3 receive the broadcast, but none of the stations in Network B receive the broadcast, because the two switches are not connected. This same configuration can be implemented through configuration options in a single switch, with the result looking like Figure 5-9.

Through the configuration of the switch there are now two virtual LANs implemented in a single switch, instead of two separate physical LANs. This is the beauty of VLANs. The broadcast, multicast, and unknown-destination traffic originating with any member of VLAN A is forwarded to all other members of VLAN A, and not to a member of VLAN B. VLAN A has the same properties as a physically separate LAN bounded by routers. The protocol behavior in Figure 5-8 is exactly the same as the protocol behavior in Figure 5-9.

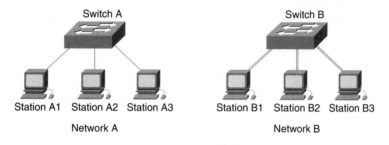

Figure 5-8   *Two Switches with Stations Attached*

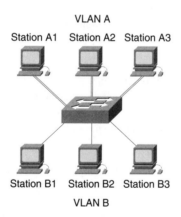

Figure 5-9   *Single Switch with Stations from Network A and Network B Attached*

VLANs can span multiple switches. In Figure 5-10, both switches contain stations that are members of VLAN A and VLAN B. This design introduces a new problem, the solution to which is specified in the IEEE 802.1Q standard and the Cisco proprietary Inter-Switch Link (ISL) protocol. The problem has to do with the forwarding of broadcast, multicast, or unknown-destination frames from a member of a VLAN on one switch to the members of the same VLAN on the other switch.

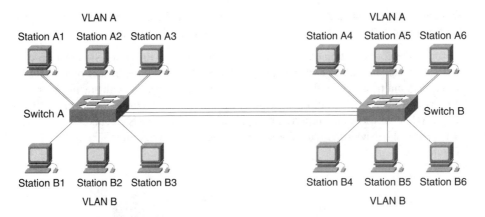

Figure 5-10   *VLAN A and VLAN B Span Two Switches*

In Figure 5-10, all frames going from Switch A to Switch B take the same interconnection path. The 802.1Q standard and the Cisco ISL protocol define a method for Switch B to recognize whether an incoming frame belongs to VLAN A or to VLAN B. As a frame leaves Switch A, a special header is added to the frame, called the *VLAN tag*. The VLAN tag contains a VLAN identifier (ID) that specifies to which VLAN the frame belongs.

Because both switches have been configured to recognize VLAN A and VLAN B, they can exchange frames across the interconnection link, and the recipient switch can determine the VLAN into which those frames should be sent by examining the VLAN tag. The link between the two switches is sometimes called a *trunk link* or simply a *trunk*.

Trunk links allow the network designer to stitch together VLANs that span multiple switches. A major design consideration is determining the scope of each VLAN and how many switches it should span. As mentioned earlier, most designers try to keep the scope small. Each VLAN is a broadcast domain, and per recommendations specified in the previous chapter, a single broadcast domain should be limited to a few hundred workstations (or other devices, such as IP phones).

Another major design consideration is the capacity of trunk links. Using methods discussed in Chapter 4, you should study network traffic to determine if Fast Ethernet, Gigabit Ethernet, or multiples of Fast or Gigabit Ethernet will be required for trunk links. Although Cisco supports 10-Mbps Ethernet trunks on some equipment, 10 Mbps is usually sufficient only for trunks that support small networks or for lab networks used for learning and testing purposes.

Wireless LANs

As discussed in Part I of this book, user mobility has become an important goal for many enterprises. In a campus network design, one or more wireless LANs (WLAN) can meet this goal by offering intranet and Internet access in open areas on the campus and in high-density areas such as auditoriums, conference rooms, and cafeterias. WLAN technology also enables deployment of LANs in offices or other parts of buildings where it may not be cost effective or practical to install cabling.

A WLAN consists of access points that communicate using radio frequency (RF) with wireless clients. The area that a single access point can cover is often called a *wireless cell*. Designing a WLAN topology requires a designer to determine the coverage area of each wireless cell and to decide how many cells will be required to meet total coverage needs. Factors that affect the coverage of a single access point include data rate, power level, antenna choice, and antenna positioning. Architectural characteristics of the wireless site also affect coverage, as described in the "Checking a Site for a Wireless Installation" section in Chapter 3, "Characterizing the Existing Internetwork."

Positioning an Access Point for Maximum Coverage

Most access points use an isotropic antenna, which means that the signal strength is theoretically the same when measured along axes in all directions. If you suspend an access point in space, the coverage should resemble that of a three-dimensional sphere with the access point at its center. In reality, the limitations of antenna design usually result in less-uniform coverage, however. The most common type of access point antenna is omnidirectional, which isn't actually "omni" or "iso." Instead of a sphere, the coverage looks more like a donut or tire inner tube.

An omnidirectional antenna is usually a 4- to 6-inch transmitting element, often attached to a rotating or positionable pivot. The signal propagating from an omnidirectional antenna is strongest in a direction perpendicular to the antenna shaft and weakest in the same direction as the antenna shaft. Remembering this can help you position your antennae for maximum coverage (and help you decide if you might need a directional antenna instead of an omnidirectional antenna).

Caution   Think about the meaning of *omni* in omnidirectional. Placing an access point near an exterior wall means that some of the signal will probably radiate strongly outside the building, where an unauthorized user sitting in the parking lot can easily receive it. Also, keep in mind that an access point in one room can propagate through a wall to potentially interfere with an access point in the next room. Walls attenuate (decrease) the strength of the signal, but they don't block it completely.

Access points can be mounted in a horizontal or a vertical position. It's important to make sure that an omnidirectional antenna points straight up. In addition to the access point antenna, also consider the antenna in receiving stations, usually notebook computers. Every wireless NIC and computer is different. Some laptops have long antennas that extend from the card up through the back of the laptop, behind the screen. Other computers might not have a built-in antenna and must rely on a smaller antenna in the NIC. You should test your WLAN design with a variety of computers and other devices that the actual users will be using.

For a given data rate, you can alter the power level or choose a different antenna to change the coverage area and coverage shape. A large cell size might result in too many clients sharing the available bandwidth. (IEEE 802.11 WLANs are shared networks, with all devices in the same bandwidth domain.) By reducing the access point power or antenna gain, you can reduce the cell size and share the bandwidth with fewer clients. This will result in more access points for a given coverage area but will provide better performance for clients.

WLANs and VLANs

You can place multiple access points throughout a facility to give users the ability to roam freely throughout an extended area while maintaining uninterrupted access to network resources. The easiest method for making sure users can roam is to put all of the users in the same IP subnet and the same VLAN. Otherwise, devices that move from subnet to subnet must acquire a new IP address and can lose packets that might have been transmitted while they were acquiring an address.

Whenever possible, a WLAN should be a separate subnet to simplify addressing while roaming and also to improve management and security. Keeping all wireless clients in their own subnet makes it easier to set up traffic filters to protect wired clients from an attack launched from the WLAN.

Redundant Wireless Access Points

In both wired and wireless campus LAN architectures, redundancy is usually desirable to ensure high availability. For campus networks with WLANs that are mission critical, Cisco has a feature called *Hot Standby mode* that supports two access points being configured to use the same channel in a single coverage area. Only one of the access points is active. The standby access point passively monitors the network and the primary access point. If the primary access point fails, the secondary access point takes over to provide coverage.

> **Note**   Don't confuse access-point Hot Standby mode with the Cisco Hot Standby Router Protocol (HSRP), which is covered in the upcoming "Workstation-to-Router Redundancy" section. Access-point Hot Standby mode addresses Layer 2 redundancy, whereas HSRP addresses Layer 3 redundancy.

You should place the standby access point near the access point it will monitor and give it the same configuration (except for a different IP address). The standby access point associates with the monitored access point as a client and queries the monitored access point regularly through both the Ethernet interface and the RF interface. If the monitored access point fails to respond, the standby access point becomes active, signals the primary access point radio to become inactive, and takes the monitored access point's place in the network.

As soon as the primary access point failure is detected, user intervention is required. The user should return the backup access point to standby mode. Failure to reset the standby access point results in both the primary and standby access points operating concurrently on the same channel when the primary access point comes back online.

Redundancy and Load Sharing in Wired LANs

In wired campus networks, it is common practice to design redundant links between LAN switches. Most LAN switches implement the IEEE 802.1D spanning-tree algorithm to avoid network loops. The 802.1D standard is a good solution for redundancy, but not for load sharing, because only one path is active. Some switch vendors, including Cisco, let you have one spanning tree per VLAN, which can be used to implement redundancy. A switch can act as the root bridge for one VLAN and as a backup for the root bridge for another VLAN.

Cisco Per VLAN Spanning Tree+ (PVST+) builds a separate logical tree topology for each VLAN. PVST+ allows load sharing by having different forwarding paths per VLAN. PVST+ is less scalable than the classic 802.1D method, where there is just one root and tree, because CPU time is required to process BPDUs for each VLAN. Cisco overcame this limitation with the Multi-Instance Spanning Tree Protocol (MISTP), which allows a set of VLANs to be grouped into a single spanning tree.

IEEE has also enhanced the original spanning-tree algorithm with its Multiple Spanning Trees (MST) standard, which is documented in IEEE 802.1s. The Multiple Spanning Tree Protocol (MSTP) uses RSTP for rapid convergence but improves RSTP scalability by aggregating a set of VLAN-based spanning trees into distinct instances, and by running only one (rapid) spanning-tree algorithm per instance. This architecture provides multiple forwarding paths for data traffic, enables load sharing, and reduces the number of spanning trees required to support a large number of VLANs.

If you use VLANs in a campus network design with switches that support 802.1s, PVST+, or MISTP, redundant links can offer load sharing in addition to fault tolerance. Figure 5-11 shows a redundant campus LAN design that uses the spanning-tree algorithm and VLANs.

The design in Figure 5-11 takes advantage of the concept of one spanning tree per VLAN. Switch A acts as the root bridge for VLANs 2, 4, and 6. (Switch B can become the root bridge for those VLANs if Switch A fails.) Switch B acts as the root bridge for VLANs 3, 5, and 7. (Switch A can become the root bridge for those VLANs if Switch B fails.) The result is that both links from an access layer switch carry traffic, and failover to a new root bridge happens automatically if one of the distribution layer switches fails. Both load sharing and fault tolerance are achieved.

The design in Figure 5-11 can scale to a large campus network. The design has been tested on a network that has 8000 users, 80 access layer switches, 14 distribution layer switches, and 4 core campus routers (not counting the routers going to the WAN).

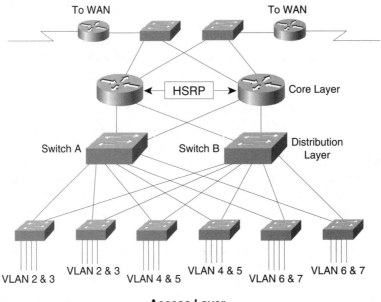

To WAN   To WAN

HSRP   Core Layer

Switch A   Switch B   Distribution
Layer

VLAN 2 & 3   VLAN 2 & 3   VLAN 4 & 5   VLAN 4 & 5   VLAN 6 & 7   VLAN 6 & 7

Access Layer

Figure 5-11   *Campus Hierarchical Redundant Topology*

Server Redundancy

This section covers guidelines for server redundancy in a campus network design. File, web, Dynamic Host Configuration Protocol (DHCP), name, and database servers are all candidates for redundancy in a campus design, depending on a customer's requirements. In a network that supports Voice over IP (VoIP), the servers that provide the mapping between a phone number and an IP address and handle call processing should be provisioned in a redundant fashion. Cisco Unified Communications Manager, for example, supports a redundancy group where servers are assigned the role of primary, secondary, or tertiary server.

DHCP servers can be placed at the access, distribution, or core layer. For large, globally distributed networks, redundant DHCP servers are usually placed in the access layer. This avoids excessive traffic between the access and distribution or core layers and allows each DHCP server to serve a smaller percentage of the user population. If the core of the network is in New York, for example, and the access and distribution layers are spread out across the world, it makes sense to have DHCP servers in the access layer. For small networks, however, DHCP servers are often centrally located in the core of the network to facilitate management by a centralized IT department.

In large campus networks, the DHCP server is often placed on a different network segment than the end systems that use it. If the server is on the other side of a router, the router can be configured to forward DHCP broadcasts from end systems. The router forwards the broadcasts to a server address configured via the **ip helper address** command on a Cisco router. The router inserts the address of the interface that received the request into the *giaddr* field of the DHCP request. The server uses the giaddr field to determine from which pool of addresses to choose an address.

Name servers are in theory less critical than DHCP servers because users can reach services by address instead of name if the name server fails; because many users do not realize this, however, it is a good idea to plan for redundant name servers. *Name servers* implement the Internet Domain Name System (DNS), the Windows Internet Naming Service (WINS), and the NetBIOS Name Service (NBNS). Name servers can be placed at the access, distribution, or core layer. For large, globally distributed networks, it makes sense to have name servers at the access layer. For small networks, however, it's more common to place name servers in the core of the network.

In any application where the cost of downtime for file servers is a major concern, mirrored file servers should be recommended. For example, in a brokerage firm where traders access data to buy and sell stocks, the data can be replicated on two or more mirrored file servers. Mirrored file servers hold identical data. Updates to the data are synchronized across the servers. The servers should be on different networks and power supplies to maximize availability.

If complete server redundancy is not feasible due to cost considerations, mirroring or duplexing of the file server hard drives is a good idea. (*Duplexing* is the same as mirroring with the additional feature that the two hard drives are controlled by different disk controllers.) Implementing a storage-area network (SAN) is another option. SANs are a popular solution for organizations seeking highly reliable, uninterrupted access to large amounts of stored information.

Redundancy has both availability and performance advantages. With mirrored file servers, it is possible to share the workload between servers. Using a content delivery network (CDN) and content services devices, users can be directed to one of many mirrored servers that all hold the same data.

Redundancy can also be achieved by adding some sophistication to DNS. When a client requests access to a resource by its DNS name, a DNS server can return multiple host addresses in its response. Whether this will provide good redundancy depends on the host software. Some implementations try additional addresses if the first one doesn't respond.

Another possibility is a feature called *DNS round robin*, where the server has a list of addresses through which it cycles. The server gives out a different address with each request, going through its list of addresses. When it gets to the end of the list, it cycles back to the beginning of the list. Due to DNS caching, where clients and other DNS servers remember a previous name-to-address mapping, DNS round robin isn't perfect, but it can be quite simple to implement and configure on a typical DNS server.

Redundancy and load balancing with DNS can also work with multiple DNS servers. Assuming that clients access different DNS servers, one server can respond with one address, while other servers respond with different addresses. Again, DNS caching can limit the effectiveness of this method.

> **Note**   There is one caveat to keep in mind with mirrored file, DHCP, web, and other types of servers. Mirrored servers offer redundancy for the hardware, cabling, LAN connection, and power supply, but they do not offer software or data redundancy. Because mirrored servers hold replicated data, if the problem is in the data or the software's capability to access the data, all the mirrored servers are affected.

Workstation-to-Router Redundancy

Workstations in a campus network must have access to a router to reach remote services. Because workstation-to-router communication is critical in most designs, you should consider implementing redundancy for this function.

A workstation has many possible ways to discover a router on its network, depending on the protocol it is running and also the implementation of the protocol. The next few sections describe methods for workstations to learn about routers and redundancy features that guarantee a workstation can reach a router.

IP implementations vary in how they implement workstation-to-router communication. Some IP workstations send an ARP frame to find a remote station. A router running proxy ARP can respond to the ARP request with the router's data link layer address. Cisco routers run proxy ARP by default.

The advantage of depending on proxy ARP to reach remote stations is that a workstation doesn't have to be configured with the address of a router. However, because proxy ARP has never been standardized, most network administrators don't depend on it. Also, many security experts recommend turning it off because it makes it easier for an attacker to reach another network. Instead, IP workstations are given the address of a default router. This can be manually configured or supplied by DHCP. A default router is the address of a router on the local segment that a workstation uses to reach remote services. The default router is usually called the default gateway for historical reasons.

An IP workstation usually knows the address of only one router: the default gateway. The result is that a workstation does not always use the most expedient method to reach a remote station. The workstation can select a path that includes an extra hop. Figure 5-12 shows the extra-hop problem. To get around the extra-hop problem and to add redundancy, some workstation IP implementations allow a network administrator to add static routes to a configuration file or to configure the workstation to run a routing protocol.

> **Note**   In UNIX environments, workstations sometimes run the RIP daemon to learn about routes. It is best if they run the RIP daemon in passive rather than active mode. In active mode, a workstation sends a RIP broadcast frame every 30 seconds. When many UNIX workstations run RIP in active mode, the amount of broadcast traffic can degrade network performance. In addition, there are security risks in allowing uncontrolled stations to run a routing protocol in active mode.

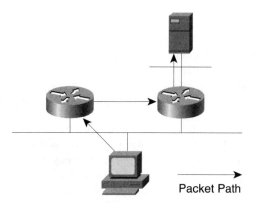

Packet Path

Figure 5-12 *Workstation-to-Router*
Extra-Hop Problem

Another alternative for IP workstation-to-router communication is the Router Discovery
Protocol (RDP). RFC 1256 specifies the RDP extension to the Internet Control Message
Protocol (ICMP). With RDP, each router periodically multicasts an ICMP *router advertisement packet* from each of its interfaces, announcing the IP address of that interface.
Workstations discover the addresses of their local routers simply by listening for advertisements, in a similar fashion to the method AppleTalk workstations use to discover the
address of a router. The default advertising rate for RDP is once every 7 to 10 minutes,
though, which is quite different from AppleTalk's default, which is once every 10 seconds.

When a workstation starts up, it can multicast an ICMP *router solicitation packet* to ask
for immediate advertisements, rather than wait for the next periodic advertisement to
arrive. RDP does not attempt to solve the extra-hop problem. Although most routers support RDP, few workstation IP implementations support it, so RDP is not widely used.

One reason that RDP has not become popular is that DHCP includes an option for a
DHCP server to return the address of a default gateway to a client. As specified in RFC
2131, a server's response to a DHCP client's request for an IP address can include an
options field in which the server can place one or more default gateway addresses. A
preference level can be used to specify which default gateway is the best option. The
server can also include a list of static routes in the options field.

These days, most IP workstations are configured with the address of a default gateway.
The configuration can be done at each workstation or at a DHCP server that supports
many workstations, which is the more common method. Running routing protocols or
router discovery protocols at workstations has proven to be a poor alternative because of
traffic and processing overhead, security issues, and the lack of implementations for
many platforms.

The problem with a default gateway configuration is that it creates a single point of failure, particularly because many implementations keep track of only one default gateway.
Loss of the default gateway results in workstations losing connections to remote sites and
being unable to establish new connections.

Hot Standby Router Protocol

Cisco *Hot Standby Router Protocol (HSRP)* provides a way for an IP workstation to keep communicating on an internetwork even if its default gateway becomes unavailable. In RFC 2338, the IETF standardized a similar protocol, the *Virtual Router Redundancy Protocol (VRRP)*. Routers in the core, distribution, or access layer can run HSRP or VRRP. The campus design shown in Figure 5-11 features HSRP at the core layer.

HSRP works by creating a *virtual router*, also called a *phantom router*, as shown in Figure 5-13. The virtual router has its own IP and MAC addresses. Each workstation is configured to use the virtual router as its default gateway. When a workstation broadcasts an ARP frame to find its default gateway, the active HSRP router responds with the virtual router's MAC address. If the active router goes offline, a standby router takes over as active router, continuing the delivery of the workstation's packets. The change is transparent to the workstation.

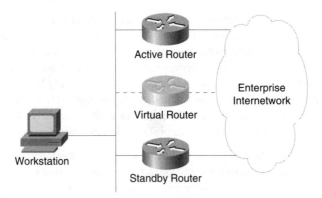

Figure 5-13   *Hot Standby Router Protocol (HSRP)*

HSRP routers on a LAN communicate among themselves to designate an active and standby router. The active router sends periodic Hello messages. The other HSRP routers listen for the Hello messages. If the active router fails, causing the other HSRP routers to stop receiving Hello messages, the standby router takes over and becomes the active router. Because the new active router assumes both the IP and MAC addresses of the phantom, workstations see no change. They continue to send packets to the virtual router's MAC address, and the new active router delivers those packets. The Hello timer should be configured to be short enough so that workstation applications and protocols do not drop connections before the standby router becomes active.

HSRP also works for proxy ARP. When an active HSRP router receives an ARP request for a station that is not on the local network, the router replies with the virtual router's MAC address. If the router becomes unavailable, the new active router can still deliver the traffic.

Cisco also has a useful enhancement to HSRP, *standby tracking*, which monitors one or more WAN interfaces on a router that has HSRP enabled on the LAN interfaces. If the software senses a problem with the WAN circuit connected to one of the WAN interfaces that it is tracking, it fails over to an active WAN interface on a standby router. The default gateway, for which HSRP provides redundancy, is the user's method of getting outside the LAN and is often connected to a WAN interface that provides access to the rest of the intranet or the Internet, so the standby tracking feature is extremely useful.

Cisco also supports an HSRP-enabled router preserving Network Address Translation (NAT) and IPsec state information. WAN edge devices can maintain NAT translations and IPsec tunnels, used in VPNs usually, when HSRP switches to a different router.

Gateway Load Balancing Protocol

To achieve load sharing along with redundancy, Cisco also has a newer protocol, the *Gateway Load Balancing Protocol (GLBP)*, which is similar, but not identical, to HSRP and VRRP. With HSRP and VRRP, the standby routers in a group are superfluous until the active router fails. These standby routers may have access to bandwidth that is wasted until a problem arises. Although multiple virtual router groups can be configured for the same set of routers, which is less wasteful, the hosts must be configured for different default gateways, which results in an extra administrative burden. GLBP provides load balancing over multiple routers using a single virtual IP address and multiple virtual MAC addresses. Each host is configured with the same virtual IP address, and all routers in the virtual router group participate in forwarding packets.

Members of a GLBP group elect one router to be the active virtual gateway (AVG) for that group. Other group members provide backup for the AVG in the event that the AVG becomes unavailable. The AVG assigns a virtual MAC address to each member of the GLBP group. Each gateway assumes responsibility for forwarding packets sent to the virtual MAC address assigned to it by the AVG. These gateways are known as *active virtual forwarders (AVF)* for their virtual MAC address. The AVG is responsible for answering ARP requests for the virtual IP address. Load sharing is achieved by the AVG replying to the ARP requests with different virtual MAC addresses.

Designing the Enterprise Edge Topology

The enterprise edge consists of a WAN edge for connecting branch offices and an Internet edge for connecting to the public Internet via a service provider's edge infrastructure. The enterprise edge might also include an extranet edge for connecting partners and an e-commerce module for selling products. This section covers enterprise edge topologies that include redundant WAN segments, multihomed connections to the Internet, and VPNs. The section also includes a few comments about the service provider edge.

Redundant WAN Segments

Because WAN links can be critical pieces of an enterprise internetwork, redundant (backup) WAN links are often included in an enterprise edge network topology. A WAN network can be designed as a full mesh or a partial mesh. A full-mesh topology provides complete redundancy. It also provides good performance because there is just a single-link delay between any two sites. However, as already discussed in this chapter, a full mesh is costly to implement, maintain, upgrade, and troubleshoot. A hierarchical partial-mesh topology, as shown previously in Figure 5-4, is usually sufficient.

Circuit Diversity

When provisioning backup WAN links, you should learn as much as possible about the actual physical circuit routing. Different carriers sometimes use the same facilities, meaning that your backup path is susceptible to the same failures as your primary path. You should do some investigative work to ensure that your backup actually is a backup. Network engineers use the term *circuit diversity* to refer to the optimum situation of circuits using different paths.

Because carriers lease capacity to each other and use third-party companies that provide capacity to multiple carriers, it is getting harder to guarantee circuit diversity. Also, carriers often merge with each other and mingle their circuits after the merge. As carriers increasingly use automated techniques for physical circuit rerouting, it becomes even more difficult to plan diversity because the rerouting is dynamic.

Nonetheless, you should work with the providers of your WAN links to gain an understanding of the level of circuit diversity in your network design. Carriers are usually willing to work with customers to provide information about physical circuit routing. Be aware, however, that carriers sometimes provide inaccurate information, based on databases that are not kept current. Try to write circuit-diversity commitments into contracts with your providers.

When analyzing circuit diversity, be sure to analyze your local cabling in addition to your carrier's services. Perhaps you have designed an ISDN link to back up a Frame Relay link. Do both of these links use the same cabling to get to the demarcation point in your building network? What cabling do the links use to get to your carrier? The cabling that goes from your building to the carrier is often the weakest link in a network. It can be affected by construction, flooding, ice storms, trucks hitting telephone poles, and other factors.

Multihoming the Internet Connection

The generic meaning of *multihoming* is to "provide more than one connection for a system to access and offer network services." The term *multihoming* is also used in many specific ways. A server, for example, is said to be multihomed if it has more than one network layer address. Content delivery networks can multihome application layer data and services.

The term *multihoming* is increasingly used to refer to the practice of providing an enterprise network with more than one entry into the Internet. Redundant entries into the Internet provide fault tolerance for applications that require Internet access. An enterprise network can be multihomed to the Internet in many different ways, depending on a customer's goals. Figure 5-14 and Table 5-2 describe some methods for multihoming the Internet connection.

Table 5-2   *Description of Options for Multihoming the Internet Connection*

	Number of Routers at the Enterprise	Number of Connections to the Internet	Number of ISPs	Advantages	Disadvantages
Option A	1	2	1	WAN backup; low cost; working with one ISP can be easier than working with multiple ISPs.	No ISP redundancy; router is a single point of failure; this solution assumes the ISP has two access points near the enterprise.
Option B	1	2	2	WAN backup; low cost; ISP redundancy.	Router is a single point of failure; it can be difficult to deal with policies and procedures of two different ISPs.
Option C	2	2	1	WAN backup; especially good for geographically dispersed company; medium cost; working with one ISP can be easier than working with multiple ISPs.	No ISP redundancy.
Option D	2	2	2	WAN backup; especially good for geographically dispersed company; ISP redundancy.	High cost; it can be difficult to deal with policies and procedures of two different ISPs.

In the case of Options C and D, the goal might be to improve network performance by allowing European enterprise sites to access the Internet using the Paris router and North American sites to use the New York router. This can be accomplished by correctly configuring a default gateway on end stations and a default route on enterprise routers in Europe and North America. A *default route* specifies where a packet should go if there is no explicit entry for the destination network in a router's routing table. The default route is also sometimes called *the gateway of last resort*.

Your customer might have more complex goals than the simple goal in the previous paragraph. Perhaps your customer wants to guarantee that European enterprise sites access North American Internet sites via the New York router. A parallel goal is that North American enterprise sites access European Internet sites via the Paris router. This could be a reasonable goal when a constant, low latency is required for an application. The latency is more predictable if the first part of the path is across the enterprise intranet instead of the Internet. This goal is harder to meet than the first goal, however. It requires that the enterprise routers understand routes from the ISP and set preferences on those routes.

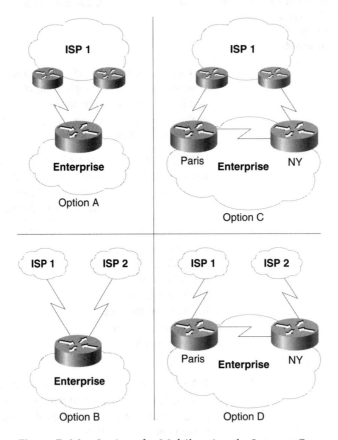

Figure 5-14   *Options for Multihoming the Internet Connection*

A related goal is to use the "best route" across the Internet to the sites that the enterprise users rely on the most. Unless an enterprise contracts (and pays) for end-to-end managed QoS, this goal cannot be met. The routing protocol used on the Internet, BGP, doesn't offer route optimality. Its only purpose is to provide reachability and stability in the global routing system. Intermediate providers with whom an enterprise has no business relationship don't care if the enterprise's traffic follows optimal routes, nor do they have any incentive to do so.

Another, more complex goal is to guarantee that incoming traffic from the Internet destined for European enterprise sites uses the Paris router and incoming traffic for North American enterprise sites uses the New York router. This goal requires the enterprise routers to advertise to the Internet routes to enterprise sites. The routes must include metrics so that routers on the Internet know the preferred path to sites on the enterprise intranet.

One other caveat when an enterprise network is multihomed is the potential to become a *transit network* that provides interconnections for other networks. Referring to Figure 5-14, consider that the enterprise router learns routes from the ISP. If the enterprise router advertises these learned routes, it risks allowing the enterprise network to become a transit network and being loaded by unintended external traffic. When an enterprise network becomes a transit network, routers on the Internet learn that they can reach other routers on the Internet via the enterprise network. To avoid this situation, enterprise routers should advertise only their own routes. Alternatively they can run without a routing protocol and rely on default and static routing.

In general, multihoming the Internet connection can be challenging if a customer's goals are complex. Encourage your customers to simplify their goals to ensure ease of implementation, scalability, availability, and affordability. If the main goal is high availability, don't assume that this means more redundancy is required. According to Howard Berkowitz in his book *WAN Survival Guide*, "Uncontrolled increases in redundancy lead to uncontrolled increases in complexity, and may actually decrease availability."

Virtual Private Networking

Virtual private networks (VPN) use advanced encryption and tunneling to permit organizations to establish secure, end-to-end, private network connections over a third-party network. The third-party network can be a private service provider network or the public Internet. An organization can connect to the third-party network using a variety of WAN and remote-access technologies, including leased lines, Frame Relay, cable modems, digital subscriber line (DSL), analog modems, ISDN, and so on. Organizations can also use VPNs to connect outside users, such as business partners, customers, resellers, and suppliers. VPNs also support mobile users and telecommuters.

Point-to-point connectivity across the third-party network is typically provided by a tunneling protocol. Tunneling is a technique for encapsulating packets of one protocol inside another protocol. For example, a tunnel can carry IPv4 packets across an internetwork that supports only IPv6. In the context of a VPN, tunneling is used to encapsulate private messages and apply encryption algorithms to the payload.

Tunnels provide a logical, point-to-point connection across a connectionless IP network, enabling application of advanced security features. Encryption is applied to the tunneled connection to scramble data, thus making data legible only to authorized systems. In applications where security and privacy are less of a concern, tunnels can be used without encryption to provide multiprotocol support.

Layer 2 tunneling methods encapsulate at the data link layer of the OSI model. Examples include Point-to-Point Tunneling Protocol (PPTP), Layer 2 Forwarding (L2F), MPLS VPNs, and Layer 2 Tunneling Protocol (L2TP). L2TP is an IETF standard (RFC 2661) that many vendors support for their VPN solutions, including Cisco and Microsoft. The IETF is also developing a new version of L2TP, called *L2*, which is emerging as a lightweight yet robust solution for Layer 2 tunneling.

Layer 3 tunneling encapsulates at the network layer. Two examples are IPsec and Cisco generic routing encapsulation (GRE). If only IP-unicast packets are being tunneled, IPsec is the best choice. GRE is used when multicast, broadcast, and non-IP packets need to be tunneled.

VPN applications for enterprise networks can be divided into two main categories:

■ **Site-to-site VPNs:** Site-to-site VPNs focus on connecting geographically dispersed offices and extending the classic enterprise WAN. A site-to-site VPN can also add interconnections between multiple organizations, in which case it is sometimes called an *extranet VPN*.

■ **Remote-access VPNs:** Remote-access VPNs focus on remote users and business partners who access the network on an as-needed basis.

The sections that follow describe these two types of VPNs in greater detail.

Site-to-Site VPNs

Site-to-site VPNs have emerged as a relatively inexpensive way for a company to connect geographically dispersed branch offices and home offices via a service provider or the Internet, as opposed to maintaining an expensive private WAN. The company's private data can be encrypted for routing through the service provider's network or the Internet. Traditionally, businesses relied on private 1.544-Mbps T1 leased lines to link remote offices together. Leased lines are expensive to install and maintain. For many companies, a leased line provides more bandwidth than is needed at too high a price. Companies also used Frame Relay and point-to-point networks for their private WANs, but they were also somewhat expensive and hard to manage. A site-to-site VPN is a more cost-effective and manageable solution.

When designing the topology of a site-to-site network, you should consider the same needs that you would for a private WAN, including the need for high availability with automatic failover, performance, security, and scalability. The most common topologies for a site-to-site VPN are as follows:

■ Hub-and-spoke

■ Mesh

■ Hierarchical network

The hub-and-spoke topology is used when there is a single regional or headquarters location with many remote offices, and most traffic is between the remote sites and the regional or headquarters location. This design minimizes configuration complexity by having a single IPsec connection or a single GRE tunnel from each remote location back to the regional or headquarters location. This design isn't appropriate when there is a high level of traffic between remote sites or when there is a need for redundancy and automatic failover. An enhancement to the design is to include multiple VPN routers at headquarters to provide better redundancy.

Mesh VPN designs can either be fully meshed, providing any-to-any connectivity, or partially meshed, providing some-to-some connectivity, depending upon customer requirements. The meshed topology is a good design to use when there are a small number of total locations (regional, headquarters, or remote locations), with a large amount of traffic flowing between some (partial mesh) or all (full mesh) of the sites. In a fully meshed design, the loss of a single location affects only traffic to or from that location. All other locations remain unaffected. This design does not scale well when there are numerous sites, due to the large number of IPsec connections or GRE tunnels with IPsec that have to be configured on each device.

A hierarchical VPN topology is a hybrid topology for a large company that has many headquarters and regional offices with a lot of traffic flowing between them, and many remote offices, with little interaction between them. The topology consists of a full- or partial-mesh core, with peripheral sites connecting into the core using a hub-and-spoke design. A hierarchical design is the most complex of the designs in terms of configuration, and might have a combination of IPsec and GRE tunnels.

Remote-Access VPNs

Remote-access VPNs permit on-demand access to an organization's internetwork, via secure, encrypted connections. Mobile or remote users, and branch offices that don't need to always be connected, can access their corporate networks via a third-party network, such as a service provider's network or the Internet. Enterprises use remote-access VPNs to reduce communications expenses by leveraging the local infrastructures of service providers who support dialup, ISDN, cable modem, DSL, or wireless access to the Internet or the provider's private network.

When implementing a remote-access VPN architecture, an important consideration is where to initiate tunneling and encryption. Should the tunnel initiate on the client PC or on a network access server (NAS) operated by the VPN service provider? In a client-initiated model, the encrypted tunnel is established by client software using IPsec, L2TP, or PPTP, thereby making the service provider network solely a means of transport to the corporate network. An advantage of a client-initiated model is that the "last mile" service provider access network used for accessing the provider point of presence (POP) is secured. A disadvantage of the client-initiated model is the need to manage software on client machines.

In a NAS-initiated model, a remote user accesses a service provider's POP, is authenticated by the service provider, and, in turn, initiates a secure tunnel to the corporate network from the POP. With a NAS-initiated architecture, VPN intelligence resides in the service provider network. There is no end-user client software for the organization to maintain, thus eliminating client management issues associated with remote access. The drawbacks, however, are lack of security on the local access network connecting the client to the service provider network and the need to interoperate with servers operated by the provider. Figure 5-15 shows a remote-access VPN topology for a retail company. The company uses both client-initiated and NAS-initiated tunnels.

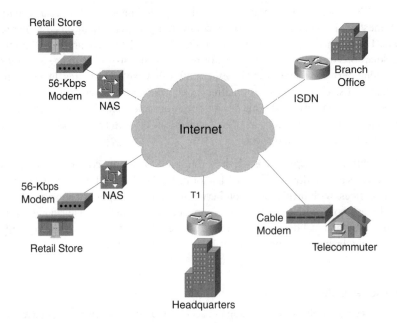

Figure 5-15 *Remote-Access VPN for a Retail Company*

At the headquarters, user VPN connections terminate in the Remote-Access VPN section of the Internet edge module, according to the Cisco SAFE architecture. Cisco recommends that one or more VPN concentrators reside within this area. A VPN concentrator is a dedicated hardware platform that aggregates a large volume of simultaneous VPN connections. Generally, enterprises place the concentrator between a router that has access to the VPN and a router that forwards traffic into the campus network. The Remote-Access VPN section also includes an authentication, authorization, and accounting (AAA) server and an intrusion detection system (IDS) or intrusion prevention system (IPS).

Service Provider Edge

Although the focus of this chapter is designing a logical topology for an enterprise network, a quick discussion of service providers is warranted at this point. An enterprise network connects to a module that can be called the *service provider edge*, and, although you aren't expected to design this module as an enterprise network designer, you need to have some understanding of it and be able to select the appropriate provider (or providers) for your design customers. The selection of a service provider is something you should consider during the logical design phase, which is the focus of Part II. Part III addresses the topic again because during that phase you should make some definite selections of WAN technologies, devices, and providers.

In the early days of data communications, there were the regional or national telephone companies and their customers, and nothing else. A customer's choice of provider was dictated by location. The level of service and pricing was dictated by the provider. Today, there is a broad range of service providers and service levels, and pricing is more negotiable.

Finding a provider that matches an enterprise's needs requires a good understanding of those needs and the culture of the enterprise and the potential provider. Many ISPs are small startups that offer wireless and cable modem service to end users. These ISPs might not have the expertise to support a large enterprise, although they might be appropriate for home users accessing the corporate network using VPN software. Some ISPs focus mostly on hosting servers and don't support end users. Some ISPs are actually network service providers (NSP), which means that their main business is connecting other ISPs rather than enterprises or end users. Selecting providers for your network design requires you to understand which of these types of services you actually need.

ISPs and NSPs are sometimes classified as being Tier 1 through Tier 5. Although these categories don't have universal meaning, if a provider calls itself a Tier 1 provider and you are looking for an inexpensive provider to connect a small office or home, you know to look elsewhere. Tier 1 ISPs are large, international providers, whereas Tier 5 ISPs are small, specialized providers, sometimes located in a town or rural area. A Tier 5 provider could be as small as an Internet café.

One important difference between the tiers has to do with the relationship a provider has with other ISPs. Using an economic definition of peer (rather than the BGP definition), a *peer relationship* means that two ISPs do not charge each other to carry each other's traffic. They are both about the same size and it is to their mutual advantage to let their customers have access to each other, without worrying about billing. This differs from the other common ISP relationship, which is a provider-customer one, where a smaller ISP pays a larger ISP for the privilege of sending traffic through the larger ISP's network. This is often called *buying transit*.

A Tier 1 provider doesn't buy transit. A Tier 1 provider has a 24/7 network operations center and a national or international backbone with at least DS-3 connectivity, and more likely OC-3 to OC-48. The provider gets all its routes from bilateral peering arrangements. Its customers are primarily other providers, but it might support a large enterprise also. Examples of Tier 1 providers include Verizon, Cable & Wireless, British Telecom, Verio, Level 3, and AT&T. Tier 2 providers also have high-bandwidth backbones and 24/7 operations, but they are limited to a regional or national presence, and they buy transit (often at a bulk discount) from a Tier 1 provider for traffic that goes outside the region. A Tier 2 provider gets all its regional routes through peering arrangements.

A Tier 3 provider is typically a regional provider for a small or medium-sized region. A Tier 3 provider buys transit from multiple upstream providers and runs a default-free routing table. There's no general definition of Tier 4 or Tier 5, but Tier 4 could be a metropolitan provider that is multihomed to two regional providers, and Tier 5 might be a small, single-homed provider that connects end users via a wireless or cable modem service.

At this point in the design process, you should have analyzed requirements and topologies to the extent that you have a good idea of the tier you will need. During the logical design phase, you should start making a list of criteria for selecting providers and develop a plan and set of standards for evaluating candidates. Investigate the availability of service providers in the relevant regions and start making inquiries. Be specific in your requests for information from candidates. Prioritize the requested information and indicate how quickly you need a response. You may also want to ask for references and to start asking questions about the provider of other users in the region. See the "Selecting a WAN Service Provider" section in Chapter 11, "Selecting Technologies and Devices for Enterprise Networks," for more information on this topic.

Secure Network Design Topologies

This section discusses network security in relation to network topologies. Chapter 8 covers network security in more detail. The focus of this section is logical topologies, but physical security is also briefly mentioned.

Planning for Physical Security

When developing the logical topology of a network, you should begin to get an idea of where equipment will be installed. You should start working with your design customer right away to make sure that critical equipment will be installed in computer rooms that have protection from unauthorized access, theft, vandalism, and natural disasters such as floods, fires, storms, and earthquakes. Physical security is not really an aspect of logical network design, but it is mentioned here because your logical topology might have an impact on it, and because the planning for physical security should start right away, in case there are lead times to build or install security mechanisms.

Meeting Security Goals with Firewall Topologies

A *firewall* is a system or combination of systems that enforces a boundary between two or more networks. A firewall can be a router with ACLs, a dedicated hardware box, or software running on a PC or UNIX system. A firewall should be placed in the network topology so that all traffic from outside the protected network must pass through the firewall. A security policy specifies which traffic is authorized to pass through the firewall.

Firewalls are especially important at the boundary between the enterprise network and the Internet. A basic firewall topology is simply a router with a WAN connection to the Internet, a LAN connection to the enterprise network, and software that has security features. This elementary topology is appropriate if your customer has a simple security policy. Simple security policies can be implemented on the router with ACLs. The router can also use NAT to hide internal addresses from Internet hackers.

For customers with the need to publish public data and protect private data, the firewall topology can include a public LAN that hosts web, FTP, DNS, and SMTP servers. Older security literature often referred to the public LAN as the *free-trade zone*, which is a good name for it. Unfortunately, the less apropos term *demilitarized zone (DMZ)* has become more popular. Security literature refers to a host in the DMZ as a *bastion host*, a secure system that supports a limited number of applications for use by outsiders. The bastion host holds data that outsiders can access, such as web pages, but is strongly protected from outsiders using it for anything other than its limited purposes.

For larger customers, it is recommended that you use a dedicated firewall in addition to a router between the Internet and the enterprise network. To maximize security, you can run security features on the router and on the dedicated firewall. (To maximize performance, on the other hand, you would not run security features on the router.) Figure 5-16 shows a DMZ secure topology.

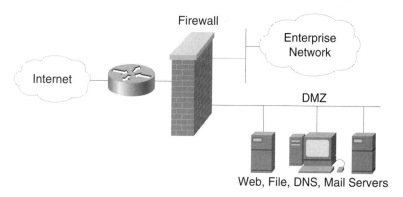

Figure 5-16   *DMZ Topology*

An alternative topology is to use two routers as the firewalls and place the DMZ between them, as shown in Figure 5-17. This topology is called a *three-part firewall topology*. A disadvantage with this approach is that the configuration on the routers might be complex, consisting of many ACLs to control traffic in and out of the private network and the DMZ. Another disadvantage is that traffic for the enterprise network flows through the DMZ. The DMZ connects public servers that can be compromised and act as launching pads for attacks into the enterprise network. You can strengthen this topology by using routers with simple ACLs at either end of the DMZ and also including firewalls at either end that are configured with more complex ACLs. Also, the bastion hosts inside the DMZ should run firewall software and be configured for a limited set of services.

Summary

This chapter focused on techniques for developing a topology for a network design. Designing a network topology is the first step in the logical design phase of the top-down network design methodology. By designing a logical topology before a physical implementation, you can increase the likelihood of meeting a customer's goals for scalability, adaptability, and performance.

Figure 5-17   *Three-Part Firewall Topology*

This chapter discussed four characteristics of network topologies:

■   Hierarchy

■   Modularity

■   Redundancy

■   Security

All of these characteristics can be applied to both campus and enterprise WAN design. The characteristics are not mutually exclusive. Your goal should be to design hierarchical, modular, redundant, and secure network architectures based on your customer's goals.

Hierarchy and modularity let you develop a network consisting of many interrelated components in a layered and structured fashion. Using a hierarchical model can help you maximize network performance, reduce the time to implement and troubleshoot a design, and minimize costs.

Redundant network designs let you meet requirements for network availability by duplicating network components. Redundancy eliminates single points of failure on the network. Redundancy also facilitates load sharing, which increases network performance. Redundancy adds complexity and cost to the network, however, and should be designed with care.

Depending on your particular network design, you should plan a secure topology that protects core routers, demarcation points, cabling, switches, servers, and so on. Adding one or more firewalls to your topology can help you protect enterprise networks from outside attackers.

After completing a logical topology for a customer, you should continue in the logical design phase by designing network addressing and naming models, selecting switching and routing protocols, and developing network security and management strategies. These topics are covered in the next few chapters. Doing a thorough job in the logical design phase can ease your transition into the design of the physical implementation of the network. It can also prepare you for the job of selecting the right products and technologies for your customer.

Review Questions

1. Many basic networking books state that there are three network topologies, a bus, a ring, and a star. Based on the knowledge you gained in this chapter, explain why these simple topologies may not meet the needs of modern networks.

2. Compare and contrast full- and partial-mesh topologies. What advantages does a partial mesh have compared to a full mesh? What advantages does a full mesh have compared to a partial mesh?

3. Why is it difficult to achieve true load balancing (as opposed to load sharing) in most networks?

4. What does *physical security* mean? What are some facets of physical security?

Design Scenario

In Chapter 1, "Analyzing Business Goals and Constraints," you learned about ElectroMyCycle, a manufacturer of new electric motorcycles. ElectroMyCycle has chosen you to design a new network that will let the company scale to a larger size. The campus network will support about 200 employees and a new data center. Another feature of the campus network will be a state-of-the-art manufacturing facility with networked equipment that communicates with servers in the data center that support real-time control and management. Engineers will access the servers from their PCs in the access layer of the campus network.

ElectroMyCycle will sell its new motorcycle both online and through a large retail company. For online sales, ElectroMyCycle plans to have a DMZ that connects a public web server, a DNS server, and an email server. The web server needs to communicate with back-end servers in the data center that hold customer billing data. ElectroMyCycle also plans to open a branch sales office in the city where the retail company's corporate headquarters reside, about 500 miles from ElectroMyCycle's headquarters.

Design and draw a logical topology that will support ElectroMyCycle's needs. In addition to meeting the specified needs, be sure to consider security.

1. Explain why you think your design meets the needs of ElectroMyCycle.

2. List the major user communities for your design.

3. List the major data stores and the user communities for each data store.

4. Identify major network traffic flows in your network topology drawing.

5. How does your design provide security for ElectroMyCycle's network?

6. What questions will you ask ElectroMyCycle about this project as you do your work?

Chapter 6

Designing Models for Addressing and Numbering

This chapter provides guidelines for assigning addresses and names to internetwork components, including networks, subnets, routers, servers, and end systems. The chapter focuses on Internet Protocol (IP) addressing and naming. To benefit most from this chapter, you should already have a basic understanding of IP addressing.

This chapter illustrates the importance of using a structured model for network layer addressing and naming. Without structure, it is easy to run out of addresses, waste addresses, introduce duplicate addresses and names, and use addresses and names that are hard to manage. To meet a customer's goals for scalability, performance, and manageability, you should assign addresses and names systematically.

This chapter also demonstrates the importance of developing policies and procedures for addressing and naming. Policies often involve a plan for distributing authority for addressing and naming to avoid one department having to manage all addresses and names. A central authority can assign blocks of addresses and names in a hierarchical fashion to departments and branch offices.

Part I of this book, "Identifying Your Customer's Needs and Goals," recommends gaining an understanding of your customer's organizational structure (for example, departments, branch offices, business units, and so on). This information is helpful when planning addresses and names. A topology map of the network is also useful, because it helps you see the hierarchy in the network and recognize where address boundaries exist. The addressing and naming step of the top-down network design process falls here in the methodology because it makes use of information you gathered in the previous phases of the network design process.

The addressing and naming step precedes selecting routing and switching protocols, which is covered in the next chapter, because the addressing model you develop might dictate which routing protocols you can select. (For example, some routing protocols do not support variable-length subnet masking [VLSM].)

Guidelines for Assigning Network Layer Addresses

Network layer addresses should be planned, managed, and documented. Although an end system can learn its address dynamically, no mechanisms exist for assigning network or subnet numbers dynamically. These numbers must be planned and administered. Many vintage networks still exist where addressing was not planned or documented. These networks are hard to troubleshoot and do not scale.

The following list provides some simple rules for network layer addressing that can help you architect scalability and manageability into a network design. These rules are described in more detail in later sections of this chapter.

■ Design a structured model for addressing before assigning any addresses.

■ Leave room for growth in the addressing model. If you do not plan for growth, you might later have to renumber many devices, which is labor-intensive.

■ Assign blocks of addresses in a hierarchical fashion to foster good scalability and availability.

■ Assign blocks of addresses based on the physical network, not on group membership, to avoid problems when groups or individuals move.

■ If the level of network management expertise in regional and branch offices is high, you can delegate authority for addressing regional and branch-office networks, subnets, servers, and end systems.

■ To maximize flexibility and minimize configuration, use dynamic addressing for end systems.

■ To maximize security and adaptability, use private addresses with Network Address Translation (NAT) in IP environments.

Using a Structured Model for Network Layer Addressing

A *structured model for addressing* means that addresses are meaningful, hierarchical, and planned. IP addresses that include a prefix and host part are structured. Assigning an IP network number to an enterprise network, then subnetting the network number and subnetting the subnets, is a structured (hierarchical) model for IP addressing.

A clearly documented structured model for addressing facilitates management and troubleshooting. Structure makes it easier to understand network maps, operate network management software, and recognize devices in protocol analyzer traces and reports. Structured addresses also facilitate network optimization and security because they make it easier to implement network filters on firewalls, routers, and switches.

A lot of companies have no model for addressing. When there is no model, and addresses are assigned in a haphazard way, the following problems can occur:

■ Duplicate network and host addresses

■ Illegal addresses that cannot be routed on the Internet

- Not enough addresses in total, or by group

- Addressees that cannot be used, and so are wasted

Administering Addresses by a Central Authority

A corporate Information Systems (IS) or enterprise networking department should develop a global model for network layer addressing. As the network designer, you should help the IS department develop the model. The model should identify network numbers for the core of the enterprise network and blocks of subnets for the distribution and access layers. Depending on the organizational structure of the enterprise, network managers within each region or branch office can further divide the subnets.

IP addresses are either public or private. Public addresses are globally unique and are registered with a numbering authority. Private addresses are never routed on the global Internet and are assigned from a special range, documented in RFC 1918. Private addresses are covered in more detail in the section "Using Private Addresses in an IP Environment" later in this chapter.

Early in the addressing design process, you need to answer the following questions about public versus private addresses:

- Are public, private, or both address types required?

- How many end systems need access to the private network only?

- How many end systems need to be visible to the public network?

- How will translation between private and public addresses occur?

- Where in the network topology will the boundary between private and public addresses exist?

The Internet Assigned Numbers Authority (IANA) is responsible for the global coordination of public IP addresses. The IANA allocates IP addresses to Regional Internet Registries (RIR). If you need a large number of public addresses, you will work with one of five RIRs:

- American Registry for Internet Numbers (ARIN) serves North America and parts of the Caribbean. Go to www.arin.net for more information.

- RIPE Network Coordination Centre (RIPE NCC) serves Europe, the Middle East, and Central Asia. Go to www.ripe.net for more information.

- Asia-Pacific Network Information Centre (APNIC) serves Asia and the Pacific region. Go to www.apnic.net for more information.

- Latin American and Caribbean Internet Addresses Registry (LACNIC) serves Latin America and parts of the Caribbean. Go to www.lacnic.net for more information.

- African Network Information Centre (AfriNIC) serves Africa. Go to www.afrinic.net for more information.

The term *provider-independent address space* refers to addresses that are assigned directly by one of the RIRs. In practice, most enterprises do not use addresses from the provider-independent address space. To become eligible for provider-independent address space, an organization must demonstrate to the RIRs that it will have thousands of Internet-connected hosts. Therefore, most enterprises work with an Internet service provider (ISP) to obtain public addresses, in which case their addresses are part of the *provider-assigned address space*. The enterprise uses these addresses for as long as it remains a subscriber of the provider. Changing to a new provider requires renumbering, which is one problem with provider-assigned addresses. Nevertheless, unless you have numerous hosts that need public addressing, you will probably use provider-assigned addresses.

Distributing Authority for Addressing

One of the first steps in developing an addressing and naming model is to determine who will implement the model. Which network administrators will actually assign addresses and configure devices? If addressing and configuration will be carried out by inexperienced network administrators, you should keep the model simple.

If there is a shortage of network administrators (which occurs in many organizations), simplicity and minimizing the amount of configuration required is important. In these situations, dynamic addressing is a good recommendation. Dynamic addressing mechanisms, such as the Dynamic Host Configuration Protocol (DHCP) for IP environments, allow each end system to learn its address automatically. Little, if any, configuration is necessary.

If network administrators in regional and branch offices are inexperienced, you might consider not delegating authority for addressing and naming. A lot of small and medium-sized companies maintain strict control of addressing and naming at a corporate (centralized) level. Maintaining strict control avoids mistakes that can cause user frustration and network failures. Maintaining strict control can be challenging, especially as regional network administrators and users become more experienced with networking and start installing devices that can assign addresses.

Using Dynamic Addressing for End Systems

Dynamic addressing reduces the configuration tasks required to connect end systems to an internetwork. Dynamic addressing also supports users who change offices frequently, travel, or work at home occasionally. With dynamic addressing, a station can automatically learn the network segment to which it is currently attached, and adjust its network layer address accordingly.

Dynamic addressing was built into legacy desktop protocols such as AppleTalk and Novell NetWare. The designers of these protocols recognized the need to minimize configuration tasks so that inexperienced users could set up small internetworks. The IP protocols, on the other hand, were designed to run on computers managed by experienced system administrators and did not originally support dynamic addressing. In recent years, however, the importance of dynamic addressing has been recognized, and most companies use DHCP to minimize configuration tasks for IP end systems.

Many networks use a combination of static and dynamic addressing. Static addresses are typically used for servers, routers, and network management systems. Static addresses are also used at the enterprise edge in the e-commerce, Internet edge, VPN/remote-access, and WAN edge modules of a modular network design. Although switches work below the network layer at the data link and physical layers, it is also a good idea to assign a static network layer address to switches for management purposes. Dynamic addresses are typically used for end systems, including workstations and IP phones.

Other criteria for using static versus dynamic addressing include the following:

- **The number of end systems:** When there are more than 30 systems, dynamic addressing is usually preferable.

- **Renumbering:** If it is likely you will need to renumber systems in the future and there are many end systems, dynamic address assignment is the better choice. Renumbering for public addresses will become necessary if a new ISP is selected. In addition, you might plan to renumber because the current plan is not well structured or will run out of numbers soon.

- **High availability:** Statically assigned IP addresses are available anytime. Dynamically assigned IP addresses have to be acquired from a server first. If the server fails, an address cannot be acquired. To avoid this problem, you can deploy redundant DHCP servers or use static addresses.

- **Security:** With dynamic address assignment, in most cases, any device that connects to the network can acquire a valid address. This imposes some security risk and might mean that dynamic addressing is not appropriate for a company with a strict security policy.

- **Address tracking:** If a management or security policy requires that addresses be tracked, static addressing might be easier to implement than dynamic addressing.

- **Additional parameters:** If end systems need information beyond an address, dynamic addressing is useful because a server can provide additional parameters to clients along with the address. For example, a DHCP server provides a subnet mask, a default gateway, and optional server information such as the address of a TFTP server for VoIP and the address of one or more name servers, including Domain Name System (DNS) and Windows Internet Naming Service (WINS) servers.

IP Dynamic Addressing

When the IP protocols were first developed, a network administrator was required to configure each host with its unique IP address. In the mid-1980s, protocols were developed to support diskless stations dynamically learning an address, which was necessary because a diskless station has no storage for saving a configuration. These protocols included the Reverse Address Resolution Protocol (RARP) and BOOTP. BOOTP has evolved into DHCP, which has gained considerable popularity since the late 1990s.

RARP is limited in scope; the only information returned to a station using RARP is its IP address. BOOTP is more sophisticated than RARP and optionally returns additional information, including the address of the default gateway, the name of a boot file to download, and 64 bytes of vendor-specific information.

Dynamic Host Configuration Protocol

DHCP is based on BOOTP, which hosts can interoperate with DHCP hosts, although DHCP adds many enhancements to BOOTP, including a larger vendor-specific information field (called the *options field* in DHCP) and the automatic allocation of reusable network layer addresses. DHCP has bypassed BOOTP in popularity because it is easier to configure. Unlike BOOTP, DHCP does not require a network administrator to maintain a MAC-to-IP address table.

DHCP uses a client/server model. Servers allocate network layer addresses and save information about which addresses have been allocated. Clients dynamically request configuration parameters from servers. The goal of DHCP is that clients should require no manual configuration. In addition, the network manager should not have to enter any per-client configuration parameters into servers.

DHCP supports three methods for IP address allocation:

- **Automatic allocation:** A DHCP server assigns a permanent IP address to a client.

- **Dynamic allocation:** A DHCP server assigns an IP address to a client for a limited period of time.

- **Manual allocation:** A network administrator assigns a permanent IP address to a client, and DHCP is used simply to convey the assigned address to the client. (Manual allocation is rarely used because it requires per-client configuration, which automatic and dynamic allocations do not require.)

Dynamic allocation is the most popular method, partly because its reallocation feature supports environments where hosts are not online all the time, and there are more hosts than addresses. With dynamic allocation, a client requests the use of an address for a limited period of time. The period of time is called a *lease*.

The allocation mechanism guarantees not to reallocate that address within the requested time, and attempts to return the same network layer address each time the client requests an address. The client can extend its lease with subsequent requests. The client can choose to relinquish its lease by sending a DHCP release message to the server.

The allocation mechanism can reuse an address if the lease for the address has expired. As a consistency check, the allocating server should probe the address before allocating the address by sending an Internet Control Message Protocol (ICMP) echo request (also known as a *ping packet*) to the address. The client should also probe the newly received address to make sure it is not currently in use by sending a ping packet to the address or by sending an Address Resolution Protocol (ARP) request for the address. If there is a reply, the address is already in use and should not be used by the client.

When a client boots, it broadcasts a DHCP discover message on its local subnet. A station that has previously received a network layer address and lease can include them in the DHCP discover message to suggest that they be used again. A router can pass the DHCP discover message on to DHCP servers not on the same physical subnet to avoid a requirement that a DHCP server resides on each subnet. (The router acts as a DHCP relay agent.)

Each server responds to the DHCP request with a DHCP offer message that includes an available network layer address in the *your address* (*yiaddr*) field. The DHCP offer message can include additional configuration parameters in the options field such as the subnet mask and the addresses of a default gateway, a DNS server, or a TFTP server.

After the client receives DHCP offer messages from one or more servers, the client chooses one server from which to request configuration parameters. The client broadcasts a DHCP request message that includes the *server identifier* option to indicate which server it has selected. This DHCP request message is broadcast and relayed through routers if necessary.

The server selected in the DHCP request message commits the configuration parameters for the client to persistent storage and responds with a DHCP ACK message, containing the configuration parameters for the requesting client.

If a client receives no DHCP offer or DHCP ACK messages, the client times out and retransmits the DHCP discover and request messages. To avoid synchronicity and excessive network traffic, the client uses a randomized exponential backoff algorithm to determine the delay between retransmissions. The delay between retransmissions should be chosen to allow sufficient time for replies from the server, based on the characteristics of the network between the client and server. For example, on a 10-Mbps Ethernet network, the delay before the first retransmission should be 4 seconds, randomized by the value of a uniform random number chosen from the range −1 to +1. The delay before the next retransmission should be 8 seconds, randomized by the value of a uniform number chosen from the range −1 to +1. The retransmission delay should be doubled with subsequent retransmissions up to a maximum of 64 seconds.

DHCP Relay Agents

DHCP clients send their messages as broadcasts. Broadcasts don't cross routers and remain local to a subnet. Without a relay agent, each subnet needs a DHCP server. As mentioned, a router can act as a DHCP relay agent. This means that the router passes DHCP broadcast messages from clients to DHCP servers that are not on the same subnet as the clients. This avoids a requirement for a DHCP server to reside on each subnet with clients.

With Cisco routers, you can use the **ip helper-address** command on each router interface where clients reside to cause the router to become a DHCP relay agent. An address parameter for the command should point to the IP address of the DHCP server. Alternatively, the address can be a broadcast address so that the router broadcasts the DHCP discover message on to the specified network. A broadcast address should be used only if the server is on a directly connected network because modern routers do not forward directed broadcasts to other networks.

When a router relays a discover message to another network or subnet, the router places the IP address for the interface on which the message arrived in the gateway address (*giaddr*) field of the DHCP header. The DHCP server can use the giaddr information to determine from which scope the assigned address should come.

Caution   When you enable an IP helper address, Cisco routers forward numerous UDP broadcasts by default, including TFTP, DNS, NetBIOS, and TACACS broadcasts. To configure the router to be more discerning in its forwarding, use the **ip forward-protocol** command for the protocols that should be forwarded and the **no ip forward-protocol** command for the protocols that should not be forwarded. To make sure DHCP packets are forwarded, use the **ip forward-protocol udp 67** command. DHCP discover and request messages use UDP destination port number 67, the port number reserved many years ago for BOOTP.

IP Version 6 Dynamic Addressing

Like IPv4, IP version 6 (IPv6) supports both static and dynamic addressing. IPv6 calls dynamic addressing *autoconfiguration*. IPv6 autoconfiguration can be stateful or stateless.

With a stateful autoconfiguration method, hosts obtain addresses and other parameters from a server. The server stores a database containing the necessary information and maintains control over address assignments. This should sound familiar. The stateful autoconfiguration model is defined in DHCPv6.

Stateless autoconfiguration requires no manual configuration of hosts, minimal (or no) configuration of routers, and no servers. For a network engineer who is not concerned about which addresses are used, as long as they are unique and routable, stateless autoconfiguration offers many benefits. Stateless autoconfiguration is discussed in RFC 4862.

With stateless autoconfiguration, a host generates its own address using locally available information plus information advertised by routers. The process begins with the generation of a link-local address for an interface. The link-local address is generated by combining the well-known link-local prefix (FE80::/10) with a 64-bit interface identifier. For more information about IPv6 prefixes, see the "Hierarchy in IP Version 6 Addresses" section later in this chapter.

The next step determines the uniqueness of the tentative address that has been derived by combining the link-local address prefix with the interface identifier. The host transmits a Neighbor Solicitation message with the tentative address as the target address. If another host is using this address, a Neighbor Advertisement is returned. In this event, autoconfiguration stops and some manual intervention is required. Because the address is usually based on a NIC address, duplicates are very unlikely. If no responses are returned, the tentative address is considered unique, and IP connectivity with local hosts is now possible.

The final step of the autoconfiguration process involves listening for IPv6 Router Advertisement messages that routers periodically transmit. A host can also force an immediate Router Advertisement by transmitting a Router Solicitation message to the all-routers multicast address. Router Advertisements contain zero or more Prefix Information options that contain information used by the host to generate a global address. Additional option fields contain a subnet prefix and lifetime values, indicating how long addresses created from the prefix remain preferred and valid.

Zero Configuration Networking

The Zero Configuration Networking (Zeroconf) working group of the Internet Engineering Task Force (IETF) carried the concept of dynamic addressing one step further than DHCP. Like AppleTalk and IPv6, Zeroconf can allocate IP addresses without a server. It can also translate between names and IP addresses without a DNS server. To handle naming, Zeroconf supports multicast DNS (mDNS), which uses multicast addressing for name resolution. Zeroconf is implemented in Mac OS, Windows operating systems, Linux, most printers from major printer vendors, and other network devices.

Zeroconf is a link-local technology. Link-local addresses and names are meaningful only on a particular network. They are not globally unique. Zeroconf is appropriate for home and small office networks, ad hoc networks at meetings and conferences (especially wireless networks), embedded systems as in an automobile, and whenever two devices need to spontaneously share or exchange information.

Although the main goal of Zeroconf is to make personal computer networking easier to use, according to the www.zeroconf.org web page, a long-term goal is "to enable the creation of entirely new kinds of networked products, products that today would simply not be commercially viable because of the inconvenience and support costs involved in setting up, configuring, and maintaining a network."

Zeroconf has many advantages, but one potential risk is that it will interfere with more structured systems for address and name assignments, although the www.zeroconf.org page does say that Zeroconf "must coexist gracefully with larger configured networks" and that Zeroconf protocols "must not cause harm to the network when a Zeroconf machine is plugged into a large network." Zeroconf has some intriguing features and, as a network designer, you should have some familiarity with it. Zeroconf can solve various problems for small, ad hoc networks.

Using Private Addresses in an IP Environment

Private IP addresses are addresses that an enterprise network administrator assigns to internal networks and hosts without any coordination from an ISP or one of the RIRs. An ISP or the RIR provides public addresses for web servers or other servers that external users access, but public addresses are not necessary for internal hosts and networks. Addressing for internal hosts that need access to outside services, such as email, FTP, or web servers, can be handled by a NAT gateway. NAT is covered later in this chapter.

In RFC 1918, the IETF reserves the following numbers for addressing nodes on internal private networks:

- 10.0.0.0 through 10.255.255.255

- 172.16.0.0 through 172.31.255.255

- 192.168.0.0 through 192.168.255.255

One advantage of private network numbers is security. Private network numbers are not advertised to the Internet. Private network numbers *must not* be advertised to the Internet because they are not globally unique. By not advertising private internal network numbers, a modicum of security is achieved. Additional security, including firewalls and intrusion detection systems, should also be deployed, as discussed in Chapter 5, "Designing a Network Topology," and Chapter 8, "Developing Network Security Strategies."

Private addressing also helps meet goals for adaptability and flexibility. Using private addressing makes it easier to change ISPs in the future. If private addressing has been used, when moving to a new ISP, the only address changes required are in the router or firewall providing NAT services and in any public servers. You should recommend private addressing to customers who want the flexibility of easily switching to a different ISP in the future.

Another advantage of private network numbers is that an enterprise network can advertise just one network number, or a small block of network numbers, to the Internet. It is good practice to avoid advertising many network numbers to the Internet. One of the goals of modern Internet practices is that Internet routers should not need to manage huge routing tables. As an enterprise network grows, the network manager can assign private addresses to new networks, rather than requesting additional public network numbers from an ISP or RIR. This avoids increasing the size of Internet routing tables.

Private network numbers let a network designer reserve scarce Internet addresses for public servers. During the mid-1990s, as the Internet became commercialized and popularized, a scare rippled through the Internet community about the shortage of addresses. Dire predictions were made that no more addresses would be available by the turn of the century. Because of this scare, many companies (and many ISPs) were given a small set of addresses that needed to be carefully managed to avoid depletion. These companies recognize the value of private addresses for internal networks.

Note The shortage of Internet addresses was mainly due to the way IPv4 addresses were divided into classes. Although the IP address space is fixed in size and will become depleted at some point, the 4-byte size of an IPv4 address is theoretically large enough to address more than 4 billion nodes. The method used to divide the address space into classes meant that many addresses were wasted, however. Approximately 50 percent of the address space was used for Class A host addresses. Another 12 percent was used for Class C host addresses.

With the invention of classless addressing, the threat of running out of addresses is less imminent. Classless addressing is covered in the "Using a Hierarchical Model for Assigning Addresses" section of this chapter.

Caveats with Private Addressing

Although the benefits of private addressing outweigh the disadvantages, it is important to be aware of the drawbacks. One drawback is that outsourcing network management is difficult. When a company delegates network management responsibility to an outside company, the outside company typically sets up network consoles at its own site that communicate with internetworking devices inside the client's network. With private addressing, however, the consoles cannot reach the client's devices, because no routes to internal networks are advertised to the outside. NAT can be used to translate the private addresses to public addresses, but then there might be problems with interoperability between NAT and network management protocols such as the Simple Network Management Protocol (SNMP).

Another drawback for private addressing is the difficulty of communicating with partners, vendors, suppliers, and so on. Because the partner companies are also probably using private addresses, building extranets becomes more difficult. Also, companies that merge with each other face a difficult chore of renumbering any duplicate addresses caused by both companies using the same private addresses.

One other caveat to keep in mind when using private addresses is that it is easy to forget to use a structured model with the private addresses. Enterprise network managers, who were once starved for addresses that were carefully doled out by ISPs and the RIRs, get excited when they move to private addressing and have all of network 10.0.0.0 at their disposal.

The excitement should not overshadow the need to assign the new address space in a structured, hierarchical fashion. Hierarchical addressing facilitates route summarization within the enterprise network, which decreases bandwidth consumption by routing protocols, reduces processing on routers, and enhances network resiliency.

Network Address Translation

Network Address Translation (NAT) is an IP mechanism that is described in RFC 3022 for converting addresses from an inside network to addresses that are appropriate for an outside network, and vice versa. NAT is useful when hosts that need access to Internet services have private addresses. NAT functionality can be implemented in a separate appliance, router, or firewall.

The NAT administrator configures a pool of outside addresses that can be used for translation. When an inside host sends a packet, the source address is translated dynamically to an address from the pool of outside addresses. NAT also has a provision for static addresses for servers that need a fixed address (for example, a web or mail server that must always map to the same well-known address).

Some NAT products also offer port translation for mapping several addresses to the same address. With *port translation*, all traffic from an enterprise has the same address. Port numbers are used to distinguish separate conversations. Port translation reduces the number of required outside addresses. Port translation is sometimes called *NAT overload or Port Address Translation (PAT)*.

When using NAT, all traffic between an enterprise network and the Internet must go through the NAT gateway. For this reason, you should make sure the NAT gateway has superior throughput and low delay, particularly if enterprise users depend on Internet video or voice applications. The NAT gateway should have a fast processor that can examine and change packets quickly. Keep in mind that, in addition to modifying IP addresses, a NAT gateway must modify the IP, TCP, and UDP checksums. (The checksums for TCP and UDP cover a pseudo header that contains source and destination IP addresses.)

In many cases, NAT must also modify IP addresses that occur inside the data part of a packet. IP addresses can appear in ICMP, FTP, DNS, SNMP, and other types of packets. Because NAT has the job of translating something so basic as network layer addresses, it can be tricky to guarantee correct behavior with all applications. A NAT gateway should be thoroughly tested in a pilot environment before it is generally deployed.

Using a Hierarchical Model for Assigning Addresses

Hierarchical addressing is a model for applying structure to addresses so that numbers in the left part of an address refer to large blocks of networks or nodes, and numbers in the right part of an address refer to individual networks or nodes. Hierarchical addressing facilitates *hierarchical routing*, which is a model for distributing knowledge of a network topology among internetwork routers. With hierarchical routing, no single router needs to understand the complete topology. This chapter focuses on hierarchical addressing and routing for IP environments, but the concepts apply to other environments also.

Why Use a Hierarchical Model for Addressing and Routing?

Chapter 5 examined the importance of hierarchy in topology design. The benefits of hierarchy in an addressing and routing model are the same as those for a topology model:

- Support for easy troubleshooting, upgrades, and manageability

- Optimized performance

- Faster routing-protocol convergence

- Scalability

- Stability

- Fewer network resources needed (CPU, memory, buffers, bandwidth, and so on)

Hierarchical addressing permits the summarization (aggregation) of network numbers. *Summarization* allows a router to group many network numbers when advertising its routing table. Summarization enhances network performance and stability. Hierarchical addressing also facilitates *variable-length subnet masking (VLSM)*. With VLSM, a network can be divided into subnets of different sizes, which helps optimize available address space.

Hierarchical Routing

Hierarchical routing means that knowledge of the network topology and configuration is localized. No single router needs to understand how to get to each other network segment. Hierarchical routing requires that a network administrator assign addresses in a hierarchical fashion. IP addressing and routing have been somewhat hierarchical for a long time, but in recent years, as the Internet and enterprise intranets have grown, it has become necessary to add more hierarchy.

To understand hierarchical routing in simple terms, consider the telephone system. The telephone system has used hierarchical routing for years. When you dial 541-555-1212 from a phone in Michigan, the phone switch in Michigan does not know how to reach this specific number in Oregon. The switch in Michigan simply knows that the number is not in Michigan and forwards the call to a national phone company. A switch at the national phone company knows that 541 is for southern Oregon but does not know specifically where calls to 555 should go. A switch in Oregon determines which central office switch handles the 555 prefix, and that switch routes the call to 1212.

With data networking, similar decisions are made as a packet travels across a routed network. However, in traditional IP networks, the decisions could not be quite as local as the decisions in the telephone example. Until recently, IP addresses for the Internet were assigned in a nonhierarchical fashion. For example, two companies in Oregon might have widely different Class C network numbers, despite the fact that they both use the same upstream provider to reach the Internet. This meant that the provider had to tell all other Internet sites about both Oregon companies. So, unlike the phone system example, a router in Michigan would know how to reach specific networks in Oregon.

Classless Interdomain Routing

In the mid-1990s, the IETF and IANA realized that the lack of a hierarchical model for assigning network numbers in the Internet was a severe scalability problem. Internet routing tables were growing exponentially, and the amount of overhead to process and transmit the tables was significant. To constrain routing overhead, it became clear that the Internet must adopt a hierarchical addressing and routing scheme. To solve the routing overhead problem, the Internet adopted the *classless interdomain routing (CIDR)* method for summarizing routes. CIDR specifies that IP network addresses should be assigned in blocks, and that routers in the Internet should group routes to cut down on the quantity of routing information shared by Internet routers.

RFC 2050 provides guidelines for IP address allocation by RIRs and ISPs. RFC 2050 states that

> An Internet Provider obtains a block of address space from an address registry, and then assigns to its customers addresses from within that block based on each customer requirement. The result of this process is that routes to many customers will be aggregated together, and will appear to other providers as a single route. For route aggregation to be effective, Internet providers encourage customers joining their network to use the provider's block, and thus renumber their computers. Such encouragement may become a requirement in the future.

At the same time that the IETF and IANA addressed the problem of nonhierarchical routing, they also addressed the problem of IP address depletion. As mentioned previously, the system of assigning addresses in classes meant that many addresses were going to waste. The IETF developed classless addressing, which provides more flexibility in specifying the length of the prefix part of an IP network number.

Classless Routing Versus Classful Routing

As shown in Figure 6-1, an IP address contains a prefix part and a host part. Routers use the prefix to determine the path for a destination address that is not local. Routers use the host part to reach local hosts.

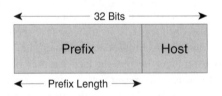

Figure 6-1   *Two Parts of an IP Address*

A prefix identifies a block of host numbers and is used for routing to that block. Traditional routing, also known as *classful routing*, does not transmit any information about the prefix length. With classful routing, hosts and routers calculate the prefix length by looking at the first few bits of an address to determine its class. The first few bits for Class A through C addresses are as shown in the following chart:

Class A	First bit = 0	Prefix is 8 bits
Class B	First 2 bits = 10	Prefix is 16 bits
Class C	First 3 bits = 110	Prefix is 24 bits

In early IP implementations, IP hosts and routers understood only three prefix lengths: 8, 16, and 24. This became a limitation as networks grew, so subnetting was introduced. With *subnets*, a host (or router) can be configured to understand that the local prefix length is extended. This configuration is accomplished with a subnet mask. For example, routers and hosts can be configured to understand that network 10.0.0.0 is subnetted into 254 subnets by using a subnet mask of 255.255.0.0.

CIDR notation indicates the prefix length with a length field, following a slash. For example, in the address 10.1.0.1/16, the 16 indicates that the prefix is 16 bits long, which means the same as the subnet mask 255.255.0.0.

Traditional IP hosts and routers had a limited capability to understand prefix lengths and subnets. They understood the length for local configurations but not for remote configurations. Classful routing did not transmit any information about the prefix length. The prefix length was calculated from the information about the address class provided in the first few bits of an address, as mentioned earlier.

Classless routing protocols, on the other hand, transmit a prefix length with an IP address. This allows classless routing protocols to group networks into one entry and use the prefix length to specify which networks are grouped. Classless routing protocols also accept any arbitrary prefix length, rather than only accepting lengths of 8, 16, or 24, which the classful system dictated.

Classless routing protocols include Routing Information Protocol (RIP) version 2, Enhanced Interior Gateway Routing Protocol (EIGRP), Open Shortest Path First (OSPF), Border Gateway Routing Protocol (BGP), and Intermediate System-to-Intermediate System (IS-IS).

Classful routing protocols include RIP version 1 and the Interior Gateway Routing Protocol (IGRP). Classful routing protocols are almost obsolete. RIP version 2 has replaced RIP version 1 and EIGRP has replaced IGRP.

Route Summarization (Aggregation)

When advertising routes into another major network, classful routing protocols automatically summarize subnets. They only advertise a route to a Class A, B, or C network, instead of routes to subnets. Because classful routers and hosts do not understand nonlocal prefix lengths and subnets, there is no reason to advertise information about prefix lengths. The automatic summarization into a major class network has some disadvantages; for example, discontiguous subnets are not supported. Chapter 3, "Characterizing the Existing Internetwork," mentioned discontiguous subnets, and they are covered in more detail later in this chapter in the section "Discontiguous Subnets."

Classless routing protocols advertise a route and a prefix length. If addresses are assigned in a hierarchical fashion, a classless routing protocol can be configured to aggregate subnets into one route, thus reducing routing overhead. The importance of route summarization on the Internet was already discussed. Summarizing (aggregating) routes on an enterprise network is also important because route summarization reduces the size of routing tables, which minimizes bandwidth consumption and processing on routers. Route summarization also means that problems within one area of the network do not tend to spread to other areas.

Route Summarization Example

This section covers a route summarization example that is based on the network shown in Figure 6-2. Looking at Figure 6-2, you can see that a network administrator assigned network numbers 172.16.0.0 through 172.19.0.0 to networks in a branch office.

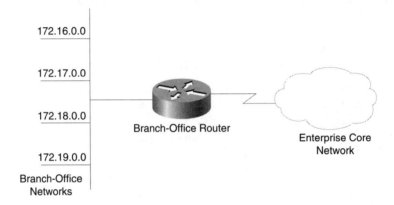

172.16.0.0

172.17.0.0

172.18.0.0

Branch-Office Router

172.19.0.0

Branch-Office
Networks

Enterprise Core
Network

Figure 6-2   *Route Summarization Example*

The branch-office router in Figure 6-2 can summarize its local network numbers and report that it can reach 172.16.0.0/14. By advertising this single route, the router is saying, "Route packets to me if the destination has the first 14 bits set to 172.16." The router is reporting a route to all networks where the first 14 bits are equal to 10101100 000100 in binary.

To understand the summarization in this example, you should convert the number 172 to binary, which results in the binary number 10101100. You should also convert the numbers 16 through 19 to binary, as shown in the following chart:

Second Octet in Decimal	Second Octet in Binary
16	00010000
17	00010001
18	00010010
19	00010011

Notice that the leftmost 6 bits for the numbers 16 through 19 are identical. This is what makes route summarization with a prefix length of 14 possible in this example. The first

8 bits for the networks are identical (all the networks have 172 for the first octet), and the next 6 bits are also identical.

Route Summarization Tips

For route summarization to work correctly, the following requirements must be met:

■ Multiple IP addresses must share the same leftmost bits.

■ Routers must base their routing decisions on a 32-bit IP address and prefix length that can be up to 32 bits. (A *host-specific route* has a 32-bit prefix.)

■ Routing protocols must carry the prefix length with 32-bit addresses.

By spending some time analyzing network numbers (and converting the addresses to binary), you can see the simplicity and elegance of classless addressing and route summarization. When you look at a block of subnets, you can determine if the addresses can be summarized by using the following rules:

■ The number of subnets to be summarized must be a power of 2 (for example, 2, 4, 8, 16, 32, and so on).

■ The relevant octet in the first address in the block to be summarized must be a multiple of the number of subnets.

Consider an example. The following network numbers are defined at a branch office. Can they be summarized?

■ 192.168.32.0

■ 192.168.33.0

■ 192.168.34.0

■ 192.168.35.0

■ 192.168.36.0

The number of subnets is 5, which is not a power of 2, so the first condition is not met. The relevant octet (third in this case) is 32, which is a not a multiple of the number of subnets. So, the second condition is not met. However, the first four subnets can be summarized. A router can summarize the first four networks as 192.168.32.0/22. The leftmost 22 bits for the first four networks are identical. The router can advertise the 192.168.36.0 network in a separate route from the 192.168.32.0/22 summary route.

Discontiguous Subnets

As mentioned earlier, classful routing protocols automatically summarize subnets. One side effect of this is that discontiguous subnets are not supported. Subnets must be next to each other (contiguous). Figure 6-3 shows an enterprise network with discontiguous subnets.

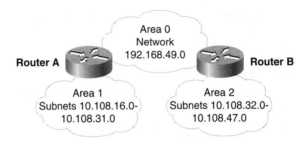

Figure 6-3   *Network with Discontiguous Subnets*

With a classful routing protocol such as RIP version 1 or IGRP, Router A in Figure 6-3 advertises that it can get to network 10.0.0.0. Router B ignores this advertisement because it can already get to network 10.0.0.0. It is directly attached to network 10.0.0.0. The opposite is also true: Router B advertises that it can get to network 10.0.0.0, but Router A ignores this information. This means that the routers cannot reach remote subnets of network 10.0.0.0.

To solve this problem, a classless routing protocol can be used. With a classless routing protocol, Router A advertises that it can get to networks 10.108.16.0/20. Router B advertises that it can get to networks 10.108.32.0/20. (To understand why the prefix length is 20, convert the network numbers to binary.) Because classless routing protocols understand prefixes of any length (not just 8, 16, or 24), the routers in Figure 6-3 can route to discontiguous subnets, assuming they are running a classless routing protocol, such as OSPF or EIGRP.

Note   To configure the devices in the previous example with an old-style subnet mask rather than a prefix length, use a mask of 255.255.240.0. The first 4 bits of the third octet are set to 1s. A trick for determining the value of the relevant octet in a subnet mask is to subtract the number of summarized subnets from 256. In this example, there are 16 summarized subnets, so the relevant octet is 256 minus 16, or 240.

Mobile Hosts

Classless routing and discontiguous subnets support mobile hosts. A *mobile host*, in this context, is a host that moves from one network to another and has a statically defined IP address. A network administrator can move a mobile host and configure a router with a host-specific route to specify that traffic for the host should be routed through that router.

In Figure 6-4, for example, host 10.108.16.1 has moved to a different network. Even though Router A advertises that network 10.108.16.0/20 is behind it, Router B can advertise that 10.108.16.1/32 is behind it.

When making a routing decision, classless routing protocols match the longest prefix. The routers in the example have in their tables both 10.108.16.0/20 and 10.108.16.1/32.

When switching a packet, the routers use the longest prefix available that is appropriate for the destination address in the packet.

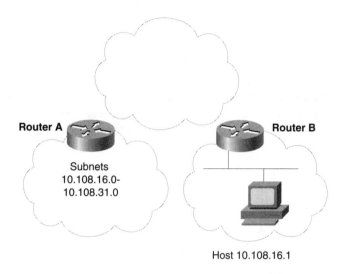

Figure 6-4   *Mobile Host*

In Figure 6-4, a better design would be to use DHCP so that hosts can be moved without requiring any reconfiguration on the hosts or routers. The example is simply used to explain the longest-prefix-match concept. It is not meant to be a design recommendation.

Variable-Length Subnet Masking

Using a classless routing protocol means that you can have different sizes of subnets within a single network. Varying the size of subnets is also known as *variable-length subnet masking (VLSM)*. VLSM relies on providing prefix length information explicitly with each use of an address. The length of the prefix is evaluated independently at each place it is used. The capability to have a different prefix length at different points supports efficiency and flexibility in the use of the IP address space. Instead of each subnet being the same size, you can have both big and small subnets.

One use for small subnets is point-to-point WAN links that only have two devices (one router on each end of the link). Such a link can use a subnet mask of 255.255.255.252, because only two devices need addresses. The two devices can be numbered 01 and 10.

Note   A disadvantage of using a separate subnet for each WAN link is that each subnet adds an entry to the routing table. With some vendors' routers, you do not need to number the serial ports on a point-to-point WAN link, which obviates the need for small WAN point-to-point subnets. One drawback with unnumbered ports, however, is that you cannot ping them, which makes troubleshooting more difficult. But if SNMP or other network management tools can identify port problems, the capability to ping a WAN port is not essential. Unnumbered WAN ports are a better solution than small WAN point-to-point subnets in this case.

Hierarchy in IP Version 6 Addresses

IPv6 increases the IP address size from 32 bits to 128 bits. The long address means that multiple levels of hierarchy can be built in to the address. Despite popular myths, the developers of IPv6 considered support for multiple levels of hierarchy a more important reason for a huge address space than the ability to address every device on the planet and possibly other planets.

An IPv6 address is written in hexadecimal rather than the dotted decimal format used by IPv4. The hexadecimal values of the eight 16-bit pieces of the address are represented as a series of fields separated by colons, in x:x:x:x:x:x:x:x format. For example, here are two IPv6 addresses:

FEDC:BA98:7654:3210:FEDC:BA98:7654:3210

1080:0:0:0:8:800:200C:417A

Note that it is not necessary to write the leading 0s in an individual field, but there must be at least one numeral in every field (except when suppressing multiple fields of 0s). Because IPv6 addresses tend to contain long strings of 0s, you can substitute double colons (::) at the start, middle, or end of an address to indicate consecutive 16-bit fields of 0s.

To avoid confusion, only one set of double colons may be used. For example, the IPv6 address 2031:0000:130F:0000:0000:09C0:876A:130B can be written as 2031:0:130F::9C0:876A:130B. However, it cannot be written as 2031::130F::9C0:876A:130B.

As is the case with IPv4, in IPv6 a source can address datagrams to either one or many destinations. IPv6 supports unicast (one to one) and multicast (one to many). IPv6 has no concept of broadcast addresses; multicast addresses are used instead. IPv6 also supports anycast (one to nearest), which is used for sending a packet to any one of a group of interfaces. An IPv6 anycast address is an address that is assigned to more than one interface (typically belonging to different nodes), with the property that a packet sent to an anycast address is routed to the "nearest" interface having that address, according to the routing protocol's measure of distance.

There are three types of unicast addresses in IPv6:

- Link-local addresses

- Global unicast addresses

- IPv6 addresses with embedded IPv4 addresses

In the past, site-local addresses were also supported but they were deprecated by RFC 3879. The sections that follow describe the three types of IPv6 unicast addresses in more detail.

Link-Local Addresses

A link-local address is useful only in the context of a single link or network. An IPv6 link-local unicast address can be automatically configured on an interface by using the link-local prefix (FE80::/10) and an interface identifier. The interface ID is 64 bits long and is often derived from the hardware address in ROM on an interface. For example, it can be based on an IEEE 802 48-bit MAC address.

A link-local address serves as a method for connecting devices on the same local network without the need for globally unique addresses. An IPv6 router must not forward packets that have either a link-local source or destination address. Link-local addresses are used in neighbor discovery and in the stateless autoconfiguration process, which was explained earlier in the chapter in the "IP Version 6 Dynamic Addressing" section.

The following Wireshark output shows a computer with a link-local unicast address sending a packet to a link-local multicast address. The computer is trying to find its router.

```
Ethernet II
    Destination: 33:33:00:00:00:02
    Source: 00:22:41:36:97:17
    Type: IPv6 (0x86dd)
Internet Protocol Version 6
    Version: 6
    Traffic class: 0x00000000
    Flowlabel: 0x00000000
    Payload length: 16
    Next header: ICMPv6 (0x3a)
    Hop limit: 255
    Source: fe80::222:41ff:fe36:9717
    Destination: ff02::2
Internet Control Message Protocol v6
    Type: 133 (Router solicitation)
    Code: 0
    Checksum: 0xca4e [correct]
    ICMPv6 Option (Source link-layer address)
        Type: Source link-layer address (1)
        Length: 8
        Link-layer address: 00:22:41:36:97:17
```

Notice that the 64-bit interface ID in the source IPv6 address is based on the computer's 48-bit MAC address. You can see the MAC address in the Ethernet II header and in the ICMPv6 option field at the end of the packet. The 0222:41ff:fe36:9717 IPv6 interface ID is the MAC address with FF:FE in the middle. Also, the value of bit 6 has been changed to a binary 1. In the MAC address, bits 0–7, counting from the left, were 00 in hexadecimal. In the IPv6 address, bit 6 is a binary 1, so bits 0–7 are 02 in hexadecimal. Bit 6 is the universal/local bit and is usually set to 1 in IPv6 to indicate a universal address rather than an address that has only local significance to an enterprise.

Global Unicast Addresses

Global unicast addresses are equivalent to public registered addresses in IPv4. These addresses are designed to support the type of provider-based aggregation currently used on the Internet. The structure of global unicast addresses enables aggregation of routing prefixes so that the number of routing-table entries in the global Internet routing table and in provider and enterprise routing tables can be minimized. Global unicast addresses are aggregated upward through organizations, then to intermediate-level ISPs, and eventually to top-level ISPs.

The general format for IPv6 global unicast addresses is as follows:

> Global routing prefix: n bits
>
> Subnet ID: m bits
>
> Interface ID: 128-n-m bits

The global routing prefix is typically a hierarchically structured value assigned to a site. It is a cluster of subnets or links. It is designed to be structured hierarchically by RIRs and ISPs. The subnet ID is an identifier of a subnet within the site and is designed to be structured hierarchically by site administrators.

RFC 3513 requires that all unicast addresses, except those that start with binary value 000, have interface IDs that are 64 bits long and are constructed in modified EUI-64 format. So, according to this RFC, the global routing prefix is n bits; the subnet ID is 64-n bits; and the Interface ID is 64 bits.

An example of a global unicast address is 2001:4860:800d::63, which belongs to Google. Note from the following DiG output that Google has many IPv6 global unicast addresses:

```
; <<>> DiG 9.4.3-P3<<>> AAAA ipv6.google.com
;; global options:  printcmd
;; Got answer:
;; ->>HEADER<<- opcode: QUERY, status: NOERROR, id: 30964
;; flags: qr rd ra; QUERY: 1, ANSWER: 7, AUTHORITY: 4, ADDITIONAL: 4

;; QUESTION SECTION:
;ipv6.google.com.          IN      AAAA

;; ANSWER SECTION:
ipv6.google.com.      10800   IN    CNAME    ipv6.l.google.com.
ipv6.l.google.com.      300   IN    AAAA     2001:4860:800d::63
```

```
ipv6.1.google.com.    300    IN    AAAA    2001:4860:800d::67
ipv6.1.google.com.    300    IN    AAAA    2001:4860:800d::68
ipv6.1.google.com.    300    IN    AAAA    2001:4860:800d::69
ipv6.1.google.com.    300    IN    AAAA    2001:4860:800d::6a
ipv6.1.google.com.    300    IN    AAAA    2001:4860:800d::93
```

IPv6 Addresses with Embedded IPv4 Addresses

Some IPv4-to-IPv6 transition strategies use an IPv4 address. For example, when tunneling IPv6 packets over an IPv4 routing infrastructure, IPv6 nodes can be assigned special IPv6 unicast addresses that carry an IPv4 address in the low-order 32 bits. The IPv6 address consists of 96 zeros, followed by a 32-bit globally unique IPv4 unicast address. This type of address is called an *IPv4-compatible IPv6 address*. An example of such an address is 0:0:0:0:0:0:66.241.68.22, or more succinctly, ::66.241.68.22.

A second type of IPv6 address that holds an embedded IPv4 address is used to represent the address of an IPv4 node as an IPv6 address. This type of address is called an *IPv4-mapped IPv6 address* and consists of 80 zero bits, 16 one bits, and a 32-bit IPv4 unicast address. An example of such an address is 0:0:0:0:0:FF:66.241.68.22, or more succinctly, ::FF:66.241.68.22.

Note   For the specific cases of IPv4 in IPv6 addresses, you write the IPv4 address in the low-order 32 bits in dotted decimal instead of hexadecimal.

Designing a Model for Naming

Names play an essential role in meeting a customer's goals for usability. Short, meaningful names enhance user productivity and simplify network management. A good naming model also strengthens the performance and availability of a network. The goal of this section is to help you design naming models for internetworks that will meet your customer's goals for usability, manageability, performance, and availability.

Names are assigned to many types of resources in a typical internetwork: routers, servers, hosts, printers, and other resources. This section covers the naming of devices and networks. Providing names for users, groups, accounts, and passwords is not covered, although some of the guidelines for naming devices apply to these items also.

A good naming model should let a user transparently access a service by name rather than address. Because networking protocols require an address, the user's system should map the name to an address. The method for mapping a name to an address can be either dynamic, using some sort of naming protocol, or static (for example, a file on the user's system that lists all names and their associated addresses). Usually, a dynamic method is preferable, despite the additional network traffic caused by dynamic naming protocols.

When developing a naming model, consider the following questions:

- What types of entities need names? Servers, routers, printers, hosts, others?

- Do end systems need names? Will the end systems offer any services, such as personal web serving?

- What is the structure of a name? Does a portion of the name identify the type of device?

- How are names stored, managed, and accessed?

- Who assigns names?

- How do hosts map a name to an address? Will a dynamic or static system be provided?

- How does a host learn its own name?

- If dynamic addressing is used, will the names also be dynamic and change when an address changes?

- Should the naming system use a peer-to-peer or client/server model?

- If name servers will be used, how much redundancy (mirroring) will be required?

- Will the name database be distributed among many servers?

- How will the selected naming system affect network traffic?

- How will the selected naming system affect security?

Distributing Authority for Naming

During the early stages of designing a naming model, consider who will actually assign names by asking the following questions:

- Will the name space be completely controlled by a centralized authority, or will the naming of some devices be carried out by decentralized agents?

- Will a corporate IS department name devices at regional and branch offices, or can departmental administrators implement naming at those sites?

- Will users be allowed to name their own systems, or are all names assigned by network administrators?

The disadvantage of distributing authority for naming is that names become harder to control and manage. If all groups and users agree on, and practice, the same policies, however, there are many advantages to distributing authority for naming.

The obvious advantage of distributing authority for naming is that no department is burdened with the job of assigning and maintaining all names. Other advantages include performance and scalability. If each name server manages a portion of the name space instead of the whole name space, the requirements for memory and processing power on the servers are lessened. Also, if clients have access to a local name server instead of depending on a centralized server, many names can be resolved to addresses locally, without causing traffic on the internetwork. Local servers can cache information about remote devices, to further reduce network traffic.

Guidelines for Assigning Names

To maximize usability, names should be short, meaningful, unambiguous, and distinct. A user should easily recognize which names go with which devices. A good practice is to include in a name some sort of indication of the device's type. For example, you can prefix or suffix router names with the characters *rtr*, switches with *sw*, servers with *svr*, and so on. Using meaningful prefixes or suffixes decreases ambiguity for end users and helps managers more easily extract device names from network management tools.

Names can also include a location code. Some network designers use airport codes in their naming models. For example, all names in San Francisco start with SFO, all names in Oakland start with OAK, and so on. The location code could be a number instead, but most people remember letters better than numbers.

Try to avoid names that have unusual characters, such as underscores, ampersands, asterisks, and so on, even if the naming protocol allows these characters (which many do). These characters are hard to type and can cause applications and protocols to behave in unexpected ways. Unusual characters might mean something special to a protocol. For example, the dollar sign when used as the last character in a NetBIOS name means that the name does not appear in network browser lists or in response to NetBIOS network-survey commands. NetBIOS names with a dollar sign at the end are for administrative use only.

It is also best if names are not case-sensitive because people usually cannot remember which case to use. Names that require a user to remember mixed cases (for instance, DBServer) are not a good idea. They are hard to type, and some protocols might not be case-sensitive anyway and might transmit the name as all lowercase or all uppercase, losing the significance of the mixed case.

You should also avoid spaces in names. Spaces confuse users and might not work correctly with some applications or protocols. Names should generally be eight characters or fewer, if possible. This is especially true for operating systems, applications, or protocols that map names to filenames and restrict the size of a filename to eight characters.

If a device has more than one interface and more than one address, you should map all the addresses to one common name. For example, on a multiport router with multiple IP addresses, assign the same name to all the router's IP addresses. This way network management software does not assume that a multiport device is actually more than one device.

Note   Security policy may dictate recommendations for naming. Names that are easily recognized by users are easily recognized by attackers also. For key devices and data sources (for example, routers and servers), it is often a good idea to use long, cryptic names. In some cases, names are used only by system software and not by users, so usability is not affected. In other cases, tradeoffs must be made between usability and security goals.

Assigning Names in a NetBIOS Environment

NetBIOS is an application programming interface (API) that includes functions for naming devices, ensuring the uniqueness of names, and finding named services. NetBIOS was developed by IBM and Sytek in the 1980s for use on PC networks. It gained popularity in the late 1980s as a way of connecting PCs using software from IBM, Microsoft, and 3Com. It is still widely used in Microsoft Windows environments. When NetBIOS is used in a TCP/IP network, which is typical these days, the implementation is often called NetBT.

NetBT makes extensive use of broadcast packets by default. Broadcast packets are used to announce named services, find named services, and elect a *master browser* in a Windows environment. Using broadcasts is not the preferred method for implementing naming functions in a TCP/IP environment, however, because of the performance implications and because routers do not forward broadcast packets by default. A router can be configured to forward NetBT broadcasts, which go to UDP port 137, but this is not an optimal solution because it requires extra configuration and spreads broadcasts, unless the configuration specifies a unicast address.

To avoid clients having to send broadcast frames to look for named services, a network administrator can place an lmhosts file on each station. The *lmhosts file* is an ASCII text file that contains a list of names and their respective IP addresses. The lmhosts file is similar to the hosts file on UNIX TCP/IP devices, although it includes some Windows-specific functionality.

The use of lmhosts files requires a lot of maintenance because the files don't dynamically change as names change. As a network grows, lmhosts files should be removed in favor of using WINS or DNS servers for dynamic resolution of NetBIOS names to IP addresses. When a PC is configured with a WINS server, the PC sends a message directly to the WINS server to resolve a name, instead of using the lmhosts file or sending broadcast packets. The PC also sends a message to the WINS server when it boots to make sure its own name is unique. To avoid configuring each PC with the address of a WINS server, a PC can receive the address of a WINS server in the options field of a DHCP response.

To ensure that a PC can reach a WINS server, you can establish redundant WINS servers. To use redundant servers, you must plan to synchronize the WINS databases on the servers. This is accomplished by establishing *WINS partners that use WINS replication*. If the redundant WINS servers are on opposite sides of a slow WAN link, replication should occur infrequently or after business hours. For international networks, WINS replication is often set to every 12 hours.

In a NetBT environment, hosts have both a NetBIOS and an IP hostname. Typically these names are the same, but they do not have to be. IP hostnames are mapped to addresses using the Domain Name System (DNS). DNS is a standard Internet service and is covered in the next section, which covers naming in a generic IP environment as opposed to a NetBT environment. It is expected that over time, naming in a Windows environment will be accomplished solely with DNS, and WINS will become obsolete. If you are designing a network from scratch, there's no need for NetBT or WINS.

Microsoft also supports dynamic hostnames, which are necessary when DHCP is used for dynamic addressing. With the DNS/WINS integration, a DNS server can query a WINS server to determine if the WINS server has learned a dynamic name. This avoids having to configure names in a DNS server, which is difficult with dynamic names.

Assigning Names in an IP Environment

Naming in an IP environment is accomplished by configuring hosts files, DNS servers, or Network Information Service (NIS) servers. DNS is used on the Internet and has also gained widespread popularity for managing names in enterprise networks. It is the recommended naming system for modern networks.

A hosts file tells a UNIX workstation how to convert a hostname into an IP address. A network administrator maintains a hosts file on each workstation in the internetwork. Both DNS and NIS were developed to allow a network manager to centralize the naming of devices, using a distributed database approach, instead of a flat file that resides on each system.

Sun Microsystems developed NIS to allow a UNIX network administrator to centralize the management of names and other configuration parameters. An administrator can use NIS to maintain names, user and password information, Ethernet addresses, mail aliases, group definitions, and protocol names and numbers. NIS was once quite common but has become less common as the Internet standard for naming (DNS) gained momentum.

The Domain Name System

DNS was developed in the early 1980s when it became clear that managing a hosts file containing the names and addresses of all the systems on the Internet would no longer work. As the Internet hosts file grew, it became difficult to maintain, store, and transmit to other hosts.

DNS is a distributed database that provides a hierarchical naming system. A DNS name has two parts: a hostname and a domain name. For example, in information.priscilla.com, information is the host, and priscilla.com is the domain. Table 6-1 shows some of the most common top-level domains.

Newer top-level domains, such as .biz, .info, .museum, and .name, may help prevent the many disputes that occur over the right to use popular and marketable names. There are also many geographical top-level domains (for example, .uk for the United Kingdom and .de for Germany).

The DNS architecture distributes the knowledge of names so that no single system has to know all names. The Internet Corporation for Assigned Names and Numbers (ICANN) is a nonprofit corporation responsible for overall DNS management and top-level domains. ICANN has accredited a set of competitive registrars that have authority over names under the top level.

Table 6-1   *Top-Level Domains*

Domain	Description
.edu	Educational institutions
.gov	Government agencies
.net	Network providers
.com	Commercial companies
.org	Nonprofit organizations

Each layer of the hierarchy can also delegate authority. For example, a registrar might delegate authority to a corporate IS department for a name such as cisco.com. The IS department can delegate authority to the engineering department for names in the engineering.cisco.com subdomain. Within the engineering department, there might be multiple hosts with names such as development.engineering.cisco.com and testing.engineering.cisco.com. Delegation allows DNS to be autonomously managed at each layer, which increases scalability and helps keep names meaningful.

DNS uses a client/server model. When a client needs to send a packet to a named station, *resolver software* on the client sends a name query to a local DNS server. If the local server cannot resolve the name, it queries other servers on behalf of the resolver. When the local name server receives a response, it replies to the resolver and caches information for future requests. The length of time that a server should cache information received from other servers is entered into the DNS database by a network administrator. Long time intervals decrease network traffic but can also make it difficult to change a name. The old name might be cached on thousands of servers in the Internet.

The management of DNS names and servers is a complex task. For more information on managing DNS names in a UNIX environment, see the classic book by Paul Albitz and Cricket Liu, *DNS and BIND*, now in its fifth edition at press time.

Dynamic DNS Names

With many DHCP implementations, when a host requests an IP address from a DHCP server, the host also receives a dynamic hostname, something like pc23.dynamic.priscilla.com. A dynamic name is not appropriate for some applications. For example, web servers, FTP servers, and some Internet telephony applications rely on static hostnames. To reach a web server, a user types in a Uniform Resource Locator (URL) that is based on the server's domain name. If the name changes dynamically, it becomes impossible to reach the server. With some Internet telephony applications, a user needs to tell people the hostname to use when placing a call to the user's system. Another example is home users who want to access a computer on their home network while traveling. The home computer might get a different IP address every time it makes a connection to its ISP. This means that there is no stable address to connect to.

For these types of applications, it is important to have a DNS implementation that can associate a static name with a dynamic address. Dynamic DNS is a service that provides the capability for a networked device, such as a home computer or router, to notify a DNS server to change, in real time, the active DNS configuration of its configured hostnames, addresses, or other information stored in the server.

Service providers and vendors offer a variety of dynamic DNS solutions. Providers supply client software (or firmware) that automates the discovery and registration of a client's public IP address. The client program runs on a computer or router and connects to the service provider's DNS server and causes the server to link the discovered IP address with a hostname. Depending on the provider, the hostname is registered within a domain owned by the provider or the customer's own domain name. These services use a variety of methods and protocols. Often they use an HTTP request because restrictive environments sometimes allow only the HTTP protocol in outbound traffic from a client.

In Microsoft Windows networks, dynamic DNS is an integral part of Active Directory. Domain controllers register their network service types in DNS so that other computers in the domain (or forest) can access them. Microsoft uses Kerberos authentication to secure this transaction. Other dynamic DNS services use the Generic Security Service Algorithm for Secret Key Transaction Authentication for DNS (GSS-TSIG), defined in RFC 3645. GSS-TSIG uses shared secret keys and one-way hashing to provide a cryptographically secure method of identifying each endpoint of a connection as being allowed to make or respond to a DNS update.

IPv6 Name Resolution

Name resolution with IPv6 can be handled statically with manual entries in a client host's local configuration files, or dynamically. Dynamic name resolution is accomplished with a DNS server that has built-in support for IPv6, usually along with IPv4. An IPv6-aware application maps a name to an IPv6 address with a request for an A6 record (an Address record for the IPv6 host). The network administrator must set up the appropriate DNS servers with IPv6 support and connect the named hosts to the IPv6 network with valid IPv6 addresses. On the client side, the administrator must either manually enter the address of a DNS server that can handle IPv6 addresses or use DHCPv6 to inform the client of the DNS server's address.

Summary

This chapter provided guidelines for assigning addresses and names in an internetwork. The chapter illustrated the importance of using a structured model for addressing and naming to make it easier to understand network maps, operate network management software, recognize devices in protocol analyzer traces, and meet a customer's goals for usability.

Structured addresses and names facilitate network optimization and security because they make it easier to code network filters on firewalls, routers, and switches. Structured addresses also help you implement route summarization, which decreases bandwidth utilization, processing on routers, and network instability.

This chapter also discussed distributing authority for addressing and naming to avoid one department having to manage all addresses and names. Another way to simplify addressing and naming tasks is to use dynamic addressing and naming. Dynamic addressing—for example, DHCP for IP environments—allows each end system to learn its address automatically. DHCP is recommended for the addressing of end systems in a campus network design.

Addressing and naming are essential elements of the logical design phase of the top-down network design process. If designed correctly, addressing and naming models can strengthen your ability to satisfy a customer's needs. They can also help you decide which routing and switching protocols to select, which is covered in the next chapter.

Review Questions

1. The following network numbers are defined at a branch office. Can they be summarized, and if so, what is the network number and prefix length?

   10.108.48.0

   10.108.49.0

   10.108.50.0

   10.108.51.0

   10.108.52.0

   10.108.53.0

   10.108.54.0

   10.108.55.0

2. Start the Wireshark application and capture packets from your computer. Using a web browser, navigate to http://www.yahoo.com. Find the DNS query that your computer sends to get an IP address for www.yahoo.com. Also, find the reply. Describe in detail the DNS data in both the query and the reply. Note, if you can't find the query and reply, you may need to clear your DNS cache. On a Windows computer, you can do this with the **ipconfig /flushdns** command. On a Mac, use the **dscacheutil -flushcache** command.

3. What is a discontiguous subnet? Why do some enterprise networks have discontiguous subnets? Why don't classful routing protocols support discontiguous subnets?

4. Discuss the configuration of IP addresses. When manually configuring IP addressing on a host, what parameters should you configure? If you suspect that there might be a problem with the addressing information that you entered, what commands can you use to troubleshoot? What are some disadvantages of manual configuration? What other options are there?

Design Scenario

In Chapter 1, "Analyzing Business Goals and Constraints," you learned about ElectroMyCycle, a manufacturer of a new electric motorcycle. ElectroMyCycle has chosen you to design a new network that will let the company scale to a larger size. In Chapter 5, you learned that ElectroMyCycle's network will support about 200 employees. The network will include a data center and a new state-of-the-art manufacturing facility. Users in the campus network will access the servers in the data center from their PCs. For online sales, ElectroMyCycle plans to have a DMZ that connects a web server, a DNS server, and an email server. ElectroMyCycle also plans to open a branch sales office in a city that is about 500 miles from ElectroMyCycle's headquarters.

Design and document an IP addressing scheme to meet ElectroMyCycle's needs. Specify which IP address blocks will be assigned to different modules of your network design. Document whether you will use public or private addressing for each module. Document whether you will use manual or dynamic addressing for each module. Specify where (if anywhere) route summarization will occur.

Chapter 7

Selecting Switching and Routing Protocols

The goal of this chapter is to help you select the right switching and routing protocols for your network design customer. The selections you make will depend on your customer's business and technical goals. To help you select the right protocols for your customer, this chapter covers the following attributes of switching and routing protocols:

- Network traffic characteristics

- Bandwidth, memory, and CPU usage

- The approximate number of peer routers or switches supported

- The capability to quickly adapt to changes in an internetwork

- The capability to authenticate route updates for security reasons

At this point in the network design process, you have created a network design topology and have developed some idea of where switches and routers will reside, but you haven't selected any actual switch or router products. An understanding of the switching and routing protocols that a switch or router must support will help you select the best product for the job.

This chapter begins with a generic discussion about decision making to help you develop a systematic process for selecting solutions for both the logical and physical components of a network design. Making sound decisions about protocols and technologies is a crucial network design skill that this chapter can help you develop.

A discussion of switching protocols follows the section on decision making. The switching section covers transparent bridging, multilayer switching, spanning-tree algorithm enhancements, and switching protocols for transporting virtual LAN (VLAN) information.

A section on routing protocols follows the bridging section. The routing section provides techniques for comparing and contrasting routing protocols. The chapter concludes with a table that summarizes the comparison of routing protocols.

Making Decisions as Part of the Top-Down Network Design Process

The next few chapters provide guidelines for selecting network design solutions for a customer. The decisions you make about protocols and technologies should be based on the information you have gathered on your customer's business and technical goals.

Researchers studying decision models say that one of the most important aspects of making a sound decision is having a good list of goals. In her book *The Can-Do Manager*, published by the American Management Association, Tess Kirby says that there are four factors involved in making sound decisions:

- Goals must be established.

- Many options should be explored.

- The consequences of the decision should be investigated.

- Contingency plans should be made.

To match options with goals, you can make a *decision table*, such as the one in Table 7-1. Table 7-1 shows a decision table that matches routing protocols to a fictional customer's business and technical goals. You can develop a similar table for switching protocols, campus-design technologies, enterprise-design technologies, WAN protocols, and so on. To develop the table, place options in the leftmost column and your customer's major goals at the top. Place the goals in priority order, starting with critical goals.

You can fill in Table 7-1 first by simply putting an X in each option that meets a critical goal. Any options that do not meet critical goals can immediately be eliminated. Other options can be evaluated on how well they meet other goals, on a scale from 1 to 10.

After a decision has been made, you should troubleshoot the decision. Ask yourself the following:

- If this option is chosen, what could go wrong?

- Has this option been tried before (possibly with other customers)? If so, what problems occurred?

- How will the customer react to this decision?

- What are the contingency plans if the customer does not approve of the decision?

This decision-making process can be used during both the logical and physical network design phases. You can use this process to help you select protocols, technologies, and devices that will meet a customer's requirements.

Table 7-1 *Example Decision Table*

	Critical Goals			Other Goals		
	Adaptability—must adapt to changes in a large internetwork within seconds	Must scale to a large size (hundreds of routers)	Must be an industry standard and compatible with existing equipment	Should not create a lot of traffic	Should run on inexpensive routers	Should be easy to configure and manage
BGP	X*	X	X	8	7	7
OSPF	X	X	X	8	8	8
IS-IS	X	X	X	8	6	6
IGRP	X	X				
EIGRP	X	X				
RIP			X			

*X = Meets critical criteria. 1 = Lowest. 10 = Highest.

Selecting Switching Protocols

Switches became popular in the mid-1990s as an inexpensive way of partitioning LANs without incurring the latency associated with bridges. Switches take advantage of fast integrated circuits to offer low latency. Bridges were much slower than switches and had fewer ports and a higher cost per port. For these reasons, switches have replaced bridges these days. The fundamental concepts, however, have not changed that much, and many discussions about switching concepts, including discussions in this chapter, use the term *bridge*.

Switches have the capability to do store-and-forward processing or cut-through processing. With *cut-through processing*, a switch quickly looks at the destination address (the first field in the Ethernet frame header), determines the outgoing port, and immediately starts sending bits to the outgoing port.

A disadvantage with cut-through processing is that it forwards illegal frames (for example, Ethernet runts) and frames with CRC errors. On a network that is prone to runts and errors, cut-through processing should not be used. Some switches have the capability to automatically move from cut-through mode to store-and-forward mode when an error threshold is reached. This feature is called *adaptive cut-through switching* by some vendors.

A switch also supports parallel forwarding, whereas bridges usually do not. When a typical bridge is forwarding a frame from one port to another, no other frame can be forwarded. There is only one forwarding path. A switch, on the other hand, allows multiple, parallel forwarding paths, which means a switch can handle a high volume of traffic more quickly than a bridge. High-end switches can support numerous simultaneous forwarding paths, depending on the structure of the switching fabric. (Manufacturers use the term *switching fabric* to describe the architecture of their switches.)

Switching and the OSI Layers

In this book, a *switch* refers to a device that operates at Layers 1 and 2 of the OSI reference model, unless otherwise specified. The term *switch* does have a more generic meaning, though. The verb *to switch* simply means to move something to a different position. An internetworking device moves data that comes in one interface to a different interface.

An Ethernet hub or repeater switches bits that come in one interface to all other interfaces. A hub works at Layer 1 of the OSI model and does not understand anything beyond bits. An Ethernet switch is a high-speed, multiport bridge that switches frames based on the Layer 2 destination address. After a switch has learned the correct interface to use for a particular unicast destination, it switches frames for that destination exclusively to that interface, unlike a hub, which switches bits to all interfaces. A router switches packets based on the Layer 3 destination address. For unicast packets, the router switches exclusively to one interface.

The noun *switch* is a good engineering term that should not be clouded by marketing hype. In electronics, a switch is a device that permits or interrupts the flow of current through an electrical circuit. In the transportation industry, a switch is a device made of two movable rails designed to turn a locomotive from one track to another. In the networking field, a switch permits or interrupts the flow of data and, although it doesn't turn a locomotive, it does turn bits, frames, and packets.

Modern routers can switch packets extremely quickly. Some manufacturers add the word *switch* to their router product names to emphasize that the routers are as fast (or almost as fast) as Layer 2 switches. Modern routers use high-speed internal data paths, parallel processors, and advanced caching methods, all essential to the high-speed switching of data. Manufacturers call their products Layer 3 switches, routing switches, switching routers, multilayer switches, and many other creative names. In general, a Layer 3 switch, routing switch, or switching router is a device that can handle both Layer 2 and Layer 3 switching of data. A Layer 3 switch is a high-speed router that can include interfaces that make a forwarding decision based solely on Layer 2 information.

Transparent Bridging

Ethernet switches and bridges use a classic technology called *transparent bridging*. A *transparent bridge* connects one or more LAN segments so that end systems on different segments can communicate with each other transparently. An end system sends a frame to a destination without knowing whether the destination is local or on the other side of a transparent bridge. Transparent bridges are so named because their presence is transparent to end systems.

To learn how to forward frames, a transparent bridge listens to all frames and determines which stations reside on which segments. The bridge learns the location of devices by looking at the source address in each frame. The bridge develops a *switching table* such as the one shown in Table 7-2. The switching table also sometimes goes by the names *bridging table*, *MAC address table*, or *Content Addressable Memory (CAM) table*.

Table 7-2   *Switching Table on a Bridge or Switch*

MAC Address	Port
08-00-07-06-41-B9	1
00-00-0C-60-7C-01	2
00-80-24-07-8C-02	3

When a frame arrives at a bridge, the bridge looks at the destination address in the frame and compares it to entries in the switching table. If the bridge has learned where the destination station resides (by looking at source addresses in previous frames), it can forward the frame to the correct port. A transparent bridge sends (floods) frames with an unknown destination address and all multicast/broadcast frames out every port (except the port on which the frame was received).

Bridges operate at Layers 1 and 2 of the OSI reference model. They determine how to forward a frame based on information in the Layer 2 header of the frame. Unlike a router, a bridge does not look at Layer 3 information or any upper layers. A bridge segments bandwidth domains so that devices on opposite sides of a bridge do not compete with each other for media access control. A bridge does not forward Ethernet collisions or MAC frames in a Token Ring network.

Although a bridge segments bandwidth domains, it does not segment broadcast domains (unless programmed by filters to do so). A bridge sends broadcast frames out every port. This is a scalability issue that was already discussed in Part I of this book. To avoid excessive broadcast traffic, bridged and switched networks should be segmented with routers or divided into VLANs.

A bridge is a store-and-forward device. *Store and forward* means that the bridge receives a complete frame, determines which outgoing port to use, prepares the frame for the outgoing port, calculates a cyclic redundancy check (CRC), and transmits the frame when the medium is free on the outgoing port.

Selecting Spanning Tree Protocol Enhancements

As discussed in Chapter 5, "Designing a Network Topology," transparent bridges and switches implement the Spanning Tree Protocol (STP) to avoid loops in a topology. An important design consideration is which enhancements to STP you should select to ensure high availability in your campus network designs. Chapter 5 discussed two important enhancements:

- IEEE 802.1w, which provides rapid reconvergence of the spanning tree and is now built into the IEEE 802.1D standard

- IEEE 802.1s, which aggregates a set of VLAN-based spanning trees into distinct instances and runs only one (rapid) spanning-tree algorithm per instance

As described in the next few sections, there are many other enhancements to STP that can increase the availability and resiliency of a campus network design that relies on STP.

PortFast

The 2004 version of 802.1D supports the concept of a *switch edge port*. An edge port corresponds to the Cisco PortFast feature (and is configured with the Cisco **spanning-tree portfast** command). A network engineer can configure a port as an edge port if it is attached to a LAN that has no other switches attached. The Rapid Spanning Tree Protocol (RSTP) can also automatically detect edge ports. Edge ports transition directly to the forwarding state, which is a major benefit for access layer ports that connect end-user systems and IP phones.

Without PortFast, a switch port lingers in the discarding and learning states before starting to forward frames, which can cause important frames to get dropped. With IP networks, the most serious problem with switch port startup delay is that a client might timeout while waiting to receive an IP address from a DHCP server. With some implementations, if this happens, the client uses an address from the Automatic Private IP Addresses range (169.254.0.1 through 169.254.255.254) rather than an address assigned by a DHCP server. This address does not allow communication across a router, which means users cannot reach the Internet and possibly corporate servers as well.

PortFast is meant to be used only on ports that do not connect another switch; however, sometimes this is unpredictable, especially as users and junior network administrators become more networking savvy and decide to install their own equipment. To protect a network that uses PortFast, Cisco supports a feature called *BPDU Guard* that shuts down a PortFast-enabled port if a bridge protocol data unit (BPDU) from another switch is received. The 2004 version of RSTP also supports a similar feature and monitors an edge port for BPDUs in case a switch is connected. As soon as the switch detects a BPDU arriving at an edge port, the port becomes a non-edge port.

UplinkFast and BackboneFast

UplinkFast is a Cisco feature that can be configured on access layer switches. UplinkFast improves the convergence time of STP if a failure of a redundant uplink from an access layer switch occurs. An uplink is a connection from an access layer switch to a higher-end switch in the distribution layer of a hierarchical network design. Figure 7-1 illustrates a typical redundant, hierarchical network design. Users are connected to Switch A in the access layer. The access layer switch is attached to two distribution layer switches. One of the uplinks is blocked by STP. (STP has also blocked one of the links between the distribution and core layers.)

If the uplink to Switch B in Figure 7-1 fails, STP eventually unblocks the uplink to Switch C, hence restoring connectivity. With the default STP parameters, the recovery takes between 30 and 50 seconds. With UplinkFast, the recovery takes about 1 second. The UplinkFast feature is based on the definition of an uplink group. On a given switch, the uplink group consists of the root port and all the ports that provide an alternate connection to the root bridge. If the root port fails or the primary uplink fails, a port from the uplink group is selected to immediately replace the root port. UplinkFast should be configured only on access layer switches at the edge of your network and not on distribution or core layer switches.

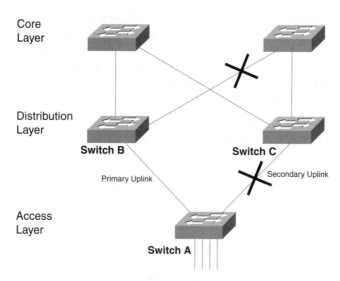

Figure 7-1 *Access Layer Switch with Two Uplinks to Distribution Layer Switches*

Note RSTP includes a form of immediate transition to the forwarding state that is similar to the Cisco proprietary UplinkFast extension to STP. When a bridge loses its root port, it can immediately transition an alternate port into the forwarding state.

Cisco also supports a feature called BackboneFast, which can save a switch up to 20 seconds (Maximum Age) when recovering from an indirect link failure that occurs on a nonlocal port. When enabled on all switches in a switched network, BackboneFast speeds converge after a failure by taking advantage of the fact that a switch involved in a nonlocal failure might be able to move into the listening state immediately. In some topologies, it is not necessary for a switch to wait for the Maximum Age timer to lapse. The switch first checks with other switches to determine if its status is valid. The checking is accomplished with two Cisco-proprietary protocol data units (PDU): Root Link Query (RLQ) and RLQ Response.

Unidirectional Link Detection

Sometimes hardware fails in such a way that connectivity between two switches works in only one direction. This is called a *unidirectional link*. Switch A can hear Switch B, but Switch B can't hear Switch A. This situation can be caused by Switch B's receiver being dead or weak, Switch A's transmitter being dead or weak, or some other component, such as a repeater or cable, being unable to transmit or receive. For example, a cable might be working at the physical layer (so the link is up) but be constructed incorrectly so that a switch port can transmit but not receive, even though its partner is unaware of the problem and can transmit and receive.

A unidirectional link can cause a loop in a switched network. If a switch port can't receive data, it can't hear BPDUs, and it might go into the forwarding state when its partner is already forwarding. If a switch port can't send data, it can't send BPDUs, and its partner might be unaware of its existence. IEEE doesn't say how to handle this situation, but vendors recognized the potential for a problem and offered fixes. Cisco provides the UniDirectional Link Detection (UDLD) protocol on high-end switches.

UDLD allows devices connected through fiber-optic or copper Ethernet cables to monitor the physical configuration of the cables and detect when a unidirectional link exists. When a unidirectional link is detected, UDLD shuts down the affected port and alerts the user. A switch port that is configured to use UDLD transmits UDLD messages periodically to neighbor devices. Devices on both ends of a link must support UDLD for the protocol to successfully identify and disable unidirectional links.

LoopGuard

Cisco also supports a feature called *LoopGuard* that is intended to provide additional protection against loops caused by a blocking port erroneously moving to the forwarding state. This usually happens because one of the ports of a physically redundant topology (not necessarily the blocking port) stops receiving BPDUs, perhaps because of a unidirectional link problem.

If LoopGuard is enabled and BPDUs are not received on a nondesignated port, the port moves into the *loop-inconsistent state* instead of moving to the listening, learning, and forwarding states. Without STP LoopGuard, the port would assume the designated port role and move to the forwarding state, and thus create a loop. When a BPDU is received on a port in a loop-inconsistent state, the port transitions into another STP state. This means that recovery is automatic, and no intervention is necessary.

You can choose either UDLD or STP LoopGuard, or both, which is recommended. UDLD works better than LoopGuard on EtherChannel (which is a grouping of Ethernet interfaces into one logical channel). UDLD disables only the failed interface. The channel remains functional with the remaining interfaces. STP LoopGuard blocks the entire channel in such a failure (by putting it into the loop-inconsistent state).

LoopGuard does not work where the link has been unidirectional since it was first brought up. The port may never receive BPDUs but not recognize that there is a problem and become a designated port. UDLD provides protection against such a problem. On the other hand, UDLD does not protect against STP failures caused by software problems that result in a designated port not sending BPDUs. Software problems are less likely than hardware problems, but they could happen. Enabling both UDLD and LoopGuard provides the highest level of protection.

Protocols for Transporting VLAN Information

Before moving to a discussion of Layer 3 routing protocols, it is important to cover some additional Layer 2 protocols that can be deployed in switched networks that use VLANs.

When VLANs are implemented in a switched network, the switches need a method to make sure intra-VLAN traffic goes to the correct interfaces. To benefit from the advantages of VLANs, the switches need to ensure that traffic destined for a particular VLAN goes to that VLAN and not to any other VLAN. This can be accomplished by tagging frames with VLAN information using the IEEE 802.1Q standard, which is discussed in the next section. Another important aspect of VLANs is configuration and management. This section also covers the Cisco VLAN management protocol: VLAN Trunking Protocol (VTP).

IEEE 802.1Q

In 1998, IEEE defined a standard method for tagging frames with a VLAN ID. The method is published in the revised 2006 version of the IEEE 802.1Q document "Virtual Bridged Local Area Networks." With 802.1Q, a VLAN tag is added inside an Ethernet frame. The frame is not encapsulated, as it is with the older Cisco Inter-Switch Link (ISL) protocol. Instead, 802.1Q adds a header that is inserted immediately following the destination and source MAC addresses of the frame to be transmitted. This is normally where an EtherType would reside for Ethernet II frames or where the length field would reside for 802.3 frames. The EtherType or length field from the original frame is pushed forward and follows the 802.1Q header.

The first 2 bytes of the 802.1Q header are the Tag Protocol Identifier (TPID) field. The TPID is set to 0x8100. Because this number is bigger than the maximum size of an Ethernet frame, a recipient knows that the field is not an 802.3 length field and that the frame is not a typical (untagged) 802.3 frame. If the recipient supports 802.1Q, it recognizes the 0x8100 as the TPID field and continues to process the rest of the fields in the 802.1Q header. If the recipient does not support 802.1Q, it sees the 2 TPID bytes as an unsupported EtherType and drops the frame.

Because 802.1Q changes an Ethernet/802.3 frame, rather than encapsulating the frame as ISL does, a switch must recompute the frame check sequence (FCS) at the end of the frame, which is a minor disadvantage of 802.1Q compared to ISL. However, the CPUs on switches these days are so fast that recomputing the FCS does not take a significant amount of time.

Some Cisco switches support only 802.1Q, and some older, obsolete Cisco switches support only ISL. Some support both. Check the Cisco product catalog for information on which trunking method is supported on a switch. Also, on some switches, you can use the **show port capabilities** command to display which trunking technologies are supported.

Aside from differences in how they tag frames, the most important difference between ISL and 802.1Q is in their interaction with STP. Depending on how recent the software is on a switch, 802.1Q might require all VLANs to be in one spanning tree, whereas ISL allows one spanning tree per VLAN. With the addition of IEEE's 802.1s Multiple Spanning Tree (MST) standard, this might no longer be a problem, but support for 802.1s with 802.1Q depends on the software on the switch.

Dynamic Trunk Protocol

The Cisco proprietary Dynamic Trunk Protocol (DTP) supports a switch negotiating with the remote side to enable or disable 802.1Q. DTP should be recommended to your design customers, but be careful with its configuration. 802.1Q on a trunk interface can be set to on, off, desirable, auto, and nonegotiate. Nonegotiate enables 802.1Q but does not send any configuration requests to the other side. Use nonegotiate when connecting to a switch that does not support DTP.

You should use the off mode whenever you do not want the local interface to be an 802.1Q trunk, but you do want it to participate in DTP to inform the remote side of its off status. Use the on mode when the remote side supports DTP, and when you want the local side to remain in trunk mode regardless of the remote side's mode.

The auto mode means that the switch can receive a request to enable 802.1Q and automatically enter into trunk mode. A switch configured in auto mode never initiates a request. The other side must be set to on or desirable.

The desirable mode causes a switch interface to inform the remote end of its intent to enable 802.1Q but does not actually enable 802.1Q unless the remote side agrees to enable it. The remote side must be set to on, auto, or desirable for the link to use 802.1Q. Do not use the desirable mode if the remote side doesn't support DTP, because receiving DTP frames may confuse the remote switch. In general, however, when both switches support DTP, Cisco recommends setting both sides to desirable. In this mode, network engineers can trust syslog and command-line status messages that a port is up and trunking, whereas with on mode, a port can appear up even though the neighbor is misconfigured.

DTP was supposed to make configuring 802.1Q simpler. With all those options, however, it is easy to make a mistake, especially because some combinations are invalid and result in an 802.1Q mode mismatch. If one side is trunking and the other side is not, the switch ports won't understand each other's traffic. One side will be tagging frames and the other side will not be tagging frames. You should avoid the following combinations:

- Nonegotiate (enable 802.1Q but don't negotiate) and off (don't enable 802.1Q)

- Nonegotiate (enable 802.1Q but don't negotiate) and auto (enable 802.1Q only if the other side says to)

VLAN Trunking Protocol

The Cisco *VLAN Trunking Protocol (VTP)* is a switch-to-switch and switch-to-router VLAN management protocol that exchanges VLAN configuration changes as they are made to the network. VTP manages the addition, deletion, and renaming of VLANs on a campus network without requiring manual intervention at each switch. VTP also reduces manual configuration by automatically configuring a new switch or router with existing VLAN information when the new switch or router is added to the network.

In large switched networks, you should divide the network into multiple VTP domains, which reduces the amount of VLAN information each switch must maintain. A switch accepts VLAN information only from switches in its domain. VTP domains are loosely analogous to autonomous systems in a routed network where a group of routers shares common administrative policies. Multiple VTP domains are recommended on large networks. On medium-sized and small networks, a single VLAN domain is sufficient and minimizes potential problems.

Cisco switches can be configured in VTP server, client, or transparent mode. Server mode is the default. In VTP server mode, you can create, modify, and delete VLANs. VTP servers save their VLAN configurations when they are powered down. VTP clients exchange information with other VTP clients and servers, but you cannot create, change, or delete VLANs on a VTP client. You must do that on a VTP server. VTP clients do not save their VLAN configurations when powered down. Nevertheless, most switches should be clients to avoid VLAN information becoming desynchronized if updates are made on many switches.

A VTP transparent switch does not advertise its VLAN configuration and does not synchronize its VLAN configuration based on received advertisements; however, VTP transparent switches do forward received VTP advertisements to other switches. Use transparent mode when a switch in the middle of the topology does not need to match other switch configurations but would cause problems for other switches if it did not forward VLAN information. You can also use transparent mode on all switches if you prefer to manually control the configuration of VLAN information.

Selecting Routing Protocols

A *routing protocol* lets a router dynamically learn how to reach other networks and exchange this information with other routers or hosts. Selecting routing protocols for your network design customer is harder than selecting switching protocols, because there are so many options. The decision is made easier if you can use a decision table, such as the one shown in Table 7-1. Armed with a solid understanding of your customer's goals and information on the characteristics of different routing protocols, you can make a sound decision about which routing protocols to recommend.

Characterizing Routing Protocols

All routing protocols have the same general goal: to share network reachability information among routers. Routing protocols achieve this goal in a variety of ways. Some routing protocols send a complete routing table to other routers. Other routing protocols send specific information on the status of directly connected links. Some routing protocols send periodic Hello packets to maintain their status with peer routers. Some routing protocols include advanced information such as a subnet mask or prefix length with route information. Most routing protocols share dynamic (learned) information, but in some cases, static configuration information is more appropriate.

Routing protocols differ in their scalability and performance characteristics. Many routing protocols were designed for small internetworks. Some routing protocols work best in a static environment and have a hard time converging to a new topology when changes occur. Some routing protocols are meant for connecting interior campus networks, and others are meant for connecting different enterprises. The next few sections provide more information on the different characteristics of routing protocols. Table 7-5 at the end of this chapter summarizes the comparison of various routing protocols.

Distance-Vector Routing Protocols

Routing protocols fall into two major classes: distance-vector protocols and link-state protocols. This chapter covers distance-vector protocols first.

The following protocols are distance-vector protocols (or derivatives of distance-vector protocols):

- Routing Information Protocol (RIP) version 1 and 2

- Interior Gateway Routing Protocol (IGRP)

- Enhanced IGRP (EIGRP) (an advanced distance-vector protocol)

- Border Gateway Protocol (BGP) (a path-vector routing protocol)

The term *vector* means direction or course. A *distance vector* is a course that also includes information on the length of the course. Many distance-vector routing protocols specify the length of the course with a hop count. A *hop count* specifies the number of routers that must be traversed to reach a destination network. (For some protocols, *hop count* means the number of links rather than the number of routers.)

A distance-vector routing protocol maintains (and transmits) a routing table that lists known networks and the distance to each network. Table 7-3 shows a typical distance-vector routing table.

A distance-vector routing protocol sends its routing table to all neighbors. It sends a broadcast packet that reaches all other routers on the local segment (and any hosts that use routing information). Distance-vector protocols can send the entire table each time, or they can simply send updates after the first transmission and send the complete routing table only occasionally.

Split-Horizon, Hold-Down, and Poison-Reverse Features of Distance-Vector Protocols

A router running a distance-vector protocol sends its routing table out each of its ports on a periodic basis. If the protocol supports the *split-horizon technique*, the router sends only routes that are reachable via other ports. This reduces the size of the update and, more important, improves the accuracy of routing information. With split horizon, a router does not tell another router information that is better learned locally.

Table 7-3   *Distance-Vector Routing Table*

Network	Distance (in Hops)	Send to (Next Hop)
10.0.0.0	0 (directly connected)	Port 1
172.16.0.0	0 (directly connected)	Port 2
172.17.0.0	1	172.16.0.2
172.18.0.0	2	172.16.0.2
192.168.1.0	1	10.0.0.2
192.168.2.0	2	10.0.0.2

Most distance-vector protocols also implement a *hold-down timer* so that new information about a route to a suspect network is not believed right away, in case the information is based on stale data. Hold-down timers are a standard way to avoid loops that can happen during convergence. To understand the loop problem, consider the network shown in Figure 7-2.

Figure 7-2   *Partial Distance-Vector Routing Tables on Router A and Router B*

When routers broadcast their routing tables, they simply send the Network and Distance columns of the table. They do not send the Send To (Next Hop) column, which is one of the causes of the loop problem.

The sequence of events that can lead to a routing loop is as follows:

1.   Router A's connection to Network 172.16.0.0 fails.

2.   Router A removes Network 172.16.0.0 from its routing table.

3. Based on previous announcements from Router A, Router B broadcasts its routing table saying that Router B can reach network 172.16.0.0.

4. Router A adds Network 172.16.0.0 to its routing table with a Send To (Next Hop) value of Router B and a distance of 2.

5. Router A receives a frame for a host on network 172.16.0.0.

6. Router A sends the frame to Router B.

7. Router B sends the frame to Router A.

The frame loops back and forth from Router A to Router B until the IP Time-To-Live (TTL) value expires (*TTL* is a field in the IP header of an IP packet that is decremented each time a router processes the frame).

To make matters worse, without split horizon, at some point Router A sends a route update saying it can get to Network 172.16.0.0, causing Router B to update the route in its table with a distance of 3. Both Router A and Router B continue to send route updates until finally the distance field reaches infinity. (Routing protocols arbitrarily define a distance that means infinity. For example, 16 means infinity for RIP.) When the distance field reaches infinity, the routers remove the route.

The route-update problem is called the *count-to-infinity problem*. A hold-down function tells a router not to add or update information for a route that has recently been removed, until a hold-down timer expires. In the example, if Router A uses hold-down, it does not add the route for network 172.16.0.0 that Router B sends. Split horizon also solves the problem in the example, because if Router B uses split horizon, it does not tell Router A about a route to 172.16.0.0.

Poison-reverse messages are another way of speeding convergence and avoiding loops. With poison reverse, when a router learns a route from another router, it responds by sending an update back to that router that lists the distance to the network as infinity. By doing so, the router explicitly states that the route is not directly reachable via itself.

Triggered updates are another advanced feature of distance-vector protocols that can speed convergence. With triggered updates, a routing protocol announces route failures immediately. Rather than simply waiting for the next regularly scheduled routing update and not including in the update any routes that have failed, a router can immediately send an update. The immediate (triggered) update lists the failed route with the distance set to infinity.

Link-State Routing Protocols

Link-state routing protocols do not exchange routing tables. Instead, routers running a link-state routing protocol exchange information about the links to which a router is connected. Each router learns enough information about links in the internetwork from peer routers to build its own routing table.

The following protocols are link-state routing protocols:

■   Open Shortest Path First (OSPF)

■   Intermediate System-to-Intermediate System (IS-IS)

■   NetWare Internetwork Packet Exchange (IPX) Link Services Protocol (NLSP)

A link-state routing protocol uses a shortest-path first algorithm, such as the Dijkstra algorithm, to determine how to reach destination networks. The Dijkstra algorithm, which is named after the computer scientist who invented the algorithm, Edsger Dijkstra, solves the problem of finding the shortest path from a source point in a mathematical graph to a destination point. One of the beauties of the algorithm is that while finding the shortest path to one destination, a source can also find the shortest path to all points in the graph at the same time. This makes the algorithm a perfect fit for a routing protocol, although it does have other uses.

With link-state routing, routers use a Hello protocol to establish a relationship (called an adjacency) with neighbor routers. Each router sends link-state advertisements (LSA) to each adjacent neighbor. The advertisements identify links and metrics. Each neighbor that receives an advertisement propagates the advertisement to its neighbors. The result is that every router ends up with an identical link-state database that describes the nodes and links in the internetwork graph. Using the Dijkstra algorithm, each router independently calculates its shortest path to each network and enters this information in its routing table.

Link-state routing requires more router CPU power and memory than distance-vector routing and can be harder to troubleshoot. Link-state routing does have some advantages over distance-vector routing, however. In general, link-state routing was designed to use less bandwidth, be less prone to loops, and converge more quickly that distance-vector routing. (Although there are distance-vector protocols, such as EIGRP, that have those qualities also.)

Choosing Between Distance-Vector and Link-State Protocols

According to Cisco design documents, you can use the following guidelines to help you decide which type of routing protocol to deploy.

Choose distance-vector protocols when

■   The network uses a simple, flat topology and does not require a hierarchical design.

■   The network uses a simple hub-and-spoke topology.

■   The administrators do not have enough knowledge to operate and troubleshoot link-state protocols.

■   Worst-case convergence times in the network are not a concern.

Choose link-state protocols when

■   The network design is hierarchical, which is usually the case for large networks.

- The administrators are knowledgeable about the selected link-state protocol.

- Fast convergence of the network is crucial.

Routing Protocol Metrics

Routing protocols use *metrics* to determine which path is preferable when more than one path is available. Routing protocols vary on which metrics are supported. Traditional distance-vector routing protocols used hop count only. Newer protocols can also take into account delay, bandwidth, reliability, and other factors. Metrics can affect scalability. For example, RIP supports only 15 hops. Metrics can also affect network performance. A router that uses hop count as its sole metric misses the opportunity to select a route that has more hops but also more bandwidth than another route.

Hierarchical Versus Nonhierarchical Routing Protocols

Some routing protocols do not support hierarchy. All routers have the same tasks, and every router is a peer of every other router. Routing protocols that support hierarchy, on the other hand, assign different tasks to routers, and group routers in areas, autonomous systems, or domains. In a hierarchical arrangement, some routers communicate with local routers in the same area, and other routers have the job of connecting areas, domains, or autonomous systems. A router that connects an area to other areas can summarize routes for its local area. Summarization enhances stability because routers are shielded from problems not in their own area.

Interior Versus Exterior Routing Protocols

Routing protocols can also be characterized by where they are used. Interior routing protocols, such as RIP, OSPF, and EIGRP, are used by routers within the same enterprise or autonomous system (AS). Exterior routing protocols, such as BGP, perform routing between multiple autonomous systems. BGP is used on the Internet by peer routers in different autonomous systems to maintain a consistent view of the Internet's topology.

Classful Versus Classless Routing Protocols

The previous chapter discussed the differences between IP classful and classless routing protocols. To summarize the concepts in Chapter 6, "Designing Models for Addressing and Naming," a classful routing protocol, such as RIP or IGRP, always considers the IP address class (Class A, B, or C). Address summarization is automatic by major network number. This means that discontiguous subnets are not visible to each other, and variable-length subnet masking (VLSM) is not supported.

Classless protocols, on the other hand, transmit prefix length or subnet mask information with IP network addresses. With classless routing protocols, the IP address space can be mapped so that discontiguous subnets and VLSM are supported. The IP address space should be mapped carefully so that subnets are arranged in contiguous blocks, allowing route updates to be summarized at area boundaries.

Dynamic Versus Static and Default Routing

A *static route* is a route that is manually configured and does not rely on updates from a routing protocol. In some cases, it is not necessary to use a routing protocol. Static routes are often used to connect to a stub network. A *stub network* resides on the edge of an internetwork and isn't used as a transit path for traffic trying to get anywhere else. An example of a stub network is a company that connects to the Internet via a single link to an Internet service provider (ISP). The ISP can have a static route to the company. It is not necessary to run a routing protocol between the company and the ISP.

A disadvantage with static routing is the amount of administration that might be required, especially on large networks. On small (and even some large) networks, static routes have many advantages, however, and should not be overlooked when designing or upgrading a network. Static routes reduce bandwidth usage and are easy to troubleshoot. Static routes allow you to use a route other than the one that dynamic routing would choose, which can be beneficial when you want traffic to follow a specific path. Static routes can also let you use a route that is more specific than the dynamic routing proto-col permits. Static routes also facilitate security because they give you more control over which networks are reachable.

Most ISPs have many static routes in their routing tables to reach their customers' net-works. At an ISP, when traffic arrives from other sites on the Internet with a destination address that matches the network address assigned to a customer, the routing decision is simple. The traffic goes in just one direction—to the router at the customer's site. There's no need for a routing protocol.

On Cisco routers, static routes take precedence over routes to the same destination that are learned via a routing protocol. Cisco IOS Software also supports a *floating static route*, which is a static route that has a higher administrative distance than dynamically learned routes and can thus be overridden by dynamically learned routes. One important application of floating static routes is to provide backup routes when no dynamic infor-mation is available.

A *default route* is a special type of static route that is used when there is no entry in the routing table for a destination network. A default route is also called "the route of last resort." In some cases, a default route is all that is necessary. Take the example of the cus-tomer network connected to an ISP again. At the customer side, it might not be necessary or practical to learn routes to all the networks on the Internet. If there's just one connec-tion to the Internet (the link to the ISP), all Internet traffic has to go in that direction any-way. So, the enterprise network designer can simply define a default route that points to the ISP's router.

Although static and default routes reduce resource usage, including bandwidth and router CPU and memory resources, the tradeoff is a loss of detailed information about routing. Routers with a default route always send traffic that is not local to a peer router. They have no way of knowing that the other router might have lost some of its routes. They also have no way of knowing if a destination is always unreachable (for example, when someone is doing a ping scan and sending multiple pings to numerous IP destination addresses, some of which are not reachable). A router with a default route forwards these packets. It has no way of distinguishing destinations that it cannot reach from destinations that no routers can reach. Default routing can also cause a router to use suboptimal paths. To avoid these types of problems, use dynamic routing.

On-Demand Routing

On-Demand Routing (ODR) is a Cisco proprietary feature that provides IP routing for stub networks. ODR uses the Cisco Discovery Protocol (CDP) to carry minimal routing information between a main site and stub routers. ODR avoids the overhead of dynamic routing without incurring the configuration and management overhead of static routing.

The IP routing information required to represent the network topology for a router in a stub network is fairly simple. For example, in a hub-and-spoke topology (see Figure 5-5 in Chapter 5), stub routers at the spoke sites have a WAN connection to the hub router and a small number of LAN segments directly connected to the stub router. These stub networks might not require the stub router to learn any dynamic IP routing information.

With ODR, the hub router provides default route information to the stub routers, thereby eliminating the need to configure a default route on each stub router. Stub routers use CDP to send IP prefix information for directly connected interfaces to the hub. The hub router installs stub network routes in its routing table. The hub router can also be configured to redistribute these routes into any configured dynamic IP routing protocols. On the stub router, no IP routing protocol is configured. This simplifies configuration and is often a good solution for the access layer of a hierarchically designed network.

Scalability Constraints for Routing Protocols

When selecting a routing protocol for a customer, consider your customer's goals for scaling the network to a large size and investigate the following questions for each routing protocol. Each of the following questions addresses a scalability constraint for routing protocols:

- Are there any limits placed on metrics?

- How quickly can the routing protocol converge when upgrades or changes occur? Link-state protocols tend to converge more quickly than distance-vector protocols. Convergence is discussed in more detail in the next section.

- How often are routing updates or LSAs transmitted? Is the frequency of updates a function of a timer, or are updates triggered by an event, such as a link failure?

- How much data is transmitted in a routing update? The whole table? Just changes? Is split horizon used?

- How much bandwidth is used to send routing updates? Bandwidth utilization is particularly relevant for low-bandwidth serial links.

- How widely are routing updates distributed? To neighbors? To a bounded area? To all routers in the AS?

■   How much CPU utilization is required to process routing updates or LSAs?

■   Are static and default routes supported?

■   Is route summarization supported?

These questions can be answered by watching routing protocol behavior with a protocol analyzer and by studying the relevant specifications or RFCs. The next few sections in this chapter can also help you understand routing protocol behavior better.

Routing Protocol Convergence

Convergence is the time it takes for routers to arrive at a consistent understanding of the internetwork topology after a change takes place. A change can be a network segment or router failing, or a new segment or router joining the internetwork. To understand the importance of quick convergence for your particular customer, you should develop an understanding of the likelihood of frequent changes on the customer's network. Are there links that tend to fail often? Is the customer's network always "under construction" either for enhancements or because of reliability problems?

Because packets might not be reliably routed to all destinations while convergence is taking place, convergence time is a critical design constraint. The convergence process should complete within a few seconds for time-sensitive applications, such as voice applications and Systems Network Architecture (SNA)-based applications. When SNA is transported across an IP internetwork, a fast-converging protocol such as OSPF is recommended. Link-state protocols were designed to converge quickly. Some newer distance-vector protocols, such as EIGRP, were also designed for quick convergence.

A router starts the convergence process when it notices that a link to one of its peer routers has failed. A Cisco router sends *keepalive frames* every 10 seconds (by default) to help it determine the state of a link. On a point-to-point WAN link, a Cisco router sends keepalive frames to the router at the other end of the link. On LANs, a Cisco router sends keepalive frames to itself.

If a serial link fails, a router can start the convergence process immediately if it notices the Carrier Detect (CD) signal drop. Otherwise, a router starts the convergence after sending two or three keepalive frames and not receiving a response. On an Ethernet network, if the router's own transceiver fails, it can start the convergence process immediately. Otherwise, the router starts the convergence process after it has been unable to send two or three keepalive frames.

If the routing protocol uses Hello packets and the Hello timer is shorter than the keepalive timer, the routing protocol can start convergence sooner. Another factor that influences convergence time is load balancing. If a routing table includes multiple paths to a destination, traffic can immediately take other paths when a path fails. Load balancing was discussed in more detail in Chapter 5.

IP Routing

The most common IP routing protocols are RIP, EIGRP, OSPF, IS-IS, and BGP. The following sections describe some of the performance and scalability characteristics of these protocols to help you select the correct protocols for your network design customer.

Routing Information Protocol

The IP *Routing Information Protocol (RIP)* was the first standard routing protocol developed for TCP/IP environments. RIP was developed originally for the Xerox Network System (XNS) protocols and was adopted by the IP community in the early 1980s. RIP was the most common interior routing protocol for many years, probably because it is easy to configure and runs on numerous operating systems. It is still in use on older networks and networks where simplicity and ease of troubleshooting are important. RIP version 1 (RIPv1) is documented in RFC 1058. RIP version 2 (RIPv2) is documented in RFC 2453.

RIP broadcasts its routing table every 30 seconds. RIP allows 25 routes per packet, so on large networks, multiple packets are required to send the whole routing table. Bandwidth utilization is an issue on large RIP networks that include low-bandwidth links. To avoid routing loops during convergence, most implementations of RIP include split horizon and a hold-down timer.

RIP uses a single routing metric (hop count) to measure the distance to a destination network. This limitation should be considered when designing networks that use RIP. The limitation means that if multiple paths to a destination exist, RIP maintains only the path with the fewest hops, even if other paths have a higher aggregate bandwidth, lower aggregate delay, less congestion, and so on.

Another limitation of RIP is that the hop count cannot go above 15. If a router receives a routing update that specifies that a destination is 16 hops away, the router purges that destination from its routing table. A hop count of 16 means the distance to the destination is infinity—in other words, the destination is unreachable.

RIPv1 is a classful routing protocol, which means that it always considers the IP network class. Address summarization is automatic by major network number. This means that discontiguous subnets are not visible to each other, and VLSM is not supported. RIPv2, on the other hand, is classless.

The Internet Engineering Task Force (IETF) developed RIPv2 to address some of the scalability and performance problems with RIPv1. RIPv2 adds the following fields to route entries within a routing table:

- **Route tag:** Distinguishes internal routes that are within the RIP routing domain from external routes that have been imported from another routing protocol or a different autonomous system

- **Subnet mask:** Contains the subnet mask that is applied to the IP address to yield the nonhost (prefix) portion of the address

■ **Next hop:** Specifies the immediate next-hop IP address to which packets to the destination in the route entry should be forwarded

Route tags facilitate merging RIP and non-RIP networks. Including the subnet mask in a route entry provides support for classless routing. The purpose of the next-hop field is to eliminate packets being routed through extra hops. Specifying a value of 0.0.0.0 in the next-hop field indicates that routing should be via the originator of the RIP update. Specifying a different value than 0.0.0.0 is useful when RIP is not in use on all routers in a network.

RIPv2 also supports simple authentication to foil hackers sending routing updates. The authentication scheme uses the space of a route entry. This means that there can be only 24 route entries in a message when authentication is used. Currently, the only authentication supported is a simple plain-text password.

Enhanced Interior Gateway Routing Protocol

Cisco developed the proprietary distance-vector *Interior Gateway Routing Protocol (IGRP)* in the mid-1980s to meet the needs of customers requiring a robust and scalable interior routing protocol. Many customers migrated their RIP networks to IGRP to overcome RIP's 15-hop limitation and reliance on just one metric (hop count). IGRP's 90-second update timer for sending route updates was also more attractive than RIP's 30-second update timer for customers concerned about bandwidth utilization.

Cisco developed the proprietary *Enhanced IGRP (EIGRP)* in the early 1990s to meet the needs of enterprise customers with large, complex, multiprotocol internetworks. EIGRP is compatible with IGRP and provides an automatic redistribution mechanism to allow IGRP routes to be imported into EIGRP, and vice versa. EIGRP can also redistribute routes for RIP, IS-IS, BGP, and OSPF.

EIGRP uses a composite metric based on the following factors:

■ **Bandwidth:** The bandwidth of the lowest-bandwidth segment on the path. A network administrator can configure bandwidth or use the default value, which is based on the type of link. (Configuration is recommended for high-speed WAN links if the default bandwidth value is less than the actual speed.)

■ **Delay:** A sum of all the delays for outgoing interfaces in the path. Each delay is inversely proportional to the bandwidth of each outgoing interface. Delay is not dynamically calculated.

■ **Reliability:** The reliability of the path, based on the interface reliability reported by routers in the path. In an EIGRP update, reliability is an 8-bit number, where 255 is 100 percent reliable and 1 is minimally reliable. By default, reliability is not used unless the **metric weights** command is configured, in which case it is dynamically calculated.

■ **Load:** The load on the path, based on the interface load reported by routers in the path. In an EIGRP update, reliability is an 8-bit number, where 255 is 100 percent loaded and 1 is minimally loaded. By default, load is not used unless the **metric weights** command is configured, in which case load is dynamically calculated.

EIGRP allows load balancing over equal-metric paths and nonequal-metric paths. The EIGRP *variance feature* means that if one path is three times better than another, the better path can be used three times more than the other path. Only routes with metrics that are within a certain range of the best route can be used as multiple paths. Refer to the Cisco configuration documentation for more information.

EIGRP has a better algorithm for advertising and selecting a default route than RIP does. RIP allows a network administrator to configure one default route, which is identified as network 0.0.0.0. EIGRP, on the other hand, allows real networks to be flagged as candidates for being a default. Periodically, EIGRP scans all candidate default routes and chooses the one with the lowest metric to be the actual default route. This feature allows more flexibility and better performance than RIP's static default route.

To reduce convergence time, EIGRP supports triggered updates. A *triggered* router sends a *update* in response to a change (for example, the failure of a link). Upon receipt of a triggered update, other routers can also send triggered updates. A failure causes a wave of update messages to propagate throughout the network, thus speeding convergence time and reducing the risk of loops.

EIGRP has many advanced features and behaviors not found in IGRP or other distance-vector protocols. Although EIGRP still sends vectors with distance information, the updates are as follows:

- *Nonperiodic* means that updates are sent only when a metric changes rather than at regular intervals.

- *Partial* means that updates include only routes that have changed, not every entry in the routing table.

- *Bounded* means that updates are sent only to affected routers.

These behaviors mean that EIGRP uses little bandwidth.

Unlike IGRP, EIGRP updates carry a prefix length with each network number, which makes EIGRP a classless protocol. By default, EIGRP summarizes routes on the classful network boundaries, however. Automatic summarization can be turned off and manual summarization used instead, which can be helpful when a network includes discontiguous subnets.

One of the main goals of EIGRP is to offer quick convergence on large networks. To meet this goal, the designers of EIGRP adopted the *diffusing-update algorithm (DUAL)* that

Dr. J. J. Garcia-Luna-Aceves developed at SRI International. DUAL specifies a method for routers to store neighbors' routing information so that the routers can quickly switch to alternative routes. Routers can also query other routers to learn alternative routes and send Hello packets to determine the reachability of neighbors. DUAL guarantees a loop-free topology, so there is no need for a hold-down mechanism, which is another feature that minimizes convergence time.

DUAL is one reason that EIGRP uses significantly less bandwidth than IGRP or other distance-vector protocols. A router using DUAL develops its routing table using the concept of a feasible successor. A *feasible successor* is a neighboring router that has the least-cost path to a destination. When a router detects that a link has failed, if a feasible successor has an alternate route, the router switches to the alternate route immediately, without causing any network traffic. If there is no successor, the router sends a query to neighbors. The query propagates across the network until a new route is found.

An EIGRP router develops a *topology table* that contains all destinations advertised by neighboring routers. Each entry in the table contains a destination and a list of neighbors that have advertised the destination. For each neighbor, the entry includes the metric that the neighbor advertised for that destination. A router computes its own metric for the destination by using each neighbor's metric in combination with the local metric the router uses to reach the neighbor. The router compares metrics and determines the lowest-cost path to a destination and a feasible successor to use in case the lowest-cost path fails.

EIGRP can scale to thousands of routing nodes. To ensure good performance in large internetworks, EIGRP should be used on networks with simple hierarchical topologies.

Open Shortest Path First

In the late 1980s, the IETF recognized the need to develop an interior link-state routing protocol to meet the needs of large enterprise networks that were constrained by the limitations of RIP. The *Open Shortest Path First (OSPF)* routing protocol is a result of the IETF's work. OSPF is defined in RFC 2328.

The advantages of OSPF are as follows:

- OSPF is an open standard supported by many vendors.

- OSPF converges quickly.

- OSPF authenticates protocol exchanges to meet security goals.

- OSPF supports discontiguous subnets and VLSM.

- OSPF sends multicast frames, rather than broadcast frames, which reduces CPU utilization on LAN hosts (if the hosts have NICs capable of filtering multicasts).

- OSPF networks can be designed in hierarchical areas, which reduces memory and CPU requirements on routers.

- OSPF does not use a lot of bandwidth.

To minimize bandwidth utilization, OSPF propagates only changes. Other network traffic is limited to database-synchronization packets that occur infrequently (every 30 minutes) and Hello packets that establish and maintain neighbor adjacencies and are used to elect a designated router on LANs. Hellos are sent every 10 seconds. On dialup and ISDN links configured as demand circuits, OSPF can be even quieter. In this case, OSPF routers suppress Hellos and the database-synchronization packets.

Upon startup and when there are changes, an OSPF router multicasts LSAs to all other routers within the same hierarchical area. OSPF routers accumulate link-state information to calculate the shortest path to a destination network. The calculation uses the Dijkstra algorithm. The result of the calculation is a database of the topology, called the *link-state database*. Each router in an area has an identical database.

All routers run the same algorithm, in parallel. From the link-state database, each router constructs a tree of shortest paths, with itself as the root of the tree. The shortest-path tree provides the route to each destination. Externally derived routing information appears on the tree as leaves. When several equal-cost routes to a destination exist, traffic is distributed equally among them.

According to RFC 2328, the cost of a route is described by "a single dimensionless metric" that is "configurable by a system administrator." A cost is associated with the output side of each router interface. The lower the cost, the more likely the interface is to be used to forward data traffic. A cost is also associated with externally derived routes (for example, routes learned from a different routing protocol).

On a Cisco router, the cost of an interface defaults to 100,000,000 divided by the bandwidth for the interface. For example, both FDDI and 100-Mbps Ethernet have a cost of 1. The cost can be manually configured. Usually it is best if both ends of a link use the same cost. If a Cisco router is at one end of a link and a non-Cisco router is at the other end, you might need to manually configure the cost. Because OSPF defines the cost metric so broadly, vendors are not required to agree on how the cost is defined.

Note Cisco OSPF implementation uses a reference bandwidth of 100 Mbps for cost calculation. The formula to calculate the cost for an interface is the reference bandwidth divided by the interface bandwidth. For example, in the case of a 10-Mbps Ethernet interface, the interface cost is 100 Mbps divided by 10 Mbps, or 10. In an internetwork with high-speed links of 100 Mbps or higher, you should change the reference bandwidth to a number higher than 100 Mbps. You can use the **ospf auto-cost reference-bandwidth** command to make that change.

OSPF Architectures

OSPF allows sets of networks to be grouped into areas. The topology of an area is hidden from the rest of the autonomous system. By hiding the topology of an area, routing traffic is reduced. Also, routing within the area is determined only by the area's own topology, providing the area protection from bad routing data. By dividing routers into areas, the memory and CPU requirements for each router are limited.

A contiguous backbone area, called *Area 0*, is required when an OSPF network is divided into areas. Every other area connects to Area 0 via an *Area Border Router (ABR)*, as shown in Figure 7-3. All traffic between areas must travel through Area 0, which should have high availability, throughput, and bandwidth. Area 0 should be easy to manage and troubleshoot. A set of routers in a rack connected via a high-speed LAN makes a good Area 0 for many customers.

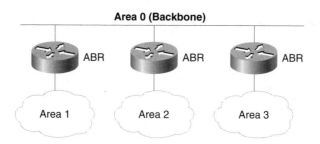

Figure 7-3   *OSPF Areas Connected via ABRs*

In addition to ABRs, an OSPF network might include one or more Autonomous System Boundary Routers (ASBR), which connects an OSPF network to a different AS or to a network that uses a routing protocol other than OSPF. For example, an ASBR could connect an internal OSPF campus network to the Internet.

When designing an OSPF network, make sure to assign network numbers in blocks that can be summarized. An ABR should summarize routes behind it to avoid routers in the backbone and other areas having to know details about a particular area. The summarization must be configured on Cisco routers with the **area-range** command.

An ABR that connects a stub network can be configured to inject a default route into the stub area for all external networks that are outside the AS or are learned from other routing protocols. The router can also be configured to inject a default route for internal summarized or nonsummarized routes to other areas. If a router injects a default route for all routes, Cisco calls the area a *totally stubby area*, which are a Cisco technique that works as long as all the stubby areas' ABRs are Cisco routers.

Cisco also supports *not-so-stubby areas*, which allows the redistribution of external routes into OSPF in an otherwise stubby area. Not-so-stubby areas are specified in RFC 1587. Not-so-stubby areas are not common, but they can be used on a stub network that includes a legacy link to another routing protocol or AS that is different from the link used by the rest of the internetwork to reach the outside world.

Because of the requirement that OSPF be structured in areas and the recommendation that routes be summarized, it can be difficult to migrate an existing network to OSPF. Also, enlarging an existing OSPF network can be challenging. If a network is subject to rapid change or growth, OSPF might not be the best choice. For most networks, however, OSPF is a good choice because of its low-bandwidth utilization, scalability, and compatibility with multiple vendors.

Intermediate System-to-Intermediate System

Intermediate System-to-Intermediate System (IS-IS) is a dynamic link-state protocol developed for use with the Open System Interconnection (OSI) protocol suite. Integrated IS-IS is an implementation of IS-IS for mixed OSI and IP networks that has gained limited popularity for use within large, hierarchical IP networks, especially within the core of large ISPs. IS-IS is a classless, interior routing protocol that is similar in operation to OSPF although somewhat more flexible, efficient, and scalable.

As with OSPF, IS-IS can be implemented in a hierarchical fashion. A router can play different roles:

- Level 1 routers route within an area.

- Level 2 routers route between areas.

- Level 1–2 routers participate in Level 1 intra-area routing and Level 2 interarea routing.

In IS-IS, the boundary between areas is on a link between routers. A router belongs to only one area. In comparison, in OSPF, area boundaries reside inside an ABR. Some router interfaces in the ABR belong to one area and other interfaces belong to another area. With IS-IS, all router interfaces are in the same area. This makes IS-IS somewhat more modular and means that in some cases, an area can be upgraded without affecting as many routers.

Level 1 routers within an area (including Level 1–2 routers) maintain an identical link-state database that defines their area's topology. Level 2 (including Level 1–2 routers) also maintain a separate link-state database for the Level 2 topology.

Unlike OSPF ABRs, Level 1–2 routers do not advertise Level 2 routes to Level 1 routers. A Level 1 router has no knowledge of destinations outside of its own area. This makes IS-IS more efficient than OSPF with regard to CPU use and the processing of routing updates, although similar functionality can be implemented on Cisco OSPF routers by configuring a totally stubby area.

Note From a Level 1 router's point of view, sending traffic outside the area involves finding the nearest Level 2 router. The Level 1 router relies on the Level 2 router to reach the destination. The path taken can be suboptimal if some of an area's exit-point Level 2 routers are poorly located or have poor connectivity to the destination network. The choice of exit router in IS-IS is not based on detailed information. On the positive side, this behavior means Level 1 routers require less processing.

The set of Level 2 routers (including Level 1–2 routers) and their interconnecting links comprise the IS-IS backbone. As with OSPF, interarea traffic must traverse this backbone. OSPF has a central backbone (Area 0) that physically attaches all the other areas. A consistent IP addressing structure is necessary to summarize addresses into the backbone and reduce the amount of information that is carried in the backbone and advertised across the network. In comparison, an IS-IS backbone can be a set of distinct areas inter-connected by a chain of Level 2 and Level 1–2 routers, weaving their way through and between Level 1 areas. Compared to OSPF, IS-IS allows a more flexible approach to extending the backbone by adding additional Level 2 routers.

Border Gateway Protocol

The IETF developed the *Border Gateway Protocol (BGP)* to replace the now-obsolete Exterior Gateway Protocol (EGP) as the standard exterior routing protocol for the Internet. BGP solves problems that EGP had with reliability and scalability. BGP4, the current version of BGP, is specified in RFC 1771.

Internal BGP (iBGP) can be used at a large company to route between domains. *External BGP (eBGP)* is used to route between companies and to participate in global Internet routing. eBGP is often used to multihome an enterprise's connection to the Internet. It is a common misconception that multihoming requires BGP, but this is not true. Depending on a customer's goals and the flexibility of their ISP's policies, you can multihome with default routes, as discussed in Chapter 5. Running eBGP can be challeng-ing, requiring an understanding of the complexities of Internet routing. eBGP should be recommended only to companies that have senior network engineers, and a good rela-tionship with their ISPs. An inexperienced network engineer can configure eBGP in such a way as to cause problems for the entire Internet. Also, eBGP should be used only on routers with a lot of memory, a fast CPU, and a high-bandwidth connection to the Internet. An Internet routing table contains more than 100,000 routes and is continually growing as the Internet expands and more companies use BGP to multihome.

The main goal of BGP is to allow routers to exchange information on paths to destination networks. Each BGP router maintains a routing table that lists all feasible paths to a par-ticular network. BGP routers exchange routing information upon initial startup, and then send incremental updates, using TCP for reliable delivery of BGP packets. An update specifies *path attributes*, which include the origin of the path information, a sequence of autonomous-system path segments, and next-hop information.

When a BGP router receives updates from multiple autonomous systems that describe different paths to the same destination, the router must choose the single best path for reaching that destination. After the best path is chosen, BGP propagates the best path to its neighbors. The decision is based on the value of attributes in the update (such as next hop, administrative weight, local preference, the origin of the route, and path length) and other BGP-configurable factors.

Using Multiple Routing Protocols in an Internetwork

When selecting routing protocols for a customer, it is important to realize that you do not have to use the same routing protocols throughout the internetwork. The criteria for selecting protocols are different for different parts of an internetwork. Also, when merg-ing a new network with an old network, it is often necessary to run more than one rout-ing protocol. In some cases, your network design might focus on a new design for the core and distribution layers and need to interoperate with existing access layer routing protocols. As another example, when two companies merge, sometimes each company wants to run a different routing protocol.

This section summarizes some recommendations for selecting a routing protocol for different layers of the hierarchical design model and then discusses redistribution between routing protocols. The section ends with a quick discussion of Integrated Routing and Bridging (IRB), a Cisco IOS method for connecting bridged and routed networks in a single router.

Routing Protocols and the Hierarchical Design Model

As discussed in Chapter 5, large internetworks are designed using a modular, hierarchical approach. One such approach is the three-layer hierarchical design model, which has a core layer that is optimized for availability and performance, a distribution layer that implements policies, and an access layer that connects users. The next three sections discuss routing protocols for the three layers of the model.

Routing Protocols for the Core Layer

The core layer should incorporate redundant links and load sharing between equal-cost paths. It should provide immediate response if a link failure occurs and adapts quickly to change. Routing protocols that meet these needs include EIGRP, OSPF, and IS-IS. The decision to use EIGRP, OSPF, or IS-IS should be based on the underlying topology, IP addressing design, vendor preferences, and other business and technical goals.

OSPF imposes a strict hierarchical design. OSPF areas must map to the IP addressing plan, which can be difficult to achieve. EIGRP and IS-IS are more flexible with regard to the hierarchical structure and IP addressing design. EIGRP is a Cisco proprietary protocol, however. Although Cisco has licensed it to a few vendors, if other vendors' products are to be used in the implementation of the network design, EIGRP might not be a good solution. Alternatively, EIGRP can be used in the core with redistribution to another routing protocol in the distribution layer.

RIP is not recommended as a core routing protocol. Its response to change is slow, which can result in disrupted connectivity.

Routing Protocols for the Distribution Layer

The distribution layer represents the connection point between the core and access layers. Routing protocols used in the distribution layer include RIPv2, EIGRP, OSPF, and IS-IS. The distribution layer also sometimes uses ODR. The distribution layer often has the job of redistributing between routing protocols used in the core layer and those used in the access layer.

Routing Protocols for the Access Layer

The access layer provides access to network resources for local and remote users. As with the distribution and core layers, the underlying topology, IP addressing design, and vendor preferences drive the choice of routing protocol. Access layer equipment may be less powerful than distribution and core layer equipment, with regard to processing power and memory, which influences the routing protocol choice.

Routing protocols that should be used in the access layer include RIPv2, OSPF, and EIGRP. The distribution layer also sometimes uses ODR. Use of static routing is also a possibility. IS-IS is not often appropriate for the access layer because it demands more knowledge to configure and is also not well suited to dialup networks. The limitations of using OSPF as an access layer routing protocol are connected to its high memory and processing power requirements and strict hierarchical design requirements. The high memory and processing power requirements of OSPF can be avoided with the use of summarization and careful area planning, however.

Redistribution Between Routing Protocols

Redistribution allows routers to run more than one routing protocol and share routes among routing protocols. Implementing redistribution can be challenging because every routing protocol behaves differently and routing protocols cannot directly exchange information about routes, prefixes, metrics, link states, and so on. Redistribution can lead to routing loops if not configured carefully, and can complicate planning and troubleshooting.

Despite the challenges, redistribution may be desirable when connecting different layers of the hierarchical model, when migrating to a new routing protocol, when different departments use different protocols, or when there is a mixed-vendor environment.

A network administrator configures redistribution by specifying which protocols should insert routing information into other protocols' routing tables. Redistribution design involves determining the routing protocols to be used in a network and the extent of each routing domain. A routing domain in this context is a set of routers that share information through the use of a single routing protocol. The designer must determine where the boundaries between routing domains reside and where redistribution must occur. Redistribution is most often needed in the distribution layer where routing domains intersect.

Another decision is whether to use one- or two-way redistribution. With one-way redistribution, routing information is redistributed from one routing protocol to another, but not vice versa. Static or default routes can be used in the opposite direction to provide connectivity. With two-way redistribution, routing information is redistributed from one routing protocol to another and vice versa. Complete routing information can be exchanged or filtering can be used to limit the information that is exchanged.

In most hierarchical designs, you will probably use one-way rather than two-way redistribution. When you do use two-way redistribution, you will probably not redistribute all routes from one domain to the other. Most designs require you to filter so that only a subset of the routes in one domain is redistributed into the other. Filtering routes may be necessary to avoid routing loops and to maintain security, availability, and performance.

You should make sure that a routing protocol does not inject routes into another routing protocol that already has a better way to reach the advertised networks. This can be accomplished with filtering. If a router is misconfigured (or maliciously reconfigured by a hacker) so that it begins advertising routes that do not belong to its domain, traffic flow can be affected. The problem might result in suboptimal routing or, worse, prevent traffic from reaching its destination. A good design practice is to filter routes so that a router receives only expected routes from other domains.

Filtering is also used to enhance performance. A large network could have hundreds or even thousands of routes. If all routes are redistributed into a network with smaller routers, the size of the routing table can overwhelm the smaller routers, degrading network performance. The router can get bogged down searching the large routing table for the next-hop address. The large routing table could also exceed the router's memory, causing the router to fail altogether.

Redistribution configuration should also be done with care to avoid *feedback*. Feedback happens when a routing protocol learns about routes from another protocol and then advertises these routes back to the other routing protocol. For example, if a router is configured to redistribute EIGRP routes into a RIPv2 domain, and also configured to redistribute routes back into EIGRP, the router must filter any routes that it learned from EIGRP before redistributing routes into EIGRP. This avoids any problems caused by the differences in metrics used by different routing protocols.

Resolving Incompatible Metrics

When redistributing from one routing protocol to another, you will need to make some decisions about metrics. Routing protocols use different metrics that cannot easily be converted to each other. Instead of attempting a conversion, you should simply make a decision on what the metric should be for routes that originated with a different routing protocol. For example, you may decide that all EIGRP routes start out with a hop count of 1 when redistributed into a RIPv2 domain. Or you may decide that all OSPF routes start out with a bandwidth of 1000 and a delay of 100 when redistributed into EIGRP.

Administrative Distances

Another factor that makes redistribution challenging is the possibility that a router can learn about a destination via more than one routing protocol. Every routing protocol and every vendor handles this issue differently. Cisco assigns an *administrative distance* to routes learned from different sources. A lower administrative distance means that a route is preferred. For example, if a router learns about a route via both OSPF and RIPv2, the OSPF route is preferred because OSPF has a default administrative distance of 110 and RIPv2 has a default administrative distance of 120. If a router also has a static route to the destination, the static route is preferred because the default administrative distance for a static route is 1. Table 7-4 outlines some common administrative distances by type of route.

Note   Cisco IOS Software also supports a *floating static route*, which is a static route that has a higher administrative distance than a dynamically learned route. Floating static routes are available for IP, IPX, and AppleTalk. A floating static route is a statically configured route that has a high administrative distance so that it can be overridden by dynamically learned routing information. A floating static route can be used to create a "path of last resort" that is used only when no dynamic information is available. One important application of floating static routes is to provide backup routes in topologies where dial-on-demand routing (DDR) is used.

Table 7-4   *Administrative Distance by Route Type*

Route Source	Default Distance Value
Connected interface	0
Static route	1
Enhanced Interior Gateway Routing Protocol (EIGRP) summary route	5
External Border Gateway Protocol (BGP)	20
Internal EIGRP	90
IGRP	100
OSPF	110
Intermediate System-to-Intermediate System (IS-IS)	115
Routing Information Protocol (RIP)	120
Exterior Gateway Protocol (EGP)	140
On-Demand Routing (ODR)	160
External EIGRP	170
Internal BGP	200
Unknown	255

Integrated Routing and Bridging

For customers who need to merge bridged and routed networks, Cisco IOS Software offers support for IRB, which connects VLANs and bridged networks to routed networks within the same router.

An older Cisco IOS feature, *Concurrent Routing and Bridging (CRB)*, supported routing and bridging within the same router, but it simply meant that you could connect bridged networks to other bridged networks and routed networks to other routed networks. IRB extends CRB by providing the capability to forward packets between bridged and routed interfaces via a software-based interface called the *bridged virtual interface (BVI)*.

One advantage of IRB is that a bridged IP subnet or VLAN can span a router. This can be useful when there is a shortage of IP subnet numbers and it is not practical to assign a different subnet number to each interface on a router. IRB can also be useful during migration from a bridged environment to a routed or VLAN environment.

A Summary of Routing Protocols

Table 7-5 provides a comparison of various routing protocols to help you select a routing protocol based on a customer's goals for adaptability, scalability, affordability, security, and network performance.

Table 7-5 *Routing Protocol Comparisons*

	Distance Vector or Link State	Interior or Exterior	Classful or Classless	Metrics Supported	Scalability	Convergence Time	Resource Consumption	Supports Security? Authenticates Routes?	Ease of Design, Configuration, and Troubleshooting
RIPv1	Distance vector	Interior	Classful	Hop count	15 hops	Can be long (if no load balancing)	Memory: low CPU: low Bandwidth: high	No	Easy
RIPv2	Distance vector	Interior	Classless	Hop count	15 hops	Can be long (if no load balancing)	Memory: low CPU: low Bandwidth: high	Yes	Easy
IGRP	Distance vector	Interior	Classful	Bandwidth, delay, reliability, load	255 hops (default is 100)	Quick (uses triggered updates and poison reverse)	Memory: low CPU: low Bandwidth: high	No	Easy
EIGRP	Advanced distance vector	Interior	Classless	Bandwidth, delay, reliability, load	1000s of routers	Very quick (uses DUAL algorithm)	Memory: moderate CPU: low Bandwidth: low	Yes	Easy
OSPF	Link state	Interior	Classless	Cost (100 million divided by bandwidth on Cisco routers)	A few hundred routers per area, a few hundred areas	Quick (uses LSAs and Hello packets)	Memory: high CPU: high Bandwidth: low	Yes	Moderate
BGP	Path vector	Exterior	Classless	Value of path attributes and other configurable factors	1000s of routers	Quick (uses update and keepalive packets, and withdraws routes)	Memory: high CPU: high Bandwidth: low	Yes	Moderate
IS-IS	Link state	Interior	Classless	Configured path value, plus delay, expense, and errors	Hundreds of routers per area, a few hundred areas	Quick (uses LSAs)	Memory: high CPU: high Bandwidth: low	Yes	Moderate

Summary

This chapter provided information to help you select the right switching and routing protocols for your network design customer. The chapter covered scalability and performance characteristics of the protocols and talked about how quickly protocols can adapt to changes.

Deciding on the right switching and routing protocols for your customer will help you select the best switch and router products for the customer. For example, if you have decided that the design must support a routing protocol that can converge within seconds in a large internetwork, you will probably not recommend a router that runs only RIP.

This chapter began with a generic discussion about decision making to help you develop a systematic process for selecting network design solutions. A discussion of bridging and switching protocols followed, which covered transparent bridging, multilayer switching, enhancements for STP, and VLAN protocols. A section on routing protocols followed the switching section. Table 7-5 summarized the comparisons that were made of various routing protocols in the routing section.

Review Questions

1. Compare and contrast distance-vector and link-state routing. If you were designing a new routing protocol, which would you use and why?

2. Analyze the routing table on your computer. In Windows you can view it with a **route print** command. On a Mac, you can view it with a **netstat -rn** command. What entries are in your routing table and why are they there? Is your default route in the table and, if yes, what is it?

3. Select a routing protocol that interests you, whether it's RIPv2, OSPF, EIGRP, BGP, or a different routing protocol. Research any security issues associated with this routing protocol and write two or three paragraphs about what you discovered.

4. Network designers use many factors when deciding which routing protocol to use. For example, they consider whether the routing protocol converges quickly. List and briefly describe five other factors that characterize routing protocols and help a designer distinguish one protocol from another.

Design Scenario

In Chapter 4, "Characterizing Network Traffic," you learned about Genome4U, a scientific research project at a large university that plans to sequence the genomes of 100,000 volunteers. The project will also create a set of publicly accessible databases with genomic, trait, and medical data associated with the volunteers. Genome4U's fund raising is going well, and the project is building a multistory lab for about 500 researchers. The project network engineers will be implementing a new internetwork for the lab using Cisco switches and routers. The network engineers plan to use EIGRP on the new routers. However, network designs are never that easy. The new internetwork also needs to communicate with many business partners, including a nearby biology lab that uses RIP and a fund-raising office that uses OSPF. The lab also needs Internet access, which it hopes can be achieved by simply connecting the network to the university's campus network, which has Internet access.

Design a plan for integrating the different routing protocols into a new network design for Genome4U's lab. What information will you redistribute between routing protocols? What problems do you expect to encounter (with different metrics, security, and so on) when you redistribute, and how will you overcome the problems? How will you provide Internet access?

Chapter 8

Developing Network Security Strategies

Developing security strategies that can protect all parts of a complicated network while having a limited effect on ease of use and performance is one of the most important and difficult tasks related to network design. Security design is challenged by the complexity and porous nature of modern networks that include public servers for electronic commerce, extranet connections for business partners, and remote-access services for users reaching the network from home, customer sites, hotel rooms, Internet cafes, and so on. To help you handle the difficulties inherent in designing network security for complex networks, this chapter teaches a systematic, top-down approach that focuses on planning and policy development before the selection of security products.

The goal of this chapter is to help you work with your network design customers in the development of effective security strategies, and to help you select the right techniques to implement the strategies. The chapter describes the steps for developing a security strategy and covers some basic security principles. The chapter presents a modular approach to security design that will let you apply layered solutions that protect a network in many ways. The final sections describe methods for securing the components of a typical enterprise network that are most at risk, including Internet connections, remote-access networks, network and user services, and wireless networks.

Security should be considered during many steps of the top-down network design process. This isn't the only chapter that covers security. Chapter 2, "Analyzing Technical Goals and Tradeoffs," discussed identifying network assets, analyzing security risks, and developing security requirements. Chapter 5, "Designing a Network Topology," covered secure network topologies. This chapter focuses on security strategies and mechanisms.

Network Security Design

Following a structured set of steps when developing and implementing network security will help you address the varied concerns that play a part in security design. Many security strategies have been developed in a haphazard way and have failed to actually secure assets and to meet a customer's primary goals for security. Breaking down the process of security design into the following steps will help you effectively plan and execute a security strategy:

1. Identify network assets.

2. Analyze security risks.

3. Analyze security requirements and tradeoffs.

4. Develop a security plan.

5. Define a security policy.

6. Develop procedures for applying security policies.

7. Develop a technical implementation strategy.

8. Achieve buy-in from users, managers, and technical staff.

9. Train users, managers, and technical staff.

10. Implement the technical strategy and security procedures.

11. Test the security and update it if any problems are found.

12. Maintain security.

Chapter 2 covered steps 1 through 3 in detail. This chapter quickly revisits steps 1 through 3 and also addresses steps 4, 5, 6, and 12. Steps 7 through 10 are outside the scope of this book. Chapter 12, "Testing Your Network Design," addresses Step 11.

Identifying Network Assets

Chapter 2 discussed gathering information on a customer's goals for network security. As discussed in Chapter 2, analyzing goals involves identifying network assets and the risk that those assets could be sabotaged or inappropriately accessed. It also involves analyzing the consequences of risks.

Network assets can include network hosts (including the hosts' operating systems, applications, and data), internetworking devices (such as routers and switches), and network data that traverses the network. Less obvious, but still important, assets include intellectual property, trade secrets, and a company's reputation.

Analyzing Security Risks

Risks can range from hostile intruders to untrained users who download Internet applications that have viruses. Hostile intruders can steal data, change data, and cause service to be denied to legitimate users. *Denial-of-service (DoS)* attacks have become increasingly common in the past few years. See Chapter 2 for more details on risk analysis.

Analyzing Security Requirements and Tradeoffs

Chapter 2 covers security requirements analysis in more detail. Although many customers have more specific goals, in general, security requirements boil down to the need to protect the following assets:

- The confidentiality of data, so that only authorized users can view sensitive information

- The integrity of data, so that only authorized users can change sensitive information

- System and data availability, so that users have uninterrupted access to important computing resources

According to RFC 2196, "Site Security Handbook:"

> One old truism in security is that the cost of protecting yourself against a threat should be less than the cost of recovering if the threat were to strike you. Cost in this context should be remembered to include losses expressed in real currency, reputation, trustworthiness, and other less obvious measures.

As is the case with most technical design requirements, achieving security goals means making tradeoffs. Tradeoffs must be made between security goals and goals for affordability, usability, performance, and availability. Also, security adds to the amount of management work because user login IDs, passwords, and audit logs must be maintained.

Security also affects network performance. Security features such as packet filters and data encryption consume CPU power and memory on hosts, routers, and servers. Encryption can use upward of 15 percent of available CPU power on a router or server. Encryption can be implemented on dedicated appliances instead of on shared routers or servers, but there is still an effect on network performance because of the delay that packets experience while they are being encrypted or decrypted.

Another tradeoff is that security can reduce network redundancy. If all traffic must go through an encryption device, for example, the device becomes a single point of failure. This makes it hard to meet availability goals.

Security can also make it harder to offer load balancing. Some security mechanisms require traffic to always take the same path so that security mechanisms can be applied uniformly. For example, a mechanism that randomizes TCP sequence numbers (so that hackers can't guess the numbers) won't work if some TCP segments for a session take a path that bypasses the randomizing function due to load balancing.

Developing a Security Plan

One of the first steps in security design is developing a security plan. A *security plan* is a high-level document that proposes what an organization is going to do to meet security requirements. The plan specifies the time, people, and other resources that will be required to develop a security policy and achieve technical implementation of the policy. As the network designer, you can help your customer develop a plan that is practical and pertinent. The plan should be based on the customer's goals and the analysis of network assets and risks.

A security plan should reference the network topology and include a list of network services that will be provided (for example, FTP, web, email, and so on). This list should specify who provides the services, who has access to the services, how access is provided, and who administers the services.

As the network designer, you can help the customer evaluate which services are definitely needed, based on the customer's business and technical goals. Sometimes new services are added unnecessarily, simply because they are the latest trend. Adding services might require new packet filters on routers and firewalls to protect the services, or additional user-authentication processes to limit access to the services, adding complexity to the security strategy. Overly complex security strategies should be avoided because they can be self-defeating. Complicated security strategies are hard to implement correctly without introducing unexpected security holes.

One of the most important aspects of the security plan is a specification of the people who must be involved in implementing network security:

- Will specialized security administrators be hired?

- How will end users and their managers get involved?

- How will end users, managers, and technical staff be trained on security policies and procedures?

For a security plan to be useful, it needs to have the support of all levels of employees within the organization. It is especially important that corporate management fully support the security plan. Technical staff at headquarters and remote sites should buy into the plan, as should end users.

Developing a Security Policy

According to RFC 2196, "Site Security Handbook:"

> A security policy is a formal statement of the rules by which people who are given access to an organization's technology and information assets must abide.

A *security policy* informs users, managers, and technical staff of their obligations for protecting technology and information assets. The policy should specify the mechanisms by which these obligations can be met. As was the case with the security plan, the security policy should have buy-in from employees, managers, executives, and technical personnel.

Developing a security policy is the job of senior management, with help from security and network administrators. The administrators get input from managers, users, network designers and engineers, and possibly legal counsel. As a network designer, you should work closely with the security administrators to understand how policies might affect the network design.

After a security policy has been developed, with the engagement of users, staff, and management, it should be explained to all by top management. Many enterprises require personnel to sign a statement indicating that they have read, understood, and agreed to abide by a policy.

A security policy is a living document. Because organizations constantly change, security policies should be regularly updated to reflect new business directions and technological shifts. Risks change over time also and affect the security policy.

Components of a Security Policy

In general, a policy should include at least the following items:

- An *access policy* that defines access rights and privileges. The access policy should provide guidelines for connecting external networks, connecting devices to a network, and adding new software to systems. An access policy might also address how data is categorized (for example, confidential, internal, and top secret).

- An *accountability policy* that defines the responsibilities of users, operations staff, and management. The accountability policy should specify an audit capability and provide incident-handling guidelines that specify what to do and whom to contact if a possible intrusion is detected.

- An *authentication policy* that establishes trust through an effective password policy and sets up guidelines for remote-location authentication.

- A *privacy policy* that defines reasonable expectations of privacy regarding the monitoring of electronic mail, logging of keystrokes, and access to users' files.

- *Computer-technology purchasing guidelines* that specify the requirements for acquiring, configuring, and auditing computer systems and networks for compliance with the policy.

Developing Security Procedures

Security procedures implement security policies. Procedures define configuration, login, audit, and maintenance processes. Security procedures should be written for end users, network administrators, and security administrators. Security procedures should specify how to handle incidents (that is, what to do and who to contact if an intrusion is detected). Security procedures can be communicated to users and administrators in instructor-led and self-paced training classes.

Maintaining Security

Security must be maintained by scheduling periodic independent audits, reading audit logs, responding to incidents, reading current literature and agency alerts, performing security testing, training security administrators, and updating the security plan and policy. Network security should be a perpetual process. Risks change over time, and so should security. Cisco security experts use the term *security wheel* to illustrate that implementing, monitoring, testing, and improving security is a never-ending process. Many overworked security engineers might relate to the wheel concept. Continually updating security mechanisms to keep up with the latest attacks can sometimes make an administrator feel a bit like a hamster on a training wheel.

Security Mechanisms

This section describes some typical ingredients of secure network designs. You can select from these ingredients when designing solutions for common security challenges, which are described in the "Modularizing Security Design" section later in this chapter.

Physical Security

Physical security refers to limiting access to key network resources by keeping the resources behind a locked door and protected from natural and human-made disasters. Physical security can protect a network from inadvertent misuses of network equipment by untrained employees and contractors. It can also protect the network from hackers, competitors, and terrorists walking in off the street and changing equipment configurations.

Depending on the level of protection, physical security can protect a network from terrorist and biohazard events, including bombs, radioactive spills, and so on. Physical security can also protect resources from natural disasters such as floods, fires, storms, and earthquakes.

Depending on your particular network design customer, physical security should be installed to protect core routers, demarcation points, cabling, modems, servers, hosts, backup storage, and so on. Work with your customer during the early stages of the network design project to make sure equipment will be placed in computer rooms that have card key access and/or security guards. Computer rooms should also be equipped with uninterruptible power supplies, fire alarms, fire-abatement mechanisms, and water-removal systems. To protect equipment from earthquakes and high winds during storms, equipment should be installed in racks that attach to the floor or wall.

Because physical security is such an obvious requirement, it is easy to forget to plan for it, but it should never be overlooked or considered less important than other security mechanisms. As mentioned in the "Secure Network Design Topologies" section of Chapter 5, you should start working with your design customer at the beginning of the design project to make sure that critical equipment will be protected. Planning for physical security should start during the early phases of the top-down design process in case there are lead times to build or install security mechanisms.

Authentication

Authentication identifies who is requesting network services. The term *authentication* usually refers to authenticating users but can also refer to authenticating devices or software processes. For example, some routing protocols support *route authentication*, whereby a router must pass some criteria before another router accepts its routing updates.

Most security policies state that to access a network and its services, a user must enter a login ID and password that are authenticated by a security server. To maximize security, one-time (dynamic) passwords can be used. With one-time password systems, a user's password always changes. This is often accomplished with a security card, also called a *Smartcard*. A *security card* is a physical device about the size of a credit card. The user types a personal identification number (PIN) into the card. The *PIN* is an initial level of security that simply gives the user permission to use the card. The card provides a one-time password that is used to access the corporate network for a limited time. The password is synchronized with a central security card server that resides on the network. Security cards are commonly used by telecommuters and mobile users. They are not usually used for LAN access.

Authentication is traditionally based on one of three proofs:

- **Something the user knows:** This usually involves knowledge of a unique secret that is shared by the authenticating parties. To a user, this secret appears as a classic password, a PIN, or a private cryptographic key.

- **Something the user has:** This usually involves physical possession of an item that is unique to the user. Examples include password token cards, security cards, and hardware keys.

- **Something the user is:** This involves verification of a unique physical characteristic of the user, such as a fingerprint, retina pattern, voice, or face.

Many systems use *two-factor authentication*, which requires a user to have two proofs of identity. An example is an access control system that requires a security card and a password. With two-factor authentication, a compromise of one factor does not lead to a compromise of the system. An attacker could learn a password, but the password is useless without the security card. Conversely, if the security card is stolen, it cannot be used without the password.

Authorization

Whereas authentication controls who can access network resources, *authorization* says what they can do after they have accessed the resources. Authorization grants privileges to processes and users. Authorization lets a security administrator control parts of a network (for example, directories and files on servers).

Authorization varies from user to user, partly depending on a user's department or job function. For example, a policy might state that only Human Resources employees should see salary records for people they don't manage.

Security experts recommend use of the *principle of least privilege* in the implementation of authorization. This principle is based on the idea that each user should be given only the minimal necessary rights to perform a certain task. Therefore, an authorization mechanism should give a user only the minimum access permissions that are necessary. Explicitly listing the authorized activities of each user with respect to every resource is difficult, so techniques are used to simplify the process. For example, a network manager can create user groups for users with the same privileges.

Accounting (Auditing)

To effectively analyze the security of a network and to respond to security incidents, procedures should be established for collecting network activity data. Collecting data is called *accounting* or *auditing*.

For networks with strict security policies, audit data should include all attempts to achieve authentication and authorization by any person. It is especially important to log "anonymous" or "guest" access to public servers. The data should also log all attempts by users to change their access rights.

The collected data should include user- and hostnames for login and logout attempts, and previous and new access rights for a change of access rights. Each entry in the audit log should be timestamped.

The audit process should not collect passwords. Collecting passwords creates a potential for a security breach if the audit records are improperly accessed. Neither correct nor incorrect passwords should be collected. An incorrect password often differs from the valid password by only a single character or transposition of characters.

A further extension of auditing is the concept of security assessment. With *security assessment*, the network is examined from within by professionals, trained in the vulnerabilities exploited by network invaders. Part of any security policy and audit procedure should be periodic assessments of the vulnerabilities in a network. The result should be a specific plan for correcting deficiencies, which might be as simple as retraining staff.

Data Encryption

Encryption is a process that scrambles data to protect it from being read by anyone but the intended receiver. An *encryption device* encrypts data before placing it on a network. A *decryption device* decrypts the data before passing it to an application. A router, server, end system, or dedicated device can act as an encryption or decryption device. Data that is encrypted is called *ciphered data* (or simply *encrypted data*). Data that is not encrypted is called *plain text* or *clear text*.

Encryption is a useful security feature for providing data confidentiality. It can also be used to identify the sender of data. Although authentication and authorization should also protect the confidentiality of data and identify senders, encryption is a good security feature to implement in case the other types of security fail.

There are performance tradeoffs associated with encryption, however, as mentioned in the "Analyzing Security Tradeoffs" section earlier in the chapter. Encryption should be used when a customer has analyzed security risks and identified severe consequences if data is not kept confidential and the identity of senders of data is not guaranteed. On internal networks and networks that use the Internet simply for web browsing, email, and file transfer, encryption is usually not necessary. For organizations that connect private sites via the Internet, using virtual private networking (VPN), encryption is recommended to protect the confidentiality of the organization's data.

Encryption has two parts:

- An *encryption algorithm* is a set of instructions to scramble and unscramble data.

- An *encryption key* is a code used by an algorithm to scramble and unscramble data.

Children sometimes play with encryption by using a simple algorithm such as "find the letter on the top row and use the letter on the bottom row instead," and a key that might look something like the following table:

A	B	C	D	E	F	G	H	I	J	K	L	M	N	O	P	Q	R	S	T	U	V	W	X	Y	Z
I	N	B	Y	G	L	S	P	T	A	R	W	Q	H	X	M	D	K	F	U	O	C	Z	V	E	J

In this example, LISA is encrypted as WTFI. The key shows only uppercase letters, but there are many other possibilities also, including lowercase letters, digits, and so on. Most algorithms are more complex than the one in the children's example to avoid having to maintain a key that includes a value for each possible character.

The goal of encryption is that even if the algorithm is known, without the appropriate key, an intruder cannot interpret the message. This type of key is called a *secret key*. When both the sender and receiver use the same secret key, it is called a *symmetric key*. The Data Encryption Standard (DES) is the best known example of a symmetric key system. DES encryption is available for most routers and many server implementations.

Although secret keys are reasonably simple to implement between two devices, as the number of devices increases, the number of secret keys increases, which can be hard to manage. For example, a session between Station A and Station B uses a different key than a session between Station A and Station C, or a session between Station B and Station C, and so on. Asymmetric keys can solve this problem.

Public/Private Key Encryption

Public/private key encryption is the best known example of an asymmetric key system. With public/private key systems, each secure station on a network has a public key that is openly published or easily determined. All devices can use a station's public key to encrypt data to send to the station.

The receiving station decrypts the data using its own private key. Because no other device has the station's private key, no other device can decrypt the data, so data confidentiality is maintained. Mathematicians and computer scientists have written computer programs that identify special numbers to use for the keys so that the same algorithm can be used by both the sender and receiver, even though different keys are used. Figure 8-1 shows a public/private key system for data confidentiality.

Figure 8-1   *Public/Private Key System for Ensuring Data Confidentiality*

Public/private key systems provide both confidentiality and authentication features. Using asymmetric keys, a recipient can verify that a document really came from the user or host that it appears to have come from. For example, suppose you are sending your tax returns to the Internal Revenue Service (IRS). The IRS needs to know that the returns came from you and not from a hostile third party that wants to make it look like you owe more than you do.

You can encrypt your document or a part of your document with your private key, resulting in what is known as a *digital signature*. The IRS can decrypt the document, using your public key, as shown in Figure 8-2. If the decryption is successful, the document came from you because nobody else should have your private key.

Figure 8-2   *Public/Private Key System for Sending a Digital Signature*

The digital signature feature of asymmetric keys can be used with the feature for data confidentiality. After encrypting your document with your private key, you can also encrypt the document with the IRS's public key. The IRS decrypts the document twice. If the result is plain-text data, the IRS knows that the document came from you and that you meant for the document to go to the IRS and not anyone else.

Some examples of asymmetric key systems include the Rivest, Shamir, and Adleman (RSA) standard, the Diffie-Hellman public key algorithm, and the Digital Signature Standard (DSS). Cisco uses the DSS standard to authenticate peer routers during the setup of an encrypted session. The peer routers use the Diffie-Hellman algorithm to send information on a secret key to use to encrypt data. The actual data is encrypted using the DES algorithm and the secret key.

Packet Filters

Packet filters can be set up on routers, firewalls, and servers to accept or deny packets from particular addresses or services. Packet filters augment authentication and authorization mechanisms. They help protect network resources from unauthorized use, theft, destruction, and DoS attacks.

A security policy should state whether packet filters implement one or the other of the following policies:

- Deny specific types of packets and accept all else

- Accept specific types of packets and deny all else

The first policy requires a thorough understanding of specific security threats and can be hard to implement. The second policy is easier to implement and more secure because the security administrator does not have to predict future attacks for which packets should be denied. The second policy is also easier to test because there is a finite set of accepted uses of the network. To do a good job implementing the second policy requires a good understanding of network requirements. The network designer should work with the security administrator to determine what types of packets should be accepted.

Cisco implements the second policy in its packet filters, which Cisco calls *access control lists (ACL)*. An ACL on a router or switch running Cisco IOS Software always has an implicit deny-all statement at the end. Specific accept statements are processed before the implicit deny-all statement. (The statement is implicit because the administrator does not have to actually enter it, although it is a good idea to enter it to make the behavior of the list more obvious.)

ACLs let you control whether network traffic is forwarded or blocked at interfaces on a router or switch. ACL definitions provide criteria that are applied to packets that enter or exit an interface. Typical criteria are the packet source address, the packet destination address, or the upper-layer protocol in the packet.

Because Cisco IOS Software tests a packet against each criteria statement in the list until a match is found, ACLs should be designed with care to provide good performance. By studying traffic flow, you can design the list so that most packets match the earliest conditions. Fewer conditions to check per packet means better throughput. Good advice for designing ACLs is to order the list with the most general statements at the top and the most specific statements at the bottom, with the last statement being the general, implicit deny-all statement.

Firewalls

As discussed in Chapter 5, a *firewall* is a device that enforces security policies at the boundary between two or more networks. A firewall can be a router with ACLs, a dedicated hardware appliance, or software running on a PC or UNIX system. Firewalls are especially important at the boundary between the enterprise network and the Internet.

A firewall has a set of rules that specifies which traffic should be allowed or denied. A *static stateless packet-filter firewall* looks at individual packets and is optimized for speed and configuration simplicity. A *stateful firewall* can track communication sessions and more intelligently allow or deny traffic. For example, a stateful firewall can remember that a protected client initiated a request to download data from an Internet server and allow data back in for that connection. A stateful firewall can also work with protocols, such as active (port-mode) FTP, that require the server to also open a connection to the client.

Another type of firewall is a *proxy firewall*. Proxy firewalls are the most advanced type of firewall but also the least common. A proxy firewall acts as an intermediary between hosts, intercepting some or all application traffic between local clients and outside servers. Proxy firewalls examine packets and support stateful tracking of sessions. These types of firewalls can block malicious traffic and content that is deemed unacceptable.

Intrusion Detection and Prevention Systems

An intrusion detection system (IDS) detects malicious events and notifies an administrator, using email, paging, or logging of the occurrence. An IDS can also perform statistical and anomaly analysis. Some IDS devices can report to a central database that correlates information from multiple sensors to give an administrator an overall view of the real-time security of a network. An intrusion prevention system (IPS) can dynamically block traffic by adding rules to a firewall or by being configured to inspect (and deny or allow) traffic as it enters a firewall. An IPS is an IDS that can detect and prevent attacks.

There are two types of IDS devices:

- **Host IDS:** Resides on an individual host and monitors that host.

- **Network IDS:** Monitors all network traffic that it can see, watching for predefined signatures of malicious events. A network IDS is often placed on a subnet that is directly connected to a firewall so that it can monitor the traffic that has been allowed and look for suspicious activity.

In the past a major concern with both IDS and IPS devices was the volume of false alarms that they tended to generate. A false alarm occurs when an IDS or IPS reports a network event as a serious problem when it actually isn't a problem. This false-alarm problem has been ameliorated by sophisticated software and services on modern IPS devices. Cisco IPS solutions, for example, include anomaly detection that learns about typical actual network traffic on a customer's network and alarms only upon deviation from that traffic.

Cisco also supports reputation filtering and global correlation services so that an IPS can keep up-to-date on global security trends and more accurately deny traffic from networks known to be currently associated with botnets, spam, and other malware.

Modularizing Security Design

Security experts promote the *security defense in depth* principle. This principle states that network security should be multilayered, with many different techniques used to protect the network. No security mechanism can be guaranteed to withstand every attack. Therefore, each mechanism should have a backup mechanism. This is sometimes called the *belt-and-suspenders approach*. Both a belt and suspenders ensure that trousers stay up. A networking example is to use a dedicated firewall to limit access to resources and a packet-filtering router that adds another line of defense.

As part of implementing security defense in depth, security design should be modular. Multiple methods should be designed and applied to different parts of the network, whether it be the Internet connection, the wireless infrastructure, or the remote-access component. Cisco provides a modular approach with its SAFE security reference architecture (described in Chapter 5).

In general, using a modular approach to security design is a good way to gain an understanding of the types of solutions that must be selected to implement security defense in depth. The next few sections cover security for the following modules or components of an enterprise network:

- Internet connections

- Remote-access and virtual private networks (VPN)

- Network services and management

- Server farms

- User services

- Wireless networks

Securing Internet Connections

Internet connections should be secured with a set of overlapping security mechanisms, including firewalls, packet filters, physical security, audit logs, authentication, and authorization. Internet routers should be equipped with packet filters to prevent DoS and other attacks. These filters should be backed up with additional filters placed on firewall devices. The Internet connection should be carefully monitored. Network and host IDS devices should monitor subnets, routers, and Internet-accessible servers to detect signs of attack or malicious network activity and identify successful breaches into the protected network.

A good rule for enterprise networks is that the network should have well-defined exit and entry points. An organization that has only one Internet connection can manage Internet security problems more easily than an organization that has many Internet connections. Some large organizations require more than one Internet connection for performance and redundancy reasons, however. This is fine as long as the connections are managed and monitored. Departments or users who add Internet connections without coordination from corporate network engineers should not be tolerated.

A common risk associated with the Internet connection is reconnaissance threats from the Internet, whereby an attacker attempts to probe the network and its hosts to discover reachable networks, hosts, and services running on exposed hosts, and to develop a network map. To manage the risk of reconnaissance attempts, routers and first-line firewall devices should block all incoming connections, except those necessary to reach specific services on public servers or to complete a transaction started by a trusted client. The routers and firewalls should also block packets typically used for reconnaissance threats, such as pings.

When selecting routing protocols for the Internet connection and for routers that inject Internet routes into the interior network, you should select a protocol that offers route authentication such as Routing Information Protocol version 2 (RIPv2), Open Shortest Path First (OSPF), Enhanced Interior Gateway Routing Protocol (EIGRP), or Border Gateway Protocol, version 4 (BGP4). Static and default routing is also a good option because with static and default routing there are no routing updates that could be compromised.

When securing the Internet connection, Network Address Translation (NAT) can be used to protect internal network addressing schemes. As discussed in Chapter 6, "Designing Models for Addressing and Naming," NAT hides internal network numbers from outside networks. NAT translates internal network numbers when outside access is required.

Securing Public Servers

Most companies have a need for public servers that are accessible from the Internet. These include World Wide Web, File Transfer Protocol (FTP), Domain Name System (DNS), email, and e-commerce servers. Public servers should be placed on a demilitarized zone (DMZ) network that is protected from other networks via firewalls. DMZ networks were discussed in more detail in Chapter 5.

To protect public servers from DoS attacks, server administrators should use reliable operating systems and applications that have been patched with the most recent security fixes. Adding Common Gateway Interface (CGI) or other types of scripts to servers should be done with great care. Scripts should be thoroughly tested for security leaks.

Public servers should run firewall software and be configured for DoS protection. For example, the server should be configured to limit the number of connection establishments that can occur in a particular timeframe. Servers should also run software that can examine the content carried by application protocols so that the software can scan, and possibly eliminate, dangerous content such as viruses or mobile code. (*Mobile code* is software that can be transmitted across a network and executed on another device.)

If a customer can afford two separate servers, security experts recommend that FTP services not run on the same server as web services. FTP users have more opportunities for reading and possibly changing files than web users do. A hacker could use FTP to damage a company's web pages, thus damaging the company's image and possibly compromising web-based electronic commerce and other applications. Security experts recommend never allowing Internet access to Trivial File Transfer Protocol (TFTP) servers, because TFTP offers no authentication features.

Email servers have long been a source for intruder break-ins, probably because email protocols and implementations have been around a long time and hackers can easily understand them. Also, by its very nature, an email server must allow outsider access. To secure email servers, network administrators should keep current on well-known bugs and security leaks by subscribing to mailing lists dedicated to security information.

DNS servers should be carefully controlled and monitored. Name-to-address resolution is critical to the operation of any network. An attacker who can successfully control or impersonate a DNS server can wreak havoc on a network. DNS servers should be protected from security attacks by packet filters on routers and versions of DNS software that incorporate security features.

Traditionally, DNS had no security capabilities. In particular, there was no way to verify information returned in a DNS response to a query. A hacker could hijack the query and return a counterfeit name-to-address mapping. Digital signatures and other security features are being added to the protocol to address this issue and other security concerns. Refer to RFC 4033, "DNS Security Introduction and Requirements," and its companion documents, RFC 4034 and RFC 4035, for more information.

Securing E-Commerce Servers

E-commerce servers are vulnerable to the same attacks that threaten all public servers, but a compromise of an e-commerce server results in more substantial loss because these servers hold highly confidential and sensitive customer and financial data. E-commerce servers are often targets of DoS attacks, directed at their operating systems or applications. E-commerce servers must be protected from DoS attacks with packet-filtering rules and rules that deny successive connection attempts in a short period of time. They should also be protected from attackers who want to compromise them to launch an attack on other servers, including other e-commerce servers.

In some network designs, e-commerce applications run on multiple servers. For example, an e-commerce application front-end web server accepts encrypted sessions from Internet clients, processes the requests, and queries a database server, which holds sensitive customer and financial data. For optimum protection of sensitive data, and to avoid a compromised server attacking another server, you can separate the servers into their own DMZ networks. For example, design the topology so that there is a firewall that protects the database server from the front-end web server, in case the web server is compromised. Servers on the same segment can also be separated by LAN switch access control mechanisms (such as private VLANs). Network and host IDS devices should monitor subnets and individual servers to detect signs of attacks and confirm successful breaches.

Securing Remote-Access and VPNs

To support mobile users, many enterprise networks include remote-access technologies, VPN concentrators, and site-to-site VPN gateways. The users' data is sent over public networks, such as the Public Switched Telephone Network (PSTN) and the Internet, so protecting the data from eavesdropping is important. Protecting from identity spoofing of remote clients or sites is also important, to avoid an attacker impersonating a legitimate client and logging in to the network. This can happen if an attacker steals a legitimate user's credentials (such as a username and password pair) or learns the authentication keys used on a VPN connection.

Securing Remote-Access Technologies

Security is critical for remote-access technologies and should consist of firewall technologies, physical security, authentication and authorization mechanisms, auditing, and possibly encryption. Authentication and authorization are the most important features and can be implemented with the Challenge Handshake Authentication Protocol (CHAP) and the Remote Authentication Dial-In User Service (RADIUS) protocol.

Remote users and remote routers that use the Point-to-Point Protocol (PPP) should be authenticated with CHAP. The Password Authentication Protocol (PAP), which offers less security than CHAP, is not recommended. The "Remote-Access Technologies" section of Chapter 11, "Selecting Technologies and Devices for Enterprise Networks," covers PPP, CHAP, and PAP in more detail.

Another option for authentication, authorization, and accounting is *RADIUS*. Livingston, Inc., developed RADIUS, which has become an industry standard and is documented in RFC 2865. RADIUS gives an administrator the option of having a centralized database of user information. The database includes authentication and configuration information and specifies the type of service permitted by a user (for example, PPP, Telnet, rlogin, and so on). RADIUS is a client/server protocol. An access server acts as a client of a RADIUS server.

Dialup services should be strictly controlled. Users should not be allowed to attach modems and analog lines to their own workstations or servers. (Some companies actually fire employees who do this.) If some remote users still need to dial in to the network using a modem and analog telephone line, it's helpful to have a single dial-in point (for example, a single modem pool or access server) so that all users are authenticated in the same way. A different set of modems should be used for any dial-out services. Both dial-in and dial-out services should be authenticated.

There are many operational security considerations with dialup networks, and if possible, dialup networks should be eliminated from modern networks. If that is not possible, modems and access servers should be carefully configured and protected from hackers reconfiguring them. Modems should be programmed to reset to the standard configuration at the start and end of each call, and modems and access servers should terminate calls cleanly. Servers should force a logout if the user hangs up unexpectedly.

If the modems and access servers support callback (which most do), callback should be used. With *callback*, when a user dials in and is authenticated, the system disconnects the call and calls back on a specified number. Callback is useful because the system calls back the actual user, not a hacker who might be masquerading as the user. Callback can easily be compromised, however, and should not be the only security mechanism used.

Securing VPNs

Organizations that use VPNs to connect private sites and end users via a public network such as the Internet should use NAT, firewalls, strong authentication, and data encryption. The client operating systems that connect via the VPN should use personal firewall and virus protection software. It is important to protect against a compromise of a client or remote site that allows an attacker to successfully attack the enterprise network over the VPN. An example is a VPN client that has been compromised by a Trojan horse that turns the client system into a relay. Such an attack could mean that when the client is connected to the enterprise network via an Internet remote-access VPN, the attacker can connect to the client over the Internet, and then from the client connect to the protected enterprise network.

In VPN topologies, private data travels across a public network, so encryption is a must. The most common solution for encryption is to use the IP Security Protocol (IPsec), which is an Internet Engineering Task Force (IETF) standard that provides data confidentiality, data integrity, and authentication between participating peers at the IP layer. IPsec provides a secure path between remote users and a VPN concentrator, and between remote sites and a VPN site-to-site gateway.

Numerous RFCs deal with Ipsec, and many Internet drafts. To learn IPsec better, the main RFCs you should read are as follows:

- RFC 4301, "Security Architecture for the Internet Protocol"

- RFC 4302, "IP Authentication Header"

- RFC 4303, "IP Encapsulating Security Payload (ESP)"

- RFC 4306, "Internet Security Association and Key Management Protocol (ISAKMP)"

IPsec enables a system to select security protocols and algorithms, and establish cryptographic keys. The Internet Key Exchange (IKE) protocol provides authentication of IPsec peers. It also negotiates IPsec keys and security associations. IKE uses the following technologies:

- **DES:** Encrypts packet data.

- **Diffie-Hellman:** Establishes a shared, secret, session key.

- **Message Digest 5 (MD5):** A hash algorithm that authenticates packet data.

- **Secure Hash Algorithm (SHA):** A hash algorithm that authenticates packet data.

- **RSA encrypted nonces:** Provides repudiation.

- **RSA signatures:** Provides nonrepudiation.

Securing Network Services and Network Management

To protect internal network services, it is important to protect internal internetworking devices, such as routers and switches. You should treat each network device as a high-value host and harden (strengthen) it against possible intrusions. This involves common practices such as running only the minimal necessary services and establishing trust only with authentic partners. For example, a router should not accept routing updates from a router that has not been authenticated. Routing protocols that support authentication should be selected, including RIPv2, OSPF, EIGRP, and BGP4. Static and default routes are also a good choice because they eliminate the need to accept routing updates.

Login IDs and passwords should be required for accessing routers and switches, whether the user accesses the device via a console port or via the network. A first-level password can be used for administrators that simply need to check the status of the devices. A second-level password should be used for administrators who have permission to view or change configurations. Avoid using a nonsecure protocol such as Telnet to access routers and switches over a network. A better choice is Secure Shell (SSH).

When administrators (or hackers posing as administrators) connect to a router or switch, they should not see the typical connect message, which often says something simple, such as Welcome to This Router. Instead, a router or switch should display warnings about authorized usage and the monitoring of all activity on the device. Many security experts recommend getting help from a lawyer when writing the connect message.

If modem access to the console ports of internetworking devices is allowed, the modems must be secured just as standard dial-in user modems are, and the phone numbers should be unlisted and unrelated to the organization's main number(s). The phone numbers should also be changed when there is staff turnover.

For customers with numerous routers and switches, a protocol such as the *Terminal Access Controller Access Control System (TACACS)* can be used to manage large numbers of router and switch user IDs and passwords in a centralized database. TACACS also offers auditing features, which can be helpful when an inexperienced network administrator tries to avoid responsibility for a misconfiguration that led to a security incident.

To protect against the misconfiguration of devices by hackers (or inexperienced network administrators), you can enforce authorization on specific configuration commands. TACACS and other authorization methods can be configured to permit only specific administrators to enter risky commands, such as commands to change IP addresses or ACLs. The use of a well-managed, centralized change-control process is also recommended.

Limiting use of the Simple Network Management Protocol (SNMP) should be considered on enterprise networks for which security goals outweigh manageability goals. One of the main issues with SNMP is the **set** operation, which allows a remote station to change management and configuration data. If SNMPv3 is used, this is not as big a concern, because SNMPv3 supports authentication for use with the **set** operation and other SNMP operations.

Network management systems should be especially protected because they host extremely sensitive data about network and security device configuration. Moreover, network management systems are sometimes connected to other devices over a separate (out-of-band) management network, which, without careful design, could provide a path around security mechanisms such as firewalls.

To minimize risk, network management systems should be placed in their own DMZ behind a firewall. They should run a hardened operating system that has been patched with the latest security fixes. All unnecessary services should be disabled.

As is the case with routers and switches, network management systems must be protected from the impersonation of administrators, where an attacker steals the credentials (usernames or passwords) of an administrator. To manage the risk of administrator impersonation, provide the administrator with strong authentication mechanisms. A good example is a two-factor, one-time password system based on security cards.

Securing Server Farms

Server farms host file, print, database, and application servers inside campus networks and branch offices. These servers often contain an enterprise's most sensitive information, so they must be protected. Because servers are accessed by a large number of users, network performance is usually a critical issue, which can limit the choice of protection mechanisms. Nonetheless, methods should be deployed to protect against the compromise of exposed applications and unauthorized access to data. Network and host IDS devices should be deployed to monitor subnets and individual servers to detect signs of attacks and confirm successful breaches.

When servers in a server farm are compromised, attackers can use those servers to attack other servers. To manage this risk, configure network filters that limit connectivity from the server. In many cases, a server has no need to initiate connections. Connection establishments generally come from the client. There are numerous exceptions, however, which can be programmed into filters. For example, with active (port-mode) FTP, the server initiates a connection. Also, various network management, naming, resource-location, and authentication and authorization protocols might require the server to initiate a connection. As part of the top-down network design process, you should have analyzed the protocols present in server farm locations (see Chapter 3, "Characterizing the Existing Internetwork" and Chapter 4, "Characterizing Network Traffic" for more information). The data you gathered can help you determine which protocols a server will need to allow.

To maximize security, both server and end-user software should be carefully selected and maintained. Server and desktop administrators should be required to keep current as to the latest hacker tricks and viruses. Known security bugs in operating systems should be identified and fixed. In addition, application software should be selected based partly on its adherence to modern, secure programming practices. With the creation of safer high-level programming languages and increasing programmer awareness of security issues, many applications are available that are reasonably secure. Most stock software, which is still used by many businesses, is vulnerable to simple attacks to defeat its security, however.

For customers with stringent security requirements, server applications might incorporate encryption. This is in addition to any client/server encryption used to protect data traveling across a network. To protect against the unauthorized use of data, cryptographic methods can protect data on a disk drive. For example, the data on disk drives can be encrypted so that it can be read only by the proper application.

File and other servers should provide authentication and authorization features. Security policies and procedures should specify accepted practices regarding passwords: when they should be used, how they should be formatted, and how they can be changed. In general, passwords should include both letters and numbers, be at least six characters, not be a common word, and be changed often.

On servers, root password knowledge (or the non-UNIX equivalent) should be limited to a few people. Guest accounts should be avoided if possible. Protocols that support the concept of *trust* in other hosts should be used with caution (examples include rlogin and rsh on UNIX systems). Hosts that permit guest accounts and support trusted hosts should be isolated from other hosts if possible.

Kerberos is an authentication system that provides user-to-host security for application-level protocols such as FTP and Telnet. If requested by the application, Kerberos can also provide encryption. Kerberos relies on a symmetric key database that uses a key distribution center (KDC) on a Kerberos server.

Securing User Services

A security policy should specify which applications are allowed to run on networked PCs and restrict the downloading of unknown applications from the Internet or other sites. The security policy should also require that PCs have personal firewall and antivirus software installed. Security procedures should specify how this software is installed and kept current.

Users should be encouraged to log out of their sessions with servers when leaving their desks for long periods of time and to turn off their machines when leaving work, to protect against unauthorized people walking up to a system and accessing services and applications. Automatic logouts can also be deployed to automatically log out a session that has had no activity for a period of time.

One other aspect of securing the end-user part of a network is ensuring that users connect only permitted computers or other devices to the LAN interfaces in their offices. In particular, one area of concern is users who connect wireless access points that are not properly secured. These unauthorized access points are sometimes called *rogue access points*. Security for wireless networks, which is discussed in more detail in the next section, should not be left to end users. It should be carefully planned and implemented and not compromised by users installing their own wireless access points.

Cisco and other vendors support an IEEE standard called 802.1X, which provides port-based security on switch ports. With 802.1X enabled on a switch port, no device can connect to the network without first using 802.1X to authenticate. This is one method for ensuring that a user doesn't install an unknown device, such as a wireless access point. With this use of 802.1X, it is the access point that is authenticated. Another use of 802.1X is to authenticate wireless client devices, such as laptops. When a legitimate wireless infrastructure is in place, 802.1X is no longer needed on the ports that connect known access points, but it can be used to authenticate wireless users, as discussed later in the "802.1X with Extensible Authentication Protocol" section of this chapter.

Securing Wireless Networks

Wireless networks are gaining widespread popularity in enterprise campus networks, at branch offices, and in home offices. Most organizations support the increases in productivity and employee satisfaction that wireless networking offers but at the same time are concerned about the security risks, as they should be. In recent years, glaring holes have been discovered in the typical methods used for wireless security, resulting in the development of new methods and models for providing security on wireless networks. This section covers some overall design guidelines first and then includes information on the following two topics:

- Authentication in wireless networks

- Data privacy in wireless networks

As mentioned in Chapter 5, it is best to place wireless LANs (WLAN) in their own subnet and their own VLAN. This simplifies addressing for stations that roam and also improves management and security. Keeping all wireless clients in their own subnet makes it easier to set up traffic filters to protect wired clients from an attack launched on the wireless network. To maximize roaming flexibility, all WLANs can be a single VLAN and IP subnet, so that there is no need to retrieve a new IP address when moving from one area to another. To maximize security, however, it might be wiser to subdivide the WLAN into multiple VLANs and IP subnets.

Keep in mind that security requirements for wireless users vary with the type of user. Guests who visit an enterprise might need easy access to the Internet but should be prevented from accessing the enterprise network. These guests cannot be expected to know an encryption key or to have VPN software installed. This is different from the employees who want wireless access while having lunch in the cafeteria or while meeting in private conference rooms. Those users could be expected to know a key or to have the corporate-approved VPN software installed. The use of VLANs comes in handy here. When you understand the different user types and where they might roam, you can divide the WLAN into multiple VLANs and apply security policies separately for each VLAN.

You should implement ACLs on wireless access points and on wired switches and routers that carry traffic that originated on a wireless network. The ACLs should allow only specific protocols, in accordance with security policies.

All wireless (and wired) laptop computers should be required to run antivirus and personal firewall software. They should also be regularly updated with the most recent operating system security patches. Depending on security requirements, you might also want to require corporate wireless laptop users to use VPN software to access the enterprise network. The final section in this chapter, "Using VPN Software on Wireless Clients," discusses using IPsec VPN software as a security option for wireless networks.

Authentication in Wireless Networks

In a wired Ethernet LAN, a device must physically plug into the network to communicate. This fundamental feature of a wired Ethernet is not present in the realm of wireless networking, however. There is nothing to plug in. The IEEE 802.11 standard provides a method for devices to authenticate to a wireless access point, thus emulating the basic security provided by a wired network where a user must have physical access to a port to communicate.

Authentication takes place after a wireless client has located an access point with a sufficiently strong signal and selected a channel. The 802.11 client initialization process consists of the following steps:

Step 1.   The client broadcasts a Probe Request frame on every channel.

Step 2.   Access points within range respond with a Probe Response frame.

Step 3.   The client decides which access point is the best for access and sends an Authentication Request frame.

Step 4.   The access point sends an Authentication Response frame.

Step 5.   Upon successful authentication, the client sends an Association Request frame to the access point.

Step 6.   The access point replies with an Association Response frame. The client can now pass traffic to the access point.

IEEE 802.11 specifies two forms of authentication: *open* and *shared key*. With open authentication, the client is always authenticated as long as the access point has been configured to allow open authentication. This is the default mode for most systems. Open authentication can be thought of as null authentication. The client asks to be authenticated and the access point permits the authentication. It might sound pointless to use such an algorithm, but open authentication has its place in 802.11 networks. Open authentication is often used for guest access, where it would be impractical to provide users with a key. Also, many 802.11-compliant devices are handheld data-acquisition units, such as barcode readers. They do not have the CPU capabilities required for complex authentication algorithms.

With shared key authentication, a Wired Equivalent Privacy (WEP) static key must be properly configured in both the client and the access point. The steps for shared key authentication are as follows:

Step 1.   The client sends an Authentication Request to the access point requesting shared key authentication.

Step 2.   The access point responds with an Authentication Response containing challenge text.

Step 3.   The client uses its locally configured WEP key to encrypt the challenge text and replies with another Authentication Request.

Step 4.   If the access point can decrypt the Authentication Request and retrieve the original challenge text, the client must be using the correct WEP key, so the access point responds with an Authentication Response that grants the client access.

In August 2001, cryptanalysts Fluhrer, Mantin, and Shamir determined that a WEP key can be derived by passively collecting particular frames from a wireless LAN. Researchers at AT&T and Rice University and the developers of the AirSnort application implemented the vulnerability and verified that either 64- or 128-bit WEP keys can be derived after as few as 4 million frames. For high-usage wireless LANs, this translates to roughly 4 hours until a 128-bit WEP key can be derived.

In addition to WEP's vulnerability to passive attacks, WEP is also vulnerable to inductive key derivation, which is the process of deriving a key by coercing information from the wireless LAN. Man-in-the-middle attacks, a form of inductive key derivation, are effective in 802.11 networks because of the lack of effective message integrity. The receiver of a frame cannot verify that the frame was not tampered with during its transmission.

The shared WEP key, as specified by IEEE 802.11, is a static key. If the key is discovered by an unauthorized user, it must be changed on access points and every individual client. Attackers can discover the key in many ways, including eavesdropping on numerous packets, but also by using simpler methods, such as asking naive users for the key or stealing users' laptop computers where the key is configured.

The 802.11 specification stipulates only the two mechanisms for authenticating wireless devices that have already been discussed: open authentication and shared key authentication. Other mechanisms that are also commonly used include setting an unpublished Service Set Identifier (SSID), authenticating devices by their client Media Access Control

(MAC) address, and using 802.1X with the Extensible Authentication Protocol (EAP). These are described in the next three sections.

Using an Unpublished Service Set Identifier

Every WLAN has an SSID that identifies it. To gain access to a wireless LAN, a client must know the correct SSID. Some network administrators rely on this as a method for security even though it doesn't truly authenticate the client and doesn't provide any data privacy. Also, an eavesdropper can easily determine the SSID with the use of a wireless protocol analyzer. The SSID is advertised in plain text in beacon messages that the access point sends.

Some access point vendors, including Cisco, offer the option to disable SSID broadcasts in beacon messages, but this does not offer much protection. The SSID can still be determined by analyzing Probe Response frames from an access point. Also, disabling SSID broadcasts might have an adverse effect on wireless interoperability for mixed-vendor deployments. Therefore, most experts do not recommend using the SSID as a mode of security.

MAC Address Authentication

MAC address authentication verifies a client's MAC address against a configured list of allowed addresses. MAC address authentication is used to augment the open and shared key authentications provided by 802.11, further reducing the likelihood of unauthorized devices accessing the network. Depending on the access point, the list of MAC addresses might be locally configured on the access point, or the access point might use an authentication protocol such as RADIUS and an external authentication server. A server is helpful for large installations where configuring individual access points would be difficult. If a server is used, redundancy must be considered so that the server does not become a single point of failure.

MAC addresses are sent as clear text per the 802.11 specification. As a result, in wireless LANs that use MAC address authentication, a network attacker might be able to subvert the MAC authentication process by spoofing a valid MAC address. Network attackers can use a protocol analyzer to determine valid MAC addresses that are being used in the network and change their own wireless NICs to use that address (on NICs that support changing the MAC address).

MAC address authentication is labor-intensive. A network administrator must know the address of every allowed NIC and configure this into the access point or server. Also, as mentioned, hackers can get around MAC address authentication by changing their own address to match an allowed address. Therefore, most experts do not recommend relying on MAC address authentication as the only mode of security.

802.1X with Extensible Authentication Protocol

IEEE 802.1X specifies a method for authenticating and authorizing a device attached to a LAN port. It is used on both wired switches and on wireless access points (where the "attachment" is not physical). 802.1X provides optional support for use of an authentication server, such as a RADIUS server, which is recommended for larger installations.

802.1X is extensible and supports a variety of authentication algorithms. The most common are varieties of EAP, which is an IETF standard, documented in RFC 2284. With 802.1X and EAP, devices take on one of three roles:

■ The supplicant resides on the wireless LAN client.

■ The authenticator resides on the access point.

■ An authentication server resides on a RADIUS server.

When 802.1X and EAP are implemented, a client that associates with an access point cannot use the network until the user is authenticated. After association, the client and the network (access point or RADIUS server) exchange EAP messages to perform authentication. An EAP supplicant on the client obtains credentials from the user, which could be a user ID and password, a user ID and one-time password, or a digital certificate. The credentials are passed to the authenticator or server and a session key is developed.

With 802.1X and EAP, session timeouts force a client to reauthenticate to maintain network connectivity. Although reauthentication is transparent to the client, the process of reauthentication generates new WEP keys at every reauthentication interval. This is important for mitigating statistical key derivation attacks and is a critical WEP enhancement. One disadvantage of 802.1X with EAP, however, is that reauthentication can cause some delay, when compared to using a static WEP key. This might cause a problem for users that roam with delay-sensitive devices, such as 802.11 phones.

Note that EAP authenticates users. Whereas 802.11 authentication is device-based, EAP is based on authenticating a user rather than a wireless LAN device. This avoids the problems caused by theft of a laptop computer using a static WEP key, which would allow the thief access to the network and would probably result in a network administrator needing to change the WEP key on the affected access points and all clients. EAP generates unique keying material for each user. This relieves network administrators from the burden of managing static keys. EAP also supports mutual authentication, which allows a client to be certain that it is communicating with the intended authentication server.

Selecting the right EAP implementation can be a challenging process due to the large number of options. The funny-sounding names, such as LEAP and PEAP, don't help matters. You must get this right though. The supplicant, authenticator, and authentication server must all support the same variety of EAP, which is mostly likely one of the following:

■ **Lightweight EAP (LEAP):** Developed by Cisco and is sometimes called *EAP-Cisco*. Cisco licenses LEAP to other vendors, including Apple Computer and Intel. LEAP supports user-based authentication and dynamic WEP keys that are generated after authentication and when session timeouts occur. User authentication is based on a user's Windows logon, which means the user does not have to supply additional logon information to access the wireless network, which makes LEAP easy to use. LEAP supports mutual authentication, which means that the client authenticates the server and the server authenticates the client. This is important for ensuring that the client talks to an authorized server and not a hacker posing as a server.

- **EAP-Transport Layer Security (EAP-TLS):** Developed by Microsoft and is documented in RFC 2716. Microsoft supports EAP-TLS in all versions of Windows XP and has released a free Windows 2000 client. Like LEAP, EAP-TLS supports mutual authentication, dynamic keys, and session timeouts. EAP-TLS requires certificates for clients and servers. Because of this, some users consider Microsoft's EAP to be more secure than other EAPs. However, the certificate requirement also means EAP-TLS needs certificate management, such as the use of a trusted certificate authority and the ability to quickly revoke certificates.

- **EAP-Tunneled TLS (EAP-TTLS):** Developed by Funk and Certicom and then turned over to the IETF, where it is currently (as of this writing) a standards-based Internet draft. EAP-TTLS is an enhancement of EAP-TLS, with support for advanced authentication methods such as token cards. A variety of vendors have signed on to support EAP-TTLS.

- **Protected EAP (PEAP):** Supported by Cisco, Microsoft, and RSA Security. Like LEAP and EAP-TLS, PEAP supports mutual authentication, dynamic keys, and session timeouts. PEAP uses a certificate for the client to authenticate the RADIUS server. The server uses a one-time password or a username and password to authenticate the client. When the client validates the server's certificate, it builds an encrypted tunnel and then uses EAP in the tunnel to authenticate. PEAP is more manageable and scalable than EAP-TLS. Organizations can avoid installing digital certificates on every client machine, as required by EAP-TLS, and select the method of client authentication that best suits them.

- **EAP-MD5:** Has no key management features or dynamic key generation. Although EAP-MD5 is supported on many platforms, it will probably be phased out of most wireless networks because it has few benefits over WEP.

Data Privacy in Wireless Networks

Previous sections discussed methods for authenticating a wireless device (or the user of a wireless device). Another important requirement for wireless networks is data privacy. The original IEEE 802.11 standard specified WEP as the method for encrypting data to meet privacy requirements. Unfortunately, WEP has been shown to be ineffective as a data-privacy mechanism because of the many ways of compromising it. Cisco and other vendors implemented many enhancements to WEP, which IEEE standardized as part of its IEEE 802.11i standard.

One set of enhancements that addresses the shortcomings with WEP is known as the Temporal Key Integrity Protocol (TKIP). TKIP provides the following:

- A message integrity check (MIC), which provides effective frame authenticity to mitigate man-in-the-middle vulnerabilities

- Per-packet keying, which provides every frame with a new and unique WEP key that mitigates WEP key derivation attacks

In addition to TKIP, the IEEE recognized the need for stronger encryption mechanisms and adopted the use of the Advanced Encryption Standard (AES) for the data-privacy section of the 802.11i standard. The development of AES was facilitated by the National Institute of Standards and Technology (NIST), which solicited the cryptography community for new encryption algorithms. The algorithms had to be fully disclosed and available royalty free. The NIST judged candidates on cryptographic strength as well as practical implementation. The finalist, and adopted method, is known as the Rijndael algorithm. The Rijndael algorithm provides for a variety of key sizes, including 128, 192, and 256 bits.

Wi-Fi Protected Access

Another development that is related to 802.11i and wireless security is Wi-Fi Protected Access (WPA). WPA is a subset of the 802.11i standard that was adopted by the Wi-Fi Alliance. The Wi-Fi Alliance is a nonprofit international association formed in 1999 to certify interoperability of wireless products based on IEEE 802.11 specifications.

The Wi-Fi Alliance introduced WPA because 802.11i was not ratified yet and also because 802.11i was expected to include specifications that would eventually require hardware upgrades for some devices. The Wi-Fi Alliance decided to introduce a subset of the specification that was stable and could be achieved via software upgrades.

WPA uses 802.1X with EAP for authentication and TKIP for data encryption. For enterprise networks, WPA should be used with an authentication server, such as a RADIUS server, to provide centralized access control and management. In small and home offices, WPA allows the use of manually entered keys or passwords. The small or home office user enters a password (also called a *master key* or a *preshared key*) in the access point and each client, and WPA takes over from there. The password ensures that only devices with a matching password can join the network. Entering a correct password also starts the TKIP encryption process.

In some configurations, a WPA1 option is distinguished from a WPA2 option. WPA1 uses TKIP and predates 802.11i. WPA2 uses AES and is compatible with 802.11i. Another distinction is WPA Personal versus WPA Enterprise. WPA Personal uses preshared keys and is appropriate for home or small office networks. WPA Enterprise uses a RADIUS server and is appropriate for larger business networks.

Using VPN Software on Wireless Clients

Although EAP and WPA solve many of the problems with WEP, they can be difficult to implement, especially in multivendor environments. Another option for customers with a strong need to protect data confidentiality is to use VPN software on the wireless clients. With this solution, the clients reach the campus network by connecting to a VPN concentrator. VPN software that uses IPsec has many advantages, including Triple Data Encryption Standard (3DES) encryption, one-time password support, and support for per-user policies.

When VPN software is installed, WLAN clients still associate with a wireless access point to establish connectivity at Layer 2. The clients then establish connectivity at Layer 3 using DHCP and DNS. The clients establish a VPN tunnel to a VPN concentrator to securely communicate with the campus network.

The wireless network should be considered an untrusted network, suitable only as a transit network for IPsec traffic once a VPN tunnel has been established. To isolate the untrusted wireless network, administrators should place the WLAN users in their own VLAN. The wireless clients should also run personal firewall software to protect them while they are connected to the untrusted WLAN network without the protection of IPsec.

Another protection mechanism is a feature called *Publicly Secure Packet Forwarding (PSPF)*, which prevents WLAN clients on the same access point from communicating with each other (or attacking each other). PSPF provides Internet access to clients without providing other typical LAN services, such as the capability to share files.

To minimize security threats, you should configure the wireless access point to allow only the protocols required for establishing a secure tunnel to a VPN concentrator. These protocols include DHCP for initial client configuration, DNS for name resolution, and IPsec VPN-specific protocols—IP protocol 50 for ESP and UDP port 500 for IKE. (The DNS traffic is necessary only if the VPN client accesses the VPN gateway by name.)

Despite the assurance of data privacy that IPsec provides, an IPsec VPN solution for wireless security has some disadvantages. For example, some VPN software requires the user to start the software and provide additional logon information before accessing the campus network. Roaming from one area to another might require the acquisition of a new IP address or a mobile IP solution. Also, when 3DES encryption is provided in software, users may notice a performance degradation.

In general, IPsec VPN in a wireless network has the same disadvantages that it has in wired networks, including diminished ease of use and performance, configuration complexity, the need for local software to be installed on the client computers, interoperability problems with various applications, the lack of support for multicast applications, and the fact that IPsec is an IP-only solution. Also, handheld devices, including 802.11 phones, might not support IPsec.

Understanding the needs of the various user communities and their applications will help you decide whether IPsec should be required instead of (or in addition to) the wireless security measures discussed in the previous sections. Determining the size of wireless user communities and the traffic volume they will generate is also important. Many VPN solutions were designed to handle a small number of remote users rather than a large number of transient wireless users. An analysis of traffic flow and volume may be necessary to determine if a VPN solution will scale to support your wireless users.

Summary

This chapter provided information to help you select methods for meeting a customer's goals for network security. Security is a major concern for most customers because of the increase in Internet connectivity and Internet applications, and because more users are accessing enterprise networks from remote sites and wireless devices. Also, at the same time that enterprises have become more dependent on their networks, the number of attacks on networks has increased.

The tasks involved with security design parallel the tasks involved with overall network design. It is important to analyze requirements, develop policies, and consider tradeoffs before selecting actual technologies and products to meet the security needs of the various users of an enterprise network. The network should be considered a modular system that requires security for many components, including Internet connections, remote-access networks, network services, end-user services, and wireless networks. To protect the network, you should develop multilayered strategies, procedures, and implementations that provide security defense in depth.

Review Questions

1. What is the difference between a security plan and a security policy? How do these two relate to each other?

2. People who are new to security often assume that security simply means encryption. Why is this a naive assumption? What are some other aspects of security that are just as important as encryption?

3. List and briefly describe four tradeoffs that often must be made in order to achieve good network security.

4. Research a case that has been in the news in the last few years where a major security breach occurred on a wireless network. Find a case where attackers got in via the wireless network but then penetrated farther into the network, resulting in severe economic or political damage to the victim organization. Write two or three paragraphs about what you found.

Design Scenario

In previous chapters you have been asked to do some design work for ElectroMyCycle. Throughout this process you have kept security requirements in mind, of course, but now the time has come to focus on security.

1. What are ElectroMyCycle's most important assets that must be protected with security mechanisms?

2. What are the biggest security risks that ElectroMyCycle faces?

3. Design a high-level security policy for ElectroMyCycle.

4. Describe how you will achieve buy-in from the major stakeholders for your security policy.

Chapter 9

Developing Network Management Strategies

This chapter concludes the discussion of logical network design. Network management is one of the most important aspects of logical network design. Management is often overlooked during the design of a network because it is considered an operational issue rather than a design issue. If you consider management from the beginning, however, you can avoid scalability and performance problems that occur when management is added to a design after the design is complete.

A good network management design can help an organization achieve availability, performance, and security goals. Effective network management processes can help an organization measure how well design goals are being met and adjust network parameters if these goals are not being met. Network management also facilitates meeting scalability goals because it can help an organization analyze current network behavior, apply upgrades appropriately, and troubleshoot any problems with upgrades. The goal of this chapter is to help you work with your network design customer in the development of management strategies and to help you select the right tools and products to implement the strategies.

Network Management Design

Approaching network management design in the same way you approach any design project is a good idea. Think about scalability, traffic patterns, data formats, and cost/benefit tradeoffs. Network management systems can be expensive. They can also have a negative effect on network performance.

Pay attention to the *Heisenberg uncertainty principle*, which states that the act of observing something can alter what is observed. Some network management systems poll remote stations on a regular basis. The amount of traffic caused by the polling can be significant. You should analyze your customer's requirements for polling timers and not arbitrarily use the defaults of a network management system.

Work with your customer to figure out which resources should be monitored and the metrics to use when measuring the performance of devices. Choose carefully the data to collect. Saving too much data can result in a requirement for a supercomputer to process and store the data. On the other hand, be careful not to throw away so much data that you cannot use the remaining data to manage the network.

Plan the format that data should be saved in carefully. You should try to use general-purpose data formats. Assume that the data you collect might be used for different applications than the ones that you have in mind. As Kathryn Cramer says in her book *Roads Home: Seven Pathways to Midlife Wisdom*: "Remain open to possibilities other than what has been imagined."

Proactive Network Management

When helping your customer design network management strategies, you should encourage the practice of proactive network management. As more companies recognize the strategic importance of their internetworks, they are putting more emphasis on proactive management. *Proactive management* means checking the health of the network during normal operation to recognize potential problems, optimize performance, and plan upgrades.

Companies that practice proactive management collect statistics and conduct tests, such as response-time measurements, on a routine basis. The statistics and test results can be used to communicate trends and network health to management and users. Network managers can write monthly or quarterly reports that document the quality of network service that has been delivered in the last period, measured against service goals. The service goals are defined by the network design: availability, response time, throughput, usability, and so on.

If your network design customer plans to implement proactive network management, which you should encourage, consider this objective when designing a network management strategy for your customer. Proactive network management is desirable but can require that network management tools and processes be more sophisticated than with reactive network management. This tradeoff can be justified with less downtime, however.

Network Management Processes

Chapter 2, "Analyzing Technical Goals and Tradeoffs," talked about analyzing a customer's goals for manageability of a network. In general, most customers have a need to develop network management processes that can help them manage the implementation and operation of the network, diagnose and fix problems, optimize performance, and plan enhancements.

The International Organization for Standardization (ISO) defines five types of network management processes, which are often referred to with the FCAPS acronym:

- Fault management

- Configuration management

- Accounting management

- Performance management

- Security management

Fault Management

Fault management refers to detecting, isolating, diagnosing, and correcting problems. It also includes processes for reporting problems to end users and managers, and tracking trends related to problems. In some cases, fault management means developing workarounds until a problem can be fixed.

Network users expect quick and reliable fault resolution. They also expect to be kept informed about ongoing problems and to be given a timeframe for resolution. After a problem is resolved, they expect the problem to be tested and then documented in some sort of problem-tracking database. A variety of tools exist to meet these fault-management requirements, including monitoring tools that alert managers to problems, protocol analyzers for fault resolution, and help-desk software for documenting problems and alerting users of problems. Monitoring tools are often based on the Simple Network Management Protocol (SNMP) and Remote Monitoring (RMON) standards, which are covered in more detail later in this chapter.

Most operating systems provide a means for the system and its running processes to report faults to a network manager. Cisco devices produce syslog messages as a result of network events. Every syslog message contains a time stamp, level, and facility. Syslog levels are as follows:

- Emergency (level 0, the most severe level)

- Alert (level 1)

- Critical (level 2)

- Error (level 3)

- Warning (level 4)

- Notice (level 5)

- Informational (level 6)

- Debugging (level 7)

Syslog messages are sent by default to the Cisco router or switch console. Network devices can be configured to send syslog messages to a network management station or a remote network host on which a syslog analyzer is installed. A syslog analyzer applies filters and sends only a predefined subset of all syslog messages to a network management station. This saves bandwidth and also reduces the amount of information a network administrator must analyze.

Configuration Management

Configuration management helps a network manager keep track of network devices and maintain information on how devices are configured. With configuration management, a network manager can define and save a default configuration for similar devices, modify the default configuration for specific devices, and load the configuration on devices.

Configuration management also lets a manager maintain an inventory of network assets and do version-logging. *Version-logging* refers to keeping track of the version of operating systems or applications running on network devices. The inventory of network assets can also include information on the hardware configuration of devices, such as the amount of RAM, the size of flash memory, and the type of cabling that the devices use.

Configuration management facilitates change management. In the past, network administrators spent a lot of their time handling configurations for new employees and configuration changes for employees that moved. These days dynamic configuration protocols, such as the Dynamic Host Configuration Protocol (DHCP), free up management time for more strategic tasks than moves, adds, and changes. A protocol such as the VLAN Trunking Protocol (VTP) is also beneficial because it automatically updates switches with VLAN information.

Accounting Management

Accounting management facilitates usage-based billing, whereby individual departments or projects are charged for network services. Even in cases in which there is no money exchange, accounting of network usage can be useful to catch departments or individuals who "abuse" the network. The abuse could be intentional (for example, a discontented employee or former employee causing network problems) or unintentional. (People playing network games do not intend to harm the network but could cause excessive traffic nonetheless.) A practical reason to track unexpected traffic growth is so that the traffic can be considered during the next capacity-planning phase.

Performance Management

According to the ISO, performance management allows the measurement of network behavior and effectiveness. Performance management includes examining network application and protocol behavior, analyzing reachability, measuring response time, and recording network route changes. Performance management facilitates optimizing a network, meeting service-level agreements (SLA), and planning for expansion. Monitoring performance involves collecting data, processing some or all of the data, displaying the processed data, and archiving some or all of the data.

You should monitor two types of performance:

■ **End-to-end performance:** Measures performance across an internetwork. It can measure availability, capacity, utilization, delay, delay variation, throughput, reachability, response time, errors, and the burstiness of traffic.

■   **Component performance:** Measures the performance of individual links or devices. For example, throughput and utilization on a particular network segment can be measured. Additionally, routers and switches can be monitored for throughput (packets per second), memory and CPU usage, and errors.

Performance management often involves polling remote parts of the network to test reachability and measure response times. Response-time measurements consist of sending a ping packet and measuring the round-trip time (RTT) to send the packet and receive a response. The ping packet is actually an Internet Control Message Protocol (ICMP) echo packet.

On large networks, reachability and RTT studies can be impractical. For example, on a network with 10,000 devices, some commercially available network management systems take hours to poll the devices, cause significant network traffic, and save more data than a human can process. Work with your customer to scale back goals for doing reachability and RTT studies if the goals are unrealistic.

Another performance management process is to use protocol analyzers or SNMP tools to record traffic loads between important sources and destinations. The objective is to document the megabytes per second between pairs of autonomous systems, networks, hosts, or applications. Source/destination traffic-load documentation is useful for capacity planning, troubleshooting, and figuring out which routers should be peers in routing protocols that use a peering system, such as the Border Gateway Protocol (BGP). Source/destination traffic-load data is also useful if an SLA includes throughput requirements.

Performance management can include processes for recording changes in routes between stations. Tracking route changes can be useful for troubleshooting reachability and performance problems. One way to document route changes is to use ICMP echo packets with the IP record-route option turned on. Be aware that turning on the record-route option might skew RTT measurements, however. The record-route option causes each router to put its address in the options field of the IP header, which can cause extra processing time. (Don't forget the Heisenberg uncertainty principle!) Plan to do route-change studies separately from RTT analyses. Another way to study route changes is with traceroute. Traceroute is somewhat unreliable, however.

Note   Traceroute determines the IP routing path to a remote device. With UNIX and Cisco IOS operating systems, a traceroute packet is a User Datagram Protocol (UDP) "probe" packet sent to a high port number, in the 33,000 to 43,000 range. Microsoft operating systems send a ping rather than a UDP packet. Traceroute works by taking advantage of the ICMP error message a router generates when a packet exceeds its Time-To-Live (TTL) value. TTL is a field in the IP header of an IP packet.

Traceroute starts by sending a UDP probe or ping packet with a TTL of 1. This causes the first router in the path to discard the packet and send back a time-exceeded (TTL exceeded) ICMP message. Traceroute then sends several packets, increasing the TTL by one after a few packets have been sent at each TTL value. For example, it sends a few packets with

TTL equal to 1, then a few packets with TTL equal to 2, then a few packets with TTL equal to 3, and so on, until the destination host is reached.

Each router in the path decrements the TTL. The router that decrements the TTL to 0 sends back the time-exceeded (TTL exceeded) message. The final destination host sends back a ping reply (if the sender were using a Microsoft operating system) or a destination unreachable (port-unreachable) ICMP message (if the sender were using UNIX or Cisco IOS), because the high UDP port number is not a well-known port. This process allows a user to see a message from every router in the path to the destination and a message from the destination.

Unfortunately, traceroute is not dependable. Some routers do not send back time-exceeded messages, either because they are simply not programmed to do so or because they are configured to rate-limit ICMP or block ICMP for security reasons. Some routers incorrectly use the TTL of the incoming packet to send the time-exceeded message, which does not work. Also, some systems do not send the port-unreachable message, which means that traceroute waits for a long time before timing out. Finally, some service providers purposely change the results of traceroute to hide internal hops so that users think the providers' paths must be shorter than competitors' paths.

Security Management

Security management lets a network manager maintain and distribute passwords and other authentication and authorization information. Security management also includes processes for generating, distributing, and storing encryption keys. It can also include tools and reports to analyze a group of router and switch configurations for compliance with site security standards.

One important aspect of security management is a process for collecting, storing, and examining security audit logs. Audit logs should document logins and logouts (but not save passwords) and attempts by people to change their level of authorization.

Collecting audit data can result in a rapid accumulation of data. The required storage can be minimized by keeping data for a short period of time and summarizing the data. One drawback to keeping less data, however, is that it makes it harder to investigate security incidents. Compressing the data, instead of keeping less data, is often a better solution. It is also a good idea to encrypt audit logs. A hacker who accesses audit logs can cause a lot of damage to a network if the audit log is not encrypted. The hacker can alter the log without detection and also glean sensitive information from the log.

A variety of tools exist for maintaining security logs, including Event Viewer on Windows systems and syslog on UNIX and Cisco IOS devices. Most contemporary operating systems, including Windows, Solaris, Mac OS X, and FreeBSD, support audit event logging because of requirements in the Common Criteria for Information Technology Security Evaluation, an international standard for computer security certification.

Network Management Architectures

This section discusses some typical decisions that must be made when selecting a network management architecture. A network management architecture consists of three major components:

■ **A managed device:** A network node that collects and stores management information. Managed devices can be routers, servers, switches, bridges, hubs, end systems, or printers.

■ **An agent:** Network management software that resides in a managed device. An agent tracks local management information and uses a protocol such as SNMP to send information to NMSs.

■ **A network management system (NMS):** Runs applications to display management data, monitor and control managed devices, and communicate with agents. An NMS is generally a powerful workstation that has sophisticated graphics, memory, storage, and processing capabilities. The NMS is typically located in a network operations center (NOC).

Figure 9-1 shows the relationship between managed devices, agents, and NMSs.

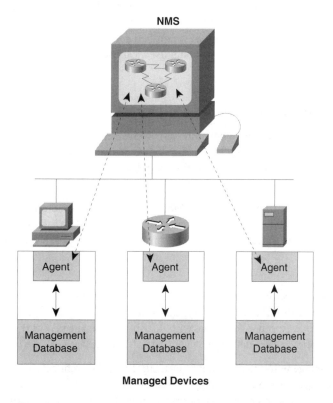

Figure 9-1   *Network Management Architecture*

A network management architecture consists of managed devices, agents, and NMSs arranged in a topology that fits into the internetwork topology. The tasks for designing a network management architecture parallel the tasks for designing an internetwork. Traffic flow and load between NMSs and managed devices should be considered. A decision should be made about whether management traffic flows in-band (with other network traffic) or out-of-band (outside normal traffic flow). A redundant topology should be considered. A decision should be made about a centralized or distributed management topology.

In-Band Versus Out-of-Band Monitoring

With *in-band monitoring*, network management data travels across an internetwork using the same paths as user traffic. This makes the network management architecture easy to develop but results in the dilemma that network management data is impacted by problems on the internetwork, making it harder to troubleshoot the problems. It is beneficial to use management tools even when the internetwork is congested, failing, or under a security attack.

Out-of-band monitoring makes the network design more complex and expensive. To keep the cost down, analog dialup lines are often used for backup, rather than ISDN or Frame Relay circuits. Another tradeoff with out-of-band monitoring is that there are security risks associated with adding extra links between NMSs and agents. To reduce the risks, the links should be carefully controlled and added only if absolutely necessary. For analog modem links, the agent should use a callback mechanism after the NMS calls the agent.

Centralized Versus Distributed Monitoring

In a centralized monitoring architecture, all NMSs reside in one area of the network, often in a corporate NOC. Agents are distributed across the internetwork and send data such as ping and SNMP responses to the centralized NMSs. The data is sent via out-of-band or in-band paths.

Distributed monitoring means that NMSs and agents are spread out across the internetwork. A hierarchical distributed arrangement can be used whereby distributed NMSs send data to sophisticated centralized NMSs using a manager-of-managers (MoM) architecture. A centralized system that manages distributed NMSs is sometimes called an *umbrella NMS*.

In an MoM architecture, distributed NMSs can filter data before sending it to the centralized stations, thus reducing the amount of network management data that flows on the internetwork. Another advantage with distributed management is that the distributed systems can often gather data even when parts of the internetwork are failing.

The disadvantage with distributed management is that the architecture is complex and hard to manage. It is more difficult to control security, contain the amount of data that is collected and stored, and keep track of management devices. A simple network management architecture that does not complicate the job of managing the network is generally a better solution.

Selecting Network Management Tools and Protocols

After you have discussed high-level network management processes with your customer, and developed a network management architecture, you can make some decisions on which network management tools and protocols to recommend to your customer. You can meet most customers' needs by recommending tools that support SNMP and RMON. Cisco Discovery Protocol (CDP) and Cisco NetFlow Accounting are also helpful.

Selecting Tools for Network Management

To ensure high network availability, management tools should support numerous features that can be used for performance, fault, configuration, security, and accounting management. At a minimum, a network management solution should include tools for isolating, diagnosing, and reporting problems to facilitate quick repair and recovery. Ideally, the system should also incorporate intelligence to identify trends that can predict a potential failure so that a network manager can take action before a fault condition occurs.

When selecting management tools, consider the flexibility of the tools and the varied audiences that may interface with them. Network management tools should provide an intuitive user interface that can react quickly to user input. In many cases, having both a browser interface and command-line interface (CLI) is beneficial.

If the tools allow dynamic configuration of devices, configuration changes should take effect without requiring a reboot of the device, if the device supports this, because disruption of service for a critical device could potentially impact thousands of users. Management software should also check the validity of any configuration changes and automatically restore operation to the last known configuration or software image in case of error. Management software that supports the dynamic configuration of devices should require authentication to avoid an unauthorized user making changes.

Simple Network Management Protocol

SNMP is supported by most commercial NMSs and many networking devices, including switches, routers, servers, and workstations. SNMP has gained widespread popularity because of its simplicity and because it is easy to implement, install, and use. Also, when used sensibly, SNMP does not place undue burden on the network. Interoperability between SNMP implementations from different vendors can be achieved with minimal effort because SNMP is so simple.

SNMPv3 should gradually supplant versions 1 and 2 because it offers better security, including authentication to protect against modification of information, and secure set operations for the remote configuration of SNMP-managed devices.

SNMPv2 was introduced in 1993 and updated in 1996. SNMPv2 added a get-bulk operation for the efficient retrieval of a block of parameters when gathering data from a table of parameters; however, neither SNMPv1 nor SNMPv2 provide security features. Without authentication, it is possible for nonauthorized users to exercise SNMP network management functions. It is also possible for nonauthorized users to eavesdrop on management information as it passes from managed systems to an NMS. SNMPv3 provides security features to help alleviate these problems. Because of its security, SNMPv3 can be used for more than just monitoring network statistics. It can also be used for control applications. Most vendors support SNMPv3. Cisco started supporting SNMPv3 in Cisco IOS Software Release 12.0(3)T.

SNMP is specified in three sets of documents:

- RFC 2579 defines mechanisms for describing and naming parameters that are managed with SNMP. The mechanisms are called the structure of managed information (SMI).

- RFC 3416 defines protocol operations for SNMP.

- Management Information Bases (MIB) define management parameters that are accessible via SNMP. Various RFCs define MIBs of different types. The core set of parameters for the Internet suite of protocols is called *MIB II* and is defined in RFC 1213. Vendors can also define private MIBs.

SNMP has seven types of packets:

- **Get Request:** Sent by an NMS to an agent to collect a management parameter

- **Get-Next Request:** Sent by an NMS to collect the next parameter in a list or table of parameters

- **Get-Bulk Request:** Sent by an NMS to retrieve large blocks of data, such as multiple rows in a table (not in SNMPv1)

- **Response:** Sent by an agent to an NMS in response to a request

- **Set Request:** Sent by an NMS to an agent to configure a parameter on a managed device

- **Trap:** Sent autonomously (not in response to a request) by an agent to an NMS to notify the NMS of an event

- **Inform:** Sent by an NMS to notify another NMS of information in a MIB view that is remote to the receiving application (not in SNMPv1, supports MoM architectures)

Management Information Bases (MIB)

A MIB stores information gathered by the local management agent on a managed device. Each object in a MIB has a unique identifier. Network management applications use the identifier to retrieve a specific object. The MIB is structured as a tree. Similar objects are grouped under the same branch of the MIB tree. For example, various interface counters are grouped under the Interfaces branch of the MIB II (RFC 1213) tree.

MIB II defines the following groups of managed objects for TCP/IP networks:

- System
- Interfaces
- Address Translation
- IP
- ICMP
- TCP
- UDP
- EGP
- Transmission
- SNMP

In addition to standard MIBs, such as MIB II for TCP/IP objects, there are vendor-specific MIB definitions. Vendors can obtain their own branch for the private definition of a MIB subtree and create custom managed objects under that branch. To use private definitions of managed objects, a network manager must import the definitions into an NMS. A Cisco router supports standard MIB II objects and private managed objects introduced by Cisco in a private section of the MIB tree. Cisco MIB definitions can be obtained at http://www.cisco.com/public/sw-center/netmgmt/cmtk/mibs.shtml.

Remote Monitoring (RMON)

The RMON MIB was developed by the IETF in the early 1990s to address shortcomings in the standard MIBs, which lacked the capability to provide statistics on data link and physical layer parameters. The IETF developed the RMON MIB to provide Ethernet traffic statistics and fault diagnosis.

RMON agents gather statistics on cyclic redundancy check (CRC) errors, Ethernet collisions, packet-size distribution, the number of packets in and out, and the rate of broadcast packets. The RMON alarm group lets a network manager set thresholds for network parameters and configure agents to automatically deliver alerts to NMSs. RMON also supports capturing packets (with filters if desired) and sending the captured packets to an NMS for protocol analysis.

RMON delivers information in nine groups of parameters. Table 9-1 lists and describes the groups.

RMON provides network managers with information about the health and performance of the network segment on which the RMON agent resides. RMON provides a view of the health of the whole segment, rather than the device-specific information that many non-RMON SNMP agents provide. The benefits of RMON are obvious, but the scope of

RMON version 1 (RMON1) is limited because it focuses on data link and physical layer parameters. The IETF is currently working on an RMON2 standard that moves beyond segment information to supply information on the health and performance of network applications and end-to-end communications. RMON2 is described in RFC 4502. Table 9-2 shows the groups in RMON2.

Table 9-1   *RMON Ethernet Groups*

Group	Description
Statistics	Tracks packets, octets, packet-size distribution, broadcasts, collisions, dropped packets, fragments, CRC/alignment errors, jabbers, and undersized and oversized packets.
History	Stores multiple samples of values from the Statistics group for the comparison of the current behavior of a selected variable to its performance over the specified period.
Alarm	Enables setting thresholds and sampling intervals on any statistic to create an alarm condition. Threshold values can be an absolute value, a rising or falling value, or a delta value.
Hosts	Provides for each active node a table that includes a variety of node statistics, including packets and octets in and out, multicast and broadcast packets in and out, and error counts.
Host Top N	Extends the host table to offer a user-defined study of sorted host statistics. Host Top N is calculated locally by the agent, thus reducing network traffic and processing on the NMS.
Matrix	Displays the amount of traffic and number of errors occurring between pairs of nodes within a segment.
Filters	Enables the user to define specific packet-match filters and have them serve as a stop or start mechanism for packet-capture activity.
Packet Capture	Captures packets that pass the filters and stores them for further analysis. An NMS can request the capture buffer and analyze the packets.
Events	Enables the user to create entries in a monitor log or generate SNMP traps from the agent to the NMS. Events can be initiated by a crossed threshold on a counter or by a packet-match count.

Table 9-2 *RMON2 Groups*

Group	Description
Protocol Directory	Provides a list of protocols supported by the device
Protocol Distribution	Contains traffic statistics for each supported protocol
Address Mapping	Contains network layer to MAC layer address mappings
Network Layer Host	Contains statistics for network layer traffic to or from each host
Network Layer Matrix	Contains network layer traffic statistics for conversations between pairs of hosts
Application Layer Host	Contains statistics for application layer traffic to or from each host
Application Layer Matrix	Contains application layer traffic statistics for conversations between pairs of hosts
User History Collection	Contains periodic samples of user-specified variables
Probe Configuration	Provides a standard way to remotely configure probe parameters such as trap destination and out-of-band management

Cisco Discovery Protocol

As mentioned in Chapter 3, "Characterizing the Existing Internetwork," CDP specifies a method for Cisco routers and switches to send configuration information to each other on a regular basis. Although some security experts recommend disabling CDP because a hacker could use the information to learn about a network's configuration and topology, many network managers leave CDP enabled because of its usefulness. CDP is enabled by default.

With the **show cdp neighbors detail** command, you can display detailed information about neighboring routers and switches, including which protocols are enabled, the network addresses for enabled protocols, the number and types of interfaces, the type of platform and its capabilities, and the version of Cisco IOS Software running on the neighbor.

CDP is a media- and protocol-independent protocol. CDP runs over the data link layer, enabling two systems that support different network layer protocols to communicate. CDP frames use a Subnetwork Access Protocol (SNAP) encapsulation and are sent to the Cisco multicast address 01-00-0C-CC-CC-CC. Although switches usually forward multicast frames, Cisco switches do not forward CDP frames. Routers also do not forward CDP frames. CDP frames are sent every 60 seconds by default, although you can change this with the **cdp timer** command.

CDP frames are sent with a holdtime of 180 seconds by default. Holdtime specifies the amount of time a receiving device should hold the information before discarding it. When an interface is shut down, CDP sends a frame with the holdtime set to zero. You can configure holdtime with the **cdp holdtime** command. Sending a CDP packet with a holdtime of zero allows a network device to quickly discover a lost neighbor.

Cisco NetFlow Accounting

As mentioned in Chapter 3, Cisco IOS NetFlow technology is an integral part of Cisco IOS Software that collects and measures data as it enters router or switch interfaces. The information gathered enables a network manager to characterize utilization of network and application resources. It can also be used to design quality of service (QoS) support. A network flow is defined as a unidirectional sequence of packets between a source and destination endpoint. A flow endpoint is identified both by IP address and by transport layer port number. NetFlow also identifies flows by IP protocol type, class of service (CoS), and an input interface identifier.

Collecting NetFlow data helps a network manager visualize traffic patterns so that proactive problem detection is possible. It also allows a network manager to implement resource utilization accounting. Service providers can use NetFlow information to migrate away from single-fee, flat-rate billing, to more flexible charging mechanisms based on time of day, bandwidth usage, application usage, QoS, and so forth. Enterprise network managers can use the information for departmental cost recovery and cost allocation for resource utilization.

Gathering NetFlow data also allows a network manager to gain a detailed, time-based view of application usage. Content and service providers can use this information to plan and allocate network and application resources to meet customer demands. For example, a content provider can decide on the capacity and location of web servers, based on NetFlow data. NetFlow data, or the information derived from it, can be warehoused for later retrieval and analysis, in support of proactive marketing and customer service programs (for example, to determine which applications and services are being used by internal and external users and target them for improved service).

Cisco recommends a carefully planned NetFlow deployment, with NetFlow services activated on strategically located routers, usually routers on the edge of a network. Although NetFlow has a performance impact on routers, the impact is minimal and is less than the impact of RMON. The benefits of NetFlow information gathering, when compared to SNMP and RMON, include the greater detail of data collected, the timestamping of data, support for different data being gathered on different interfaces, and greater scalability. Also, with NetFlow, external RMON probes are not required.

Estimating Network Traffic Caused by Network Management

After you have determined which management protocols will be used, you can estimate the amount of traffic caused by network management. Probably the main management protocol will be SNMP, although other options exist, such as CDP, pings, IP traceroute, and so on.

After selecting management protocols, you should determine which network and device characteristics will be managed. The goal is to determine what data an NMS will request from managed devices. This data could consist of reachability information, response-time measurements, network layer address information, and data from the RMON MIB or other MIBs. After you have determined what characteristics will be gathered from managed devices, you should then determine how often the NMS requests the data (this is called the polling interval).

To calculate a rough estimate of traffic load, multiply the number of management characteristics by the number of managed devices and divide by the polling interval. For example, if a network has 200 managed devices and each device is monitored for 10 characteristics, the resulting number of requests is as follows:

$$200 \times 10 = 2000$$

The resulting number of responses is also

$$200 \times 10 = 2000$$

If the polling interval is every 5 seconds and you assume that each request and response is a single 64-byte packet, the amount of network traffic is as follows:

(4000 requests and responses) $\times$ 64 bytes $\times$ 8 bits/byte = 2,048,000 bits every 5 seconds or 409,600 bps

In this example, on a shared 10-Mbps Ethernet, network management data would use 4 percent of the available network bandwidth, which is significant but probably acceptable. A good rule of thumb is that management traffic should use less than 5 percent of a network's capacity.

Note   To get a more precise estimate of traffic load caused by management data, you should use a protocol analyzer. Many SNMP implementations ask for more than one characteristic in a request packet, which uses bandwidth more efficiently than was described in the example.

Summary

One of your goals as a network designer should be to help your customer develop some strategies and processes for implementing network management. You should also help your customer select tools and products to implement the strategies and processes. This chapter provided information to help you select the right processes and tools to meet a customer's goals for network manageability. The tasks involved with management design parallel the tasks involved with overall network design: analyzing requirements and goals, making tradeoffs, characterizing network management traffic flow, and developing an appropriate topology.

Management is often overlooked during the design of a network because it is considered an operational issue rather than a design issue. However, by considering network management upfront, instead of tacking it on at the end of the design process or after the network is already operational, your design will be more scalable and robust.

Review Questions

1. This chapter covered network management, whereas the previous chapter covered network security. Note that network design tasks are often interwoven, however, and shouldn't be considered discrete just because a book is divided into discrete chapters. In what ways are network management and network security interrelated? When designing network management for your customer, what security concerns will you address? When designing network security for your customer, what network management concerns will you address?

2. What are the pros and cons of out-of-band network management versus in-band network management?

3. A network management system can communicate with a managed device using a request-response protocol or a trap mechanism. What are the pros and cons of these two methods?

4. Research a network management product or tool of your choice. Describe the product or tool in two or three paragraphs.

Design Scenario

You are in the process of developing a network design proposal for Genome4U, a large-scale university project that has been discussed in previous chapters. As you considered network management for this project, you came to a preliminary decision that Cisco Discovery Protocol (CDP) should be enabled on the Cisco routers and switches. When you discussed this idea with the university network engineers, however, you suddenly found yourself in the middle of a Layer 8 (office politics) quagmire. As it turns out, the network engineers have been arguing among themselves for years about the benefits of CDP. The security-focused engineers want it disabled. The engineers who focus on day-to-day operations want it enabled. The desktop support technicians agree with the operations group because the Cisco VoIP phones that they install can take advantage of CDP. The IT architects insist that the decision is theirs but they don't return phone calls when you ask for their opinion.

What will be your recommendation and why? Should CDP be enabled? Should it be enabled on all devices and interfaces? How will you convince your customers that your decision is the best one and they should abide by it, even the IT architects?

Summary for Part II

This chapter concludes Part II of *Top-Down Network Design*. Part II concentrated on the logical design phase of the top-down network design methodology. During the logical design phase, a network designer develops a network topology based on knowledge gained about traffic flow and load in the requirements-analysis phase of network design. The designer also devises network layer addressing and naming models, and selects bridging, switching, and routing protocols. The designer also develops security and network management strategies.

Developing a logical design is an important early step in network design. The logical design provides a network designer with a chance to focus on design goals, without delving too deeply into the details of the physical components of the network. By concentrating first on the logical architecture of the network, a designer can more accurately select technologies, capacities, and devices that will support the customer's goals. The logical design phase glues together the requirements-analysis phase, in which traffic flow and technical and business goals are analyzed, and the physical design phase, in which cabling, data link layer technologies, and devices are added to the final network architecture.

Part III

Physical Network Design

Chapter 10

Selecting Technologies and Devices for Campus Networks

Physical network design involves the selection of LAN and WAN technologies for campus and enterprise network designs. During this phase of the top-down network design process, choices are made regarding cabling, physical and data link layer protocols, and internetworking devices (such as switches, routers, and wireless access points). A logical design, which Part II, "Logical Network Design," covered, forms the foundation for a physical design. In addition, business goals, technical requirements, network traffic characteristics, and traffic flows, all of which were discussed in Part I, "Identifying Your Customer's Needs and Goals," influence a physical design.

A network designer has many options for LAN and WAN implementations. No single technology or device is the right answer for all circumstances. The goal of Part III, "Physical Network Design," is to give you information about the scalability, performance, affordability, and manageability characteristics of typical options, to help you make the right selections for your particular customer.

This chapter covers technologies for campus network designs. A *campus network* is a set of LAN segments and building networks in an area that is generally less than a mile in diameter. The next chapter covers technologies for an enterprise network that includes WAN and remote-access services.

An effective design process is to develop campus solutions first, followed by remote-access and WAN solutions. After you have designed a customer's campus networks, you can more effectively select WAN and remote-access technologies based on the bandwidth and performance requirements of traffic that flows from one campus to another.

This chapter begins with a discussion of LAN cabling-plant design, including cabling options for building and campus networks. The chapter then provides information about LAN technologies. The section "Selecting Internetworking Devices for a Campus Network Design" provides some selection criteria you can use when selecting switches, routers, and wireless access points for a campus design. The chapter concludes with an example of a campus network design that was developed for the Wandering Valley Community College.

Note   Although the example is a design for a college campus, it should not be assumed that campus network design only refers to college campuses. Many commercial businesses, government organizations, and other establishments have campus networks.

LAN Cabling Plant Design

Because cabling is more of an implementation issue than a design issue, it is not covered in detail in this book. However, the importance of developing a good cabling infrastructure should not be discounted. Whereas other components of a network design generally have a lifetime of a few years before the technology changes, the cabling infrastructure often must last for many years. It is important to design and implement the cabling infrastructure carefully, keeping in mind availability and scalability goals, and the expected lifetime of the design.

In many cases, your network design must adapt to existing cabling. Chapter 3, "Characterizing the Existing Internetwork," discussed the process for documenting the cabling already in use in building and campus networks, including the following:

- Campus- and building-cabling topologies

- Types and lengths of cables between buildings

- Location of telecommunications closets and cross-connect rooms within buildings

- Types and lengths of cables for vertical cabling between floors

- Types and lengths of cables for horizontal cabling within floors

- Types and lengths of cables for work-area cabling going from telecommunications closets to workstations

Cabling Topologies

Companies such as AT&T, IBM, Digital Equipment Corporation (DEC), Hewlett-Packard, and Northern Telecom all published cabling specifications and guidelines for developing a cabling topology. Their work still influences cabling topologies in use today. In addition, the Electronics Industry Alliance and the Telecommunications Industry Association publish the EIA/TIA guidelines for unshielded twisted-pair (UTP) cabling and installation. Though the guidelines from the different organizations differ slightly, the main goal of all of them is to help a network engineer develop a structured cabling system that is manageable and scalable.

Without going into detail on cabling topologies, a generalization can be made that two types of cabling schemes are possible:

- A *centralized cabling scheme* terminates most or all of the cable runs in one area of the design environment. A star topology is an example of a centralized system.

- A *distributed cabling scheme* terminates cable runs throughout the design environment. Ring, bus, and mesh topologies are examples of distributed systems.

Building-Cabling Topologies

Within a building, either a centralized or distributed architecture can be used, depending on the size of the building. For small buildings, a centralized scheme with all cables terminating in a communications room on one floor is possible, as shown on the left side of Figure 10-1. A centralized scheme offers good manageability but does not scale. For larger buildings, a distributed topology is more appropriate. Many LAN technologies make an assumption that workstations are no more than 100 meters (m) from a telecommunications closet where hubs or switches reside. For this reason, in a tall building with large floors, a distributed topology is more appropriate, as shown on the right side of Figure 10-1.

Campus-Cabling Topologies

The cabling that connects buildings is exposed to more physical hazards than the cabling within buildings. A construction worker might dig a trench between buildings and inadvertently cut cables. Flooding, ice storms, earthquakes, and other natural disasters can also cause problems, as can manmade disasters such as terrorist attacks. In addition, cables might cross properties outside the control of the organization, making it hard to troubleshoot and fix problems. For these reasons, cables and cabling topologies should be selected carefully.

A distributed scheme offers better availability than a centralized scheme. The top part of Figure 10-2 shows a centralized topology. The bottom part of Figure 10-2 shows a distributed topology. The centralized topology in Figure 10-2 would experience a loss of all interbuilding communication if the cable bundle between Buildings A and B were cut. With the distributed topology, interbuilding communication could resume if a cable cut between Buildings A and B occurred.

In some environments, because of right-of-way issues or environmental obstructions such as creeks or swamps, it might not be practical to have multiple cable conduits on the campus, as shown in the topology in the bottom part of Figure 10-2. In this case, you can recommend a wireless technology (for example, a laser, microwave, or 802.11 bridged link between Buildings A and D).

One disadvantage of a distributed scheme is that management can be more difficult than with a centralized scheme. Changes to a distributed cabling system are more likely to require that a technician walk from building to building to implement the changes. Availability versus manageability goals must be considered.

Types of Cables

Campus network implementations use three major types of cables:

- Shielded copper, including shielded twisted-pair (STP), coaxial (coax), and twinaxial (twinax) cables

■   Unshielded copper (typically UTP) cables

■   Fiber-optic cables

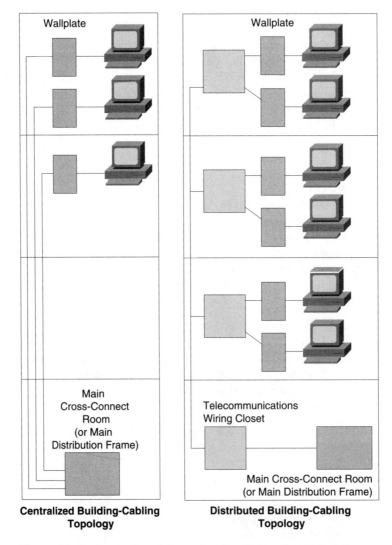

Figure 10-1   *Examples of Centralized and Distributed Building-Cabling Topologies*

STP cabling was widely used in Token Ring networks in the 1980s and 1990s. Token Ring networks have been replaced by Ethernet networks these days. Ethernet generally uses UTP and fiber-optic cabling, although it is possible to make Ethernet work on STP cabling.

Coax cable was popular in the early days of LANs. Thick Ethernet (10BASE5) used a double-shielded, 50-ohm coax cable that was about 0.4 inches in diameter, and thin

Ethernet (10BASE2 or "Cheapernet") used standard RG-58 cable that was about half that size. IBM terminals used 75-ohm coax cable, or, in some cases, twinax cables. The cabling was usually installed in a bus topology and was hard to manage in large installations without multiport repeaters. With the introduction of standards for running LAN protocols on UTP cabling (such as 10BASE-T Ethernet), coax cable became less popular. Coax and other types of shielded copper cabling are generally not recommended for new installations, except perhaps for short cable runs between devices in a telecommunications closet or computer room, or in cases where specific safety and shielding needs exist.

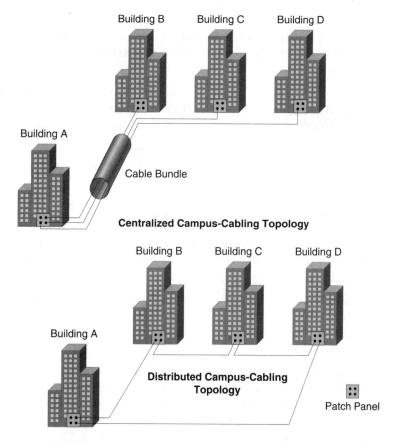

Figure 10-2 *Examples of Centralized and Distributed Campus-Cabling Topologies*

UTP is the typical wiring found in most buildings these days. It is generally the least expensive of the three types of cables. It also has the lowest transmission capabilities because it is subject to crosstalk, noise, and electromagnetic interference. Adherence to distance limitations minimizes the effects of these problems.

There are numerous categories of UTP cabling, including the following:

- Category 1 and 2 are not recommended for data transmissions because of their lack of support for high bandwidth requirements.

- Category 3 is tested to 16 MHz. Category 3 is often called *voice-grade cabling*, but it is used for data transmission also, particularly in older 10BASE-T Ethernet and 4-Mbps Token Ring networks.

- Category 4 is tested at 20 MHz, allowing it to run 16-Mbps Token Ring with a better safety margin than Category 3. Category 4 is not common, having been made obsolete by Category 5.

- Category 5 is tested at 100 MHz, allowing it to run high-speed protocols such as 100-Mbps Ethernet and Fiber Distributed Data Interface (FDDI). When four pairs are used, Category 5 supports Gigabit Ethernet.

- Category 5 Enhanced (Category 5e) is suitable for 100-Mbps Ethernet, Gigabit Ethernet, and ATM. Many companies sell 350-MHz Category 5e cabling, although the standard for the cabling (Addendum 5 to TIA/EIA-568-A) states 100 MHz.

- Category 6 is suitable for 100-Mbps Ethernet, Gigabit Ethernet, and ATM. The standard for the cabling (ANSI/TIA/EIA-568-B.2-1) states 200 MHz, although vendors support higher bandwidths.

New installations should run a minimum of Category 5e. The Telecommunications Industry Association (TIA) recommends that Category 6 be installed to support future applications that will demand high bandwidth. Category 6 improves performance characteristics such as insertion loss, near-end crosstalk (NEXT), return loss, and equal-level far-end crosstalk (ELFEXT). These enhancements provide a higher signal-to-noise ratio (SNR).

Fiber-optic cabling should be used for vertical and horizontal wiring between telecommunications closets and between buildings. Some companies also use fiber-optic cabling for work-area wiring, but the cost of network interface cards (NIC) with fiber-optic support is still high, so that is not common yet.

Fiber-optic cabling is not affected by crosstalk, noise, and electromagnetic interference, so it has the highest capacity of the three types of cables. With multiplexing technologies, such as wavelength-division multiplexing (WDM), a single strand of fiber-optic cabling can handle a capacity of 40 Gbps and beyond.

One disadvantage with fiber-optic cabling is that it can be difficult to install, which can add to the cost of deployment. When connecting an optical source to fiber or when coupling two or more fibers together, even a small deviation from the ideal position of the connector can result in misalignment and unacceptable signal loss. Some connectors introduce more loss than others. When selecting connectors, research their ease of use and the decibel (dB) loss associated with the connectors.

Fiber-optic connectors can also introduce reflection noise by reflecting light back into the optical source. Reflection noise is reduced by index-matching gels, physical contact polishes, and antireflection coatings. When selecting connectors, reflection noise is one more parameter that you should research.

Fiber-optic cabling is either *single-mode* or *multimode*. A *mode* means an allowable path for light to travel down a fiber. With multimode fiber, there are multiple modes or paths that light can follow. Some of the paths are longer than others, which means that the time it takes for light to travel down each path differs, resulting in intermodal dispersion of the light as it exits the fiber cable. Intermodal dispersion limits multimode bandwidth.

Single-mode fiber has a smaller core diameter than multimode fiber. The small core ensures that only one path is taken, which eliminates intermodal dispersion and means that single-mode fiber supports higher bandwidth rates over longer distances than multi-mode fiber. The smaller diameter makes it harder to couple sufficient optical power into the fiber, however, which adds to the cost of manufacturing and installing connectors. Single-mode interfaces for switches, routers, and workstations are also more expensive than multimode interfaces.

LAN Technologies

Chapter 1, "Analyzing Business Goals and Constraints," discussed analyzing the following business constraints, all of which have an effect on the LAN technologies you should recommend:

- Biases (technology religion)

- Policies about approved technologies or vendors

- The customer's tolerance to risk

- Technical expertise of the staff and plans for staff education

- Budgeting and scheduling

Technical goals, as discussed in Chapter 2, "Analyzing Technical Goals and Tradeoffs," also have a big impact on technology selections. The next few sections of this chapter demonstrate that LAN technologies vary in how well they can meet scalability, availability, manageability, adaptability, affordability, and other technical goals.

Chapter 2 recommended making a list of a customer's major technical goals. At this point in the design process, you should reference that list to make sure your technology selections are appropriate for your network design customer.

You should also take a look at Table 2-2, "Network Applications Technical Requirements," to determine if your customer has strict requirements about throughput, delay, and delay variation for any network applications. You should also consider the types of applications the customer plans to run on the network. Applications that allow users to share videos, collaborate with desktop sharing, watch high-definition television, and so on are more bandwidth hungry and delay sensitive than text-based applications.

Table 4-4, "Network Applications Traffic Characteristics," can also help you select the right technologies for your customer. In that table you documented bandwidth and QoS requirements for applications. The next few sections can help you determine which solutions are appropriate for applications with demanding bandwidth and QoS requirements.

Ethernet Basics

Ethernet is a physical and data link layer standard for the transmission of frames on a LAN. Since its invention in the 1970s by Xerox Corporation, Ethernet has gained widespread popularity and adapted to new demands for capacity, reliability, and low prices. An Ethernet LAN that is accurately provisioned to meet bandwidth requirements and outfitted with high-quality components, including NICs, cables, and internetworking devices, can meet even the most stringent demands for availability. Many troubleshooting tools, including cable testers, protocol analyzers, and network management applications, are available for isolating the occasional problems caused by cable breaks, electromagnetic interference, failed ports, or misbehaving NICs.

Ethernet and IEEE 802.3

DEC, Intel, and Xerox published Version 2.0 of the Ethernet specification in 1982. Version 2.0, also known as the *DIX standard* or *Ethernet II*, formed the basis for the work the Institute of Electrical and Electronic Engineers (IEEE) did on the 802.3 standard, which was finalized in 1983. Since then, 802.3 has evolved to support UTP and fiber-optic cabling, and faster transmission speeds.

Although there are some minor differences between the two technologies, the terms *Ethernet* and *802.3* are generally used synonymously. At the physical layer, 802.3 is the de facto standard. At the data link layer, both Ethernet Version 2.0 and 802.3 implementations are common.

Note   One important difference between Ethernet Version 2.0 and 802.3 is frame formats. 802.3 is used with an 802.2 Logical Link Control (LLC) header, except in early implementations of Novell NetWare. The 802.2 header includes a Destination Service Access Point (DSAP) and Source Service Access Point (SSAP) field to identify the receiving and sending processes. Ethernet Version 2.0 does not use 802.2 and instead includes an EtherType field to specify the sending/receiving process. Internet Protocol (IP) uses Ethernet Version 2.0. Most control-plane protocols, such as Cisco Discovery Protocol (CDP), VLAN Trunking Protocol (VTP), and Spanning Tree Protocol bridge protocol data units (BPDU) use 802.3 with 802.2. Figure 10-3 shows the frame formats.

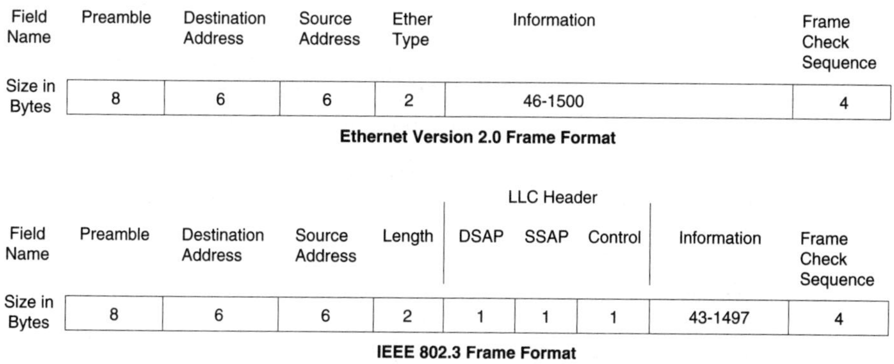

Field Name	Preamble	Destination Address	Source Address	Ether Type	Information	Frame Check Sequence
Size in Bytes	8	6	6	2	46-1500	4

Ethernet Version 2.0 Frame Format

Field Name	Preamble	Destination Address	Source Address	Length	LLC Header DSAP	SSAP	Control	Information	Frame Check Sequence
Size in Bytes	8	6	6	2	1	1	1	43-1497	4

IEEE 802.3 Frame Format

Figure 10-3 *Ethernet Version 2.0 and IEEE 802.3 Frame Formats*

Ethernet Technology Choices

Ethernet is a scalable technology that has adapted to increasing capacity requirements. The following options for implementing Ethernet networks are available:

- Half- and full-duplex Ethernet

- 100-Mbps Ethernet

- 1000-Mbps (1-Gbps or Gigabit) Ethernet

- 10-Gbps Ethernet

- Metro Ethernet

- Long-Reach Ethernet (LRE)

- Cisco EtherChannel

Each of these technologies is a possibility for the access, distribution, or core layers of a campus topology, although usually the higher speeds, such as Gigabit Ethernet, are reserved for the core layer.

The choice of an Ethernet technology for the access layer depends on the location and size of user communities, bandwidth and QoS requirements for applications, broadcast and other protocol behavior, and traffic flow, as discussed in Chapter 4, "Characterizing Network Traffic." The choice of an Ethernet technology for the distribution and core layers depends on the network topology, the location of data stores, and traffic flow. The section, "An Example of a Campus Network Design," at the end of this chapter provides an example of a network design that was accomplished by analyzing these factors.

Half-Duplex and Full-Duplex Ethernet

Ethernet was originally defined for a shared medium with stations using the carrier sense multiple access collision detection (CSMA/CD) algorithm to regulate the sending of frames and the detection of collisions when two stations send at the same time.

With shared Ethernet, a station listens before it sends data. If the medium is already in use, the station defers its transmission until the medium is free. Shared Ethernet is *half duplex*, meaning that a station is either transmitting or receiving traffic, but not both at once.

An important design rule for half-duplex Ethernet is that the round-trip propagation delay in one collision domain must not exceed the time it takes a sender to transmit 512 bits, which is 51.2 microseconds for 10-Mbps Ethernet. A single collision domain must be limited in size to make sure that a station sending a minimum-sized frame (64 bytes or 512 bits) can detect a collision reflecting back from the opposite side of the network while the station is still sending the frame. Otherwise, the station would be finished sending and not listening for a collision, thus losing the efficiency of Ethernet to detect a collision and quickly retransmit the frame.

Most Ethernet links these days are point-to-point and hence do not use half-duplex communications. A point-to-point Ethernet link supports simultaneous transmitting and receiving, which is called *full-duplex Ethernet*. On a link between a switch port and a single station, for example, both the switch and the station can transmit at the same time. This is especially beneficial if the station is a server that processes requests from many users. The switch can transmit the next request at the same time the server is sending a response to a previous request. Full-duplex operation is also common in switch-to-switch links, allowing both switches to transmit to each other at the same time. The advantage of full-duplex Ethernet is that the transmission rate is theoretically double what it is on a half-duplex link.

Note   Full-duplex operation requires the cabling to dedicate one wire pair for transmitting and another for receiving. Full-duplex operation does not work on cables with only one path (for example, coax cable). Full-duplex also does not work with 100BASE-T4 (100-Mbps Ethernet on Category 3 UTP). Unlike 10BASE-T and 100BASE-TX, with 100BASE-T4, no separate dedicated transmit and receive pairs are present. 100BASE-T4 uses three pairs for transmit/receive and one pair for collision detection.

100-Mbps Ethernet

100-Mbps Ethernet, also known as *Fast Ethernet* and *100BASE-T Ethernet*, was originally standardized in the IEEE 802.3u specification and is now merged into the full IEEE 802.3 standard. It is similar to the older 10-Mbps Ethernet standard, which is one of the reasons it is popular. For network engineers who had experience with 10-Mbps Ethernet, 100-Mbps Ethernet was easy to understand, install, configure, and troubleshoot. With some exceptions, 100-Mbps Ethernet is simply standard Ethernet, just ten times faster. In most cases, design parameters for 100-Mbps Ethernet are the same as for 10-Mbps Ethernet, just multiplied or divided by 10.

100-Mbps Ethernet is defined for four physical implementations:

- **100BASE-TX:** Two pairs of Category 5 (or better) UTP cabling

- **100BASE-T2:** Two pairs of Category 3 (or better) UTP cabling

- **100BASE-T4:** Four pairs of Category 3 (or better) UTP cabling

- **100BASE-FX:** Two multimode optical fibers

100BASE-TX is the most popular form of 100-Mbps Ethernet. With 100BASE-TX, stations are connected to switches using Category 5, Category 5e, or Category 6 UTP cabling.

Gigabit Ethernet

Gigabit Ethernet was originally defined in the IEEE 802.3z standard and is now merged into the full IEEE 802.3 standard. It operates essentially like 100-Mbps Ethernet, except that it is 10 times faster. It uses CSMA/CD with support for one repeater per collision domain and handles both half- and full-duplex operations. It uses a standard 802.3 frame format and frame size.

To avoid the need to reduce the size of a half-duplex Gigabit Ethernet network to 1/10th the size of a 100-Mbps Ethernet network, Gigabit Ethernet includes some minor changes to the MAC layer. It's helpful to compare the changes the standards developers made when they introduced 100-Mbps Ethernet to the changes they made when they introduced Gigabit Ethernet.

With half-duplex 10- and 100-Mbps Ethernet, the minimum frame size is equal to the maximum round-trip propagation delay of the network (less an allowance for jamming, synchronization, and so on). To ensure that a sender is still sending if a collision occurs on the opposite side of the largest possible network, a sender must transmit for the time it takes 512 bits (64 bytes) to travel to the opposite side of the network and back. This ensures that the sending Ethernet NIC will recognize the collision, back off, and retransmit.

To ensure that collision recognition works correctly on 100-Mbps Ethernet, where senders can send ten times as fast as they can with 10-Mbps Ethernet, the standards developers reduced the maximum network size to about 1/10th the maximum size for 10-Mbps Ethernet. Using such an approach with half-duplex Gigabit Ethernet would have resulted in impractically small networks, however. Instead, the minimum frame is maintained at 512 bits (64 bytes), but the sender is required to send for the time it takes 4096 bits (512 bytes) to travel to the opposite side of the network and back.

Frames that are shorter than 4096 bits are artificially extended by appending a carrier-extension field so that the frames are exactly 4096 bits in length. The contents of the carrier-extension field are nondata symbols. By increasing the minimum time a station sends, the standards can support a larger maximum network topology.

Carrier extension could cause performance degradation for some applications, although the developers included a workaround in the standards to avoid problems. Consider an application that is trying to output many small frames at a quick rate—for example, a Voice over IP (VoIP) application. If the interface adds bits to reach 4096 bits, will the application be able to send at the proper rate? When the application is finished and releases control of the medium, will some other application jump in, causing the first application to defer? The Gigabit Ethernet designers addressed these problems by allowing a sender to send multiple frames.

A Gigabit Ethernet station may choose to burst frames if there is a frame in its transmit queue when it has finished sending its first frame (plus extension, if one was necessary). The station may send again without contending for use of the channel. During the interframe gap, the station sends nondata symbols. Only the first frame requires a carrier extension. The station may start the transmission of frames for up to one burstLimit. IEEE defines the *burstLimit parameter* as 8192 bytes.

Gigabit Ethernet is most appropriate for building and campus-backbone networks. It can act as a trunk network, aggregating traffic from up to ten 100-Mbps Ethernet segments. Despite the carrier-extension and bursting features of half-duplex Ethernet, Gigabit Ethernet usually uses full-duplex mode and connects a switch to another switch or a switch to a router. Gigabit Ethernet is also used on high-performance servers that require a large amount of bandwidth.

The 802.3 standard for Gigabit Ethernet specifies multimode and single-mode fiber-optic cabling, UTP cabling, and shielded twinax copper cabling. Table 10-1 shows the variations of Gigabit Ethernet.

Table 10-1   *Gigabit Ethernet Specifications*

	1000BASE-SX	1000BASE-LX	1000BASE-CX	1000BASE-T
Type of cabling	850-nm wavelength multimode fiber	1300-nm wavelength multimode and single-mode fiber	Twinax	UTP
Distance limitations (in meters)	220–550, depending on the cable	550 for multimode and 5000 for single mode	25	100 between a hub and station; a total network diameter of 200 m

1000BASE-SX, also known as the *short-wavelength specification* (hence the *S* in the name), is appropriate for multimode horizontal cabling and backbone networks.

1000BASE-LX uses a longer wavelength (hence the *L* in the name) and supports both multimode and single-mode cabling. 1000BASE-LX is appropriate for building and campus-backbone networks.

1000BASE-CX is appropriate for a telecommunications closet or computer room where the distance between devices is 25 m or less. 1000BASE-CX runs over 150-ohm balanced, shielded, twinax cable.

1000BASE-T is intended for horizontal and work-area Category 5 or better UTP cabling. 1000BASE-T supports transmission over four pairs of UTP cable and covers a cabling distance of up to 100 m, or a network diameter of 200 m. Only one repeater is allowed.

10-Gbps Ethernet

One of the reasons that Ethernet is such a good choice for campus network designs is that it continues to grow with increasing bandwidth demands. In 2002, the IEEE standardized 10-Gbps Ethernet, which is now part of the full 802.3 standard. 10-Gbps Ethernet differs in some important ways from the other Ethernet implementations, but it is also remarkably similar to the other implementations. The frame format and other Layer 2 specifications remain the same, which means that applications that use Ethernet do not need to change.

In the near future, Ethernet will live up to its name. The name *Ethernet* comes from the term *ether*, the rarefied element that scientists formerly believed filled all space. Ethernet will be everywhere. An Internet transaction, for example, might start on a 100BASE-T home or business network, zoom across a fiber-optic metropolitan Ethernet to a local ISP, travel a WDM 10-Gbps Ethernet to a larger provider, and travel across various Ethernet links to reach an e-commerce server that is furnished with a Gigabit or 10-Gbps Ethernet NIC. The transaction will be encapsulated in an Ethernet frame the entire time.

Currently, most 10-Gbps Ethernet products are in the form of modules or line cards for high-end switches and routers, but some vendors also support 10-Gbps Ethernet interfaces for servers. Both ISPs and enterprise networks use 10-Gbps Ethernet as a backbone technology. Some enterprise networks also use 10-Gbps Ethernet in server farms, storage-area networks (SAN), and digital video studios.

10-Gbps Ethernet supports full-duplex transmission over fiber-optic or copper cabling. It doesn't support half-duplex mode. 10-Gbps supports LAN applications and metropolitan-area network (MAN) and WAN applications. When single-mode fiber-optic cabling is used, a 10-Gbps Ethernet link can extend in distance to 40 km (25 miles).

Like the other implementations of Ethernet, 10-Gbps Ethernet supports serial transmission, where bits are sent one after the other, one at a time in a series. Networking experts learned long ago that parallel transmission (the opposite of serial transmission) was relegated to ancient printers and legacy protocols from the 1970s. Not so anymore! The 10GBASE-LX4 variety of 10-Gbps Ethernet simultaneously launches four bit streams as four wavelengths of light. This is called *wide wavelength-division multiplexing* (WWDM), and is categorized as a parallel transmission mechanism in IEEE 802.3.

In addition to 10GBASE-LX4, 10-Gbps Ethernet supports many other physical layer specifications that use parallel and serial transmission. Table 10-2 shows distance limitations for the various 10-Gbps Ethernet implementations.

Table 10-2   *10-Gbps Ethernet Implementations*

Implementation	Wavelength	Medium	Minimum Modal Bandwidth	Operating Distance
10GBASE-LX4	1310 nm	62.5-micron multimode fiber	500 MHz/km	2–300 m
10GBASE-LX4	1310 nm	50-micron multimode fiber	400 MHz/km	2–240 m
10GBASE-LX4	1310 nm	50-micron multimode fiber	500 MHz/km	2–300 m
10GBASE-LX4	1310 nm	10-micron single-mode fiber	Not applicable	2–10 km
10GBASE-S	850 nm	62.5-micron multimode fiber	160 MHz/km	2–26 m
10GBASE-S	850 nm	62.5-micron multimode fiber	200 MHz/km	2–33 m
10GBASE-S	850 nm	50-micron multimode fiber	400 MHz/km	2–66 m
10GBASE-S	850 nm	50-micron multimode fiber	500 MHz/km	2–82 m
10GBASE-S	850 nm	50-micron multimode fiber	2000 MHz/km	2–300 m
10GBASE-L	1310 nm	10-micron single-mode fiber	Not applicable	2–10 km
10GBASE-E	1550 nm	10-micron single-mode fiber	Not applicable	2–30 km[*]
10GBASE-CX4	Not applicable	Twinax	Not applicable	15 m
SFP+ Direct Attach	Not applicable	Twinax	Not applicable	10 m
10GBASE-T	Not applicable	UTP or STP	Not applicable	100 m

The standard permits 40-km lengths if link attenuation is low enough.

Metro Ethernet

Metro Ethernet blends the capabilities and behavior of LAN technologies with those of WAN technologies. Metro Ethernet is covered in more detail in the next chapter, "Selecting Technologies and Devices for Enterprise Networks," but it is mentioned here because it is an Ethernet technology and this section covers Ethernet, and because it is relevant to the case study at the end of this chapter.

Carriers offer Metro Ethernet to customers who are looking for a cost-effective method to interconnect campus networks and to access the Internet. With Metro Ethernet, a customer can use a standard 10/100-Mbps Ethernet interface, or a Gigabit or 10-Gbps interface, to access the service provider's network. The customer can set up virtual circuits to reach other sites and to reach an ISP. Metro Ethernet supports a copper or fiber-optic interface but uses fiber-optic cabling inside the provider's network. It can use a variety of transport protocols, including Synchronous Optical Network (SONET), Asynchronous Transfer Mode (ATM), dense-mode wavelength-division multiplexing (DWDM), and Multiprotocol Label Switching (MPLS).

Long-Reach Ethernet

Metro Ethernet should not be confused with another LAN and MAN technology, called Long-Reach Ethernet (LRE), which can be used to connect buildings and rooms within buildings in campus networks. LRE provides a point-to-point link that can deliver a symmetrical, full-duplex, raw data rate of 11.25 Mbps over distances of up to 1 mile (1.6 km).

LRE enables the use of Ethernet over existing, unconditioned, voice-grade copper twisted-pair wire that is ubiquitous in many cities and even rural areas, having been installed and upgraded over many years by telephone companies. Owners of multiunit structures such as hotels, apartment buildings, business complexes, and government agencies can use LRE to provide Ethernet connectivity to customers even though the building wiring uses old Category 1, 2, or 3 cabling.

LRE allows Ethernet LAN transmissions to coexist with telephone, ISDN, or PBX signaling services over a pair of ordinary copper wires. LRE technology uses coding and digital modulation techniques from the digital subscriber line (DSL) world in conjunction with Ethernet, the most popular LAN protocol. Chapter 11, "Selecting Technologies and Devices for Enterprise Networks," covers DSL in more detail.

Cisco EtherChannel

The previous three sections migrated into the realm of MAN applications. Getting back to smaller campus networks, one more technology that is a part of many network designers' toolbox of LAN choices is Cisco EtherChannel technology. EtherChannel is a trunking technology that groups full-duplex 802.3 Ethernet links together so that the links can provide extremely high speeds, support load sharing, and back each other up if one link fails. EtherChannel was first introduced by Kalpana in its switches in the early 1990s. Cisco has extended the technology, while remaining compatible with IEEE 802.3 standards.

EtherChannel can be used between routers, switches, and servers on point-to-point links that require more bandwidth than a single Ethernet link can provide. Cisco provides EtherChannel ports for many of its high-end switches and routers. Intel and other vendors make EtherChannel NICs for servers.

With Fast EtherChannel, up to four Fast Ethernet links can be grouped to provide a maximum aggregate bandwidth of 800 Mbps (full duplex). With Gigabit EtherChannel, up to four Gigabit Ethernet links can be grouped to provide a maximum aggregate bandwidth of 8 Gbps. With 10-Gbps Ethernet, up to four 10-Gbps Ethernet links can be grouped to provide a maximum aggregate bandwidth of 80 Gbps.

EtherChannel distributes unicast, broadcast, and multicast traffic across the links in a channel, providing high-performance load sharing and redundancy. If a link failure occurs, traffic is redirected to remaining links without user intervention.

Note EtherChannel selects a link within a channel by performing an XOR operation on the last 2 bits of the source and destination addresses in a frame. The XOR operation can result in one of four values that are mapped to the four possible links. (If only two links are used, the XOR operation is done using only the last bit from each address.) This method may not evenly balance traffic if a majority of traffic is between two hosts, such as two routers or two servers. However, for typical network traffic with a mix of senders and receivers, EtherChannel provides high-performance load balancing.

When designing EtherChannel trunks, you can increase its effectiveness as a redundancy feature by grouping links that run on cables in different parts of a campus network. Figure 10-4 shows a topology where the network designer increased bandwidth between a data center and a wiring closet to an aggregate of 800 Mbps (full duplex) and also used the physical diversity of the fiber plant to decrease the chances of a network outage.

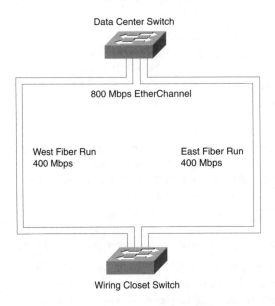

Figure 10-4 *EtherChannel Redundancy*

The EtherChannel connection consists of four Fast Ethernet links. Two fiber runs on the east side of the building provide 400 Mbps, and two fiber runs on the west side of the building provide the remaining 400 Mbps. In this example, if a fiber cut occurs on one side of the building, the remaining side will pick up the traffic in less than 1 second and wiring closet clients will probably not even notice the change.

Selecting Internetworking Devices for a Campus Network Design

At this point in the network design process, you have developed a network topology and should have an idea of which segments will be interconnected. Table 10-3 provides a review of the major differences between internetworking devices that can be used to connect network segments. In most cases, the choice will be between a switch and a router. Hubs and bridges are generally no longer used, although hubs are sometimes placed in a network to facilitate tapping into a network for protocol analysis, and bridges are still sometimes used in wireless networks.

Table 10-3 *Comparing Hubs, Bridges, Switches, and Routers*

	OSI Layers Implemented	How Bandwidth (Collision) Domains Are Segmented	How Broadcast Domains Are Segmented	Typical Deployment	Typical Additional Features
Hub	1	All ports are in the same bandwidth domain.	All ports are in the same broadcast domain.	Connects individual devices in small LANs	Autopartitioning to isolate misbehaving nodes
Bridge	1–2	Each port delineates a bandwidth domain.	All ports are in the same broadcast domain.	Connects networks	User-configured packet filtering
Switch	1–2	Each port delineates a bandwidth domain.	All ports are in the same broadcast domain unless VLANs are used.	Connects individual devices or networks	Filtering, cell-relay capabilities, cut-through processing, multimedia (multicast) features
Router	1–3	Each port delineates a bandwidth domain.	Each port delineates a broadcast domain.	Connects networks	Filtering, firewalling, high-speed WAN links, compression, advanced queuing and forwarding processes, multimedia (multicast) features

After you have designed a network topology and made some decisions about the placement and scope of shared, switched, and routed network segments, you should then recommend actual switches, bridges, and routers from various vendors. This section covers selection criteria you can use when making decisions.

Criteria for Selecting Campus Internetworking Devices

Criteria for selecting internetworking devices in general include the following:

- Number of ports

- Processing speed

- Amount of memory

- Amount of latency introduced when the device relays data

- Throughput in packets per second

- Ingress/egress queuing and buffering techniques

- LAN and WAN technologies supported

- Autosensing of speed (for example, 10 or 100 Mbps)

- Autodetection of half- versus full-duplex operation

- Media (cabling) supported

- Ease of configuration

- Manageability (for example, support for Simple Network Management Protocol [SNMP] and Remote Monitoring [RMON], status indicators)

- Cost

- Mean time between failure (MTBF) and mean time to repair (MTTR)

- Support for packet filters and other security measures

- Support for hot-swappable components

- Support for in-service software upgrades

- Support for redundant power supplies

- Support for optimization features

- Support for QoS features

- Availability and quality of technical support

- Availability and quality of documentation

- Availability and quality of training (for complex switches and routers)

- Reputation and viability of the vendor

■   Availability of independent test results that confirm the performance of the device

For switches and bridges (including wireless bridges), the following criteria can be added to the first bulleted list in this section:

■   Bridging technologies supported (transparent bridging, Spanning Tree Algorithm, remote bridging, and so on)

■   Advanced spanning-tree features supported (rapid reconfiguration of spanning trees and multiple spanning trees [802.1s])

■   The number of MAC addresses that the switch or bridge can learn

■   Support for stacking or virtual switching where multiple switches can be managed as one switch

■   Support for port security (802.1X)

■   Support for cut-through switching

■   Support for adaptive cut-through switching

■   VLAN technologies supported, such as the VLAN Trunking Protocol (VTP) and IEEE 802.1Q

■   Support for multicast applications (for example, the ability to participate in the Internet Group Management Protocol [IGMP] to control the spread of multicast packets)

■   Amount of memory available for switching tables, routing tables (if the switch has a routing module), and memory used by protocol routines

■   Availability of a routing module

■   802.3af Power over Ethernet (PoE) or 802.3at PoE+

For routers (and switches with a routing module), the following criteria can be added to the first bulleted list in this section:

■   Network layer protocols supported

■   Routing protocols supported

■   Support for multicast applications

■   Support for advanced queuing, switching, and other optimization features

■   Support for compression (and compression performance if it is supported)

■   Support for encryption (and encryption performance if it is supported)

For wireless access points and bridges, the following criteria can be added to the first bulleted list in this section:

■   Wireless speeds supported (11 Mbps, 5.5 Mbps, 54 Mbps, and 600 Mbps)

■   Wireless standards supported (802.11a, 802.11b, 802.11g, and 802.11n)

- Speed of uplink Ethernet port

- Support for Dynamic Host Configuration Protocol (DHCP), Network Address Translation (NAT), and IP routing

- Support for VLANs

- Support for inline power over Ethernet if the access point is unlikely to be mounted near power outlets

- Antenna range and support for higher-end antenna attachments

- Transmit power and receive sensitivity

- Ability to tune the transmit power

- Availability of a rugged model for outside use

- Support for authenticating client devices by MAC address

- Support for user authentication with 802.1X and the Extensible Authentication Protocol (EAP)

- Support for mutual authentication, which allows a client to be certain that it is communicating with the intended authentication server

- An option for disabling Service Set Identifier (SSID) broadcasts

- Support for 128-bit or better encryption

- Support for dynamic keys, unique keys for each user, per-packet keying, and a message integrity check (MIC)

- Support for one-time passwords or token cards

- Support for Publicly Secure Packet Forwarding (PSPF)

- Support for security standards such as WPA or 802.11i

Optimization Features on Campus Internetworking Devices

Chapter 13, "Optimizing Your Network Design," covers optimization and QoS in more detail, but it is worth mentioning here that optimization and QoS features are more important in campus network designs than many designers might expect. Not only is QoS required in the WAN, where the available bandwidth is lower than in the campus, but stringent requirements for low latency and jitter drive the need for QoS in LAN switches and routers as well. Even in campus networks, bandwidth demand on the network often exceeds the available bandwidth. In addition, VoIP drives the need for QoS because of its requirement for low latency. QoS features should be considered when selecting internetworking devices for campus networks.

In most networks, at least some elements are oversubscribed and therefore require QoS features. QoS features are most often required on uplinks from the distribution layer to the core layer of a hierarchical network design. Sometimes QoS is required on uplinks from the access layer to the distribution layer also. The sum of the speeds on all ports on a switch where end devices are connected is usually greater than that of the uplink port. When the access ports are fully used, congestion on the uplink port is unavoidable.

Access layer switches usually provide QoS based only on Layer 2 information, if at all. For example, access layer switches can base QoS decisions on the input port for traffic. Traffic from a particular port can be defined as high-priority traffic on an uplink port. The scheduling mechanism on the output port of an access layer switch ensures that traffic from such ports is served first. Input traffic can be marked to ensure the required service when traffic passes through distribution and core layer switches.

Distribution and core layer switches can provide QoS based on Layer 3 information, including source and destination IP addresses, port numbers, and QoS bits in an IP packet. QoS in distribution and core layer switches must be provided in both directions of traffic flow. See Chapter 13 for more information on QoS and optimization.

Example of a Campus Network Design

The goal of this section is to present a campus network design that was developed using the design methodology in this book. The example is based on a real network design. Some of the facts have been changed or simplified to preserve the privacy of the design customer, to protect the security of the customer's network, and to make it possible to present a simple and easy-to-understand example.

Background Information for the Campus Network Design Project

Wandering Valley Community College (WVCC) is a small college in the western United States that is attended by about 600 full- and part-time students. The students do not live on campus. Approximately 50 professors teach courses in the fields of arts and humanities, business, social sciences, mathematics, computer science, the physical sciences, and health sciences. Many of the professors also have other jobs in the business community, and only about half of them have an office on campus. Approximately 25 administration personnel handle admissions, student records, and other operational functions.

Enrollment at WVCC has doubled in the past few years. The faculty and administration staff has also doubled in size, with the exception of the IT department, which is still quite small. The IT department consists of one manager, one server administrator, two network administrators, and two part-time student assistants.

Because of the increase in enrollment and other factors covered in the next three sections, the current network has performance and reliability problems. The administration has told the IT department that both student and faculty complaints about the network have increased. Faculty members claim that, due to network problems, they cannot efficiently submit grades, maintain contact with colleagues at other colleges, or keep up with research. Students say they have handed in homework late due to network problems. The late submissions have impacted their grades. Despite the complaints about the network, faculty, staff, and student use of the network has doubled in the past few years.

Wireless access has become a point of contention between the IT department and other departments. Students often place wireless access points in the Computing Center and the Math and Sciences building without permission from the IT department. The IT manager is concerned about network security and has assigned part-time students to roam the network to locate and remove unauthorized access points. The part-time students resent this task because in many instances the rogue access points were installed by peers and associates. Also, they think that wireless access should be allowed. Many students, faculty, and staff members agree.

Business Goals

The college still wants to attract and retain more students. The college board of trustees believes that the best way to remain fiscally sound is to continue to increase enrollment and reduce attrition.

The college administration and board of trustees identified the following business goals:

- Increase the enrollment from 600 to 1000 students in the next 3 years.

- Reduce the attrition rate from 30 to 15 percent in the next 3 years.

- Improve faculty efficiency and allow faculty to participate in more research projects with colleagues at other colleges.

- Improve student efficiency and eliminate problems with homework submission.

- Allow students to access the campus network and the Internet wirelessly using their notebook computers.

- Allow visitors to the campus to access the Internet wirelessly using their notebook computers.

- Protect the network from intruders.

- Spend a grant that the state government issued for upgrading the campus network. The money must be spent by the end of the fiscal year.

Technical Goals

The IT department developed the following list of technical goals, based on research about the causes of network problems, which is covered in more detail in the "The Current Network at WVCC" section:

- Redesign the IP addressing scheme.

- Increase the bandwidth of the Internet connection to support new applications and the expanded use of current applications.

- Provide a secure, private wireless network for students to access the campus network and the Internet.

- Provide an open wireless network for visitors to the campus to access the Internet.

- Provide a network that offers a response time of approximately 1/10th of a second or less for interactive applications.

- Provide a campus network that is available approximately 99.90 percent of the time and offers an MTBF of 3000 hours (about 4 months) and an MTTR of 3 hours (with a low standard deviation from these average numbers).

- Provide security to protect the Internet connection and internal network from intruders.

- Use network management tools that can increase the efficiency and effectiveness of the IT department.

- Provide a network that can scale to support future expanded usage of multimedia applications.

Network Applications

Students, faculty, and staff use the WVCC network for the following purposes:

- **Application 1, homework:** Students use the network to write papers and other documents. They save their work to file servers in the Computing Center and print their work on printers in the Computing Center and other buildings.

- **Application 2, email:** Students, faculty, and administrative staff make extensive use of email.

- **Application 3, web research:** Students, faculty, and administrative staff use Mozilla Firefox or Microsoft Internet Explorer to access information, participate in chat rooms, play games, and use other typical web services.

- **Application 4, library card catalog:** Students and faculty access the online card catalog.

- **Application 5, weather modeling:** Meteorology students and faculty participate in a project to model weather patterns in conjunction with other colleges and universities in the state.

- **Application 6, telescope monitoring:** Astronomy students and faculty continually download graphical images from a telescope located at the state university.

- **Application 7, graphics upload:** The Art department uploads large graphics files to an off-campus print shop that can print large-scale images on a high-speed laser printer. The print shop prints artwork that is file-transferred to the shop via the Internet.

- **Application 8, distance learning:** The Computer Science department participates in a distance-learning project with the state university. The state university lets WVCC students sign up to receive streaming video of a computer science lecture course that is offered at the state university. The students can also participate in a real-time "chat room" while attending the class.

- **Application 9, college management system:** The college administration personnel use the college management system to keep track of class registrations and student records.

User Communities

Table 10-4 shows the user communities at WVCC. The expected growth of the communities is also included. Growth is expected for two reasons:

- New PCs and Macintoshes will be purchased.

- Wireless access will allow more students and visitors to access the network with their personal laptop computers.

Table 10-4   *WVCC User Communities*

User Community Name	Size of Community (Number of Users)	Location of Community	Applications Used by Community
PC users in Computing Center	30, will grow to 60	Basement of library	Homework, email, web research, library card catalog
Mac users in the Computing Center	15, will grow to 30	Basement of library	Homework, email, web research, library card catalog
Library patrons	15, will grow to 30	Floors 1–3 of library	Email, web research, library card catalog
Business/Social Sciences PC users	15, will grow to 30	Business and Social Sciences building	Homework, email, web research, library card catalog
Arts/ Humanities Mac users	15, will grow to 25	Arts and Humanities building	Homework, email, web research, library card catalog, graphics upload
Arts/ Humanities PC users	25, will grow to 50	Arts and Humanities building	Homework, email, web research, library card catalog, graphics upload
Math/Science PC users	25, will grow to 50	Math and Sciences building	Homework, email, web research, library card catalog, weather modeling, telescope monitoring, distance learning
Administration PC users	25, will grow to 50	Administration building	Email, web research, library card catalog, college management system
Visitors to the campus	10, will grow to 25	All locations	Web research, library card catalog, email
Outside users	Hundreds	Internet	Surfing the WVCC website

Data Stores (Servers)

Table 10-5 shows the major data stores (servers) that have been identified at WVCC.

Table 10-5 *WVCC Data Stores*

Data Store	Location	Application	Used by User Community (or Communities)
Library card cata-log Windows server	Computing Center server farm	Library card catalog	All
Apple Filing Protocol (AFP) file server	Computing Center server farm	Homework	Mac users in the Computing Center and in Arts and Humanities building
Windows file/print server	Computing Center server farm	Homework	PC users in all buildings
Windows web server	Computing Center server farm	Hosts the WVCC website	All
Windows email server	Computing Center server farm	Email	All users except visitors (who use their own servers)
Windows college management server	Computing Center server farm	College management system	Administration
Windows DHCP server	Computing Center server farm	Addressing	All
Windows network management server	Computing Center server farm	Management	Administration
UNIX DNS server	State community college network system	Naming	All

Current Network at WVCC

A few years ago, the college buildings were not even interconnected. Internet access was not centralized, and each department handled its own network and server management. Much progress has been made since that time, and today a Layer 2 switched, hierarchical network design is in place. A single router that also acts as a firewall provides Internet access.

The logical topology of the current campus-backbone network at WVCC consists of a hierarchical, mesh architecture with redundant links between buildings. Figure 10-5 shows the logical topology of the campus backbone.

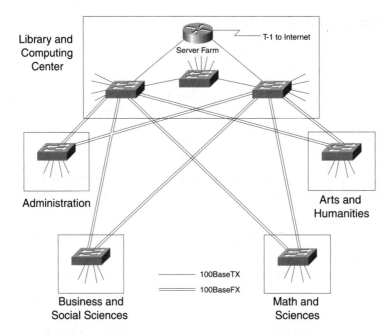

Figure 10-5 *Wandering Valley Community College's Current Campus-Backbone Network*

The campus network design has the following features:

■ The network uses switched Ethernet. A high-end switch in each building is redundantly connected to two high-end switches in the Computing Center. Figure 10-5 shows these switches.

■ Within each building, a 24- or 48-port Ethernet switch on each floor connects end-user systems. Figure 10-6 shows the building network architecture.

■ The switches run the IEEE 802.1D Spanning Tree Protocol.

■ The switches support SNMP and RMON. A Windows-based network management software package monitors the switches. The software runs on a server in the server farm module of the network design.

■ All devices are part of the same broadcast domain. All devices (except two public servers) are part of the 192.168.1.0 subnet using a subnet mask of 255.255.255.0.

■ Addressing for end-user PCs and Macs is accomplished with DHCP. A Windows server in the server farm acts as the DHCP server.

■ The email and web servers use public addresses that the state community college network system assigned to the college. The system also provides a DNS server that the college uses.

■ The router acts as a firewall using packet filtering. The router also implements NAT. The router has a default route to the Internet and does not run a routing protocol. The WAN link to the Internet is a 1.544-Mbps T1 link.

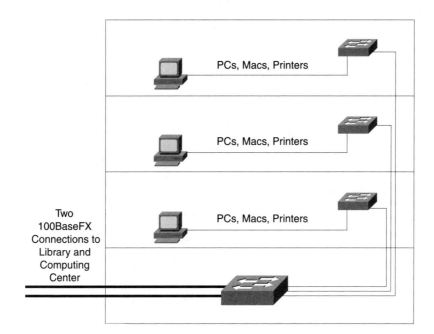

Figure 10-6   *Building Network Design for WVCC*

The physical design of the current network has the following features:

■ Buildings are connected via full-duplex 100BASE-FX Ethernet.

■ Within buildings, 100-Mbps Ethernet switches are used.

■ Every building is equipped with Category 5e cabling and wallplates in the various offices, classrooms, and labs.

■ The router in the Computing Center supports two 100BASE-TX ports and one T1 port with a built-in CSU/DSU unit. The router has a redundant power supply.

■ A centralized (star) physical topology is used for the campus cabling. Underground cable conduits hold multimode fiber-optic cabling. The cabling is off-the-shelf cabling that consists of 30 strands of fiber with a 62.5-micron core and 125-micron cladding, protected by a plastic sheath suitable for outdoor wear and tear.

Figure 10-7 shows the campus-cabling design.

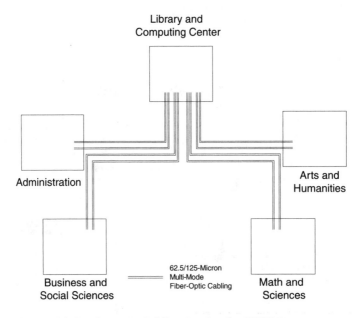

Figure 10-7   *Campus-Cabling Design for WVCC*

Traffic Characteristics of Network Applications

The student assistants in the IT department conducted an analysis of the traffic characteristics of applications. The analysis methods included capturing typical application sessions with a protocol analyzer, interviewing users about their current and planned uses of applications, and estimating the size of network objects transferred on the network.

The students determined that the homework, email, web research, library card catalog, and college management system applications have nominal bandwidth requirements and are not delay sensitive. The other applications, however, use a significant amount of bandwidth, in particular a high percentage of the WAN bandwidth to the Internet. The distance-learning application is also delay sensitive.

The users of the weather-modeling and telescope-monitoring applications want to expand their use of these applications, but are currently hindered by the amount of bandwidth available to the Internet. The graphics-upload application users are also hindered from sending large files in a timely fashion by the shortage of bandwidth to the Internet.

The distance-learning application is an asymmetric (one-way) streaming-video application. The state university uses digital video equipment to film the class lectures in real time and send the video stream over the Internet, using the Real-Time Streaming Protocol (RTSP) and the Real-Time Transport Protocol (RTP). The remote students do not send any audio or video data; they simply have the ability to send text questions while the class is happening, using a chat room web page.

A user subscribes to the distance-learning class by accessing a web server at the state university, entering a username and password, and specifying how much bandwidth the user has available. The web page currently does not let a user specify more than 56 Kbps of available bandwidth.

At this time, the distance-learning service is a point-to-point system. Each user receives a unique 56-Kbps video stream from the video system at the state university. For this reason, WVCC limits the number of users who can access the distance-learning system to ten students who are located in the Math and Sciences building.

In the future, the distance-learning system will support IP multicast technologies. In the meantime, however, students and IT staff agree that a solution must be found for allowing more than ten students to use the distance-learning system at one time.

Summary of Traffic Flows

The student assistants used their research about user communities, data stores, and application traffic characteristics to analyze traffic flows. They represented cross-campus traffic flows in a graphical form, which Figure 10-8 shows.

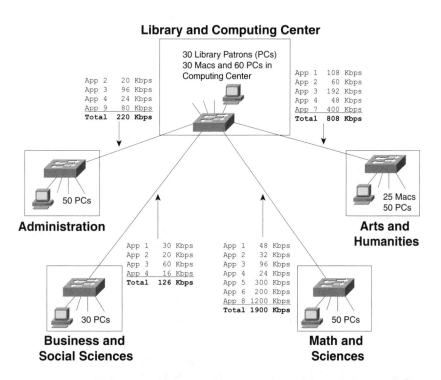

Figure 10-8   *Cross-Campus Traffic Flows on the WVCC Campus Network*

In addition to the cross-campus traffic flows, the students documented traffic flows inside the library and Computing Center and traffic flows to and from the Internet. Inside the library and Computing Center, traffic travels to and from the various servers at about the following rates:

Application 1	96 Kbps
Application 2	72 Kbps
Application 3	240 Kbps
Application 4	60 Kbps
Total	**468 Kbps**

Traffic travels to and from the router that connects the campus network to the Internet at about the following rates:

Application 2	120 Kbps
Application 3	740 Kbps
Application 5	240 Kbps
Application 6	200 Kbps
Application 7	400 Kbps
Application 8	600 Kbps
Total	**2300 Kbps**

Performance Characteristics of the Current Network

From the analysis conducted by the student assistants and from switch, router, and server logs, the IT department determined that bandwidth on the Ethernet campus network is lightly used. However, three major problems are likely the cause of the difficulties that users are experiencing:

- The IP addressing scheme supports just one IP subnet with a subnet mask of 255.255.255.0. In other words, only 254 addresses are allowed. A few years ago, the IT department assumed that only a small subset of students and faculty would use the network at one time. This is no longer the case. As use of the network grows and students place wireless laptops on the network, the number of addresses has become insufficient. Users who join the network midmorning after many other users have joined often fail to receive an IP address from the DHCP server.

- The 1.544-Mbps connection to the Internet is overloaded. Average network utilization of the serial WAN link, measured in a 10-minute window, is 95 percent. The router drops about 5 percent of packets due to utilization peaks of 100 percent.

- The router itself is overloaded. The student assistants wrote a script to periodically collect the output of the **show processes cpu** command. The assistants discovered that the 5-minute CPU utilization is often as high as 90 percent and the 5-second CPU utilization often peaks at 99 percent, with a large portion of the CPU power being consumed by CPU interrupts. Using a lab network, the assistants simulated actual network traffic going through a similar router with and without access lists and NAT enabled. The assistants determined that the Internet router CPU is overused not just because of the large amount of traffic but also because of the access lists and NAT tasks.

Network Redesign for WVCC

Using a modular approach, the network administrators and student assistants designed the following enhancements to the campus network:

- Optimized routing and addressing for the campus backbone that interconnects buildings provides access to the server farm and routes traffic to the Internet

- Wireless access in all buildings, both for visitors and users of the private campus network (students, faculty, and administrative staff)

- Improved performance and security on the edge of the network where traffic is routed to and from the Internet

Optimized IP Addressing and Routing for the Campus Backbone

The network administrators and student assistants decided to keep the hierarchical, mesh logical topology that their predecessors so wisely chose. However, to fix the IP addressing problems, a routing module was added to each of the building high-end switches, essentially turning the switches into fast routers. With this new approach, the administrators were able to subdivide the network logically into multiple subnets. The administrators decided to stay with private addresses. They assigned the following address ranges to the campus network:

- **Server farm:** 192.168.1.1–192.168.1.254

- **Library:** 192.168.2.1–192.168.2.254

- **Computing Center:** 192.168.3.1–192.168.3.254

- **Administration:** 192.168.4.1–192.168.4.254

- **Business and Social Sciences:** 192.168.5.1–192.168.5.254

- **Math and Sciences:** 192.168.6.1–192.168.6.254

- **Arts and Humanities:** 192.168.7.1–192.168.7.254

- **Users of the secure, private wireless network:** 192.168.8.1–192.168.8.254 (This is a campuswide subnet that spans all buildings and outside grounds.)

- **Users of the open, public wireless network:** 192.168.9.1–192.168.9.254 (This is a campuswide subnet that spans all buildings and outside grounds.)

- The email and web servers use public addresses that the state community college network system assigned to the college.

Instead of relying on the Layer 2 Spanning Tree Protocol for loop avoidance, the designers chose a Layer 3 routing protocol. They chose Open Shortest Path First (OSPF) because it is not proprietary and runs on many vendors' routers, converges quickly, supports load sharing, and is moderately easy to configure and troubleshoot.

Wireless Network

The wireless enhancements to the network represented the biggest challenge due to biases and other Layer 8 (nontechnical) issues. The IT department preferred a single solution that was extremely secure. Many students and faculty wanted secure access to the campus network and support for visitors using the wireless network to access the Internet.

The solution was to provide two access points in each building, with different security policies implemented on them. An open access point in each building provides access for visitors, while a secure access point in each building provides secure access for students, faculty, and staff. The open access points are on a different channel from the other access points to avoid interference and boost performance. The access points support IEEE 802.11n and each provides a nominal bandwidth of 600 Mbps.

From an IP addressing point of view, two separate subnets were used, as mentioned in the "Optimized IP Addressing and Routing for the Campus Backbone" section—one for the secure, private wireless LAN (WLAN) and one for the open, public WLAN. Each of these subnets is a campus-wide subnet. With this solution, a wireless user can roam the entire campus and never require the lease of a new address from the DHCP server.

In each building, a switch port on the routing switch connects the access point that supports the open network. A different switch port connects the access point that supports the secure, private network. Each of these switch ports is in its own VLAN. Another VLAN is used for the ports that connect wired switches and users within the building.

The open access points are not configured for WEP or MAC address authentication, and the SSID is announced in beacon frames so that users can easily associate with the WLAN. To protect the campus network from users of the open WLAN, the routing switches are configured with access lists that forward only a few protocols. Packets sent from users of the open WLAN to TCP ports 80 (HTTP), 25 (SMTP), and 110 (POP), and UDP ports 53 (DNS) and 67 (DHCP) are permitted. All other traffic is denied. Some students and faculty wanted to support more protocols, but the IT department insisted that, at least for now, these are the only supported protocols. This protects the network from security problems and avoids visitors using too much bandwidth for other applications.

The private access points implement many more security features. The SSID is hidden and not announced in beacon frames. Although a determined user could still discover the SSID, removing it from beacon packets hides it from the casual user and avoids confusing visitors, who see only the public SSID. Students, faculty, and staff who want to use the private WLAN must know the private SSID and type it into the configuration tool for their wireless adapters.

To protect the privacy of data that travels across the private WLAN, access points and clients will use Wi-Fi Protected Access (WPA) and the Temporal Key Integrity Protocol (TKIP). The private access points are also configured to use 802.1X and Lightweight

Extensible Authentication Protocol (LEAP). Users of the private WLAN must have a valid user ID and password. To accomplish user authentication, the IT department will purchase a dedicated one-rack-unit (one-RU) hardened appliance that operates as a centralized Remote Authentication Dial-In User Service (RADIUS) server for user authentication. They chose an appliance rather than software for a generic PC platform to avoid security vulnerabilities found in typical industry-standard operating systems. The appliance must be reliable and easy to configure and troubleshoot.

Improved Performance and Security for the Edge of the Network

To fix the problems with high CPU utilization on the Internet router, the designers chose to break apart the network functions of security and traffic forwarding. The Internet router will now focus on traffic forwarding. The administrators reconfigured the router with a simpler list of access filters that provide initial protection from intruders, and they removed NAT functionality from the router. Instead, a dedicated firewall was placed into the topology between the router and the campus network. The firewall provides security and NAT.

The IT department chose a one-RU appliance firewall with a hardened operating system that supports OSPF routing, NAT, URL filtering, and content filtering. For now, four interfaces on the firewall will be used. The outside interface will connect the Internet router; two inside interfaces will connect the campus network; and the demilitarized zone (DMZ) interface will connect the email and web servers.

To fix the problem of high utilization on the WAN link to the Internet and the high incidence of packet dropping, the WAN link was replaced with a 10-Mbps Metro Ethernet link. The IT department discovered that a few service providers in the area were willing to bring in a single-mode fiber-optic link and support Ethernet rather than a WAN protocol. The IT department ordered a 10/100BASE-FX interface for the router and chose a service provider that offers a reasonable monthly charge and has a good reputation for reliability. In addition, the provider makes it easy for its customers to upgrade to more bandwidth. For example, if the college decides it needs a 100-Mbps Ethernet link, the college can make a single phone call to the provider and the provider guarantees to make the change that day.

The IT department also factored into the choice of provider the experience level and knowledge of the installation and support staff. In particular, the provider's network engineers had many practical ideas for addressing redundancy for future network designs.

Figure 10-9 shows the new design for the WVCC campus network.

Although the network design in the example is simple, and some decisions were more obvious than they would be for a more complex design, the example demonstrated the use of the following top-down network design steps:

Step 1. Analyze requirements, including both business and technical goals, and any "workplace politics" that are relevant to technology choices.

Step 2. Characterize the existing network.

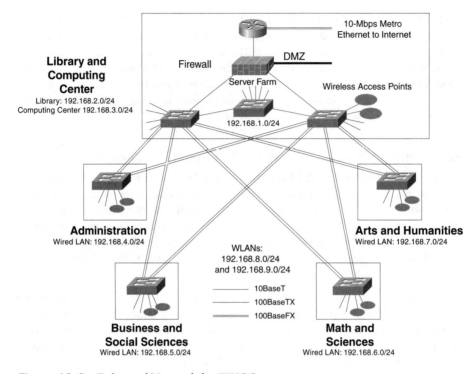

Figure 10-9   *Enhanced Network for WVCC*

Step 3.   Identify network applications and analyze bandwidth and QoS requirements for the applications.

Step 4.   Analyze traffic flows.

Step 5.   Choose a logical topology.

Step 6.   Select building access technologies.

Step 7.   Select campus-backbone technologies.

Step 8.   Select Internet connectivity technologies.

Step 9.   Select security solutions.

Summary

This chapter covered the first step in the physical design phase of the top-down network design methodology: selecting technologies and devices for campus network designs. A physical design consists of cabling, Layer 2 protocol implementations, and network devices. The physical design depends on business objectives, technical requirements, traffic characteristics, and traffic flows, which Part I of this book discusses. The physical design builds on the logical design, which Part II discusses.

This chapter covered LAN cabling plant design and LAN technologies, such as Ethernet, Metro Ethernet, and EtherChannel. The chapter also provided some selection criteria you can use when choosing internetworking devices. The chapter concluded with an example of a campus network design that was developed for the Wandering Valley Community College.

Review Questions

1. What are the most important criteria for selecting an internetworking device?

2. What is the difference between single-mode and multimode fiber? Which is faster?

3. Why are QoS features often necessary in LAN switches and routers?

4. Modern campus networks are almost always built with Ethernet technology these days. Why is that? Why did Ethernet outlast older technologies such as Token Ring, FDDI, and ATM LAN Emulation (LANE)?

Design Scenario

The WVCC case study in this chapter left some design decisions to the reader. In particular, the case study doesn't mention actual product selections made by the network designers. Making these selections is your job. Read through the case study and answer the following questions.

1. Based on the design requirements and decisions that have been made, what wireless access points would you recommend for WVCC? Do some Internet research to find an access point that will meet WVCC's needs and write two or three paragraphs about the product and why you chose it.

2. To accomplish user authentication for the private WLAN, WVCC's IT department will purchase a dedicated one-RU hardened appliance that will operate as a centralized RADIUS server. Do some Internet research to find such a server that will meet WVCC's needs and write two or three paragraphs about the product and why you chose it.

3. WVCC has decided to purchase a standalone firewall. Reread the "Improved Performance and Security for the Edge of the Network" section of the chapter to understand WVCC's requirements for the firewall. Do some Internet research to find a firewall that will meet WVCC's needs, and write two or three paragraphs about the product and why you chose it.

4. WVCC's IT department would like to deploy a solution for managing the wireless network. The solution should allow the network administrators to remotely manage the access points and discover any rogue access points that students or faculty might install without permission from the IT department. Either a hardware appliance or a software application that runs on a shared server will meet the need. Do some Internet research to find a wireless management product that will meet WVCC's needs, and write two or three paragraphs about the product and why you chose it.

5. The work of an IT department is never finished. The WVCC network administrators and student assistants have many plans for the next network upgrade. Their main concern at this point is availability. Although the hierarchical mesh network has some redundancy, there are many single points of failure. Availability of applications can be adversely affected by any one of these points failing. Write a short paper that identifies the most significant single points of failure in WVCC's new network design. Discuss the changes to the network design that you would make (or additional products that you would recommend) to avoid these single points of failure.

Chapter 11

Selecting Technologies and Devices for Enterprise Networks

This chapter presents technologies for the remote-access and wide-area network (WAN) components of an enterprise network design. The chapter discusses physical and data link layer protocols and enterprise network devices, such as remote-access servers, routers, firewalls, and virtual private network (VPN) concentrators.

The chapter begins with a discussion of the following remote-access technologies:

■ Point-to-Point Protocol (PPP)

■ Cable modems

■ Digital subscriber line (DSL)

After discussing remote-access technologies, the chapter presents options for selecting WAN and remote-access capacities with the North American Digital Hierarchy, the European E system, or the Synchronous Digital Hierarchy (SDH). The chapter continues with a discussion of the following WAN technologies:

■ Leased lines

■ Synchronous Optical Network (SONET)

■ Frame Relay

■ Asynchronous Transfer Mode (ATM)

■ Metro Ethernet

The chapter then covers two topics that will help you complete your WAN design:

■ Selecting routers for an enterprise WAN design

■ Selecting a WAN service provider

The chapter concludes with an example of a WAN network design that was developed for a medium-sized company, Klamath Paper Products, Inc. The example indicates what technologies and devices were chosen for this customer based on the customer's goals.

The technologies and devices you select for your particular network design customer will depend on bandwidth and quality of service (QoS) requirements, the network topology, business requirements and constraints, and technical goals (such as scalability, affordability, performance, and availability). An analysis of traffic flow and load, as discussed in Chapter 4, "Characterizing Network Traffic," can help you accurately select capacities and devices.

For some organizations, scalability is a key design goal. The selected WAN solution must have enough headroom for growth. As discussed in this chapter, some WAN technologies are more scalable than others.

Another key design goal for many organizations is to minimize the cost of WAN and remote-access circuits. Optimization techniques that reduce costs play an important role in most WAN and remote-access designs. Methods for merging separate voice, video, and data networks into a combined, cost-effective WAN also play an important role. These methods must handle the diverse QoS requirements of different applications.

Remote-Access Technologies

As organizations have become more mobile and geographically dispersed, remote-access technologies have become an important ingredient of many enterprise network designs. Enterprises use remote-access technologies to provide network access to telecommuters, employees in remote offices, and mobile workers who travel.

An analysis of the location of user communities and their applications should form the basis of your remote-access design. It is important to recognize the location and number of full- and part-time telecommuters, how extensively mobile users access the network, and the location and scope of remote offices. Remote offices include branch offices, sales offices, manufacturing sites, warehouses, retail stores, regional banks in the financial industry, and regional doctors' offices in the health-care industry. Remote offices are also sometimes located at a business partner's site (for example, a vendor or supplier).

Typically, remote workers use such applications as email, web browsing, sales order-entry, and calendar applications to schedule meetings. Other, more bandwidth-intensive applications include downloading software or software updates, exchanging files with corporate servers, providing product demonstrations, managing the network from home, videoconferencing, and attending online classes.

In the past, telecommuters and mobile users typically accessed the network using an analog modem line. Analog modems take a long time to connect and have high latency and low speeds. (The highest speed available for analog modems is 56 kbps.) These days remote users need higher speeds, lower latency, and faster connection-establishment times. Analog modems have been replaced with small office/home office (SOHO) routers that support a cable or DSL modem. The sections that follow discuss these options and provide information on PPP, a protocol typically used with remote-access and other WAN technologies.

PPP

The Internet Engineering Task Force (IETF) developed PPP as a standard data link layer protocol for transporting various network layer protocols across serial, point-to-point links. PPP can be used to connect a single remote user to a central office, or to connect a remote office with many users to a central office. PPP is used with Integrated Services Digital Network (ISDN), analog lines, digital leased lines, and other WAN technologies. PPP provides the following services:

- Network layer protocol multiplexing

- Link configuration

- Link-quality testing

- Link-option negotiation

- Authentication

- Header compression

- Error detection

PPP has four functional layers:

- The physical layer is based on various international standards for serial communication, including EIA/TIA-232-C (formerly RS-232-C), EIA/TIA-422 (formerly RS-422), V.24, and V.35.

- The encapsulation of network layer datagrams is based on the standard High-Level Data Link Control (HDLC) protocol.

- The Link Control Protocol (LCP) is used for establishing, configuring, authenticating, testing, and terminating a data-link connection.

- A family of Network Control Protocols (NCP) is used for establishing and configuring various network layer protocols, such as IP, IPX, AppleTalk, and DECnet.

Multilink PPP and Multichassis Multilink PPP

Multilink PPP (MPPP) adds support for channel aggregation to PPP. Channel aggregation can be used for load sharing and providing extra bandwidth. With channel aggregation, a device can automatically bring up additional channels as bandwidth requirements increase. Channel aggregation was popular with ISDN links, but it can be used on other types of serial interfaces also (a PC connected to two analog modems can use channel aggregation, for example). MPPP ensures that packets arrive in order at the receiving device. To accomplish this, MPPP encapsulates data in PPP and assigns a sequence number to datagrams. At the receiving device, PPP uses the sequence number to re-create the original data stream. Multiple channels appear as one logical link to upper-layer protocols.

Multichassis MPPP is a Cisco IOS Software enhancement to MPPP that allows channel aggregation across multiple remote-access servers at a central site. Multichassis MPPP allows WAN administrators to group multiple access servers into a single *stack group*. User traffic can be split and reassembled across multiple access servers in the stack group.

Multichassis MPPP makes use of the *Stack Group Bidding Protocol (SGBP)*, which defines a bidding process to allow access servers to elect a server to handle aggregation for an application. The server has the job of creating and managing a bundle of links for an application that requests channel aggregation.

SGBP bidding can be weighted so that CPU-intensive processes, such as bundle creation, fragmentation and reassembly of packets, compression, and encryption, are offloaded to routers designated as *offload servers*. You can deploy a high-end router as an offload server. An Ethernet switch can connect members of the stack group and the offload server, as shown in Figure 11-1.

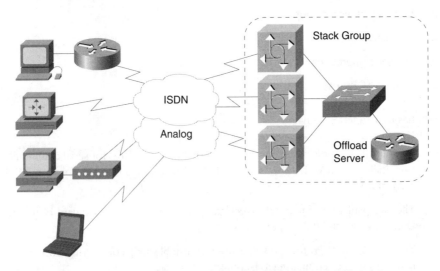

Figure 11-1 *Multichassis Multilink PPP Stack Group and Offload Server*

Password Authentication Protocol and Challenge Handshake Authentication Protocol

PPP supports two types of authentication:

- Password Authentication Protocol (PAP)

- Challenge Handshake Authentication Protocol (CHAP)

CHAP is more secure than PAP and is recommended. (In fact, the RFC that discusses CHAP and PAP, RFC 1334, has been obsoleted by RFC 1994, which no longer mentions

PAP.) With PAP, a user's password is sent as clear text. An intruder can use a protocol analyzer to capture the password and later use the password to break into the network. CHAP provides protection against such attacks by verifying a remote node with a three-way handshake protocol and a variable challenge value that is unique and unpredictable. Verification happens upon link establishment and can be repeated any time during a session.

Figure 11-2 shows a CHAP sequence of events. When a remote node connects to an access server or router, the server or router sends back a challenge message with a challenge value that is based on an unpredictable random number. The remote station feeds the challenge value and the remote node's password through a hash algorithm, resulting in a one-way hashed challenge response. The remote node sends the hashed challenge response to the server, along with a username that identifies the remote node. The server looks up the username and runs the associated password and the challenge through the same hash algorithm that the remote node used. If the remote node sent the correct password, the hash values will match and the server sends an accept message; otherwise, it sends a deny message.

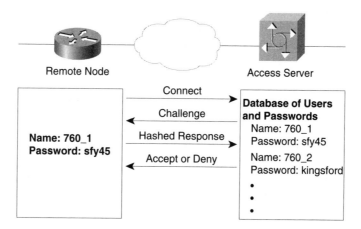

Figure 11-2   *Connection Establishment with the Challenge Handshake Authentication Protocol*

Cable Modem Remote Access

A popular option for remote access is a *cable modem*, which operates over the coax cable used by cable TV (CATV) providers. Coax cable supports higher speeds than telephone lines, so cable modem solutions are much faster than analog modem solutions. Another benefit of cable modems is that no dialup is required. This is an advantage over analog modems that take a long time to dial and connect to a remote site.

Note   The term *cable modem* is somewhat misleading. A cable modem works more like a LAN interface than an analog modem.

Cable-network service providers offer *hybrid fiber/coax (HFC)* systems that connect CATV networks to the service provider's high-speed fiber-optic network. The HFC systems allow users to connect their PCs or small LANs to the coax cable that enters their home or small office, and use this connection for high-speed access to the Internet or to an organization's private network using VPN software.

The cable-network service provider operates a cable modem termination system (CMTS) that provides high-speed connectivity for numerous cable modems. Many cable providers use a specialized CMTS router for this purpose. The router is designed to be installed at a cable operator's headend facility or distribution hub, and to function as the CMTS for subscriber end devices. The router forwards data upstream to connect with the Internet and/or the public switched telephone network (PSTN) if telephony applications are deployed.

Challenges Associated with Cable Modem Systems

A challenge with implementing a remote-access solution based on cable modems is that the CATV infrastructure was designed for broadcasting TV signals in just one direction: from the cable TV company to a person's home. Data transmission, however, is bidirectional. Data travels from the provider to the home (or small office) and from the home to the provider.

Because of the design of CATV networks, most cable-network services offer much more bandwidth for downstream traffic (from the service provider) than for upstream traffic (from the customer). An assumption is made that a lot of the data traveling from the home or small office consists of short acknowledgment packets and requires less bandwidth. This assumption is accurate for such applications as web browsing, but might not be accurate for other applications that will be deployed in your network design. A cable modem solution is not the best answer for peer-to-peer applications or client/server applications in which the client sends lots of data.

A typical cable-network system offers 25 to 50 Mbps downstream bandwidth and about 2 to 3 Mbps upstream bandwidth. Multiple users share the downstream and upstream bandwidth. Downstream data is seen by all active cable modems. Each cable modem filters out traffic that is not destined for it. Upstream bandwidth is allocated using timeslots. There are three types of timeslots:

- **Reserved:** A timeslot that is available only to a particular cable modem. The headend system at the provider's site allocates reserved timeslots to cable modems using a bandwidth allocation algorithm.

- **Contention:** A timeslot that is available to all cable modems. If two cable modems transmit in the same timeslot, the packets collide and the data is lost. The headend system signals that no data was received, and the cable modems can try again after waiting a random amount of time. Contention timeslots are used for short data transmissions (including requests for a quantity of reserved timeslots for transmitting more data).

- **Ranging:** A timeslot that is used for clock correction. The headend system tells a cable modem to transmit during a ranging timeslot. The headend system measures the time to receive the transmission, and gives the cable modem a small positive or negative correction value for its local clock.

If you plan to use a cable modem solution for remote users or remote offices, be sure to query the service provider about the number of users who share a single cable and the types of applications they use. Provide the service provider with information about the bandwidth requirements of your users' applications, based on the analysis of traffic characteristics that you did as part of the requirements-analysis phase of the network design project.

Typically a service provider can give you an approximation of how much bandwidth is available per user of a cable-network system. Some systems also have the capability to guarantee a level of bandwidth for heavy-usage applications. If your users require more bandwidth than the service provider can offer, then you should investigate using a leased line or Frame Relay circuit instead of a cable modem.

Another concern with shared media such as cable modem systems is how to offer QoS for voice, video, and other delay-sensitive applications. If the service provider doesn't have any good solutions for this problem, consider using a different WAN technology if your users rely on these delay-sensitive applications.

Digital Subscriber Line Remote Access

Another technology for remote access is *digital subscriber line (DSL)*. Telephone companies offer DSL for high-speed data traffic over ordinary telephone wires. With DSL, a home office or small office can connect a DSL modem (or DSL router with a built-in modem) to a phone line and use this connection to reach a central-site intranet and/or the Internet.

DSL operates over existing telephone lines between a telephone switching station and a home or office. Speeds depend on the type of DSL service and many physical layer factors, including the length of the circuit between the home or branch office and the telephone company, the wire gauge of the cable, the presence of bridged taps, and the presence of crosstalk or noise on the cable.

DSL supports asymmetric and symmetric communication. With asymmetric DSL (ADSL), traffic can move downstream from the provider and upstream from the end user at different speeds. An ADSL circuit has three channels:

- A high-speed downstream channel with speeds ranging from 1.544 to 12 Mbps

- A medium-speed duplex channel with speeds ranging from 16 to 640 kbps

- A plain old telephone service (POTS) 64-kbps channel for voice

With symmetric DSL (SDSL), traffic in either direction travels at the same speed, up to 1.544 Mbps. Unlike ADSL, SDSL does not allow POTS to run on the same line as data (although VoIP is feasible with SDSL). SDSL is a viable business solution that is a good choice for a small enterprise or branch office that hosts web or other services that send data as well as receive data.

Other DSL Implementations

DSL is sometimes called *xDSL* because of the many types of DSL technologies. In addition to ADSL and SDSL, providers in your area may support the following services:

- **ISDN DSL (IDSL):** A cross between ISDN and DSL. As with ISDN, IDSL uses a single wire pair to transmit data at 128 kbps in both directions and at distances of up to 15,000 to 18,000 feet (about 4600 to 5500 m). Unlike ISDN, IDSL does not use a signaling channel (a D channel).

- **High-bit-rate DSL (HDSL):** A mature technology that provides symmetric communications up to 1.544 Mbps over two wire pairs or 2.048 Mbps over three wire pairs. HDSL is a cost-effective alternative to a T1 or E1 circuit. HDSL is less expensive than T1 or E1 partly because it can run on poorer-quality lines without requiring any line conditioning. HDSL's range is 12,000 to 15,000 feet (about 3700 to 4600 m). Providers can extend the range with signal repeaters. HDSL does not support access to the PSTN.

- **HDSL-2:** Provides symmetric communications of up to 1.544 Mbps, but it is different from HDSL in that it uses a single wire pair. Engineers developed HDSL-2 to serve as a standard by which different vendors' equipment could interoperate. The biggest advantage of HDSL-2 is that it is designed not to interfere with other services, in particular ADSL, which is the most popular type of DSL. A disadvantage with HDSL-2 is that it supports only a full rate, offering services only at 1.544 Mbps.

- **G.SHDSL:** Combines the best of SDSL and HDSL-2. The standard defines multiple rates, as SDSL does, but provides spectral compatibility with HDSL-2.

- **Very-high-bit-rate DSL (VDSL):** Provides data and PSTN service on a single twisted pair of wires at speeds up to 52 Mbps downstream and 16 Mbps upstream. VDSL is reserved for users in close proximity to a central office. Long-Reach Ethernet (LRE) uses VDSL technology.

PPP and ADSL

ADSL designs use two popular PPP implementations: PPP over ATM (PPPoA) and PPP over Ethernet (PPPoE). In a PPPoA architecture, the customer premises equipment (CPE) acts as an Ethernet-to-WAN router and a PPP session is established between the CPE and a Layer 3 access concentrator in the service provider's network. In a PPPoE architecture, the CPE acts as an Ethernet-to-WAN bridge. The client initiates a PPP session by encapsulating PPP frames into MAC frames and then bridging the frames over ATM/DSL to a gateway router at the service provider. From this point, the PPP sessions can be established, authenticated, and addressed. The client receives its IP address from the service provider, using PPP negotiation.

A PPPoA implementation involves configuring the CPE with PPP authentication information (login and password). This is the main advantage of this architecture over pure bridging implementations, as it provides per-session authentication, authorization, and accounting. Another advantage with PPPoA is that it uses ATM end to end. Therefore, the provider might find it easier to put a subscriber into a specific traffic class.

Selecting Remote-Access Devices for an Enterprise Network Design

The previous sections discussed remote-access technologies. This section covers selecting devices to implement those technologies. Selecting remote-access devices for an enterprise network design involves choosing devices for remote users and for a central site. Remote users include telecommuters, users in remote offices, and mobile users. The central site could be the corporate headquarters of a company, the core network of a university that has branch campuses, a medical facility that connects doctors' offices, and so on.

Selecting Devices for Remote Users

The most important consideration when selecting a cable or DSL modem is that the modem must interoperate with the provider's equipment. In some cases, the provider supplies the modem to avoid problems. In other cases, the provider supplies a list of products or standards that must be supported in a modem purchased by the end user, such as the Data Over Cable Service Interface Specification (DOCSIS) for cable modems in the United States.

Criteria for selecting a router for remote sites include the following:

- Security and VPN features

- Support for NAT

- Reliability

- Cost

- Ease of configuration and management

- Support for one or more high-speed Ethernet interfaces

- Support for the router to act as a wireless access point (if desired)

- Support for features that reduce line utilization, such as snapshot routing and compression

- Support for channel aggregation

- Support for QoS features to support VoIP or other applications with specific QoS requirements

Selecting Devices for the Central Site

The central site connects remote users who access the corporate network with cable modems, DSL modems, and VPN software. With a VPN, users gain network access through a service provider's local network and send their data over encrypted tunnels to a VPN firewall or concentrator at the central site. Criteria for selecting central-site devices to support remote users include the criteria listed previously for a remote-site router as well as additional criteria related to VPN functionality.

Both routers and firewalls at the central site can act as the termination point for VPN tunnels. A generic router can become overwhelmed if a network supports many tunnels, however. If you expect the peak number of simultaneous users to reach 100, a dedicated firewall or VPN concentrator should be deployed. (A VPN concentrator is a standalone hardware platform that aggregates a large volume of simultaneous VPN connections.)

Generally, enterprises place the VPN firewall between a router that has access to the VPN and a router that forwards traffic into the campus network. Hence, the firewall should support at least two Ethernet interfaces of the flavor used in this module of the network design (Fast Ethernet, Gigabit Ethernet, and so on).

When selecting a VPN firewall, make sure it will interoperate with the VPN client software on the users' systems. Cisco, Microsoft, and other vendors provide client software. Also pay attention to the number of simultaneous tunnels the firewall supports and the amount of traffic it can forward. The firewall should have a fast processor, high-speed RAM, and support for redundant power supplies and hardware-assisted encryption. It should also support the following software features:

- Tunneling protocols, including IPsec, PPTP, and L2TP

- Encryption algorithms, including 56-bit DES, 168-bit Triple DES, Microsoft Encryption (MPPE), 40- and 128-bit RC4, and 128-, 192-, and 256-bit AES

- Authentication algorithms, including Message Digest 5 (MD5), Secure Hash Algorithm (SHA-1), Hashed Message Authentication Coding (HMAC) with MD5, and HMAC with SHA-1

- Network system protocols, such as DNS, DHCP, RADIUS, Kerberos, and LDAP

- Routing protocols

- Support for certificate authorities, such as Entrust, VeriSign, and Microsoft

- Network management using Secure Shell (SSH) or HTTP with Secure Sockets Layer (SSL)

WAN Technologies

This section covers WAN technologies that are typical options for connecting geographically dispersed sites in an enterprise network design. The section covers the most common and established WAN technologies, but the reader should also research new technologies as they gain industry acceptance. Wireless WAN technologies, for example, are not covered in this book, but are expected to expand the options available for WAN (and remote-access) networks in the future.

Recent changes in the WAN industry continue an evolution that began in the mid-1990s when the bandwidth and QoS requirements of corporations changed significantly due to new applications and expanded interconnectivity goals. As the need for WAN bandwidth accelerated, telephone companies upgraded their internal networks to use SONET and ATM technologies, and started offering new services to their customers. Today, an enterprise network architect has many options for WAN connectivity. The objective of this section is to present some of these options to help you select the right technologies for your customer.

Systems for Provisioning WAN Bandwidth

Regardless of the WAN technology you select, one critical network design step you must complete is selecting the amount of capacity that the WAN must provide. You need to consider capacity requirements for today and for the next 2 to 3 years. Selecting the right amount of capacity is often called *provisioning*. Provisioning requires an analysis of traffic flows, as described in Chapter 4, and an analysis of scalability goals, as described in Chapter 2, "Analyzing Technical Goals and Tradeoffs." This section provides an overview of the bandwidth capacities that are available to handle traffic flows of different sizes.

WAN bandwidth for copper cabling is provisioned in North America and many other parts of the world using the North American Digital Hierarchy, which is shown in Table 11-1. A channel in the hierarchy is called a *digital signal* (DS). Digital signals are multiplexed together to form high-speed WAN circuits. DS-1 and DS-3 are the most commonly used capacities.

Table 11-1   *North America Digital Hierarchy*

Signal	Capacity	Number of DS-0s	Colloquial Name
DS-0	64 kbps	1	Channel
DS-1	1.544 Mbps	24	T1
DS-1C	3.152 Mbps	48	T1C
DS-2	6.312 Mbps	96	T2
DS-3	44.736 Mbps	672	T3
DS-4	274.176 Mbps	4032	T4
DS-5	400.352 Mbps	5760	T5

In Europe, the Committee of European Postal and Telephone (CEPT) has defined a hierarchy called the *E system*, which is shown in Table 11-2.

Table 11-2   *Committee of European Postal and Telephone (CEPT) Hierarchy*

Signal	Capacity	Number of
E0	64 kbps	N/A
E1	2.048 Mbps	1
E2	8.448 Mbps	4
E3		16
E4		64
E5		256

The *Synchronous Digital Hierarchy (SDH)* is an international standard for data transmission over fiber-optic cables. SDH defines a standard rate of transmission of 51.84 Mbps, which is also called *Synchronous Transport Signal level 1 (STS-1)*. Higher rates of transmission are a multiple of the basic STS-1 rate. The STS rates are the same as the SONET Optical Carrier (OC) levels, which are shown in Table 11-3.

Table 11-3   *Synchronous Digital Hierarchy (SDH)*

STS Rate	OC	Speed
STS-1	OC-1	51.84 Mbps
STS-3	OC-3	
STS-12	OC-12	622.08 Mbps
STS-24	OC-24	1.244 Gbps
STS-48	OC-48	2.488 Gbps
STS-96	OC-96	4.976 Gbps
STS-192	OC-192	9.952 Gbps

Leased Lines

The first WAN technology this chapter covers is the leased-line service offered by many telephone companies and other carriers. A *leased line* is a dedicated circuit that a customer leases from a carrier for a predetermined amount of time, usually for months or years. The line is dedicated to traffic for that customer and is used in a point-to-point topology between two sites on the customer's enterprise network. Speeds range from 64 kbps (DS-0) to 45 Mbps (DS-3). Enterprises use leased lines for both voice and data traffic. Data traffic is typically encapsulated in a standard protocol such as PPP or HDLC.

Dedicated leased lines have the advantage that they are a mature and proven technology. Historically, they had the disadvantage that they were expensive, especially in some parts of Europe and Asia. As carriers upgrade their internal networks with more capacity, costs are dropping, however.

Leased lines also have the advantage over most other services that they are dedicated to a single customer. The customer does not share the capacity with anyone. Most newer systems, such as cable modems, DSL, ATM, and Frame Relay, are based on a shared network inside the provider's network.

Leased lines tend to be overlooked as a potential WAN solution because they are not a new technology. In some situations, however, they are the best option for simple point-to-point links. Leased lines are a good choice if the topology is truly point to point (and not likely to become point to multipoint in the near future), the pricing offered by the local carrier is attractive, and applications do not require advanced QoS features that would be difficult to implement in a simple leased-line network.

Synchronous Optical Network

The next WAN technology this chapter covers is *Synchronous Optical Network (SONET)*, which is a physical layer specification for high-speed synchronous transmission of packets or cells over fiber-optic cabling. SONET was proposed by Bellcore in the mid-1980s and is now an international standard. SONET uses the SDH system with STS-1 as its basic building block. Service providers and carriers are making wide use of SONET in their internal networks. SONET is also gaining popularity within private networks to connect remote sites in a WAN or metropolitan-area network (MAN).

Both ATM and packet-based networks can be based on SONET. With packet transmission, SONET networks usually use PPP at the data link layer and IP at the network layer. Packet over SONET (POS) is expected to become quite popular as Internet and intranet traffic grows, and as new applications, such as digital video, demand the high speed, low latency, and low error rates that SONET can offer.

One of the main goals of SONET and SDH was to define higher speeds than the ones used by the North American Digital Hierarchy and the European E system, and to alleviate problems caused by incompatibilities in those systems. The creators of SONET and SDH defined high-speed capacities, starting with the 51.84-Mbps STS-1, that were approved by both North American and European standards bodies.

Another goal of SONET was to support more efficient multiplexing and demultiplexing of individual signals. With SONET (SDH), it is easy to isolate one channel from a multiplexed circuit (for example, one phone call from a trunk line that carries numerous phone calls). With *plesiochronous systems*, such as the North American Digital Hierarchy and the European E system, isolating one channel is more difficult. Although isolating a 64-kbps channel from a DS-1 circuit is straightforward, isolating a 64-kbps channel from a DS-3 trunk requires demultiplexing to the DS-1 level first.

> **Note** The North American Digital Hierarchy and European E system are called *plesiochronous systems*. Plesio means "almost" in Greek. A truly synchronous system, such as SONET, supports more efficient multiplexing and demultiplexing than a plesiochronous ("almost synchronous") system.

The SONET specification defines a four-layer protocol stack. The four layers have the following functions:

- **Photonic layer:** Specifies the physical characteristics of the optical equipment
- **Section layer:** Specifies the frame format and the conversion of frames to optical signals
- **Line layer:** Specifies synchronization and multiplexing onto SONET frames
- **Path layer:** Specifies end-to-end transport

Terminating multiplexers (implemented in switches or routers) provide user access to the SONET network. Terminating multiplexers turn electrical interfaces into optical signals and multiplex multiple payloads into the STS-*N* signals required for optical transport.

A SONET network is usually connected in a ring topology using two self-healing fiber paths. A path provides full-duplex communication and consists of a pair of fiber strands. One path acts as the full-time working transmission facility. The other path acts as a backup protection pair, remaining idle while the working path passes data. If an interruption occurs on the working path, data is automatically rerouted to the backup path within milliseconds. If both the working and protected pairs are cut, the ring wraps, and communication can still survive. Figure 11-3 shows a typical SONET network.

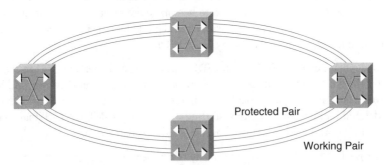

Figure 11-3 *Redundant SONET Ring*

Frame Relay

Frame Relay is a high-performance WAN protocol that operates at the physical and data link layers of the OSI reference model. Frame Relay emerged in the early 1990s as an enhancement to more complex packet-switched technologies, such as X.25. Whereas X.25 is optimized for excellent reliability on physical circuits with a high error rate,

Frame Relay was developed with the assumption that facilities are no longer as error prone as they once were. This assumption allows Frame Relay to be more efficient and easier to implement than X.25.

Frame Relay offers a cost-effective method for connecting remote sites, typically at speeds from 64 kbps to 1.544 Mbps (a few providers offer DS-3 speeds for Frame Relay). Frame Relay offers more granularity in the selection of bandwidth assignments than leased lines, and also includes features for dynamic bandwidth allocation and congestion control to support bursty traffic flows. Frame Relay has become a popular replacement for both X.25 and leased-line networks because of its efficiency, flexible bandwidth support, and low latency.

Frame Relay provides a connection-oriented data link layer service. A pair of devices communicate over a Frame Relay virtual circuit, which is a logical connection created between two data terminal equipment (DTE) devices across a Frame Relay packet-switched network (PSN). Routers, for example, act as DTE devices and set up a virtual circuit for the purpose of transferring data. A virtual circuit can pass through any number of intermediate data circuit-terminating equipment (DCE) devices (switches) located within the Frame Relay PSN.

Frame Relay virtual circuits fall into two categories:

- **Switched virtual circuits (SVC):** Temporary connections for supporting occasional data transfer

- **Permanent virtual circuits (PVC):** Permanently configured circuits that are established in advance of any data transfer

An SVC requires call setup and termination whenever there is data to send. With PVCs, the circuit is established by the provider, which means that troubleshooting is simplified. Most networks use PVCs rather than SVCs.

A Frame Relay virtual circuit is identified by a 10-bit data-link connection identifier (DLCI). DLCIs are assigned by a Frame Relay service provider (for example, a telephone company). Frame Relay DLCIs have local significance. Two DTE devices connected by a virtual circuit might use a different DLCI value to refer to the same circuit. Although you can think of the DLCI as an identifier for the entire virtual circuit, practically speaking, the DLCI refers to the connection from a DTE router to the DCE Frame Relay switch at the provider's site. The DLCI might be different for the DTE-DCE connection at each end of the virtual circuit.

Frame Relay Hub-and-Spoke Topologies and Subinterfaces

Frame Relay networks are often designed in a hub-and-spoke topology, such as the topology shown in Figure 11-4. A central-site router in this topology can have many logical connections to remote sites with only one physical connection to the WAN, thus simplifying installation and management.

One problem with a hub-and-spoke topology is that split horizon can limit routing. With *split horizon*, distance-vector routing protocols do not repeat information out the interface it was received on. This means that devices on network 300 in Figure 11-4 cannot learn about devices on network 400, and vice versa, because the central-site router only advertises network 100 when it sends its routing table out the WAN interface.

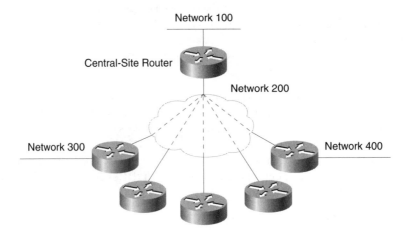

Figure 11-4   *Frame Relay Hub-and-Spoke Topology*

Some routing protocols support disabling the split-horizon function. Split horizon is automatically disabled in a Frame Relay hub-and-spoke topology when the Cisco Interior Gateway Routing Protocol (IGRP) and Enhanced IGRP (EIGRP) are used. Split horizon can be disabled for the IP Routing Information Protocol (RIP). However, some older protocols, such as Novell's RIP and Service Advertising Protocol (SAP) and AppleTalk's Routing Table Maintenance Protocol (RTMP), require split horizon.

A solution to the split-horizon problem is to use a full-mesh design with physical circuits between each site. The drawback to this approach is cost. For example, in the network portrayed in Figure 11-4, a full mesh would comprise 15 circuits instead of 6. Because each circuit costs money, this would not be an optimum solution.

The other alternative is to use subinterfaces. A *subinterface* is a logical interface that is associated with a physical interface. In Figure 11-4, the central-site router could have five point-to-point subinterfaces defined, each communicating with one of the remote sites. With this solution, the central-site router applies the split-horizon rule based on logical subinterfaces, instead of the physical interface, and includes remote sites in the routing updates it sends out the WAN interface.

One downside of using subinterfaces is that router configurations are slightly more complex. Another disadvantage is that more network numbers are required. In Figure 11-4, the entire WAN "cloud" is network 200 when subinterfaces are not used. When subinterfaces are used, each circuit within the cloud requires a network number.

Frame Relay Congestion Control Mechanisms

Although Frame Relay devices generally do not use all of their available bandwidth all of the time, a Frame Relay device does have the capability to transmit data at its physical access rate for extended periods of time. For this reason, the Frame Relay standard includes congestion control mechanisms to ensure fair bandwidth allocation, and feedback mechanisms to inform user devices about the availability of network bandwidth.

The Frame Relay packet header includes a *discard eligibility (DE)* bit used to identify less-important traffic that can be dropped when congestion occurs. In addition, Frame Relay includes two congestion-notification schemes:

- **Forward explicit congestion notification (FECN):** Informs the receiver of a frame that the frame traversed a path that is experiencing congestion

- **Backward explicit congestion notification (BECN):** Informs a sender that congestion exists in the path that the sender is using

Service providers are able to keep prices for their Frame Relay service reasonably low because of the bursty nature of the traffic typically offered to Frame Relay networks. The service provider generally oversubscribes its internal network, making the assumption that not all virtual circuits use all of their available bandwidth all of the time. Switches within the service provider's network can use the FECN and BECN mechanisms to notify end-system devices of any congestion problems. The resulting behavior at the end systems depends on which protocol and which implementation of the protocol is being used.

Note   Congestion control in a Transmission Control Protocol (TCP) application is usually independent of the FECN and BECN mechanisms. Upon packet loss, TCP decreases its transmit window size, effectively slowing its transmission rate. It then gradually increases the window size until congestion occurs again.

Frame Relay Traffic Control

When you subscribe to a Frame Relay service with a provider, you establish an access rate and order the appropriate line service and interface for the router to support this access rate. The access rate is the maximum number of bits per second that a DTE, such as a router, can transmit into the Frame Relay network. In addition, many service providers let you specify other parameters related to bandwidth usage, including a committed information rate (CIR), a committed burst (Bc) size, and an excess burst (Be) size.

The CIR specifies that as long as the data input by a device to the Frame Relay network is below or equal to the CIR, then the network will continue to forward data for that virtual circuit. If the data input rate exceeds the CIR, there is no longer any guarantee. The network might discard traffic beyond the CIR limit, although if there is sufficient bandwidth it might continue to forward traffic. CIR is measured over a time interval *T*. CIR is expressed in bits per second.

The relationship between CIR and Bc is as follows:

CIR = Bc/T

Bc is the maximum number of bits that the network is committed to transfer for a virtual circuit during the T timeframe. Bc is expressed in bits.

The Be parameter is the number of bits in excess of Bc that a virtual circuit can send during the T time period. The network sends these bits if there is no congestion, but the first Frame Relay switch can mark the frames as eligible to be discarded (DE). Be is expressed in bits.

Bc, Be, T, and CIR are defined per DLCI. The access rate is valid per each user-network interface. For Bc, Be, and CIR, incoming and outgoing values can be distinguished. If the connection is symmetrical, the values in both directions are the same. For PVCs, the incoming and outgoing Bc, Be, and CIR are defined at subscription time.

When planning a Frame Relay network, if the service provider supports CIR, Bc, and Be, you must determine the values to use. This decision is based on the pricing model of the service provider and the analysis of traffic volume and flow that you did as part of the requirements-analysis phase of the network design process. The access rate and CIR of the Frame Relay connection at the hub of a hub-and-spoke topology should be more than the sum of the CIRs at the remote sites and less than or equal to the sum of the burst capacities of the remote sites.

Many service providers don't let you specify Be or Bc. Some providers don't let you specify CIR either. To keep things simple, some providers base their Frame Relay offerings simply on the physical access rate. These carriers often offer a *zero CIR*, which means that they make only a best effort to send your traffic. The advantage of a zero CIR is that it is inexpensive.

Although it is recommended that the CIR and other parameters be based on a careful analysis of traffic, keep in mind that the CIR and other parameters are based on a probabilistic service. Although some carriers market the CIR as a true guarantee, carriers actually oversubscribe their networks and cannot guarantee that their customers will correctly react to congestion feedback mechanisms, which means that no customer's CIR or Bc is truly a guarantee.

Frame Relay/ATM Interworking

Some service providers offer WAN solutions that use both ATM and Frame Relay technologies. The term *Frame Relay/ATM interworking* is used to describe the protocols and processes for connecting ATM and Frame Relay WANs. Interworking can be implemented in two different ways, depending on the goals of the network design:

- **Network interworking:** Two or more Frame Relay networks are connected via an ATM core network. This is a common topology used by service providers who use ATM for their internal networks and offer Frame Relay to their customers.

■ **Service interworking:** An ATM network connects to a Frame Relay network. This topology is less common, but might be used during a transition from Frame Relay to ATM or vice versa.

ATM

Despite the complexity of ATM, ATM is a good choice for WAN backbone networks for customers with accelerating bandwidth requirements and applications with advanced QoS requirements. ATM supports very high bandwidth requirements. When used on copper cabling, ATM can run at T3 or higher speeds. When used on fiber-optic cabling, ATM theoretically supports speeds up to OC-192 (9.952 Gbps) and beyond, especially if technologies such as wavelength-division multiplexing (WDM) are used.

ATM facilitates the efficient sharing of bandwidth among applications with various QoS requirements. Applications can theoretically share bandwidth more fairly in a cell-based system compared to a frame-based system, because in a frame-based system, large frames can monopolize bandwidth. In addition, with a connection-oriented technology such as ATM, an application can specify upon connection establishment the QoS it requires, including peak and minimum cell rates, a cell-loss ratio, and a cell-transfer delay.

Ethernet over ATM

A disadvantage with ATM is that ATM interfaces for routers and switches are expensive. Some service providers allow the customer to use an Ethernet interface to access the provider's ATM WAN. This service is often called *Ethernet over ATM*. In some cases, the provider places an Ethernet-to-ATM converter at the customer's premises. In other cases, the customer doesn't need any extra equipment. The conversion happens inside the provider's network.

Ethernet over ATM is gaining popularity with service providers. Many providers already have large ATM WANs. Allowing their customers to connect to the ATM WAN using Ethernet benefits both the provider and the customer. The provider can offer a new service without making major changes to its network. The customer gets the benefit of a lower-cost entry into the network through the use of an Ethernet interface.

Note   Metro Ethernet, which is discussed in the next section, can be implemented using Ethernet over ATM technology. Metro Ethernet can use a variety of transport protocols, including ATM, SONET, WDM, and MPLS.

An Ethernet over ATM solution combines the advantages of Ethernet with those of ATM. Ethernet advantages include low cost, simplicity, ease of maintenance, interoperability with existing equipment, high speeds, and ease of upgrading to even faster speeds. ATM advantages include high speeds, reliability, and support for categorizing applications into different classes based on the service and QoS that the applications require.

Separating applications into different service classes benefits multipurpose networks where high-bandwidth applications are mixed with delay-sensitive applications, such as voice and video. ATM supports a set of parameters that describe the traffic presented to the ATM network. ATM also supports a set of traffic-control mechanisms that the network can use to meet service requirements. The network can implement connection admission control and resource allocation differently for different service classes.

A service provider can map Ethernet VLANs to ATM virtual circuits and set up service classes for particular VLANs or applications. Although many users of Ethernet over ATM won't opt for the complexity and extra cost associated with service classes, customers with specialized applications can benefit from service classes. To reduce complexity, some service providers have the capability of mapping QoS parameters more familiar to LAN engineers (such as IEEE 802.1p QoS parameters) to the more complicated ATM QoS parameters.

Metro Ethernet

Chapter 10, "Selecting Technologies and Devices for Campus Networks," briefly covered Metro Ethernet. This chapter covers it in more detail. Metro Ethernet is a service offered by providers and carriers that traditionally had only classic WAN offerings, such as dialup, T1, and Frame Relay. Metro Ethernet blends the capabilities and behavior of WAN technologies with those of Ethernet. Carriers offer Metro Ethernet to customers who are looking for a cost-effective method to interconnect campus networks and to access the Internet.

One of the many advantages of Metro Ethernet is that the customer can use a standard 10/100-Mbps Ethernet interface, or a Gigabit or 10-Gbps interface, to access the service provider's network. The customer can set up virtual circuits to reach other sites and to reach an ISP. Metro Ethernet supports a copper or fiber-optic interface, but uses fiber-optic cabling inside the provider's network. It can use a variety of transport protocols, including SONET, ATM, dense-mode wavelength-division multiplexing (DWDM), and Multiprotocol Label Switching (MPLS).

Metro Ethernet service providers allow subscribers to add bandwidth as needed. Compared to adding WAN bandwidth, adding bandwidth to a Metro Ethernet service can happen extremely quickly, sometimes as quickly as a few minutes or hours. Metro Ethernet providers offer a wide range of bandwidth options. In addition to the standard Ethernet speeds, many providers offer a 1-Mbps service and allow customers to add bandwidth in 1-Mbps increments.

Some Metro Ethernet implementations use what is called an Ethernet virtual circuit (EVC). An EVC is similar to a Frame Relay PVC. An EVC is an association of two or more User-Network Interfaces (UNI), where a UNI is a standard Ethernet interface at a customer's site. Three basic service types use EVCs:

- Ethernet line service (E-line service) provides a point-to-point EVC between two UNIs.

- Ethernet LAN service (E-LAN service) provides multipoint connectivity. It can connect two or more UNIs. It is also known as Virtual Private LAN Services (VPLS) or Transparent LAN Services (TLS).

- Ethernet tree service (E-Tree service) provides point-to-multipoint connectivity.

Metro Ethernet is a blending of WAN and LAN technologies. It supports virtual circuits like a WAN and also provides support for a committed information rate (CIR), committed burst size, peak information rate (PIR), and peak burst size, like a WAN often does. In a similar fashion to a LAN, Metro Ethernet also supports VLANs, 802.1X port authentication, and the Spanning Tree Protocol. Metro Ethernet also supports many QoS features to optimize the forwarding of latency-sensitive traffic. Cisco routers and switches that implement Metro Ethernet, for example, support advanced queuing techniques, traffic shaping, and Random Early Detection (RED).

Metro Ethernet is used to connect intranet and extranet sites. ISPs are also starting to use Metro Ethernet. The ISP typically multiplexes multiple subscribers over a high-speed Ethernet UNI. An ISP's customer uses an EVC to connect to the ISP's local point of presence (POP).

The most common method for using Metro Ethernet for dedicated Internet access is to use the E-line service. If the customer wants to use the same UNI to support both Internet access and an intranet or extranet connection, this is also possible with the use of separate EVCs. A customer can also use multiple EVCs to access multiple ISPs for redundancy, thus multihoming the Internet connection.

For more information about Metro Ethernet, see the Metro Ethernet Forum's website at http://www.metroethernetforum.org.

Selecting Routers for an Enterprise WAN Design

An enterprise WAN connects high-performance routers. Chapter 10 covered typical criteria for the selection of internetworking devices in general. The criteria in Chapter 10 (such as the number of ports, processing speed, media and technologies supported, mean time to repair [MTTR], mean time between failure [MTBF], and so on) apply to enterprise and campus devices. In addition, enterprise routers should offer high throughput, high availability, and advanced features to optimize the utilization of expensive WAN circuits. Routers for an enterprise WAN network design should be selected carefully to avoid performance problems caused by an underpowered router that aggregates traffic from many networks.

When provisioning enterprise routers, keep in mind that in a hierarchical design, such as the designs discussed in Chapter 5, "Designing a Network Topology," a concentration of traffic from lower layers of the hierarchy aggregates at routers at the top of the hierarchy. This means you need to plan for adequate performance on the routers at the upper layers of the hierarchy.

Based on an analysis of traffic flow, you should select routers that provide the necessary WAN interfaces to support bandwidth requirements, provide an appropriate packets-per-second level, and have adequate memory and processing power to forward data and handle routing protocols. In addition, you should select routers that provide optimization features such as advanced switching and queuing techniques, traffic shaping, RED, and express forwarding. Chapter 13, "Optimizing Your Network Design," discusses router optimization techniques in more detail.

Selecting a WAN Service Provider

In addition to selecting technologies and devices for a WAN network design, you must also select service providers or carriers. One obvious criterion for selecting a service provider is the cost of services. Using cost as the main selection criterion, however, can make the choice difficult because providers offer distinct services and define terms and conditions differently. Also, for many network designs, cost is not the main criterion. The following criteria are often more important than cost:

- The extent of services and technologies offered by the provider

- The geographical areas covered by the provider

- Reliability and performance characteristics of the provider's internal network

- The level of security offered by the provider

- The level of technical support offered by the provider

- The likelihood that the provider will continue to stay in business

- The provider's willingness to work with you to meet your needs

When selecting a service provider, try to investigate the structure, security, and reliability of the provider's internal network to help you predict the reliability of your WAN, which depends on the provider's network. Learning about the provider's network can be challenging because providers generally do not share detailed information about their internal networks, but nonetheless, you should talk to systems engineers and current customers of the provider to try to determine the following characteristics of the provider's network:

- The physical routing of network links

- Redundancy within the network

- The extent to which the provider relies on other providers for redundancy

- The level of oversubscription on the network

- Bandwidth allocation mechanisms used to guarantee application QoS requirements

- The types of switches that are used and the bandwidth-allocation and -optimization features available on the switches

- The frequency and typical causes of network outages

- Security methods used to protect the network from intruders

- Security methods used to protect the privacy of a customer's data

- Disaster recovery plans in case of earthquakes, fires, hurricanes, asteroids that collide with satellites, or other natural or man-made disasters

Most service providers can furnish customers with a *service-level agreement (SLA)* that defines the specific terms of the service and how the service will be measured and guaranteed. Some SLAs address only network availability, which is not sufficient for many applications. An SLA should also address application performance, including latency and throughput.

An SLA should also specify the level of technical support that can be expected. Generally you should get a contract for 24-hour, 7-day support for a mission-critical WAN. In addition to specifying specific terms and conditions for support and service in an SLA, when negotiating a contract with a provider, try to get answers to the following support-related questions:

- What is the experience level of the installation and support staff?

- Does the support staff have experience with your particular protocols and applications?

- If necessary, can you request a dedicated single-point-of-contact support representative who will take responsibility for resolving all problems and questions?

- Does the provider adhere to industry standards for service quality such as the IT Service Management (ITSM) framework?

- How difficult is it for a typical customer to provision and price new services?

- Does the provider offer a customer training program on services and pricing structures?

Example of a WAN Design

This section presents a WAN design that was developed using some of the design steps in this book. The section describes an actual network design that was developed for Klamath Paper Products. The name of the company has been changed. The example is based on a real network design, but some of the facts have been changed to preserve the privacy of the company and protect the security of the company's network, and to make it possible to present a simple and easy-to-understand example.

Background Information for the WAN Design Project

Klamath Paper Products, Inc. manufactures paper and packaging products, including office paper, newsprint, cartons, and corrugated boxes. They also manufacture wood pulp and chemicals used in the manufacturing of pulp and paper.

Klamath Paper Products (which will be called Klamath from now on) has approximately 15 sites in the western United States. Headquarters are in Portland, Oregon. Klamath employs around 1500 people and has customers all over the world, with a large customer base in Asia.

Klamath is concerned about reduced profit margins caused by fewer sales in Asia in recent years and the scarcity of lumber used to manufacture Klamath's products. Klamath recently completed a strategic re-engineering project that identified ways to increase profits by improving the efficiency of internal processes and making more use of recycled postconsumer paper in the production of new paper products.

As a result of the re-engineering project, the Conservation Initiative Task Force at Klamath plans to roll out an ongoing distance-learning program that will train all employees on ways to conserve raw materials, use recycled materials, and work more efficiently. Executive management considers the new training program vital to the continued success of Klamath, and approved funding to equip the training rooms at most sites with digital videoconferencing systems.

After Klamath installs the videoconferencing system and the WAN to support it, there are plans to offer classes to other companies in the wood and paper manufacturing industries. Klamath has recognized a business opportunity associated with the federal government's plan to help pay for workers in the timber industry to attend classes in modern methods for sustainable forest management and environmentally sound lumber and paper production.

Business and Technical Goals

Klamath's main business goals for the WAN design project are as follows:

- Increase profits by implementing a WAN that will support the goals of the Conservation Initiative Task Force, in particular the new distance-learning program.

- Improve the performance of the existing WAN to support more efficient operations.

- Contain the rising costs associated with operating the existing WAN.

- Provide a network that will let employees more easily share ideas for further improving efficiency and increasing the use of recycled materials.

- Provide a new source of revenue from the timber-industry distance-learning program.

Engineers in the telecommunications and networking departments added the following technical goals:

- Update the capacity and QoS capabilities of the existing WAN, which in its current state cannot support the new videoconferencing system.

- Design a network that uses currently available technologies from the WAN service providers in the region.

- Provide a network that offers a response time of 1/10th of a second or less for interactive applications.

- Provide a network that is available 99.98 percent of the time and offers an MTBF of 4000 hours (about 5.5 months) and an MTTR of 1 hour (with a low standard deviation from these average numbers).

- Improve the manageability of the network by simplifying the topology, which is currently a complex mesh of voice and data circuits.

- Design a network that will scale as new high-bandwidth applications are added in the future.

- Design a network that can support voice traffic in the future.

Network Applications

The new distance-learning application will use a two-way compressed digital video service based on the H.323 standards for videoconferencing. Each site with a training room will be equipped with a high-end digital video camera. Both synchronous and asynchronous distance learning will be supported. With *synchronous distance learning*, remote students attend classes taught by instructors at headquarters or other sites in "real time." With *asynchronous distance learning*, students can check out a video class from a video server at headquarters and have the video transmitted to their site.

Other applications in use at Klamath include the following:

- The manufacturing support system runs on a mainframe in Portland. The system keeps track of manufacturing schedules and work orders. Members of the various manufacturing departments access the system from their PCs. This system is considered critical to Klamath's mission to deliver products by the dates that were promised to customers.

- The financial modeling system runs on UNIX and makes use of an Oracle database that resides on UNIX servers in Portland. Financial analysts use applications on their PCs to access this system.

- The sales order-entry and tracking system runs on Windows servers. Sales and marketing personnel use their PCs to access this system.

- The graphics production system runs on Macintosh computers and uses Apple Filing Protocol (AFP) servers.

- Most users also deploy a standard set of desktop applications that includes email, calendaring, web browsing, file sharing, and printing. These applications use TCP/IP and NetBIOS.

User Communities

Table 11-4 shows a summarized view of the user communities at Klamath.

Table 11-4   *Klamath User Communities*

User Community Name	Size of Community (Number of Users)	Location(s) of Community	Application(s) Used by Community
Headquarters	350	Portland	All
Office paper manufacturing and sales	200	Seattle	All
Newsprint, cartons, and boxes manufacturing and sales	250	Spokane	All
Wood pulp and chemicals manufacturing and sales	150	Boise	All
Other smaller manufacturing and sales offices	25–75	Western United States	All

Data Stores (Servers)

Table 11-5 shows the data stores that were identified at Klamath.

Table 11-5   *Klamath Data Stores*

Data Store	Location	Application(s)	Used by User Community (or Communities)
Mainframe	Portland	Manufacturing support system	All manufacturing sites
UNIX servers	Two in Portland	Financial modeling	Finance departments in Portland, Seattle, Spokane, and Boise
Windows servers	Portland, Seattle, Spokane, Boise	Sales order-entry and tracking system	All sales sites
AFP servers	Portland, Seattle, Spokane, Boise	Graphics production	Graphics departments in Portland, Seattle, Spokane, and Boise
Video server (new)	Portland	Distance learning	All

Current Network

The current WAN consists of dedicated 64-kbps data circuits that connect the 15 sites in a partial-mesh topology. Voice traffic is carried on separate 64-kbps circuits. A WAN service provider leases the 64-kbps lines to Klamath and also provides Internet access via a T1 circuit that connects a router at the Portland headquarters to a router at the provider's site. The router at the Portland headquarters acts as a packet-filtering firewall.

The core of the data network is a full mesh of 64-kbps circuits that connects the major sites. A router at each site connects Ethernet LANs to the WAN, as shown in Figure 11-5.

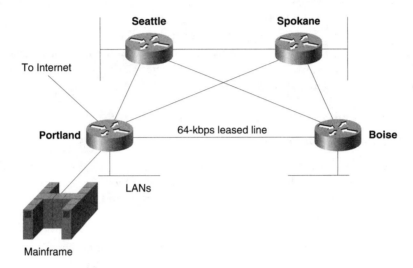

Figure 11-5   *Existing Core WAN at Klamath*

Traffic Characteristics of the Existing WAN

As Klamath has grown over the years, network performance has degraded. Users report that the network is slow, especially during the busiest hour between 10 a.m. and 11 a.m. Users of the manufacturing support system report that it sometimes takes 2 or 3 minutes for their screens to unlock after they enter information. Users of the sales order-entry system and the financial modeling applications also report slow response times.

A WAN protocol analyzer was used at each of the major sites to measure current bandwidth usage on the 64-kbps data circuits. It was determined that every circuit in Portland was approaching saturation, with an average utilization of 80 percent in a 10-minute window. WAN circuits between Seattle and Spokane, Spokane and Boise, and Boise and Seattle were also heavily used, with an average utilization in a 10-minute window of 70 percent.

The protocol analyzer was also used to study protocol and traffic characteristics. The following conclusions were made:

- No single protocol was causing any serious problems.

- Although there were quite a few retransmissions, no applications appeared to retransmit too quickly.

- Applications appeared to have been optimized to use large frame sizes and large window sizes.

- Broadcast traffic accounted for about 5 percent of the network utilization and appeared to be normal routing and service-advertising packets.

- The average error rate for the circuits was one cyclic redundancy check (CRC) error per two million bytes of data (which is acceptable).

The status of the routers in the core of the network was also checked. The following Cisco IOS commands, which were discussed in Chapter 3, "Characterizing the Existing Internetwork," were used to check the routers:

- The **show processes** command indicated no problems with CPU overutilization.

- The **show buffers** command indicated no problems with buffers.

- The **show interfaces** command indicated that the routers were dropping frames from the output queue of the serial WAN ports at a rate of about 1 in 20 frames, or 5 percent. This appeared to be caused by too much network traffic destined for the 64-kbps circuits, and was considered a problem.

The end result of the analysis of the existing core WAN was that the core WAN was congested due to too much traffic caused by normal application behavior.

WAN Design for Klamath Paper Products

A decision table was used as part of the design process for Klamath. Klamath's major goals were consolidated and critical goals were placed at the top of the table, as shown in Table 11-6. Potential options were placed in the leftmost column and evaluated on whether they met a critical goal.

Note If all options had met all critical goals, then other goals could have been listed also to further the decision-making process. Options could have been evaluated on how well they met noncritical goals on a scale from 1 to 10, as shown in Table 7-1, "Example Decision Table," in Chapter 7. However, in the case of Klamath, it was not necessary to go beyond evaluating how well options met critical goals.

After analyzing business and technical goals, characterizing the existing core WAN, and analyzing the options available from the WAN service providers in the area, Klamath decided to update the core WAN architecture from 64-kbps lines to Metro Ethernet using an E-LAN service and MPLS transport. This choice will keep costs low and benefit from the QoS features of Metro Ethernet.

Table 11-6   *WAN Technologies Decision Table*

	Critical Goals for the WAN Technology				
	Must have the capacity and QoS capabilities to support video training without disrupting the manufacturing application	Must use currently available technologies from WAN service providers in the region	Response time must be 1/10 of a second or less for interactive applications	Availability must be 99.98 percent or higher	The short- and long-term costs for operating the WAN must be contained
Add more 64-kbps leased lines		X	X	X	
SONET	X		X	X	
Frame Relay		X		X	X
Ethernet over ATM	X		X	X	X
ATM	X	X	X	X	
Metro Ethernet	X	X	X	X	X

The three main contenders, besides Metro Ethernet, were ATM, Ethernet over ATM, and Frame Relay. ATM was ruled out because ATM router interfaces are too expensive. Ethernet over ATM was ruled out because the services providers in the area don't offer it. Frame Relay was seriously considered, but Metro Ethernet was selected instead of Frame Relay because it was designed to handle environments with diverse applications, such as the delay-sensitive videoconferencing and interactive manufacturing-support and financial-modeling applications at Klamath.

In the new design, the delay-sensitive traffic will be carried on virtual circuits that are distinct from the circuits that carry other data. Traffic management parameters will be specified and implemented so that the network accepts and carries traffic according to the QoS needs of the different applications.

The current WAN service provider that leases the existing 64-kbps circuits was selected as the service provider for the new Metro Ethernet WAN. The current provider was selected because it offers the following advantages over other providers:

■ A proven history of supplying highly reliable Metro Ethernet services to customers

■ Excellent pricing for Metro Ethernet that was comparable in price to the cost of adding numerous 64-kbps circuits to meet capacity requirements

■ The ability to allow Klamath to keep their current IP addressing scheme

■ 24-hour support, 7-days a week, with a guaranteed MTTR of 1 hour

■ A single point of contact who is responsible for Klamath's service

Each site in the core of the network will connect to the network via a 10/100 Ethernet interface in a router. For now, 10-Mbps Ethernet will be used. Upgrading to 100 Mbps or 1000 Mbps will be possible in the future, but for now, 10-Mbps Ethernet was chosen because the service provider offers attractive pricing for 10-Mbps Metro Ethernet and because 10 Mbps is sufficient capacity for the current network applications.

Klamath will replace the existing routers in the core of the network with new high-end routers that provide superior packets-per-second throughput, high-availability features, and support for optimization features. The routers will support Ethernet interfaces for connectivity to the service provider's Metro Ethernet and to the internal LANs and mainframe. Figure 11-6 shows the new design for Klamath's core network.

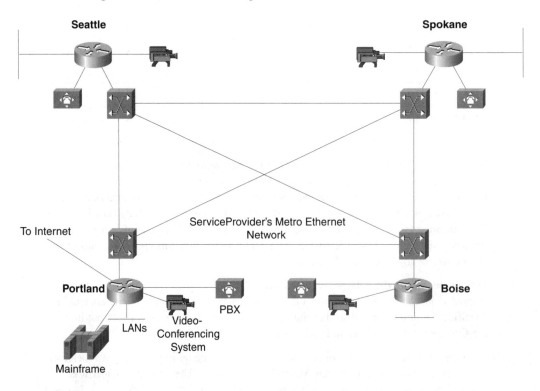

Figure 11-6 *New Core WAN at Klamath*

Summary

This chapter continued the discussion of physical network design that was started in the previous chapter. It covered selecting technologies and devices for enterprise network designs, with a focus on the remote-access and WAN components of an enterprise network.

Remote-access technologies include PPP, cable modems, and DSL. WAN technologies include the North American Digital Hierarchy, the European E system, SDH, leased lines, SONET, Frame Relay, ATM, and Metro Ethernet. You can use many selection criteria when choosing remote-access devices, central-site servers and concentrators, enterprise routers, and a WAN service provider to implement these technologies. These criteria include the types of ports, protocols, and optimization and security features offered by the device or service provider.

The chapter concluded with an example of a WAN network design that was developed for Klamath Paper Products, Inc. To keep the example simple, not all steps of the top-down network design methodology were documented. The example demonstrated the use of the following steps:

- Analyzing requirements, including both business and technical goals

- Identifying existing and future network applications

- Identifying user communities and data stores

- Characterizing the existing network, including the existing topology, bandwidth utilization, bandwidth utilization by protocol, and network performance

- Selecting a WAN technology and service provider based on requirements and goals

Review Questions

1. Define CIR, Bc, and Be and explain how a Frame Relay service provider uses them.

2. What are the most important criteria for selecting a WAN service provider?

3. Why are QoS features often necessary in WAN routers?

4. Some people think that Frame Relay will disappear over time. Do you think that is likely, and if so, why, and what do you think will replace it?

Design Scenario

This chapter included a detailed case study about Klamath Paper Products. Reread the case study and answer the following questions.

1. Based on the design requirements and decisions that have been made, what routers would you recommend for Klamath? Do some Internet research to find a router that will meet Klamath's needs and write two or three paragraphs about the product and why you chose it.

2. In the future, Klamath's separate voice network will be dismantled. All voice, data, and video traffic will traverse the Metro Ethernet network. This will simplify the topology of the current voice/data network and facilitate manageability. It will also

allow Klamath to reduce the costs of operating separate data and voice networks. Research a VoIP solution that would work for Klamath. Write two or three paragraphs about the solution and why you chose it.

3. Klamath doesn't seem too concerned about security. This should concern you. Write a proposal for Klamath that discusses a security project that you would like to do for Klamath to help them understand their network assets, the security risks that they face, and the steps they should take to become more secure.

4. Research a Metro Ethernet service that is offered by a vendor in your country (or another country if your country doesn't have Metro Ethernet). Write a one-page paper that describes the service in technical terms. Also include pricing information if it is available.

Summary for Part III

This chapter concludes Part III, "Physical Network Design." Physical design involves the selection of media, technologies, and devices for campus and enterprise networks. A physical design consists of cabling, Layer 1 and Layer 2 protocol implementations, and network devices. The physical design depends on business objectives, technical requirements, traffic characteristics, and traffic flows, which Part I of this book discussed. The physical design builds on the logical design, which Part II discussed.

A network designer has many options for LAN and WAN technology for campus and enterprise networks. No single technology or device is the right answer for all circumstances. The goal of Part III was to present characteristics of typical options to help you make the right selections for your particular customer.

Part IV, "Testing, Optimizing, and Documenting Your Network Design," covers the final steps in designing a network: testing the network design, optimizing the network design, and documenting the design with a design proposal. Testing and optimizing a network design are two of the most significant steps in a systems-analysis approach to network design. Writing a comprehensive network design proposal that documents how the design fulfills business and technical goals is also a crucial step in the top-down network design methodology.

Testing, Optimizing, and Documenting Your Network Design

Chapter 12

Testing Your Network Design

Part IV, "Testing, Optimizing, and Documenting Your Network Design," of *this book* covers the final steps in network design: testing, optimizing, and documenting your design. This chapter discusses testing your design, which is a critical step in a systems analysis approach to network design. Testing will help you prove to yourself and to your network design customer that your solution meets the customer's business and technical goals.

This chapter covers techniques for using industry tests to predict the performance of network components. It also covers building and testing a prototype system, and using network management and modeling tools to anticipate the end-to-end performance and quality of service (QoS) that your design will provide.

Testing a network design is a broad subject. This book covers the topic at a high level. Complete books could be written on network design testing. Two recommended books relevant to network design testing include Raj Jain's *The Art of Computer Systems Performance Analysis* and Robert Buchanan's *The Art of Testing Network Systems* (both published by John Wiley & Sons, Inc.).

Notice that both Jain and Buchanan use the word *art* in the titles of their books. Testing a network system, and predicting and measuring its performance, is in many ways an art rather than a science. For one thing, every system is different, so selecting the right testing methods and tools requires technical awareness, creativity, ingenuity, and a thorough understanding of the system to be evaluated. No single methodology or tool is right for every project or for every network designer.

Selecting the right testing procedures and tools depends on your goals for the testing project, which typically include the following:

- Verifying that the design meets key business and technical goals.

- Validating LAN and WAN technology and device selections.

- Verifying that a service provider provides the agreed-upon service.

- Identifying any bottlenecks or connectivity problems.

- Testing the redundancy of the network.

- Analyzing the effects on performance of network link failures.

- Determining optimization techniques that will be necessary to meet performance and other technical goals.

- Proving that your design is better than a competing design (in cases where a customer plans to select one design from proposals provided by multiple vendors or consultants).

- Passing an "acceptance test" that gives you approval to go forward with the network implementation (and possibly to get paid for completing the design phase of the project).

- Convincing managers and coworkers that your design is effective.

- Identifying any risks that might impede implementation and planning for contingencies.

- Determining how much additional testing might be required. For example, perhaps you will decide that the new system should first be deployed as a pilot and undergo more testing before being rolled out to all users.

Using Industry Tests

Vendors, independent test labs, and trade journals often publish information on the tests they have completed to verify the features and performance of particular network devices or network design scenarios. Some respected, independent testing labs include the following:

- **University of New Hampshire InterOperability Laboratory (UNH-IOL):** Go to http://www.iol.unh.edu for more information.

- **ICSA Labs:** Go to http://www.icsalabs.com for more information.

- **Miercom:** Go to http://www.miercom.com for more information.

- **AppLabs:** Go to http://www.applabs.com for more information.

- **The Tolly Group:** Go to http://www.tolly.com for more information.

Sometimes, for simple network designs, you can rely on test results from vendors, independent labs, or trade journals to prove to your customer that your design will perform as intended. For example, if you have proposed a campus network design based solely on a particular vendor's switching technology, and an independent trade journal has verified the features and performance of the vendor's products, the journal's testing results might adequately convince your customer of your design's effectiveness. For more complex network designs, you generally should do your own testing, in addition to presenting to your customer independent studies that help sell your case.

Test results published by vendors or independent parties, such as trade journals or testing labs, can be informative, but they can also be misleading. For one thing, vendors obviously make every effort to ensure that their products appear to perform better than their competitors' products. Keep in mind that some trade journals and labs are also reluctant to publish negative results about vendors' products because the vendors help pay their bills. (Vendors pay labs to run tests and publish advertisements in trade journals.)

In addition, most tests run by vendors, independent labs, and trade journals are component tests rather than system tests. Component testing is generally not sufficient to measure the performance of a network design. Furthermore, the test configuration used by the vendor or testing lab almost certainly does not match your actual configuration. This means that the testing results might not be relevant to your particular design.

To understand how network components will behave in your configuration with your applications, network traffic, and unique requirements, building a prototype system or model of the network is usually necessary. The prototype or model will let you go beyond component testing and estimate the design's probable performance, including end-to-end delay, throughput, and availability.

Building and Testing a Prototype Network System

The goal of this section is to help you itemize the tasks to build a prototype that verifies and demonstrates the behavior of a network system. A secondary goal is to help you determine how much of a network system must be implemented in a prototype to verify the design.

A *prototype* is an initial implementation of a new system that provides a model on which the final implementation will be patterned. A prototype allows a designer to validate the operation and performance of a new system. It should be functional, but does not need to be a full-scale implementation of the new system. It should, however, result from both a thorough analysis of needs and a design review with the end customer.

Determining the Scope of a Prototype System

Based on a clear understanding of your customer's goals, you should determine how much of the network system you must implement to convince your customer that the design will meet requirements. Because it is generally not practical to implement a complete, full-scale system, you should isolate which aspects of a network design are most important to your customer. Your prototype should verify important capabilities and functions that might not perform adequately. Risky functions can include complex, intricate functions and component interactions, functions whose design was influenced by business or technical constraints, and functions for which tradeoffs had to be made because of conflicting goals.

The scope of a network prototype can depend on both technical and nontechnical goals. Pay attention to nontechnical factors, such as your customer's biases, business style, and history with network projects. Perhaps the customer already refused a network design because of its lack of manageability and usability features and so might be predisposed to look for these problems in your system. If this is the case, one goal of your prototype should be to develop a demonstration that showcases manageability and usability benefits.

Your ability to implement a prototype depends on available resources. Resources include people, equipment, money, and time. You should use sufficient resources to produce a valid test without requiring so many resources that testing pushes the project over budget, delays it, or negatively affects network users.

A prototype can be implemented and tested in three ways:

- As a test network in a lab

- Integrated into a production network but tested during off hours

- Integrated into a production network and tested during normal business hours

It is a good idea to implement at least part of a prototype system on a test network before implementing it on a production network. This will allow you to work out bugs without impacting the productivity of workers who depend on the network. A test network also helps you evaluate product capabilities, develop initial device configurations, and model predicted network performance and quality of service (QoS). You can also use a test network to demonstrate your design and selected products to a customer.

Testing a Prototype on a Production Network

After a design has been accepted on a provisional basis, it is important to test an initial implementation of the design on a production network to identify possible bottlenecks or other problems that real traffic might trigger. Initial tests can be done during off-hours to minimize possible problems, but final testing should be done during normal business hours to evaluate performance during normal load.

A few key tips to keep in mind when planning a "live" test are as follows:

- Warn users in advance about the timing of tests so that they can expect some performance degradation, but ask the users to work as they typically do to avoid invalidating the test by abnormal behavior.

- Warn network administrators and other designers in advance to avoid the possibility that they could be running tests at the same time.

- Warn network managers in advance so that they are not confused by unexpected alarms on network management consoles and so that they can account for test traffic when documenting load and availability statistics.

- If possible, run multiple, short (less than 2-minute) tests to minimize user impact and lessen the effects on baseline measurements.

- Run tests that start with small traffic and configuration changes, and then incrementally increase the changes.

- Monitor test results and discontinue them when test objectives are met or the production network is severely impacted or fails.

Writing and Implementing a Test Plan for Your Network Design

After you have decided on the scope of your testing project, write a test plan that describes how you will implement your testing. The test plan should include each of the following topics, which the next few sections of this chapter describe in more detail:

- Test objectives and acceptance criteria

- The types of tests that will be run

- Network equipment and other resources required

- Test scripts

- The timeline and milestones for the testing project

Developing Test Objectives and Acceptance Criteria

The first and most important step in writing a test plan is to list the objectives of the test or tests. Objectives should be specific and concrete, and should include information on determining whether the test passed or failed. The following are some examples of specific objectives and acceptance criteria that were written for a particular customer:

- Measure the response time for Application XYZ during peak usage hours (between 10 a.m. and 11 a.m.). The acceptance criterion, per the network design proposal, is that the response time must be half a second or less.

- Measure Application XYZ's throughput during peak usage hours (between 10 a.m. and 11 a.m.). The acceptance criterion, per the network design proposal, is that throughput must be at least 2 Mbps.

- Measure the amount of time it takes for a user of the new Voice over IP (VoIP) system to hear a dial tone after picking up a telephone handset. The acceptance criterion is that the average (mean) amount of time must be less than or equal to the average amount of time for a user of the private branch exchange (PBX) corporate telephone system. The variance from the average must also be equal or smaller.

Objectives and acceptance criteria should be based on a customer's business and technical goals for the network design but may be more formally or specifically defined. The criteria for declaring that a test passed or failed must be clear and agreed upon by the tester and the customer. This avoids a common problem in which, after the test is completed, the testers and customers agree on the results, but they disagree on the interpretation of the results.

Even though the underlying goal of your testing might be to show that your system is better than a competitor's, you should avoid incorporating biases or preconceived notions about outcomes into test objectives (and test scripts). The test objective should simply be to measure the outcome, not prove that the outcome is in your favor; and it should be based as much as possible on industry standards for all relevant technologies and services (for example, VoIP and International Telecommunication Union [ITU] voice acceptability standards).

Objectives and acceptance criteria can reference a baseline measurement for the current network. For example, an objective might be to measure the cyclic redundancy check (CRC) error rate on a WAN segment and compare the results to a baseline measurement. The acceptance criterion might be that there must be 20 percent fewer errors than there are today. To determine whether the criterion has been met, a baseline measurement must exist, as discussed in Chapter 3, "Characterizing the Existing Internetwork." Chapter 3 also includes a Network Health checklist that can help you write objectives and acceptance criteria.

Determining the Types of Tests to Run

In general, tests should include performance, stress, and failure analyses. Performance analysis should examine the level of service that the system offers in terms of throughput, delay, delay variation, response time, and efficiency. Stress analysis should examine any degradation of service due to increased offered load on the network. Failure analysis should calculate network availability and accuracy, and analyze the causes of any network outages. Depending on a customer's business and technical goals, other tests that might be necessary are manageability, usability, adaptability, and security tests.

The specific types of tests to run against your particular design depend on test objectives. Typical tests include the following:

- **Application response-time testing:** This type of test measures performance from a user's point of view and evaluates how much time a user must wait when executing typical operations that cause network activity. These operations include starting an application, switching between screens, forms, and fields within the application, and executing file opens, reads, writes, searches, and closes. With this type of testing, the tester watches actual users or simulates user behavior with a simulation tool. The test should start with a predetermined number of users and actions, and then gradually increase the number of users and actions to expose any increases in response time due to additional network or server load.

- **Throughput testing:** This type of test measures throughput for a particular application and throughput for multiple applications in kilobytes or megabytes per second. It can also measure throughput in terms of packets per second through a switching device (for example, a switch or router). As in response-time testing, throughput testing should begin with several users and actions that are gradually increased.

- **Availability testing:** With availability testing, tests are run against the system for 24 hours to 72 hours, under medium to heavy load. The rate of errors and failures is monitored.

■   **Regression testing:** Regression testing makes sure the new system doesn't break any applications or components that were known to work and perform to a certain level before the new system was installed. Regression testing does not test new features or upgrades. Instead, it focuses on existing applications. Regression testing should be comprehensive and is usually automated to facilitate comprehensiveness.

Documenting Network Equipment and Other Resources

A test plan should include a network topology drawing and a list of required devices. The topology drawing should include major devices, addresses, names, network links, and some indication of link capacities. The topology drawing should also document any WAN or LAN links that must connect to the production network or to the Internet.

The list of devices should include switches, routers, workstations, servers, telephone-equipment simulators, wireless access points, firewalls, cables, and so on. The list should document version numbers for hardware and software, and availability information. Sometimes testing requires new equipment that might not be available yet or equipment that for other reasons has a long lead time for procurement. If this is the case, it should be noted in the test plan.

In addition to network equipment, a test plan should include a list of required testing tools. The "Tools for Testing a Network Design" section later in this chapter describes useful tools for testing a network design. Typical tools include network management and monitoring tools, traffic-generation tools, modeling and simulation tools, and QoS and service-level-management tools.

The test plan should also list any applications that will increase testing efficiency, such as software distribution applications or remote-control programs that facilitate the configuring and reconfiguring of nodes during a test.

Note   In a Microsoft Windows environment, if your testing requires loading new software applications or versions on multiple systems, Microsoft System Center Configuration Manager software (formerly known as SMS) can be a useful addition to the testing environment.

The test plan should document any other resources you will need, including the following:

■   Scheduled time in a lab either at your site or the customer's site

■   Power, air conditioning, rack space, and other physical resources

■   Help from coworkers or customer staff

■   Help from users to test applications

■   Network addresses and names

Writing Test Scripts

For each test, write a test script that lists the steps to be taken to fulfill the test objective. The script should identify which tool is used for each step, how the tool is used to make relevant measurements, and what information should be logged during testing. The script should define initial values for parameters and how to vary those parameters during testing. For example, the test script might include an initial traffic-load value and incremental increases for the load.

The following is an example of a simple test script for the network test environment shown in Figure 12-1.

■   **Test objective:** Assess the firewall's capability to block Application ABC traffic during both light and moderately heavy load conditions.

■   **Acceptance criterion:** The firewall should block the TCP SYN request from every workstation on Network A that attempts to set up an Application ABC session with Server 1 on Network B. The firewall should send each workstation a TCP RST (reset) packet.

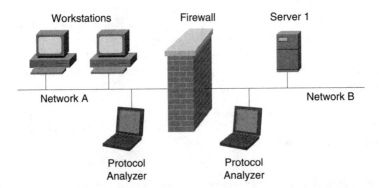

Figure 12-1   *Test Environment for the Example Test Script*

Following are the testing steps:

Step 1.   Start capturing network traffic on the protocol analyzer on Network A.

Step 2.   Start capturing network traffic on the protocol analyzer on Network B.

Step 3.   Run Application ABC on a workstation located on Network A and access Server 1 on Network B.

Step 4.   Stop capturing network traffic on the protocol analyzers.

Step 5.   Display data on Network A's protocol analyzer and verify that the analyzer captured a TCP SYN packet from the workstation. Verify that the network layer destination address is Server 1 on Network B, and the destination port is port 1234 (the port number for Application ABC). Verify that the firewall responded to the workstation with a TCP RST packet.

Step 6. Display data on Network B's protocol analyzer and verify that the analyzer did not capture any Application ABC traffic from the workstation.

Step 7. Log the results of the test in the project log file.

Step 8. Save the protocol analyzer trace files to the project trace-file directory.

Step 9. Gradually increase the workload on the firewall, by increasing the number of workstations on Network A one at a time, until 50 workstations are running Application ABC and attempting to reach Server 1. Repeat Steps 1 through 8 after each workstation is added to the test.

Documenting the Project Timeline

For complex testing projects, the test plan should document the project timeline, including the start and finish date for the project and major milestones. The timeline should list major tasks and the person who has been assigned to each task. The following list shows typical tasks, including some tasks that should have already been completed by the time the test plan is written:

1. Write test objectives and acceptance criteria.
2. Design the network topology for the testing environment.
3. Determine what networking hardware and software will be necessary.
4. Place a purchase order for the hardware and software if necessary.
5. Determine which testing tools will be necessary.
6. Place a purchase order for the testing tools if necessary.
7. Determine other resources that will be necessary and arrange for their availability.
8. Write test scripts.
9. Install and configure hardware and software.
10. Start testing.
11. Log the results of the testing.
12. Review and analyze the results.
13. Reduce results data (if necessary).
14. Present results to the customer.
15. Archive results.

Implementing the Test Plan

Implementing the test plan is mostly a matter of following your test scripts and documenting your work. Realize, however, that sometimes test scripts cannot be followed precisely, because it is difficult to consider all contingencies and potential problems when writing a script. For this reason, it is important to maintain logs, either electronically or in a paper notebook. An electronic log is preferable because it enables easier searching for information later.

In addition to keeping a log that documents collected test data and test results, it is a good idea to keep a daily activity log that documents progress and any changes made to test scripts or equipment configurations. The daily activity log can also be used to record any problems that were encountered and theories about causes. These theories might be helpful later when analyzing results and might help with future testing projects.

Tools for Testing a Network Design

This section discusses the types of tools that can be used to test a network design. The section also recommends some specific tools.

Types of Tools

In general, the types of tools you can use to test your network design include the following:

- Network management and monitoring tools

- Traffic-generation tools

- Modeling and simulation tools

- QoS and service-level-management tools

Network management and monitoring tools are usually used in a production environment to alert network managers to problems and significant network events, but they also help when testing a network design. Network management applications, such as the CiscoWorks offerings from Cisco or the HP Operations Manager software, can alert you to problems on your test network. These types of tools usually run on a dedicated network management station (NMS).

Network management and monitoring software can also include applications that reside on network devices. For example, some network operating systems include software that monitors server CPU and memory usage, which can be useful when isolating performance problems in a new network design. As another example, many Cisco IOS Software commands are useful tools for checking the performance of Cisco routers and switches in a test environment.

You can also use a protocol analyzer to monitor a new design. A *protocol analyzer* can help you analyze traffic behavior, errors, utilization, efficiency, and rates of broadcast and multicast packets. You can also use a protocol analyzer to generate traffic. If it is impractical to purchase, install, and configure all the devices required to develop a large-scale prototype, you can purchase a subset of the devices and generate traffic to induce the load that would be present if all the devices were installed. This will give you an approximation of the behavior of the new system.

Depending on your budget for the network testing project, instead of using a protocol analyzer to generate traffic, you can use expensive but powerful multiport traffic generators. These tools can send multiple streams of network traffic, emulate protocols, and analyze performance and conformance to standards specifications.

For a sophisticated model of the new network system, you can use modeling and simulation tools. *Simulation* is the process of using software and mathematical models to analyze the behavior of a network without requiring an actual network. A *simulation tool* enables you to develop a model of a network, estimate the performance of the network, and compare alternatives for implementing the network. A simulation tool, if accurate, is often preferable to implementing and measuring an extensive prototype system because it allows alternatives to be more easily compared.

A good simulation tool is only as good as its developer's understanding of computer networking, statistical analysis, and modeling techniques. Because a complete simulation of a system would require the simulator to be more powerful than the sum of the components it is modeling, a sophisticated simulation tool allows the development of a model that factors in only those aspects of the network that have a significant impact on performance. Developing good simulation tools is an art that requires great awareness of how real networks and components work and interact.

Effective simulation tools include device libraries that model the behavior of major networking devices (for example, switches and routers). Because the performance limitations of switches and routers often arise from the way processes, buffers, and queues are implemented, switch and router models should take into account the architecture of the device.

Modeling switch and router behavior can be challenging, however, because every vendor has numerous optimization techniques and configuration options. One solution to this problem is that a simulation tool can incorporate measurements of actual network traffic, rather than relying solely on device libraries that model theoretical device behavior. This approach not only solves the problem of modeling complex devices, but also allows the tool to calibrate assumptions made about traffic load and characteristics. There is less reliance on the network designer to accurately predict traffic load and more reliance on real measurements.

QoS and service-level-management tools analyze end-to-end performance for network applications. These tools measure application response times. They collect data from a variety of sources, including packets, traffic flows, and device MIBs. Some QoS management tools sort traffic in terms of the differentiated services codepoint (DSCP) bits in the IP header and report how much bandwidth each category uses. QoS and service-level-management tools also provide a variety of other features such as baseline, threshold, trending, and anomaly detection reporting.

Examples of Network Testing Tools

This section describes some specific tools that can be used to test your network design. There are many other tools in addition to the ones listed here, so be sure to do some research on the best tool for your project. The tools listed here are network management, modeling, simulation, and service-level-management tools that can be used for testing networks and for managing operational networks.

CiscoWorks Internetwork Performance Monitor

CiscoWorks Internetwork Performance Monitor (IPM) is a network troubleshooting and monitoring application that gauges network response time and availability. It helps network administrators discover end-to-end network performance problems, locate bottlenecks, measure response time, and diagnose latency problems. CiscoWorks IPM is a component of CiscoWorks LAN Management Solution (LMS).

IPM features include

- Continuous response time and latency monitoring between network device pairs

- Monitoring and measurement of jitter

- Integration with Cisco IP Service Level Agreement technology available in most Cisco IOS devices

- Threshold-crossing alerts

- Comprehensive reporting based on response time, availability, and statistics

WANDL Network Planning and Analysis Tools

WANDL, Inc., developed the Network Planning and Analysis Tools (NPAT) software suite to help customers handle the design, planning, and management of large-scale WANs. WANDL's customers, who include carriers, Fortune 500 companies, and government organizations, use NPAT to plan and analyze networks ranging in size from 30 to more than 300 backbone nodes. WANDL's IP/MPLSView is a network design, testing, traffic management, and traffic engineering solution for IP and Multiprotocol Label Switching (MPLS) networks.

The WANDL tools support capacity planning, network testing, and optimization. They allow a user to test the redundancy of a network and analyze the effects of network outages. They facilitate analyzing alternatives for WAN technologies with sophisticated what-if analysis tools. A unique feature of the WANDL tools is the capability to estimate monthly tariff charges for WAN circuits.

OPNET Technologies

OPNET Technologies software embeds expert knowledge about how network devices, protocols, applications, and servers operate. This intelligence enables users to optimize performance and availability of their networks and applications.

OPNET Modeler is a network technology development environment that allows users to design and study network systems. Modeler's object-oriented modeling approach and graphical editors mirror the structure of actual networks and network components.

OPNET IT Guru Network Planner is another product from OPNET that models Cisco and other vendors' device configurations and includes tools for taking captured data and analyzing which components are the bottlenecks.

Ixia Tools

Ixia has a set of sophisticated network testing tools ranging from IxAutomate, which automates performance, scalability, and functional testing of network devices, to IxLoad, which generates Layer 4 through 7 traffic for content-aware assessment. The IxNetwork tool supports routing, switching, authentication, Ethernet, and Fiber Channel over Ethernet (FCoE) protocols. Ixia's K2 40-Gbps and 100-Gbps modules provide Layer 2 through Layer 7 measurement and analysis at extremely fast speeds, facilitating the generation and analysis of network traffic for IP-TV, VoIP, video on demand, HDTV, Internet gaming, and multimedia streaming services.

In October 2009, Ixia bought Agilent Technologies' N2X network tester. Now called *IxN2X*, this tool is designed to test IP forwarding devices such as routers and switches that deliver video, VoIP, data services, and business VPNs. It is used in "out-of-service" lab environments to test at real-world scale with realistic traffic. IxN2X lets its users test next-generation networks by generating deterministic, repeatable test stimuli and making nanosecond-accurate measurements.

NetIQ Voice and Video Management Solution

NetIQ has numerous products for planning network upgrades and testing network designs. NetIQ products that help a network designer assess whether a network can handle new voice and video applications are especially helpful. NetIQ's Vivinet Assessor, in particular, can help you before deployment to determine quickly and easily how well VoIP will work on a network. Vivinet Assessor predicts the overall call quality you can expect from the network and generates reports detailing the network's VoIP readiness.

NetPredict's NetPredictor

NetPredictor is a performance and service-level-management tool that predicts and monitors the QoS provided by a network as it would be perceived by a user. NetPredictor analyzes the interrelated effects on network applications of end-to-end latency, load, and packet loss. It bases its analysis on models of both network and protocol behavior that are automatically calibrated by actual network management and protocol analyzer data.

NetPredictor facilitates the following design tasks:

- Determining what network and server resources are needed to deliver a required QoS level

- Predicting end-to-end performance before deploying new applications or technologies

- Developing service-level agreements (SLA) based on verifiable performance predictions

- Monitoring actual performance and comparing it with expectations or SLAs

NetPredictor lets you model an existing network and then simulate replacing existing devices with other network components to determine how performance will change. The model can be based on knowledge about the network and applications that you provide and information from a device library. The model automatically adapts to data that NetPredictor captures from the actual network.

Summary

Testing your network design is an important step in the design process that allows you to confirm that your design meets business and technical goals. By testing your design, you can verify that the solutions you have developed will provide the performance and QoS that your customer expects.

This chapter presented a systems-analysis approach to testing that includes writing concrete test objectives, verifiable acceptance criteria, test scripts, and test logs. The chapter also provided information on design and testing tools, including tools from Cisco, WANDL, OPNET, and NetIQ.

The next chapter talks about optimization techniques you can use to ensure that your design meets performance requirements. It is not uncommon during the testing phase to determine that an initial implementation of a design requires some manipulation to meet QoS requirements and other goals, such as scalability, availability, security, manageability, affordability, and so on. Based on the results of your network design testing, you can select and test optimization techniques, such as those described in the next chapter.

Review Questions

1. List and describe five typical goals for a network design testing project.

2. What are some advantages of using industry tests for your network design testing project? What are some disadvantages of using industry tests?

3. What are some advantages of testing a new network design component on a production network during normal business hours? What are some disadvantages of taking this approach?

4. What is regression testing? Why is regression testing usually an important part of a network testing project? In what cases is regression testing not necessary?

Design Scenario

In Chapter 10, "Selecting Technologies and Devices for Enterprise Networks," you learned about the network design project for Wandering Valley Community College (WVCC). Write a test plan that WVCC can use to test the new wireless network. Consider WVCC's goals for this part of the network, in particular the need to have an open access point for visitors and a separate secure, private access point for employees and students. The test plan should include at least one detailed test script. The topic for the test script is your choice.

Chapter 13

Optimizing Your Network Design

Optimization is a critical design step for organizations that use high-bandwidth and delay-sensitive applications. To achieve business goals, these organizations expect their networks to use bandwidth efficiently, to control delay and jitter, and to support preferential service for essential applications. Internetworking vendors, such as Cisco, and standards bodies, such as the Institute of Electrical and Electronics Engineers (IEEE) and the Internet Engineering Task Force (IETF), offer numerous options to meet these expectations. This chapter introduces you to some of these options.

At this point in the top-down network design process, you should have a solid understanding of the logical and physical topology of your network. You should know about any links that will be shared by applications with different requirements, and you should have tested a pilot implementation of the network design to determine which links are in most need of optimization techniques.

This chapter covers optimization solutions. It assumes you have already analyzed requirements, especially application requirements for low delay or high throughput. As mentioned in Chapter 4, "Characterizing Network Traffic," during the early phases of a design project, you should work with your customer to classify network applications into service categories so that you can determine which optimization and quality of service (QoS) options the applications will require. After you have classified an application, you should fill in the "QoS Requirements" column in Table 4-4, "Network Applications Traffic Characteristics." As mentioned in Chapter 2, "Analyzing Technical Goals and Tradeoffs," you should also fill in application throughput and delay goals in Table 2-2, "Network Applications Technical Requirements."

The chapter starts with a discussion of IP multicast techniques that minimize bandwidth utilization for multimedia applications. Reducing delay is also important for multimedia applications that are sensitive to delay, such as voice and video. The "Reducing Serialization Delay" section describes some methods for ensuring that delay is minimized.

The chapter continues with a discussion of methods for optimizing network performance to meet QoS requirements. These methods allow applications to inform routers of their load and latency requirements, and let routers share QoS information among themselves and with policy servers. Later in this chapter, the section "Cisco IOS Features for Optimizing Network Performance" describes an assortment of optimization techniques offered by Cisco, including advanced switching, queuing, and traffic-shaping techniques.

Optimizing Bandwidth Usage with IP Multicast Technologies

One of the main reasons optimization techniques are required on internetworks is the increasing use of high-bandwidth, multiple-user, multimedia applications. Such applications as distance learning, videoconferencing, and collaborative computing have a need to send streams of data to multiple users, without using excessive amounts of bandwidth or causing performance problems on many systems.

The IETF has developed several IP multicast standards that optimize the transmission of multimedia and other types of traffic across an internetwork. The standards identify multicast addressing techniques that avoid the extra traffic caused by many unicast point-to-point or broadcast traffic streams. They also specify how routers learn which network segments should receive multicast streams, and how routers route multicast traffic.

Older multimedia applications that do not use multicast technologies send a data stream to every user. Such applications use a unicast point-to-point method of handling multimedia traffic that wastes bandwidth. An alternative to multiple point-to-point streams is to send a single stream and use a broadcast destination address. The obvious disadvantage with this technique is that the data stream goes to all devices, even devices for which no application is installed to handle the stream. This approach has a negative effect on performance for every device receiving the stream, including workstations, switches, and routers.

With IP multicast technologies, on the other hand, a single data stream is sent to only those stations that request the stream, thus optimizing bandwidth usage and reducing performance problems on end stations and internetworking devices.

Businesses, universities, and other organizations can use IP multicast technologies for many information-dissemination applications, including online training classes, virtual meetings, and electronic newscasts. In addition, IP multicast technologies are used in computer-simulation applications. An example is simulated military scenarios. Because it is impractical to prepare for large-scale battles with real equipment, some military institutions conduct training exercises with thousands of simulated planes, tanks, troops, weather satellites, and other devices. A plane or tank can register to receive weather and topography information for its current location by joining an IP multicast group for that location. As the plane moves, it leaves and joins new groups. This way the plane can avoid receiving information on the weather and topography for all areas (which would be overwhelming), and instead receive information relevant only to its current location. This type of application must support multicast addressing and dynamic multicast group membership, which are discussed in the next few sections.

IP Multicast Addressing

IP multicasting transmits IP data to a group of hosts that is identified by a single Class D IP address. In dotted decimal notation, host group addresses range from 224.0.0.0 to 239.255.255.255. Network stations recognize an address as being a Class D address because the first 4 bits must be 1110 in binary.

A multicast group is also identified by a MAC layer multicast address. Using a MAC layer multicast address optimizes network performance by allowing network interface cards (NIC) that are not part of a group to ignore a data stream that is not for them.

The Internet Assigned Numbers Authority (IANA) owns a block of MAC layer addresses that are used for group multicast addresses. The range of addresses for Ethernet is 01:00:5E:00:00:00 to 01:00:5E:7F:FF:FF. When a station sends a frame to an IP group that is identified by a Class D address, the station inserts the low-order 23 bits of the Class D address into the low-order 23 bits of the MAC layer destination address. The top 9 bits of the Class D address are not used. The top 25 bits of the MAC address are 01:00:5E followed by a 0, or, in binary, the following:

> 00000001 00000000 01011110 0

For example, when a router running the Open Shortest Path First (OSPF) routing protocol sends to the *All OSPF Routers* 224.0.0.5 multicast IP address, the address is converted to 01:00:5e:00:00:05 for use as the destination MAC address. Note that MAC addresses are written in hexadecimal, whereas IP addresses are written in dotted decimal notation.

As another example, when a host sends to the 233.252.16.1 multicast IP address, the address is converted to 01:00:5E:7C:10:01 for use as the destination MAC address. Follow these steps to make the conversion:

Step 1. The top 9 bits of the Class D IP address are not used, so to start, drop the first octet. In other words, drop the 233.

Step 2. Also drop the first bit of the second octet. The second octet is 252 in decimal, or 11111100 in binary. You only want the last 7 bits, however, because IEEE says the first bit must be a 0. So the number becomes 01111100 in binary, or 124 in decimal. That is 0x7C in hexadecimal.

Step 3. Use the entire third octet, which is 16 in decimal, but convert it to hexadecimal, giving you 0x10.

Step 4. Use the entire fourth octet, which is 1 in decimal, but convert it to hexadecimal, giving you 0x01.

Step 5. Prepend 01:00:5E to give you the final result of 01:00:5E:7C:10:01.

Internet Group Management Protocol

Internet Group Management Protocol (IGMP) enables a host to join a group and inform routers of the need to receive a particular data stream. IP hosts use IGMP to report their multicast group memberships to immediately neighboring multicast routers.

When a user (or system process) starts an application that requires a host to join a multicast group, the host transmits a *membership-report* message to inform routers on the segment that traffic for the group should be multicast to the host's segment. Although it is possible that the router is already sending data for the group to the host's segment, the specification states that a host should send a *membership-report* message in case it is the first member of the group on the network segment.

In addition to allowing hosts to join groups, IGMP specifies that a multicast router sends an IGMP query out every interface at regular intervals to see if any hosts belong to the group. A host responds by sending an IGMP *membership-report* message for each group in which it is still a member (based on the applications running on the host).

To lessen bandwidth utilization, hosts set a random timer before responding to queries. If the host sees another host respond for a group to which the host belongs, the host cancels its response. The router does not need to know how many or which specific hosts on a segment belong to a group. It only needs to recognize that a group has at least one member on a segment, so that it sends traffic to that segment using the IP and MAC multicast addresses for the group.

By default, a data link layer switch floods multicast frames out every port. The Cisco Group Management Protocol (CGMP) and the IETF IGMP snooping methods allow switches to participate in the process of determining which segments have hosts in a particular multicast group. CGMP is a Cisco proprietary method that lets a router send a message to switches to tell the switches about hosts joining and leaving groups. IGMP snooping is an IETF standard that causes no extra traffic but allows a switch to learn from the IGMP messages sent to routers.

Multicast Routing Protocols

In addition to determining which local network segments should receive traffic for particular multicast groups, a router must also learn how to route multicast traffic across an internetwork. Multicast routing protocols provide this function.

Whereas a standard unicast routing protocol learns paths to destination networks, a multicast routing protocol learns paths to multicast destination addresses. Multicast routing protocols help routers learn which interfaces should send each multicast stream. This section covers two multicast routing protocols: Distance Vector Multicast Routing Protocol (DVMRP) and Protocol Independent Multicast (PIM).

Distance Vector Multicast Routing Protocol

The IETF developed DVMRP to experiment with multicast routing. DVMRP is historically interesting and useful for understanding multicast routing concepts, but PIM, which is covered in the next section, is a better choice when implementing multicast routing on operational networks. DVMRP was based on the unicast Routing Information Protocol (RIP). Like RIP, DVMRP was an Interior gateway protocol (IGP), suitable for use within an autonomous system (AS) but not between different autonomous systems. DVMRP used IGMP to exchange routing updates.

The key difference between RIP and DVMRP is that RIP learns the path to a particular destination, whereas DVMRP keeps track of the return paths to the source of multicast packets. DVMRP combines many of the features of RIP with the Truncated Reverse Path Broadcasting (TRPB) algorithm.

TRPB learns how to forward multicast packets by computing the shortest (reverse) path tree between the source of a multicast packet and all possible recipients of the packet. Each multicast router determines its place in the tree, relative to the particular source, and then determines which of its interfaces are in the shortest path tree. Multicast packets are forwarded out these interfaces. A process for excluding interfaces not in the shortest path tree also exists and is called *pruning*.

Protocol Independent Multicast

Like DVMRP, PIM works in tandem with IGMP and with a unicast routing protocol, such as RIP, OSPF, Cisco Enhanced Interior Gateway Routing Protocol (EIGRP), and so on.

PIM has two modes: *dense mode* and *sparse mode*. The adjectives *dense* and *sparse* refer to the density of group members. Dense groups have many members. An example of a dense group is employees at a corporation who listen to the company president's quarterly report when it is multicast on the corporate intranet. A sparse group might be a much smaller group of employees who have signed up for a particular distance-learning course.

Dense-Mode Protocol Independent Multicast

Dense-mode PIM is similar to DVMRP. Both protocols use a reverse-path forwarding (RPF) mechanism to compute the shortest (reverse) path between a source and all possible recipients of a multicast packet. Dense-mode PIM is simpler than DVMRP, however, because it does not require the computation of routing tables.

If a router running dense-mode PIM receives a multicast packet from a source to a group, it first verifies in the standard unicast routing table that the incoming interface is the one that it uses for sending unicast packets toward the source. If this is not the case, it drops the packet and sends back a prune message. If it is the case, the router forwards a copy of the packet on all interfaces for which it has not received a prune message for the source/group destination pair. If there are no such interfaces, it sends back a prune message.

The first packet for a group is flooded to all interfaces. After this has occurred, however, routers listen to *prune* messages to help them develop a map of the network that lets them send multicast packets only to those networks that should receive the packets. The *prune* messages also let routers avoid loops that would cause more than one router to send a multicast packet to a segment.

Dense-mode PIM works best in environments with large multicast groups and a high likelihood that any given LAN has a group member, which limits the router's need to send prune messages. Because of the flooding of the first packet for a group, dense-mode PIM does not make sense in environments where a few sparsely located users want to participate in a multicast application. In this case, sparse-mode PIM, which is described in the next section, is a better solution.

Sparse-Mode Protocol Independent Multicast

Sparse-mode PIM is quite different from dense-mode PIM. Rather than allowing traffic to be sent everywhere and then pruned back where it is not needed, sparse-mode PIM defines a rendezvous point. The *rendezvous point* provides a registration service for a multicast group.

Sparse-mode PIM relies on IGMP, which lets a host join a group by sending a *membership-report* message, and detach from a group by sending a leave message. A designated router for a network segment tracks *membership-report* and *leave* messages on its segment, and periodically sends *join* and *prune* PIM messages to the rendezvous point. The *join* and *prune* messages are processed by all the routers between the designated router and the rendezvous point. The result is a distribution tree that reaches all group members and is centered at the rendezvous point.

The *distribution tree* for a multicast group is initially used for any source, but the sparse-mode PIM specification, RFC 4601, also provides a mechanism to let the rendezvous point develop source-specific trees to further the pruning of network traffic.

When a source initially sends data to a group, the designated router on the source's network unicasts *register* messages to the rendezvous point with the source's data packets encapsulated within. If the data rate is high, the rendezvous point can send *join/prune* messages back toward the source. This enables the source's data packets to follow a *source-specific shortest path tree*, and eliminates the need for the packets to be encapsulated in *register* messages. Whether the packets arrive encapsulated or not, the rendezvous point forwards the source's decapsulated data packets down the distribution tree toward group members.

Reducing Serialization Delay

On slow WAN links, the time to output a large packet is significant. The time to output a packet is called *transmission delay* or *serialization delay*. Serialization delay becomes an issue when a WAN link is used by applications that send large packets, such as file transfer, and applications that are delay-sensitive, such as voice, video, and interactive applications such as Telnet. Solutions to this problem include the use of link-layer fragmentation and interleaving (LFI) and the use of compression for multimedia packet headers. This section covers these solutions.

Link-Layer Fragmentation and Interleaving

LFI reduces delay on slow WAN links by breaking up large packets and interleaving the resulting small packets with packets for applications that are delay sensitive. PPP, Frame Relay, ATM, and other WAN technologies can all benefit from LFI on low-speed links, such as 56-kbps Frame Relay or 64-kbps ISDN B channels.

LFI for PPP is defined by the Multilink Point-to-Point Protocol (MPPP) standard, which is RFC 1990. LFI for PPP is relatively simple. Large packets are multilink encapsulated based on RFC 1990 and fragmented to packets of a size small enough to satisfy the delay requirements of delay-sensitive traffic. Small delay-sensitive packets are not multilink encapsulated but are interleaved between fragments of the large packets.

MPPP allows packets to be sent at the same time over multiple point-to-point links to the same remote address. The multiple links come up in response to a load threshold that you define. The load can be calculated on inbound traffic, outbound traffic, or on either, as needed for the traffic between specific sites. MPPP provides bandwidth on demand and reduces delay on WAN links.

When you configure MPPP on a Cisco router, packets arriving at an output interface are sorted into queues based on classifications that you define. After the packets are queued, large packets are fragmented into smaller packets in preparation for interleaving with time-sensitive packets. If weighted fair queuing (WFQ) is configured for an interface, packets from each queue are interleaved and scheduled (fairly and based on their weight) for transmission in the output interface queue. To ensure the correct order of transmission and reassembly, LFI adds multilink headers to the packet fragments after the packets are dequeued and ready to be sent.

In addition to supporting LFI for classic MPPP uses, such as aggregated ISDN channels, Cisco also supports LFI for Frame Relay and ATM virtual circuits. This feature implements LFI using MPPP over Frame Relay and ATM. LFI for Frame Relay and ATM supports low-speed Frame Relay and ATM virtual circuits and Frame Relay/ATM interworking (FRF.8). LFI for Frame Relay and ATM works concurrently with and on the same switching path as other QoS features, including Frame Relay traffic shaping (FRTS), low-latency queuing (LLQ), and class-based weighted fair queuing (CBWFQ).

Cisco also supports the following three methods for performing Frame Relay fragmentation:

■ End-to-end Frame Relay fragmentation in accordance with the FRF.12 standard

■ Trunk Frame Relay fragmentation in accordance with the FRF.11 Annex C standard

■ Cisco proprietary fragmentation for voice encapsulation

Compressed Real-Time Transport Protocol

The Real-Time Transport Protocol (RTP), which is defined in RFC 3550, provides end-to-end network transport functions suitable for transmitting real-time data over multicast or unicast network services. Applications typically run RTP on top of the User Datagram Protocol (UDP) to make use of UDP's multiplexing and checksum services. Working together with UDP, RTP implements Layer 4 (transport) functionality. Compressed RTP compresses the RTP, UDP, and IP headers to reduce serialization delay on slow links.

The RTP packet header includes several fields that specify the attributes of the data carried in the RTP packet:

- The *payload type* indicates the format of the payload (for example, MPEG audio or video data, JPEG video, or an H.261 video stream).

- The *sequence number* indicates the location of the packet in the data stream. The sequence number increments by one for each RTP data packet sent and can be used by the receiver to detect packet loss and to restore packet sequence.

- The *timestamp* reflects the sampling instant of the first byte in the data packet.

- The *synchronization source (SSRC) field* identifies the source of a stream of RTP packets (for example, a microphone or video camera). All packets from a synchronization source form part of the same timing and sequence number space, so a receiver groups packets by SSRC for playback.

- The *contributing source (CSRC) list* identifies sources that have contributed to the payload in the packet. An example application is audioconferencing, where the CSRC field indicates all the talkers whose speech was combined to produce the outgoing packet.

The RTP header adds important functionality that is used by multimedia applications, including video and voice over IP (VoIP). The downside of RTP is that it adds bytes to every packet, which can be an issue when a design goal is to reduce serialization delay and minimize bandwidth usage. Compressed RTP reduces delay and saves network bandwidth by compressing the RTP/UDP/IP header from 40 bytes to 2 or 4 bytes. The header can be 2 bytes when no UDP checksum is used and 4 bytes when a UDP checksum is used. The compression scheme takes advantage of the fact that, although several fields change in every packet, the difference from packet to packet is often constant. Compressing the headers is especially beneficial for slow links and small packets (such as VoIP traffic), where the compression can reduce overhead and serialization delay significantly.

Optimizing Network Performance to Meet Quality of Service Requirements

In addition to optimizing bandwidth usage by adding IP multicast, LFI, and compression features to a network design, you might determine that optimization is also needed to meet QoS requirements. The "Characterizing Quality of Service Requirements" section in

Chapter 4 talked about specifying the QoS that an application requires. This section covers some techniques for meeting those requirements.

As discussed in Chapter 4, the Integrated Services working group defines two types of service that offer QoS assurances beyond *best-effort service* (which offers no QoS assurances):

■ **Controlled-load service:** Provides a client data flow with a QoS closely approximating the QoS that the flow would receive on an unloaded network. The controlled-load service is intended for applications that are highly sensitive to overload conditions.

■ **Guaranteed service:** Provides firm bounds on end-to-end packet-queuing delays. Guaranteed service is intended for applications that need a guarantee that a packet will arrive no later than a certain time after it was transmitted by its source.

Many optimization options are available to accommodate applications with controlled-load or guaranteed service requirements. The next few sections describe some of these options, starting with one that has been available for many years: the precedence and type-of-service functionality built in to the IP packet.

IP Precedence and Type of Service

Although specialized features to support QoS have recently become a hot topic of conversation among network engineers and designers, the concept that a network must support applications with varying requirements for service is not new. The creators of IP incorporated support for different levels of precedence and types of service into the IP packet format when IP was first developed in the 1970s. Figure 13-1 shows the fields in the original IP version 4 (IPv4) header, with an emphasis on the historical Type of Service field near the beginning of the header.

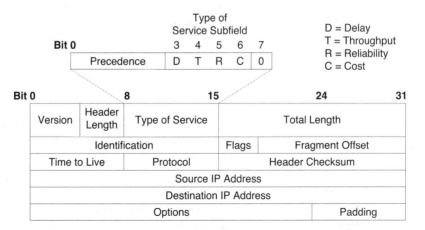

Figure 13-1   *Internet Protocol (IP) Header with Historical Type of Service Field*

The IP Type of Service field specified both precedence and type of service. *Precedence* helped a router determine which packet to send when several packets were queued for transmission to the same output interface. *Type of service* helped a router select a routing path when multiple paths were available.

The Type of Service field was divided into two subfields (that were followed by a bit that was always set to 0):

■ The 3-bit Precedence subfield supported eight levels of priority.

■ The 4-bit Type of Service subfield supported four types of service.

An application used the *Precedence* subfield to specify the importance of a packet. The importance ranged from routine priority (the bits were set to 000) to high priority (the bits were set to 111). A value of 5 decimal was typical for VoIP and other real-time applications and is still recognized by many modern routers.

The purpose of the *Type of Service* subfield was to help a router select a route from a set of routes with different characteristics. The Type of Service subfield within the Type of Service field in an IP header had 4 bits (see Figure 13-1):

■ **Delay bit (D):** Tells routers to minimize delay

■ **Throughput bit (T):** Tells routers to maximize throughput

■ **Reliability bit (R):** Tells routers to maximize reliability

■ **Cost bit (C):** Tells routers to minimize monetary cost

In practice, routing protocols and routers never had good methods for addressing the needs of applications that set the type-of-service bits. Selecting a path based on the setting of the D, T, R, or C bit proved to be impractical. Although early versions of the OSPF and Border Gateway Protocol (BGP) routing protocols specified support for the bits, newer versions of OSPF and BGP specifications do not require support for routing based on the setting of the bits.

The path-selection service offered by the Type of Service subfield never materialized. The prioritization service offered by the Precedence subfield, on the other hand, is now specified by RFC 2474, "Definition of the Differentiated Services Field (DS Field) in the IPv4 and IPv6 Headers," and RFC 2475, "An Architecture for Differentiated Services."

IP Differentiated Services Field

Per RFCs 2474 and 2475, the Type of Service field became the Differentiated Services (DS) field in IPv4. Bits 0 through 5 of that field are called the *differentiated services codepoint* (DSCP), as shown in Figure 13-2. (Per RFC 3168, bits 6 and 7 are designated as the Explicit Congestion Notification field, which is beyond the scope of this discussion.)

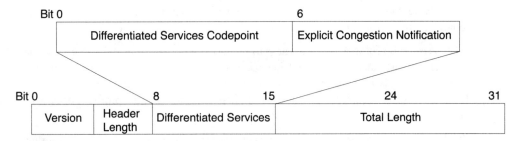

Figure 13-2 *Differentiated Services (DS) Field*

The DSCP has essentially the same goal as the Precedence subfield, which is to influence queuing and packet-dropping decisions for IP packets on an output interface of a router. RFC 2474 refers to these decisions as per-hop behaviors (PHB). The DSCP can have 1 of 64 possible values, each of which outlines a PHB. The DSCP field is backward compatible with the Precedence subfield. No attempt was made to retain compatibility with the Type of Service subfield, however.

The Assured Forwarding (AF) PHB describes a means for a provider to offer different levels of forwarding assurances for IP packets received from a customer. The AF PHB guarantees a certain amount of bandwidth to an AF class and allows access to extra bandwidth, if available. There are four AF classes, AF1 through AF4, and within each class, there are three packet-drop probabilities.

The Expedited Forwarding (EF) PHB can be used to build an assured-bandwidth, end-to-end service with low loss, latency, and jitter. Such a service appears to the endpoints like a point-to-point connection or a virtual leased line. This service has also been described as a *premium service*.

Note The IPv6 header doesn't include a DS field, but it does include an 8-bit *traffic class* field. This field takes on the responsibility of the IP precedence bits from the original IPv4 header and the DSCP field from the newer IPv4 header.

Resource Reservation Protocol

The *Resource Reservation Protocol (RSVP)* complements the IP type-of-service, precedence, DSCP, and traffic-class capabilities inherent in an IP header. RSVP supports more sophisticated mechanisms for hosts to specify QoS requirements for individual traffic flows. RSVP can be deployed on LANs and enterprise WANs to support multimedia applications or other types of applications with strict QoS requirements.

Both the IP header type-of-service capabilities and RSVP are examples of *QoS signaling protocols*. QoS signaling is a means of delivering QoS requirements across a network. The Type of Service field in the IP header offers *in-band signaling*, meaning that bits within the frame header signal to routers how the frame should be handled. RSVP offers *out-of-band signaling*, meaning that hosts send additional frames, beyond data frames, to indicate that a certain QoS service is desired for a particular traffic flow.

RSVP is a setup protocol used by a host to request specific qualities of service from the network for particular application data streams or flows. RSVP is also used by routers to deliver QoS requests to other routers along the path of a flow. RSVP operates on top of IP version 4 or 6, occupying the place of a transport protocol in the protocol stack (although it does not transport application data).

RSVP is not a routing protocol; it operates in tandem with unicast and multicast routing protocols. Whereas a routing protocol determines where packets get forwarded, RSVP is concerned with the QoS those packets receive. RSVP consults the local unicast or multi-cast routing database to obtain routes. In the multicast case, for example, a host sends IGMP messages to join a multicast group and then sends RSVP messages to reserve resources along the delivery path(s) for that group.

According to the RSVP specification, a receiver is responsible for requesting a specific QoS, not a source. Putting the onus on the receiver lets RSVP more easily accommodate large groups, dynamic group membership, and heterogeneous receiver requirements.

An application residing on a receiver host passes a QoS request to the local RSVP process. The RSVP protocol then carries the request to all the nodes (routers and hosts) along the reverse data path(s) to the data source(s) (only as far as the router located where the receiver's data path joins the multicast distribution tree). RSVP requests should result in resources being reserved in each node along the path.

RSVP provides a general facility for creating and maintaining information on resource reservations across a mesh of unicast or multicast delivery paths. RSVP transfers QoS parameters, but does not define the parameters or the different types of services that an application can request. RSVP simply passes parameters to the appropriate traffic-control and policy-control modules for interpretation.

As part of the requirements-analysis phase of the network design process, you should have identified applications that can benefit from RSVP. You should have also selected routers to implement the design during the physical design phase. At this point in the design process, analyze your selections and take another look at the network topology to make sure routers that support RSVP are available to the applications that need it. For RSVP to be effective, each router on the path from a receiver to a source must support RSVP, including routers in redundant paths that may come into service during network outages or when the traffic load is high.

Note   Remember, network design is an iterative process that allows you to adjust your plans as you consider the details and ramifications of choices made so far.

When considering RSVP, be sure to read RFC 2208 (or any updates published after publi-cation of this book). RFC 2208, "Resource Reservation Protocol Version 1 Applicability Statement," points out the problems with running RSVP on a backbone router that aggregates traffic from many networks. The processing and storage requirements for running RSVP on a router increase proportionally with the number of separate sessions and RSVP reservations. Supporting RSVP on a critical backbone router that handles many data streams can overtax the router, and is inadvisable.

RSVP is more suited for private intranets than for the Internet or other public networks that cross multiple service providers' domains. Not only are there scalability issues associated with the amount of information that routers must maintain for each RSVP session, there are also economic concerns. One service provider might be willing to provide resources (bandwidth and low delay, for example) that another service provider is not equipped to offer. A provider might not have the capacity to offer the services or the procedures to bill customers for them.

In addition, RSVP is best suited for long-duration flows, such as those present in video applications. A lot of Internet traffic consists of short-duration flows. For these reasons, RSVP is more appropriate for private networks than for the Internet. (Although this might change in the future as applications on the Internet change and more progress is made on methods for providers to cooperate.)

Common Open Policy Service Protocol

As mentioned in the previous section, RSVP simply transports QoS requests and provides techniques for routers to maintain information about the state of resource reservations. For RSVP to be effective, it needs support from additional protocols that understand actual services and policies about the services. One such protocol is *Common Open Policy Service (COPS)*, which is specified in RFC 2748.

COPS defines a simple client/server model for supporting policy control with QoS signaling protocols such as RSVP. The COPS specification describes a basic query-and-response protocol that can be used to exchange policy information between a policy server and its clients, which will typically be RSVP routers.

The COPS specification calls a policy server a *policy-decision point (PDP)*. It calls a client a *policy-enforcement point (PEP)*. The protocol lets a PEP send requests, updates, and deletions to a remote PDP and lets the PDP return decisions to the PEP. In this fashion, RSVP-based routers can exchange information with centralized servers that store a network's QoS policies, and learn how to correctly handle flows for which resources have been reserved.

Classifying LAN Traffic

The IEEE specifies a method for tagging LAN frames with a class of service (CoS) in its 802.1D document, "Standard for Local Area Network MAC (Media Access Control) Bridges." CoS for LAN frames was originally published as a supplement to 802.1D called 802.1p. Most vendors still refer to the technology as 802.1p, and this book continues to call it 802.1p, which specifies mechanisms for switches to expedite the delivery of time-critical traffic and to limit the extent of high-bandwidth multicast traffic within a switched LAN.

IEEE 802.1p provides an in-band QoS signaling method for classifying traffic on the basis of MAC frame information. It also specifies an optional protocol mechanism in switches to support end stations dynamically registering for time-critical frame delivery or filtering services. Optional protocols between switches to convey registration information in a switched LAN are also supported.

IEEE 802.1p supports eight classes of service. A value of 0 means routine service (in other words, no priority). Different switches within a LAN, and even different ports on switches, can be configured for a different number of priority levels. A switch should have a separate queue for each priority level used by a port.

> **Note**   It could be argued that LANs do not need QoS features. LANs that have been migrated to switched technologies and high speeds, such as 100-Mbps and Gigabit Ethernet, often have excess capacity. When backbone networks and uplink segments to upper layers of a hierarchical topology are considered, however, it becomes clear that QoS methods are necessary on LANs and enterprise networks. As new networked multimedia and voice applications become a central part of normal business practices, switched campus LANs can take advantage of 802.1p capabilities, in addition to the other capabilities already covered in this chapter.

Cisco IOS Features for Optimizing Network Performance

Cisco IOS Software provides a toolbox of optimization techniques to help you meet the challenges related to increasing traffic demands on campus and enterprise networks. The techniques include advanced switching and queuing services to improve throughput and offer QoS functionality.

Switching Techniques

In addition to running routing protocols to develop a routing topology, the major job of a router is to switch (forward) packets from incoming interfaces to outgoing interfaces. Switching involves receiving a packet, determining how to forward the packet based on the routing topology and QoS and policy requirements, and switching the packet to the right outgoing interface or interfaces. The speed at which a router can perform this task is a major factor in determining network performance in a routed network. Cisco supports many switching methods, with varying speeds and behaviors. This section describes some of these switching methods.

In general, you should use the fastest switching method available for an interface type and protocol. Using a speedy switching mode is especially important on backbone and core enterprise routers. Depending on the version of Cisco IOS Software you are running, the fastest mode might need to be configured. (It is not always the default.) You might also need to watch memory usage. The faster switching methods use more memory, so after enabling one of them, be sure to monitor free memory in the router for a brief time afterward.

This section starts by describing some older, but still used, technologies for Layer 3 switching, called the *classic methods for switching*, and continues with two newer technologies: NetFlow switching and Cisco Express Forwarding (CEF).

Classic Methods for Layer 3 Packet Switching

Process switching is the slowest of the switching methods. With process switching, when an interface processor receives an incoming packet, it transfers the packet to input/output memory on the router. The interface processor also generates a receive interrupt of the central processor. The central processor determines the type of packet and places it in the appropriate input queue. For example, if it is an IP packet, the central processor places the packet in the *ip_input* queue. The next time the Cisco IOS scheduler runs, it notes the packet in the input queue, and schedules the appropriate process to run. For example, for an IP packet, it schedules the ip_input process to run.

The input process, after the scheduler tells it to run, looks in the routing table to determine the exit interface that should be used for the Layer 3 destination address in the packet. The process rewrites the packet with the correct data link layer header for that interface and copies the packet to the interface. It also places an entry in the fast-switching cache so that subsequent packets for the destination can use fast switching.

Note that the forwarding decision is made by a process scheduled by the Cisco IOS scheduler. This process runs as a peer to other processes running on the router, such as routing protocols. Processes that normally run on the router are not interrupted to process-switch a packet. This makes process switching slow.

Fast switching allows higher throughput by switching a packet using an entry in the fast-switching cache that was created when a previous packet to the same destination was processed. With fast switching, a packet is handled immediately. The interface processor generates a receive interrupt. During this interrupt, the central processor determines the type of packet and then begins to switch the packet. The process currently running on the processor is interrupted to switch the packet. Packets are switched on demand, rather than switched only when the forwarding process can be scheduled. Based on information in the fast-switching cache, the data link layer header is rewritten and the packet is sent to the outgoing interface that services the destination.

Note If you are using load sharing across multiple interfaces with fast switching enabled, the load might not be balanced equally if a large portion of the traffic goes to only one destination. Packets for a given destination always exit the same interface even if routing supports multiple interfaces. In other words, fast switching uses per-destination load sharing. If this is a problem, you should use CEF, which supports both per-destination and per-packet load sharing. In addition, with CEF, per-destination load sharing is based on source/destination pairs rather than simply the destination address, which may provide a better balance than fast switching does.

NetFlow Switching

NetFlow switching is optimized for environments where services must be applied to packets to implement security, QoS features, and traffic accounting. An example of such an environment is the boundary between an enterprise network and the Internet.

NetFlow switching identifies traffic flows between hosts and then quickly switches packets in these flows at the same time that it applies services. NetFlow switching also lets a network manager collect data on network usage to enable capacity planning and bill users based on network and application resource utilization. The statistics can be collected without slowing down the switching process.

To maximize network scalability, a good design practice is to use NetFlow switching on the periphery of a network to enable features such as traffic accounting, QoS functionality, and security, and to use an even faster switching mode in the core of the network. At the core of the network, the switching mode should forward packets based on easily accessible information in the packet, and generally should not spend time applying services. The next switching mode covered in this section, *Cisco Express Forwarding (CEF)*, is optimized for the core of a network to provide high performance, predictability, scalability, and resilience.

Cisco Express Forwarding

CEF is a Cisco-patented technique for switching packets quickly across large backbone networks and the Internet. Rather than relying on the caching techniques used by classic switching methods, CEF depends on a *forwarding information base (FIB)*. The FIB allows CEF to be much less processor-intensive than other Layer 3 switching methods because the FIB tables contain forwarding information for all routes in the routing tables (whereas a cache contains only a subset of routing information).

CEF evolved to accommodate web-based applications and other interactive applications that are characterized by sessions of short duration to multiple destination addresses. CEF became necessary when it became clear that a cache-based system is not optimized for these types of applications.

Consider a web-surfing application, for example. When a user jumps to a new website, TCP opens a session with a new destination address. It is unlikely that the new destination is in the router's cache, unless it happens to be a destination the user, or other users, visited recently. This means that the first packet is process switched, which is slow. Also, the router's CPU is significantly impacted if there are many first packets to new destinations. CEF improves switching speed, and avoids the overhead associated with a cache that continually changes, through the use of the FIB, which mirrors the entire contents of the IP routing table.

As mentioned in the "Classic Methods for Layer 3 Packet Switching" section, CEF supports both per-destination and per-packet load sharing. Per-destination load sharing is the default, which means that packets for a given source/destination pair are guaranteed to exit the same interface. Traffic for different pairs tend to take different paths. Unless traffic consists of flows for a small number of source/destination pairs, traffic tends to be equally distributed across multiple paths with CEF per-destination load sharing.

CEF also supports per-packet load sharing. Per-packet load sharing allows a router to send successive data packets over paths without regard to source and destination addresses. Per-packet load sharing uses a round-robin method to select the exit interface for a packet. Each packet takes the next interface that routing allows. Per-packet load sharing provides a better balance of traffic over multiple links. You can use per-packet load sharing to help ensure that a path for a single source/destination pair does not become overloaded.

Although path utilization with per-packet load sharing is optimized, packets for a given source/destination host pair might take different paths, which could cause packets to arrive out of order. For this reason, per-packet load sharing is inappropriate for certain types of data traffic, such as VoIP, that depend on packets arriving at the destination in sequence.

Queuing Services

The high-speed switching techniques discussed in the previous sections only go so far in optimizing a network that is experiencing congestion. Intelligent and fast queuing methods are also necessary. Queuing allows a network device to handle an overflow of traffic. Cisco IOS Software supports the following queuing methods:

- First-in, first-out (FIFO) queuing

- Priority queuing

- Custom queuing

- Weighted fair queuing (WFQ)

- Class-based WFQ (CBWFQ)

- Low-latency queuing (LLQ)

First-In, First-Out Queuing

FIFO queuing provides basic store-and-forward functionality. It involves storing packets when the network is congested and forwarding them in the order they arrived when the network is no longer congested. FIFO has the advantage that it is the default queuing algorithm in some instances, so requires no configuration. FIFO has the disadvantage that it makes no decision about packet priority. The order of arrival determines the order a packet is processed and output.

Note   With FIFO queuing, if there are many packets awaiting transmission, a new packet that arrives for transmission experiences delay. You may have experienced this at the grocery store. Have you ever wondered whether you should use the FIFO express checkout line even when it's longer than the FIFO nonexpress checkout lines?

FIFO provides no QoS functionality and no protection against an application using network resources in a way that negatively affects the performance of other applications. Bursty sources can cause high delays in delivering time-sensitive application traffic, and potentially defer network control and signaling messages. Long packets can cause unfair delays for applications that use short packets. For these reasons, Cisco has developed advanced queuing algorithms that provide more features than basic FIFO queuing, including priority queuing, custom queuing, and WFQ. These algorithms are described in the next few sections.

Priority Queuing

Priority queuing ensures that important traffic is processed first. It was designed to give strict priority to a critical application and is particularly useful for time-sensitive protocols such as Systems Network Architecture (SNA). Packets can be prioritized based on many factors, including protocol, incoming interface, packet size, and source or destination address.

Priority queuing is especially appropriate in cases where WAN links are congested from time to time. If the WAN links are constantly congested, the customer should investigate protocol and application inefficiencies, consider using compression, or possibly upgrade to more bandwidth. If the WAN links are never congested, priority queuing is unnecessary. Because priority queuing requires extra processing and can cause performance problems for low-priority traffic, it should not be recommended unless necessary.

Priority queuing has four queues: high, medium, normal, and low. The high-priority queue is always emptied before the lower-priority queues are serviced, as shown in Figure 13-3. Priority queuing is analogous to a first-class line at an airport where all the clerks serve that line first until the line empties.

Custom Queuing

Custom queuing was designed to allow a network to be shared among applications with different minimum bandwidth or latency requirements. Custom queuing assigns different amounts of queue space to different protocols and handles the queues in round-robin fashion. A particular protocol can be prioritized by assigning it more queue space. Custom queuing is more "fair" than priority queuing, although priority queuing is more powerful for prioritizing a single critical application.

You can use custom queuing to provide guaranteed bandwidth at a potential congestion point. Custom queuing helps you ensure that each traffic type receives a fixed portion of available bandwidth and that, when the link is under stress, no application achieves more than a predetermined proportion of capacity. Custom queuing is analogous to a first-class line at an airport where the clerks serve that line first up to a point. After a set number of first-class passengers have been served, the clerks move on to the other people.

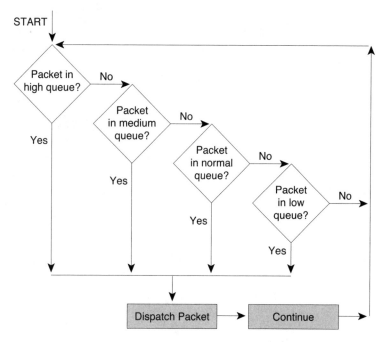

Figure 13-3 *Behavior of Priority Queuing*

Custom queuing places a message in 1 of 17 queues. The router services queues 1 through 16 in round-robin order. (Queue 0 holds system messages, such as keepalive and signaling messages, and is emptied first.) A network administrator configures the transmission window size of each queue in bytes. After the appropriate number of packets has been transmitted from a queue such that the transmission window size has been reached, the next queue is checked, as shown in Figure 13-4.

Weighted Fair Queuing

WFQ is a sophisticated set of algorithms designed to reduce delay variability and provide predictable throughput and response time for traffic flows. A goal of WFQ is to offer uniform service to light and heavy network users alike. WFQ ensures that the response time for low-volume applications is consistent with the response time for high-volume applications. Applications that send small packets are not unfairly starved of bandwidth by applications that send large packets. Bandwidth is divided up equitably in an automated way.

WFQ is a flow-based queuing algorithm that recognizes a flow for an interactive application and schedules that application's traffic to the front of the queue to reduce response time. Low-volume traffic streams for interactive applications, which includes a large percentage of the applications on most networks, are allowed to transmit their entire offered loads in a timely fashion. High-volume traffic streams share the remaining capacity.

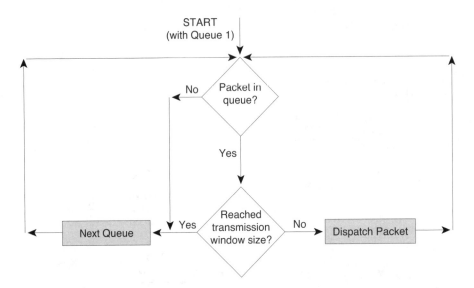

Figure 13-4   *Behavior of Custom Queuing*

Unlike custom and priority queuing, WFQ adapts automatically to changing network traffic conditions and requires little to no configuration. It is the default queuing mode on most serial interfaces configured to run at or below E1 speeds (2.048 Mbps).

For applications that use the IP Precedence subfield in the IP header, WFQ can allot bandwidth based on precedence. The algorithm allocates more bandwidth to conversations with higher precedence, and makes sure those conversations get served more quickly when congestion occurs. WFQ assigns a weight to each flow, which determines the transmit order for queued packets. IP precedence helps determine the weighting factor.

WFQ also works with RSVP, which uses WFQ to allocate buffer space, schedule packets, and guarantee bandwidth based on resource reservations. Additionally, WFQ understands the discard eligibility (DE) bit and the forward explicit congestion notification (FECN) and backward explicit congestion notification (BECN) mechanisms in a Frame Relay network. After congestion has been identified, the weights used by WFQ are altered so that a conversation encountering congestion transmits less frequently.

Class-Based Weighted Fair Queuing

CBWFQ combines the best elements of priority, custom, and weighted-fair queuing. CBWFQ results in a more complex configuration than the other queuing methods, but the complexity adds flexibility not found in the other methods. CBWFQ lets you define traffic classes based on match criteria such as protocols, access control lists, and input interfaces. Packets satisfying the criteria for a class constitute the traffic for that class. A

FIFO queue is reserved for each class, and traffic belonging to a class is directed to the queue for that class.

After a class has been defined, you can assign characteristics to it such as bandwidth and the maximum number of packets that can be queued for the class, called the *queue limit*. The bandwidth assigned to a class is the guaranteed bandwidth delivered to the class during congestion. The queue limit for the class is the maximum number of packets allowed to accumulate in the queue for the class. To optimize how packets are dropped if they exceed the queue limit, you can enable weighted random early detection (WRED), which is covered later in this chapter.

Flow classification for CBWFQ is based on WFQ. That is, packets with the same source IP address, destination IP address, source TCP or UDP port, and destination TCP or UDP port are classified as belonging to the same flow. WFQ allocates an equal share of bandwidth to each flow. Flow-based WFQ is also called fair queuing because all flows are equally weighted.

When CBWFQ is enabled, packets that arrive at an output interface are classified according to the match criteria you defined. The weight for a packet belonging to a specific class is derived from the bandwidth you assigned to the class when you configured it. In this sense, the weight for a class is user configurable. After the weight for a packet is assigned, the packet is placed in the appropriate queue. CBWFQ uses the weights assigned to the queued packets to ensure that the class queue is serviced fairly.

Low-Latency Queuing

LLQ combines priority queuing with CBWFQ and was originally called PQ-CBWFQ, but even Cisco recognized that acronyms can only be so long before they lose their mnemonic value. LLQ brings strict priority queuing to CBWFQ. Strict priority queuing allows delay-sensitive data such as voice to be sent before packets in other queues are sent.

Without LLQ, CBWFQ provides WFQ based on defined classes with no strict priority queue available for real-time traffic. As mentioned in the preceding section, CBWFQ allows you to define traffic classes and then assign characteristics to each class. For example, you can specify the minimum bandwidth delivered to a class during congestion. When you are using CBWFQ, the weight for a packet belonging to a specific class is derived from the bandwidth you assigned to the class when you configured it. Therefore, the bandwidth assigned to the packets of a class determines the order in which packets are sent. All packets are serviced fairly based on weight, and no class of packets is granted strict priority. This scheme poses problems for voice traffic that is intolerant of delay and variation in delay (jitter).

LLQ enables use of a single, strict-priority queue within CBWFQ at the class level, allowing you to direct traffic belonging to a class to the CBWFQ strict-priority queue. Although it is possible to place various types of real-time traffic in the strict-priority queue, Cisco strongly recommends that you direct only voice traffic to the queue. Voice traffic requires that delay be nonvariable. Real-time traffic such as video could introduce variation in delay, thereby thwarting the steadiness of delay required for successful voice transmission. LLQ is an essential tool for network designers who plan to transmit voice traffic on low-bandwidth links that also carry other types of traffic.

Random Early Detection

The queuing mechanisms discussed in the previous sections are essentially congestion-management techniques. Although such techniques are necessary for controlling congestion, they fall short of avoiding congestion before it occurs. A new class of congestion-avoidance algorithms is gaining popularity.

One such algorithm is *random early detection (RED)*, which works by monitoring traffic loads at points in a network and randomly discarding packets if congestion begins to increase. The result is that source nodes detect the dropped traffic and slow their transmission rate. RED is primarily designed to work with applications based on the Transmission Control Protocol (TCP).

Upon packet loss, a TCP session decreases its transmit window size, effectively slowing its transmission rate. It then gradually increases the window size until congestion occurs again. The term *porpoising* is sometimes used to refer to the closing and reopening of windows. (Picture a porpoise jumping in and out of water.)

Experience shows that if routers do not apply some sort of randomization to the dropping of packets, multiple TCP sessions tend to slow their transmission rate simultaneously. (The sessions take a synchronized porpoise dive, which in more technical terms is often called *global synchronization*.) Multiple applications lower and increase their transmission rate simultaneously, which means that bandwidth is not used effectively. When multiple applications slow down, bandwidth is wasted. When they increase their rate, they tend to increase bandwidth utilization to the point where congestion occurs again.

The advantage of RED is that it randomizes the dropping of packets, thus reducing the potential for multiple sessions synchronizing their behavior. RED is a good solution for a central-site router in a hub-and-spoke topology. RED distributes the dropping of packets across many of the spoke networks and avoids causing congestion problems for multiple application sessions from one site.

Weighted Random Early Detection

Weighted Random Early Detection (WRED) is the Cisco implementation of RED. WRED combines the capabilities of the standard RED algorithm with IP precedence. This combination provides for preferential traffic handling for higher-priority packets. It selectively discards lower-priority traffic when an interface starts to get congested, rather than using simply a random method. WRED can also adjust its behavior based on RSVP reservations. If an application registers for the Integrated Services working group controlled-load QoS service, WRED is made aware of this and adjusts its packet discarding accordingly.

Flow-based WRED classifies incoming traffic into flows based on parameters such as destination and source addresses and ports. Flow-based WRED uses this classification and state information to ensure that each flow does not consume more than its permitted share of the output buffer resources. Flow-based WRED determines which flows monopolize resources and more heavily penalizes these flows.

Traffic Shaping

Another tool that is available to network designers using Cisco equipment is *traffic shaping, which* enables you to manage and control network traffic to avoid bottlenecks and meet QoS requirements. It avoids congestion by reducing outbound traffic for a flow to a configured bit rate, while queuing bursts of traffic for that flow. In topologies with routers and links of varying capabilities, traffic can be shaped to avoid overwhelming a downstream router or link.

Traffic shaping is configured on a per-interface basis. The router administrator uses access control lists to select the traffic to shape. Traffic shaping works with a variety of Layer 2 technologies, including Frame Relay, ATM, Switched Multimegabit Data Service (SMDS), and Ethernet.

On a Frame Relay interface, you can configure traffic shaping to adapt dynamically to available bandwidth using the BECN mechanism. In addition, Cisco has a specific feature for Frame Relay networks called *Frame Relay traffic shaping* that supports optimization techniques specific to Frame Relay.

Committed Access Rate

Cisco also supports a feature called *committed access rate (CAR)* that enables you to classify and police traffic on an incoming interface. CAR supports specifying policies regarding how traffic that exceeds a certain bandwidth allocation should be handled. CAR looks at traffic received on an interface (or a subset of that traffic selected by an access control list), compares its rate to a configured maximum, and then takes action based on the result. For example, it can drop a packet or change the IP precedence bits in the packet to indicate that the packet should be handled with lower priority.

Summary

To meet a customer's goals for network performance, scalability, availability, and manageability, you can recommend a variety of optimization techniques. Optimization provides the high bandwidth, low delay, and controlled jitter required by many critical business applications.

To minimize bandwidth utilization for multimedia applications that send large streams of data to many users, you can recommend IP multicast technologies. These technologies include multicast addressing, Internet Group Management Protocol (IGMP) for allowing clients to join multicast groups, and multicast routing protocols such as DVMRP and PIM.

Multimedia and other applications that are sensitive to network congestion and delay can inform routers in the network of their QoS requirements using both in-band and out-of-band methods. An in-band method involves setting bits within packets to specify how the packet should be handled. For example, IPv4 includes the Differentiated Services field, and IPv6 includes the traffic class field. IEEE 802.1p also has a way of specifying priority within data link layer frames.

Resource Reservation Protocol (RSVP) is an out-of-band method for specifying QoS. It can be used with the Common Open Policy Service (COPS) protocol, which standardizes the client/server communication between policy-enforcement points (PEP), such as routers, and policy servers, also known as policy-decision points (PDP).

After a network has been upgraded to include QoS features, applications that use RTP can be deployed. Real-Time Transport Protocol (RTP) provides a transport layer service suitable for transmitting real-time audio and video data over multicast or unicast network services. To avoid extra serialization delay caused by the addition of an RTP header to multimedia packets, compressed RTP should be used, especially with voice packets.

Cisco supplies a number of features for optimizing a network, including NetFlow switching, Cisco Express Forwarding (CEF), advanced queuing services, random early detection (RED), and traffic shaping.

Review Questions

1. How does multicast routing differ from unicast routing?

2. This chapter mentions serialization delay (also sometimes called *transmission delay*). What other types of delay are there? List and describe three other types of delay.

3. What are some techniques for reducing serialization delay?

4. As mentioned in the "Link-Layer Fragmentation and Interleaving" section, PPP, Frame Relay, ATM, and other WAN technologies support fragmenting packets (frames) at Layer 2. As you may have learned in basic networking classes, IP can also fragment packets at Layer 3. What are some advantages and disadvantages of fragmenting at Layer 3 versus fragmenting at Layer 2?

5. Research the problem known as "TCP global synchronization." How can RED reduce the likelihood of TCP global synchronization?

Design Scenario

In Chapter 11, "Selecting Technologies and Devices for Enterprise Networks," you learned about the network design project for Klamath Paper Products. Klamath plans to roll out an ongoing distance-learning program that will train employees and other companies on ways to conserve raw materials, use recycled materials, and work more efficiently. Executive management considers the new training program vital to the continued success of Klamath and approved funding to equip the training rooms at most sites with digital videoconferencing systems.

1. Based on Klamath's requirements, select some network optimization technologies that will help maintain video quality for the distance-learning program. Based on Figure 11-6, "New Core WAN at Klamath," draw a network topology map for Klamath and indicate where your optimization techniques will be deployed. Include with the network drawing a written explanation of the optimization techniques.

2. As discussed in Chapter 11, in the future, Klamath plans to dismantle its legacy voice network. The legacy voice traffic that is currently carried on dedicated 64-kbps circuits will be updated to use VoIP technology. All voice, video, and data traffic will traverse Klamath's new Metro Ethernet network. What additional optimization techniques will you add to your network design to support the VoIP traffic? Update your network topology drawing and written explanation to indicate optimization techniques for the VoIP traffic.

Chapter 14

Documenting Your Network Design

This chapter starts by providing advice on responding to a customer's request for proposal (RFP), and concludes with information on writing a network design document when no RFP exists. The section "Contents of a Network Design Document" provides an outline of a typical design document and specifies the topics that should be included in each part of the document. The section serves as a summary for *Top-Down Network Design* because it references each of the major steps of the top-down design methodology presented in this book.

At this point in the design process, you should have a comprehensive design that is based on an analysis of your customer's business and technical goals, and includes both logical and physical components that have been tested and optimized. The next step in the process is to write a design document.

A *design document* describes your customer's requirements and explains how your design meets those requirements. It also documents the existing network, the logical and physical design, and the budget and expenses associated with the project.

It is also important that a design document contain plans for implementing the network, measuring the success of the implementation, and evolving the network design as new application requirements arise. The network designer's job is never complete. The process of analyzing requirements and developing design solutions begins again as soon as a design is implemented. Figure 14-1 shows the cyclical nature of the top-down network design process.

As mentioned in earlier chapters, in addition to being cyclical, network design is also iterative. Some steps take place during multiple phases of a design. Testing occurs during the design-validation phase and also during implementation. Optimization occurs while finalizing the design and also after implementation during the network-monitoring phase. Documentation is an ongoing effort. Documentation that is completed before the implementation stage can facilitate the approval process for a design and help expedite the rollout of new technologies and applications.

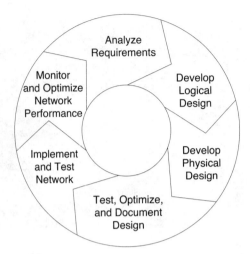

Figure 14-1   *Network Design and Implementation Cycle*

Responding to a Customer's Request for Proposal

A *Request for Proposal (RFP)* lists a customer's design requirements and the types of solutions a network design must include. Organizations send RFPs to vendors and design consultants and use the responses they receive to weed out suppliers that cannot meet requirements. RFP responses help organizations compare competing designs, product capabilities, pricing, and service and support alternatives.

Every RFP is different, but typically an RFP includes some or all of the following topics:

- Business goals for the project
- Scope of the project
- Information on the existing network and applications
- Information on new applications
- Technical requirements, including scalability, availability, network performance, security, manageability, usability, adaptability, and affordability
- Warranty requirements for products
- Environmental or architectural constraints that could affect implementation
- Training and support requirements
- Preliminary schedule with milestones and deliverables
- Legal contractual terms and conditions

Some organizations specify the required format for the RFP response. If this is the case, your initial design document should follow the customer's prescribed format and structure precisely. Organizations that specify a format might refuse to read responses that do not follow the requested format. In some cases, the customer might request a follow-up document in which you can provide more detailed information on your logical and physical network design.

Some RFPs are in the form of a questionnaire. In this case, the questions should drive the proposal's organization. Embellishments that focus on key requirements and the selling points of your design can sometimes be added, unless the RFP specifically states that they should not be added.

Although every organization handles RFPs slightly differently, typically an RFP states that the response must include some or all of the following topics:

■ A network topology for the new design

■ Information on the protocols, technologies, and products that form the design

■ An implementation plan

■ A training plan

■ Support and service information

■ Prices and payment options

■ Qualifications of the responding vendor or supplier

■ Recommendations from other customers for whom the supplier has provided a solution

■ Legal contractual terms and conditions

Despite the fact that a response to an RFP must stay within the guidelines specified by the customer, you should nonetheless use ingenuity to ensure that your response highlights the benefits of your design. Based on an analysis of your customer's business and technical goals, and the flow and characteristics of network traffic (as covered in Part I, "Identifying Your Customer's Needs and Goals"), write your response so that the reader can easily recognize that the design satisfies critical selection criteria.

When writing the response, be sure to consider the competition. Try to predict what other vendors or design consultants might propose so that you can call attention to the aspects of your solution that are likely to be superior to competing designs. In addition, pay attention to your customer's business style. Chapter 1, "Analyzing Business Goals and Constraints," covered the importance of understanding your customer's biases and any office politics or project history that could affect the perception of your design.

Contents of a Network Design Document

When your design document does not have to follow a format dictated by an RFP, or when a customer requests a follow-up document to a basic RFP response, you should write a design document that fully describes your network design. The document should include the logical and physical components of the design, information on technologies and devices, and a proposal for implementing the design. The following sections describe the topics that should be included in a comprehensive design document.

Executive Summary

A comprehensive design document can be many pages in length. For this reason, it is essential that you include at the beginning of the document an Executive Summary that succinctly states the major points of the document. The Executive Summary should be no more than one page and should be targeted at the managers and key project participants who will decide whether to accept your design.

Although the Executive Summary can include some technical information, it should not provide technical details. The goal of the summary is to sell the decision makers on the business benefits of your design. Technical information should be summarized and organized in order of the customer's highest-priority objectives for the design project.

Project Goal

This section should state the primary goal for the network design project. The goal should be business-oriented and related to an overall objective that the organization has to become more successful in its core business. The Project Goal section should be no more than one paragraph; it often can be written as a single sentence. Writing it carefully will give you a chance to make it obvious to the decision makers reading the document that you understand the primary purpose and importance of the network design project.

An example of a Project Goal section that was written for an actual design customer follows:

> The goal of this project is to develop a wide-area network (WAN) that will support new high-bandwidth and low-delay multimedia applications. The new applications are key to the successful implementation of new training programs for the sales force. The new WAN should facilitate the goal of increasing sales in the United States by 50 percent in the next fiscal year.

Project Scope

The Project Scope section provides information on the extent of the project, including a summary of the departments and networks that will be affected by the project. The Project Scope section specifies whether the project is for a new network or modifications to an existing network. It indicates whether the design is for a single network segment, a set of LANs, a building or campus network, a set of WAN or remote-access networks, or possibly the whole enterprise network.

An example of a Project Scope section follows:

> The scope of this project is to update the existing WAN that connects all major sales offices in the United States to corporate headquarters. The new WAN will be accessed by sales, marketing, and training employees. It is beyond the scope of this project to update any LANs that these employees use. It is also beyond the scope of this project to update the networks in satellite and telecommuter offices.

The scope of the project might intentionally not cover some matters. For example, fixing performance problems with a particular application might be intentionally beyond the scope of the project. By stating up front the assumptions you made about the scope of the project, you can avoid any perception that your solution inadvertently fails to address certain concerns.

Design Requirements

Whereas the Project Goal section is generally short, the Design Requirements section is your opportunity to list all the major business and technical requirements for the network design. The Design Requirements section should list the goals in priority order. Critical goals should be marked as such. To review some examples of design requirements, see the case studies in Chapter 10, "Selecting Technologies and Devices for Campus Networks," and Chapter 11, "Selecting Technologies and Devices for Enterprise Networks."

Business Goals

Business goals explain the role the network design will play in helping an organization provide better products and services to its customers. Executives who read the design document will be more likely to accept the network design if they recognize from the Business Goals section that the network designer understands the organization's business mission.

Many network designers have a hard time writing the Business Goals section because they are more interested in technical goals. However, it is critical that you focus your network design document on the ability of your design to help a customer solve real-world business problems.

As discussed in Chapter 1, most businesses embark on a network design project to help them increase revenue, reduce operational costs and inefficiencies, and improve corporate communications. Other typical goals include building partnerships with other companies and expanding into worldwide markets. At this point in the network design process, you should have a comprehensive understanding of your customer's business goals and be able to list them in the design document in priority order.

Technical Goals

The Technical Goals section documents the following goals discussed in Chapter 2, "Analyzing Technical Goals and Tradeoffs":

- **Scalability:** How much growth a network design must support.

- **Availability:** The amount of time a network is available to users, often expressed as a percent uptime, or as a mean time between failure (MTBF) and mean time to repair (MTTR). Availability documentation can also include any information gathered on the monetary cost associated with network downtime.

- **Network performance:** The customer's criteria for accepting the service level of a network, including its throughput, accuracy, efficiency, delay, delay variation (jitter), and response time. Specific throughput requirements for internetworking devices, in packets per second (pps), can also be stated. Specific throughput requirements for applications should be included in the Network Applications section.

- **Security:** General and specific goals for protecting the organization's capability to conduct business without interference from intruders inappropriately accessing or damaging equipment, data, or operations. This section should also list the various security risks that the customer identified during the requirements-analysis phase of the design project.

- **Manageability:** General and specific goals for performance, fault, configuration, security, and accounting management.

- **Usability:** The ease with which network users can access the network and its services. This section can include information on goals for simplifying user tasks related to network addressing, naming, and resource discovery.

- **Adaptability:** The ease with which a network design and implementation can adapt to network faults, changing traffic patterns, additional business or technical requirements, new business practices, and other changes.

- **Affordability:** General information on the importance of containing the costs associated with purchasing and operating network equipment and services. Specific budget information should be included in the Project Budget section.

The Technical Goals section should also describe any tradeoffs the customer is willing to make. For example, some customers might indicate that affordability can be sacrificed to meet strict availability goals, or usability can be sacrificed to meet strict security goals. As discussed in Chapter 2, including a chart that categorizes the comparative weights of goals can help the readers of a network design document understand some of the design choices that were made.

User Communities and Data Stores

This section lists major user communities, including their sizes, locations, and the principal applications they use. You can use Table 4-1, "User Communities," to summarize information about user communities. This section should also list major data stores (servers and hosts) and their locations. Use Table 4-2, "Data Stores," to summarize information about data stores.

Network Applications

The Network Applications section lists and characterizes the new and existing network applications. Information about applications can be summarized in the "Network Applications Technical Requirements" chart shown in Table 2-2, and in the "Network Applications Traffic Characteristics" chart shown in Table 4-4. If you want, you can merge these two tables so that there is just one row for each application.

The case studies in Chapters 10 and 11 provide good examples of the information regarding network applications, user communities, and data stores that should be included in a design document.

Current State of the Network

This section briefly describes the structure and performance of the existing network. It should include a high-level network map that identifies the location of major internetworking devices, data processing and storage systems, and network segments. The high-level map should document the names and addresses of major devices and segments and indicate the types and lengths of principal network segments. For large internetworks, two or three high-level maps might be necessary. Detailed maps, however, should be placed in the Appendix rather than in this section.

The network maps should include logical and physical components (for example, the location and reach of any virtual private networks [VPN], virtual LANs [VLAN], firewall segments, server clusters, and so on). The maps should also characterize the logical topology of the internetwork and the networks that make up the internetwork. Network drawings, or text associated with drawings, should indicate whether networks are hierarchical or flat, structured or unstructured, layered or not, and so on. They should also indicate network geometry (for example, star, ring, bus, hub and spoke, or mesh). The documentation of the current state of the network also briefly describes any strategies or standards your customer uses for network addressing and device naming. If the customer uses address-summarization techniques, for example, this should be indicated in the design document.

A portion of the Current State of the Network section of the network design document should be dedicated to an analysis of the health and performance of the present network. See Chapter 3, "Characterizing the Existing Internetwork," for more information on the documentation you should gather about the existing network.

Detailed health and performance reports can be placed in the Appendix of the design document to avoid overwhelming the reader with too much information at this stage. It is important that the reader be able to quickly reach the Logical Design and Physical Design sections of the document, because those sections contain the essence of your design proposal.

Logical Design

The Logical Design section documents the following aspects of your network design:

- The network topology, including one or more drawings that illustrate the logical architecture of the new network.

- A model for addressing network segments and devices.

- A model for naming network devices.

- A list of the switching and routing protocols that have been selected to implement the design, and any specific implementation recommendations associated with those protocols.

- Recommended security mechanisms and products, including a summary of security policies and procedures. (If a detailed security plan was developed as part of the network design, it can be submitted as an addendum to the design document.)

- Recommended network management architectures, processes, and products.

- Design rationale, outlining why various choices were made, in light of the customer's goals and the current state of the network.

Note   Not all designs include all these components. Based on your customer's requirements, you should recognize whether it is necessary to address all the issues included in the preceding list in your network design document.

Physical Design

The Physical Design section describes the features and recommended uses for the technologies and devices you selected to implement the design. It can include information for campus networks (as discussed in Chapter 10) and remote-access and WANs (as discussed in Chapter 11). This section can also include information about any service providers selected.

If appropriate, the Physical Design section should include information on the pricing for network devices and services. Sometimes pricing is negotiable and is not appropriate to include in the design document. Pricing can also be a distraction, taking away focus from the quality of the design solution. In many cases, however, customers expect to see product and service pricing in the design document.

The Physical Design section should also contain information on the availability of products. If your design recommends products that are not yet shipping, you should document a predicted ship date, as provided by the product vendor. If you have information about the lifecycle of a product (for example, when the vendor will obsolete it), include that also.

Results of Network Design Testing

This section describes the results of the testing that you did to verify your network design. It is one of the most important portions of the design document because it gives you a chance to prove to your customer that your design will likely meet requirements for performance, security, usability, manageability, and so on. You can describe any prototype or pilot systems that you implemented and the following testing components:

- Test objectives

- Test acceptance criteria

- Testing tools

- Test scripts

- Results and observations

In the Results and Observations segment, be sure to include any optimization techniques you recommend be applied to the design to ensure that it meets requirements. Based on the results of your testing, you might recommend mechanisms for minimizing broadcast and multicast traffic, advanced features for meeting quality of service (QoS) requirements, and sophisticated router switching and queuing services. See Chapter 13, "Optimizing Your Network Design," for more information on optimization techniques.

Implementation Plan

The Implementation Plan includes your recommendations for deploying the network design. The level of detail in this section varies from project to project, and depends on your relationship to your customer.

If you are a member of an Information Systems (IS) department that is responsible for the design and implementation of the new network, this section should be quite detailed. If you are a sales engineer for a vendor of networking products, on the other hand, your role is probably to recommend solutions but not implement them, so this section should be short. (You should avoid appearing as if you are telling your customers how to do their jobs.)

The following topics are suitable for the Implementation Plan section:

- A project schedule.

- Plans with vendors or service providers for the installation of links, equipment, or services.

- Plans or recommendations for outsourcing the implementation or management of the network.

- A plan for communicating the design to end users, network administrators, and management. This section can also explain how implementation progress will be communicated (possibly via regularly scheduled status meetings or email messages).

- A training plan for network administrators and end users.

- A plan for measuring the effectiveness of the design after it has been implemented.

- A list of known risks that could delay the project.

- A fallback plan if the network implementation fails.

- A plan for evolving the network design as new application requirements and goals arise.

Project Schedule

The Implementation Plan should include a project schedule or timeline. The level of detail you include in a schedule depends on your role on the project. In general, the schedule should at least include the dates and deliverables for major milestones. Table 14-1 shows an example of a high-level schedule that was developed by a sales engineer for an actual customer.

Table 14-1   *High-Level Schedule Developed for a Network Design Customer*

Date of Completion	Milestone
June 1	Design completed and a beta version of the design document distributed to key executives, managers, network administrators, and end users
June 15	Comments on the design document due
June 22	Final design document distributed
June 25	Installation of leased lines between all buildings completed by WAN service provider
June 28–29	Network administrators trained on new system
June 30–July 1	End users trained on new system
July 6	Pilot implementation completed in Building 1
July 20	Feedback received on pilot from network administrators and end users
July 27	Implementation completed in Buildings 2–5
August 10	Feedback received on Buildings 2–5 implementation from network administrators and end users
August 17	Implementation completed in the rest of the buildings
Ongoing	New system monitored to verify that it meets goals

Project Budget

The Project Budget section should document the funds the customer has available for equipment purchases, maintenance and support agreements, service contracts, software licenses, training, and staffing. The budget can also include consulting fees and outsourcing expenses.

Return on Investment

In many cases the best way to sell a customer on a new network design is to convince the customer that the design will pay for itself in a reasonable time period. The network design document can include a *return-on-investment (ROI)* analysis that explains how quickly the design or new equipment will pay for itself.

Following is an example of an ROI that was completed for an actual customer, Customer ABC. The goal of this ROI analysis was to prove to the customer that the recommended WAN switching equipment will pay for itself quickly because it will enable the customer to decrease the number of required T1 lines, and thus reduce the cost of leasing those lines from the local phone company.

ROI Analysis for Customer ABC   Customer ABC is considering spending $1 million on new WAN switching equipment.

If Customer ABC does not spend the $1 million on equipment and instead puts the money into other investments for 5 years, Company ABC can earn approximately 5 percent interest, and the original $1 million would be worth $1.05 million. This means that the investment in the equipment should actually be considered $1.05 million.

An assumption was made that the WAN switching equipment will have a 5-year life span before it is obsolete. So, the cost per year for owning the equipment was calculated as $1.05 million divided by 5, or $210,000. The cost per month for owning the equipment is $210,000 divided by 12, or $17,500.

The monthly cost must be compared to the cost of owning the existing time-division multiplexers (TDMs) that comprise the current design. That cost is 0 because the TDMs are old and fully paid for and depreciated.

However, the cost of operating the old network must be compared to the cost of operating the new network. The new design will make it possible for Customer ABC to use 8 T1 lines instead of the 20 T1 lines required in the old design. Each line costs Customer ABC $1500 per month. This means that 20 lines cost $30,000 per month, and 8 lines cost $12,000 per month.

The savings to Customer ABC with the new network design is $30,000 − $12,000, or $18,000 per month. Considering that the cost for the new equipment is approximately $17,500 per month, a conclusion can be drawn that the equipment will pay for itself.

Design Document Appendix

Most design documents include one or more appendixes that present supplemental information about the design and implementation. Supplemental information can include detailed topology maps, device configurations, network addressing and naming details, and comprehensive results from the testing of the network design.

You can also include business information such as a list of contacts at the customer's site and in your organization, including email addresses, phone numbers, beeper numbers, and physical addresses. Information on where to ship equipment and any special shipping requirements or procedures is a useful addition in some cases.

If necessary, the Appendix can include exact information on pricing and payment options. Sometimes copies of purchase orders are included. The Appendix can also contain legal and contractual terms and conditions, and nondisclosure agreements.

Some design documents include information about the company presenting the design proposal, including pages from annual reports, product catalogs, or recent press releases favorable to the company. The goal of this type of information is to make sure the reader understands that the company is qualified to develop and implement the proposed network design. If appropriate, this section can include recommendations from other customers for whom the company has provided a solution.

Summary

When a customer provides an RFP, your network design proposal should follow the format prescribed in the RFP. When not bound by an RFP, or when a customer expects comprehensive design documentation, you should develop a document that describes requirements, the existing network, the logical and physical design, and the budget and expenses associated with implementing the design.

The design document should include an executive summary and a primary project goal. It should also document the network topology, any addressing and naming schemes you designed, security recommendations, and information about protocols, technologies, and products. Results of your network design testing can be included to convince your customer of the validity of your design.

It is also important that a design document contain a plan for implementing the network and measuring the success of the implementation. The plan should recommend network management and monitoring processes that can confirm that the implementation meets requirements for performance, availability, security, manageability, usability, and affordability.

The plan should also mention a process for evolving the network design as new application requirements arise. Enterprise networks continue to change at a rapid rate as organizations increasingly rely on their networks to help them achieve critical business goals. A network design must keep pace with new applications that let organizations increase revenue, reduce operational costs, and communicate more effectively with customers, business partners, and employees. Organizations that have not yet implemented modern applications such as collaboration applications, IP telephony, unified communications and messaging, and videoconferencing will likely want to deploy these or other new applications in the near future.

Vendors and standards bodies rapidly introduce new products and protocols to keep up with changing requirements. By following a systematic design process, you can keep pace with the evolving networking industry. With a focus on your customer's business and technical goals, you can develop solutions that accommodate changing technologies and requirements.

Many inexperienced network designers make the mistake of immediately jumping to the design step of selecting vendors and products. *Top-Down Network Design* has presented the benefits of first analyzing requirements and traffic flows, and then developing a logical design, followed by a physical design that specifies products and technologies. Using this approach will strengthen your competency as a network designer and promote the success of your network design customers.

Review Questions

1. In what ways is network design an iterative process? Why does the need for network documentation arise in many phases of a network design project?

2. When responding to an RFP, why is it important to pay attention to the business style of the organization that is requesting the proposal?

3. How does the Project Goal section of a network design document differ from the Design Requirements section? Why is it important to have both sections?

4. What items often appear in the Appendix of a network design document?

Design Scenario

In Chapters 11 and 13, you learned about the network design project for Klamath Paper Products. Develop a high-level project schedule for Klamath's design project. Include the dates of completion for major design, testing, and implementation tasks. You may not know the exact nature of all the tasks or how long they will take, but based on what you have learned in this book, try to include realistic tasks and completion dates.

Glossary

A

ABR   1. Area Border Router. Router located on the border of one or more OSPF areas that connects those areas to the backbone network. 2. available bit rate. QoS class for ATM networks. ABR provides a feedback mechanism that lets traffic sources adapt their transmissions to changing network conditions to facilitate low cell loss and the fair sharing of available bandwidth. ABR provides no guarantees in terms of cell loss or delay. Compare with *CBR*, *UBR*, and *VBR*.

access control list   See *ACL*.

access layer   One of three layers in a hierarchical network topology, provides users on local segments access to the internetwork. Compare with *core layer* and *distribution layer*. See also *hierarchical network design*.

access server   See *remote-access server*.

accuracy   The amount of useful traffic that is correctly transmitted on a network, relative to total traffic. Accuracy is negatively affected by the bit error rate (BER), cell error rate (CER), or the number of frame errors compared to the total number of bytes transmitted. See also *BER* and *CER*.

ACL   access control list. List kept by a router or firewall to control access to or from the router for several services (for example, to prevent packets with a certain IP address from leaving a particular interface on the router).

adaptability   The ease with which a network design and implementation can adapt to network faults, changing traffic patterns, additional business or technical requirements, and other changes.

Address Resolution Protocol   See *ARP*.

administrative distance   Rating of the trustworthiness of a route in a routing table. A route with a low administrative distance is preferred over routes with higher administrative distances.

ADSL   asymmetric digital subscriber line. One of many DSL technologies. ADSL is designed to deliver more bandwidth downstream (from the provider to the customer site) than upstream. See also *DSL* and *HDSL*.

affordability   A common network design goal that specifies the importance of containing the costs associated with developing and implementing a network design, including the purchasing and operating of network equipment and services.

AFP   Apple Filing Protocol. Application and presentation layer protocol that enables users to share data files and application programs that reside on a file server.

agent   In network management, a process that resides in a managed device and reports the values of specified variables to management stations.

Apple Filing Protocol   See *AFP*.

AppleTalk   Series of communications protocols designed by Apple Computer that featured ease of use, dynamic addressing, and simplified resource discovery.

application layer   Layer 7 of the OSI reference model. This layer provides services to application processes (such as electronic mail, file transfer, and terminal emulation) that are outside the OSI model. The application layer identifies and establishes the availability of intended communication partners (and the resources required to connect with them), synchronizes cooperating applications, and establishes agreement on procedures for error recovery and control of data integrity.

area   Logical set of network segments and their attached devices. Areas are usually connected to other areas via routers.

area border router   See *ABR*.

ARP   Address Resolution Protocol. Internet protocol used to map an IP address to a MAC address. Defined in RFC 826. Compare with *RARP*. See also *proxy ARP*.

asymmetric digital subscriber line   See *ADSL*.

asymmetric encryption   An encryption technique in which a different key is used to encrypt a message than is used to decrypt the message. Compare with *symmetric encryption*.

asynchronous routing   A function of a remote-access server that provides Layer 3 routing functionality to connect LANs via an asynchronous serial WAN link.

ATM   Asynchronous Transfer Mode. International standard for cell relay in which multiple service types (such as voice, video, or data) are conveyed in fixed-length (53-byte) cells.

authentication   In security, the verification of the identity of a person or process.

authorization   Securing a network by specifying which areas of the network (applications, devices, and so forth) a user is allowed to access.

autonomous system   Collection of networks or areas under a common administration sharing a common routing strategy.

availability   The amount of time a network is available to users, often expressed as a percent uptime, or as a mean time between failure (MTBF) and mean time to repair (MTTR). See also *MTBF* and *MTTR*.

available bit rate   See *ABR*.

B

backbone   A network that connects many other networks and acts as the primary path for traffic between those networks.

backup links   Physical redundant connections between network devices.

backward explicit congestion notification   See *BECN*.

bandwidth   See *capacity*.

bandwidth domain   In a LAN, the set of devices that share and compete for bandwidth. Bandwidth domains are bounded by switches, bridges, or routers. A hub or repeater does not bound a bandwidth domain. Also called a *collision domain* on Ethernet networks.

baseline   Characterization of the normal traffic flow and performance of a network, used as input to a new or enhanced design for the network.

beacon   Frame sent by a wireless access point during normal operation. Wireless clients listen to beacon frames to locate access points.

BECN   backward explicit congestion notification. Bit set by a Frame Relay network in frames traveling in the opposite direction of frames encountering a congested path. Compare with *FECN*.

BER   bit error rate. Ratio of received bits that contain errors to the total number of received bits.

BERT   bit error rate tester. Device that determines the BER on a given communications channel.

BGP   Border Gateway Protocol. Interdomain routing protocol that exchanges reachability information with other BGP systems. BGP Version 4 (BGP4) is the predominant interdomain routing protocol used on the Internet.

BIND   Berkeley Internet Name Domain. Implementation of DNS developed and distributed by the University of California at Berkeley (United States).

bit error rate   See *BER*.

bit error rate tester   See *BERT*.

BOOTP   Bootstrap Protocol. Protocol used by a network node to determine the IP address of its interfaces to achieve network booting. See also *DHCP*.

Border Gateway Protocol   See *BGP*.

BPDU   bridge protocol data unit. Spanning Tree Protocol frame that is sent out at configurable intervals to exchange information among bridges in a network.

bridge   Device that connects and passes frames between two network segments. Bridges operate at the data link layer (Layer 2) of the OSI reference model. A bridge filters, forwards, or floods an incoming frame based on the MAC destination address of the frame.

bridge protocol data unit   See *BPDU*.

broadcast   Message that is sent to all nodes on a network. Compare with *multicast* and *unicast*.

broadcast address   Special address reserved for sending a message to all nodes. At Layer 2, a broadcast address is a MAC destination address of all 1s (FF:FF:FF:FF:FF:FF in hexadecimal). At Layer 3, for IP, a broadcast address is 255.255.255.255. Compare with *multicast address* and *unicast address*.

broadcast domain   The set of all devices that receives broadcast frames originating from any device within the set. Broadcast domains are bounded by routers (which do not forward broadcast frames). A switch or hub does not bound a broadcast domain.

broadcast storm   Undesirable network event in which many broadcasts are sent in quick succession across numerous network segments. A broadcast storm uses substantial network bandwidth, causes extra processing at network nodes, and can cause network timeouts.

building network   Multiple LANs within a building, usually connected to a building-backbone network.

bursty traffic   Network traffic characterized by short intervals of intense activity with lulls between the intervals.

C

cable modem   A modem that operates over the coaxial cable that is used by cable TV providers. Because the coaxial cable provides greater bandwidth than telephone lines, a cable modem offers much faster access than an analog modem.

caching   Form of replication in which information learned during a previous transaction is used to process later transactions.

campus network   A set of LAN segments and building networks in a geographical area that is a few miles in diameter.

capacity   The data-carrying capability of a circuit or network, measured in bits per second (bps). Because this book focuses on digital transmission technologies, it uses the terms *capacity* and *bandwidth* synonymously.

Carrier Detect   See *CD*.

carrier sense multiple access with collision avoidance   See *CSMA/CA*.

carrier sense multiple access with collision detection   See *CSMA/CD*.

CBR   constant bit rate. QoS class for ATM networks. CBR is used for connections that depend on precise clocking to ensure undistorted delivery. Compare with *ABR*, *UBR*, and *VBR*.

CD   Carrier Detect. Signal that indicates whether an interface is active. Also, a signal generated by a modem indicating that a call has been connected.

CDP   Cisco Discovery Protocol. Device-discovery protocol that runs on Cisco-manufactured equipment, including routers, remote-access servers, and switches. Using CDP, a device can advertise its existence to other devices and receive information about other devices on the same LAN or on the remote side of a WAN.

CDV   cell delay variation. In ATM, component of cell transfer delay (CTD) that is induced by buffering and cell scheduling. CDV is a QoS delay parameter associated with CBR and VBR service.

cell   Basic data unit for ATM switching and multiplexing. Cells contain identifiers that specify the data stream to which they belong. Each cell consists of a 5-byte header and 48 bytes of payload.

cell delay variation   See *CDV*.

cell error ratio   See *CER*.

cell loss ratio   See *CLR*.

cell transfer delay   See *CTD*.

CER   cell error ratio. In ATM, the ratio of transmitted cells that have errors to the total cells sent in a transmission for a specific period of time.

Challenge Handshake Authentication Protocol   See *CHAP*.

channel aggregation   A process wherein a device can automatically bring up multiple circuits as bandwidth requirements increase.

channel service unit   See *CSU*.

CHAP   Challenge Handshake Authentication Protocol. Security feature supported on links using PPP encapsulation that identifies the remote end of a PPP session using a handshake protocol and a variable challenge value that is unique and unpredictable. Compare with *PAP*.

CIDR   classless interdomain routing. Technique supported by BGP4 and other routing protocols based on route summarization (aggregation). CIDR allows routers to group routes together to cut down on the quantity of routing information carried by the core routers.

CIR   committed information rate. Rate at which a Frame Relay network agrees to transfer information under normal conditions, averaged over a minimum increment of time. CIR, measured in bits per second, is one of the key negotiated tariff metrics for a Frame Relay service.

circuit   Communications path between two or more points.

Cisco Discovery Protocol   See *CDP*.

Cisco IOS   Cisco Internetwork Operating System. Cisco software that provides common functionality, scalability, and security for Cisco products. Cisco IOS Software supports a wide variety of protocols, media, services, and platforms.

classless interdomain routing   See *CIDR*.

client   Node or software program that requests services from a server.

client/server   Distributed-computing network systems in which transaction responsibilities are divided into two parts: client and server. Clients rely on servers for services such as file storage, printing, and processing power.

CLR   cell loss ratio. In ATM, the ratio of discarded cells to cells that are successfully transmitted. CLR can be set as a QoS parameter when a connection is set up.

coaxial cable   Cable consisting of a single inner wire conductor that is surrounded by a flexible, tubular insulating layer that is surrounded by a tubular conductive shield. Also known simply as *coax cable*.

codec   coder-decoder. Device that typically uses pulse-code modulation to transform analog signals into a digital bit stream and digital signals back into analog.

collision   In Ethernet, the result of two nodes transmitting simultaneously.

collision domain   In Ethernet, the network area within which frames that have collided are propagated. Repeaters and hubs propagate collisions; LAN switches, bridges, and routers do not. See also *bandwidth domain*.

committed information rate   See *CIR*.

Common Open Policy Service   See *COPS*.

compression   The running of data through an algorithm that reduces the space required to store or the bandwidth required to transmit the data.

congestion   A condition whereby network traffic has reached or is approaching network capacity.

connection admission control   Set of actions taken by an ATM switch during connection setup that determines whether a connection's requested QoS violates the QoS guarantees for established connections.

connection-oriented   Data transfer that requires the establishment of a virtual circuit.

connectionless   Data transfer without the existence of a virtual circuit.

constant bit rate   See *CBR*.

convergence   Speed and ability of a group of internetworking devices running a specific routing protocol to agree on the topology of an internetwork after a change in that topology.

COPS   Common Open Policy Service. An IETF protocol that defines a client/server model for supporting policy control with QoS-reservation protocols such as RSVP.

core layer   The high-speed backbone of an internetwork in a hierarchical topology. The core layer should be highly reliable and adapt to changes quickly. Compare with *access layer* and *distribution layer*. See also *hierarchical network design*.

cost   Arbitrary value, typically based on hop count, media bandwidth, a configurable parameter, or other measures, that is used by routing protocols to determine the most favorable path to a particular destination. The lower the cost, the better the path. See also *routing metric*.

count to infinity   Problem that can occur in routing algorithms that are slow to converge, in which routers continuously increment the hop count to particular networks. Typically, some arbitrary hop-count limit is imposed to prevent this problem.

CRC   cyclic redundancy check. Error-checking technique in which the frame recipient calculates a remainder by dividing frame contents by a prime binary divisor and compares the calculated remainder to a value stored in the frame by the sending node.

CSMA/CA   carrier sense multiple access with collision avoidance. Media-access mechanism wherein devices try to avoid collisions by waiting a random period of time following a transmission before starting their own transmission. Devices sense the medium to determine if another device is already transmitting. If no transmission is sensed, a device can transmit. If the medium is busy, devices defer their transmissions for a random period of time. CSMA/CA is used by IEEE 802.11 wireless networks.

CSMA/CD   carrier sense multiple access with collision detection. Media-access mechanism wherein devices determine if another device is already transmitting before starting their own transmissions. If no transmission is sensed for a specific period of time, a device can transmit. If multiple devices transmit at once, a collision occurs and is detected by all colliding devices. This collision subsequently delays retransmission from those devices for some random length of time. CSMA/CD is used by Ethernet and IEEE 802.3.

CSU   channel service unit. Digital interface device that connects end-user equipment to the local digital telephone loop. Often referred to together with DSU, as *CSU/DSU*.

CTD   cell transfer delay. In ATM, the elapsed time between a cell-exit event at the source UNI and the corresponding cell-entry event at the destination UNI for a particular connection.

custom queuing   Cisco IOS routing feature that assigns different amounts of queue space to different protocols and handles queues in a round-robin fashion. Custom queuing assures each specified traffic type a fixed portion of available bandwidth. Compare with *priority queuing*.

cut-through switching   Frame-switching approach that streams data through a switch so that the leading edge of a frame exits the switch at the output port before the frame finishes entering the input port. A device using cut-through switching forwards frames as soon as the destination address is looked up and the outgoing port determined. Compare with *store-and-forward switching*.

cyclic redundancy check   See *CRC*.

D

Data Encryption Standard See *DES*.

data link layer Layer 2 of the OSI reference model. This layer provides reliable transit of data across a physical link. The data link layer is concerned with physical addressing, network topology, line discipline, error notification, ordered delivery of frames, and flow control. The IEEE has divided this layer into two sublayers: the MAC sublayer and the LLC sublayer.

data service unit See *DSU*.

data store An area in a network where application layer data resides. A data store can be a server, a set of servers, a mainframe, a tape backup unit, a digital video library, or any device or component of an internetwork where large quantities of data are stored. Sometimes called a *data sink*.

data terminal equipment See *DTE*.

datagram Logical grouping of information sent as a network layer unit over a transmission medium without prior establishment of a virtual circuit.

DCE data communications equipment or data circuit-terminating equipment. Devices and connections of a communications network that comprise the network end of the user-to-network interface. Modems and interface cards are examples of DCE. Compare with *DTE*.

DDR dial-on-demand routing. Technique whereby a router can automatically initiate and close a circuit-switched session as transmitting stations demand.

decapsulation The reverse application of encapsulation. Decapsulation unwraps data from a protocol header that was added by a device or process before transmitting the data. Compare with *encapsulation*.

decryption The reverse application of an encryption algorithm to encrypted data, thereby restoring the data to its original, unencrypted state. See also *encryption*.

default gateway See *default router*.

default route Routing table entry that is used to direct frames for which a next hop is not explicitly listed in the routing table.

default router IP address of a router configured on an end station to allow the station to get to the rest of the internetwork. Also called *default gateway*.

delay 1. Time between the initiation of a transaction by a sender and the first response received by the sender. 2. Time required to move a frame from source to destination over a given path.

delay variation The amount of time average delay varies. See also *jitter*.

demultiplexing Separating of multiple input streams that were multiplexed into a common physical signal back into multiple output streams. See also *multiplexing*.

denial of service A security attack where an intruder disables a network service by flooding it with requests, making it unusable by legitimate users.

dense-mode PIM One of two PIM operational modes. With dense-mode PIM, packets are forwarded on all outgoing interfaces until pruning occurs. Receivers are densely populated, and it is assumed that many downstream networks want to receive and will probably use multicast datagrams that are forwarded to them. See also *PIM*, *prune*, and *sparse-mode PIM*.

DES Data Encryption Standard. Standard cryptographic algorithm developed by the U.S. National Bureau of Standards (now called the National Institute of Standards and Technology, or NIST).

DHCP   Dynamic Host Configuration Protocol. Provides a mechanism for allocating IP addresses dynamically to minimize configuration and allow addresses to be reused when hosts no longer need them.

dial-on-demand routing   See *DDR*.

differentiated services codepoint   See *DSCP*.

Diffusing Update Algorithm   See *DUAL*.

digital signal level 1   See *DS-1*.

digital signature   String of bits appended to a message that provides authentication and data integrity.

digital subscriber line   See *DSL*.

discontiguous subnet   An IP subnet that is made up of two or more physical networks that are separated by routers.

distance learning   A training method wherein students attend a class from remote sites using videoconferencing or other digital or analog video and audio techniques.

Distance Vector Multicast Routing Protocol   See *DVMRP*.

distance vector routing algorithm   Class of routing algorithms that calls for each router to send its routing table in periodic update packets to its neighbors. Compare with *link-state routing algorithm*.

distribution layer   Connects network services to the access layer in a hierarchical topology, and implements policies regarding security, traffic loading, and routing. Compare with *access layer* and *core layer*. See also *hierarchical network design*.

DNS   Domain Name System. System used in the Internet for translating names of network nodes into addresses.

DS-1   digital signal level 1. Framing specification used in transmitting digital signals at 1.544 Mbps on a WAN circuit.

DSCP   differentiated services codepoint. A 6-bit field in the IP header used for packet classification purposes and indicating how packets should be forwarded. Replaces the outdated IP precedence field.

DSL   digital subscriber line. Public network technology that delivers high bandwidth over conventional telephone wiring at limited distances. See also *ADSL* and *HDSL*.

DSU   data service unit. Device used in digital transmission that adapts the physical interface on a DTE device to a transmission facility such as T1 or E1. Often referred to together with CSU, as *CSU/DSU*. See also *CSU*.

DTE   data terminal equipment. Device at the user end of a user-network interface that serves as a data source, destination, or both. DTE connects to a data network through a DCE device (for example, a modem) and typically uses clocking signals generated by the DCE. DTE includes such devices as computers, internetworking devices, and multiplexers. Compare with *DCE*.

DUAL   Diffusing Update Algorithm. Convergence algorithm used in EIGRP that provides loop-free operation. DUAL allows routers involved in a topology change to synchronize, while not involving routers that are unaffected by the change. See also *Enhanced Interior Gateway Routing Protocol*.

DVMRP   Distance Vector Multicast Routing Protocol. Multicast routing protocol, largely based on RIP. Packets are forwarded on all outgoing interfaces until pruning occurs. See also *prune*.

Dynamic Host Configuration Protocol (DHCP)   See *DHCP*.

dynamic password   Security mechanism that incorporates a dynamically generated password that can be used only once.

E

E1   Wide-area digital transmission scheme used predominantly in Europe that carries data at a rate of 2.048 Mbps. E1 lines can be leased for private use from common carriers.

efficiency   A measure of how much overhead is required to produce a certain amount of data throughput on a network. Overhead includes frame headers and trailers, acknowledgments, media access methods, and flow-control mechanisms.

EIGRP   See *Enhanced Interior Gateway Routing Protocol*.

encapsulation   Wrapping of data in a particular protocol header.

encryption   Application of a specific algorithm to alter the appearance of data, making it incomprehensible to those who are not authorized to see the information. See also *decryption*.

encryption key   A code used by an encryption algorithm to scramble and unscramble data.

Enhanced Interior Gateway Routing Protocol   Advanced version of IGRP developed by Cisco. Provides superior convergence properties and operating efficiency, and combines the advantages of link-state protocols with those of distance vector protocols.

enterprise network   Large and diverse internetwork connecting most major points in an organization. An enterprise network typically consists of building and campus networks, remote-access services, and one or more WANs.

Ethernet   LAN technology invented by Xerox Corporation and developed jointly by Xerox, Intel, and Digital Equipment Corporation. Ethernet networks use CSMA/CD and run over a variety of cable types at 10 Mbps. Ethernet is similar to IEEE 802.3.

F

Fast Ethernet   Any of several 100-Mbps Ethernet specifications. Fast Ethernet offers a speed increase ten times that of the original IEEE 802.3 specification, while preserving such qualities as frame format, MAC mechanisms, and frame size.

FDDI   Fiber Distributed Data Interface. LAN standard specifying a 100-Mbps token-passing network using fiber-optic cable and a dual-ring architecture to provide redundancy.

FECN   forward explicit congestion notification. Bit set by a Frame Relay network to inform a device receiving the frame that congestion was experienced in the path from source to destination. Compare with *BECN*.

Fiber Distributed Data Interface   See *FDDI*.

fiber-optic cable   Physical medium capable of conducting modulated light transmission. Fiber-optic cable is not susceptible to electromagnetic interference and is capable of high data rates.

fiber-optic interrepeater link   See *FOIRL*.

FIFO   first in, first out. Method of sending traffic through a device whereby the first packet received is the first packet transmitted. Does not support prioritization.

File Transfer Protocol   See *FTP*.

filter   Generally, a process or device that screens network traffic for certain characteristics, such as a source address, destination address, or protocol, and determines whether to forward or discard that traffic based on the established criteria.

firewall   Router, software, appliance, or remote-access server designated as a buffer between connected networks. A firewall uses access lists and other methods to ensure the security of a network.

first in, first out   See *FIFO*.

flat network design   A network design that has little or no hierarchy or modularity and is generally only appropriate for small shared or switched LANs.

flooding   Traffic-passing technique used by switches and bridges, in which traffic received on an interface is sent out all interfaces except the interface on which the information was received.

flow   Stream of data traveling between two endpoints across a network.

flow control   Technique for ensuring that a transmitting entity does not overwhelm a receiving entity with data. When the buffers on the receiving device are full, a message is sent to the sending device to suspend transmission until the data in the buffers has been processed.

FOIRL   fiber-optic interrepeater link. Fiber-optic signaling methodology for transmitting Ethernet frames on fiber-optic cables, based on the IEEE 802.3 fiber-optic specification.

forward explicit congestion notification   See *FECN*.

forwarding   Process of sending a frame toward its ultimate destination by way of an internetworking device.

fragmentation   Process of breaking a packet into smaller units when transmitting over a network medium that cannot support the original size of the packet. See also *reassembly*.

frame   Logical grouping of information sent as a data link layer unit over a transmission medium. Often refers to the header and trailer, used for synchronization and error control, that surround the user data contained in the unit.

Frame Relay   Industry-standard, switched data link layer protocol that handles multiple virtual circuits between connected devices. Frame Relay is more efficient than X.25, the protocol for which it is generally considered a replacement. See also *X.25*.

FTP   File Transfer Protocol. Application protocol, part of the TCP/IP protocol stack, used for transferring files between network nodes. FTP is defined in RFC 959.

full duplex   Capability for simultaneous data transmission between a sending station and a receiving station. Compare with *half duplex*.

full mesh   Term describing a network in which devices are organized in a mesh topology, with each network node having either a physical circuit or a virtual circuit connecting it to every other network node. See also *mesh* and *partial mesh*.

G–H

Gigabit Ethernet   1000-Mbps LAN technologies specified in IEEE 802.3z. Gigabit Ethernet offers a speed increase 100 times that of the original IEEE 802.3 specification, while preserving such qualities as frame format, MAC mechanisms, and frame size.

group address   See *multicast address*.

H.320   Suite of international standard specifications for videoconferencing over circuit-switched media such as ISDN, fractional T1, or switched-56 lines.

H.323   Extension of H.320 that enables videoconferencing over LANs and other packet-switched networks, and video over the Internet.

half duplex   Capability for data transmission in only one direction at a time between a sending station and a receiving station. Compare with *full duplex*.

handshaking   Process whereby two protocol entities synchronize during connection establishment.

hardware address   See *MAC address*.

hash   Resulting string of bits from a hash function. See also *message digest*.

hash function   Any well-defined procedure or mathematical function that converts a large, possibly variable-sized piece of data into a small hash code, or hash. The hash is generally a single integer that serves as an index into an array or as an integrity check of the input. The function is not reversible to produce the original input.

HDLC   High-Level Data Link Control. Synchronous data link layer protocol for WAN links that specifies framing and error control.

HDSL   high-data-rate digital subscriber line. One of many DSL technologies. HDSL delivers 1.544 Mbps of bandwidth each way over two copper twisted pairs. See also *DSL* and *ADSL*.

hello packet   Packet that is used by networking devices for neighbor discovery and recovery, and to indicate that a device is still operating.

helper address   Address configured on a router interface to which broadcasts received on that interface will be sent, commonly used to forward DHCP requests.

hierarchical network design   A technique for designing scalable campus and enterprise network topologies using a layered, modular model. See also *access layer*, *core layer*, and *distribution layer*.

hierarchical routing   A model for distributing knowledge of a network topology among internetwork routers. With hierarchical routing, no single router needs to understand the complete topology. See also *route summarization*.

high-data-rate digital subscriber line   See *HDSL*.

High-Level Data Link Control   See *HDLC*.

holddown   State into which a route is placed so routers will neither advertise the route nor accept advertisements about the route for a specific length of time (the holddown period). Holddown is used to flush bad information about a route from all routers in the network. A route is typically placed in holddown when a link to that route fails.

hop   Term describing the passage of a data packet between two network nodes (for example, between two routers).

hop count   Routing metric used to measure the distance between a source and a destination in number of routers or hops between the source and destination.

host   A system on an IP network.

HSRP   Hot Standby Router Protocol. Provides high network availability and transparent network topology changes. HSRP creates a Hot Standby router group with a lead router that services all packets sent to the Hot Standby address. The lead router is monitored by other routers in the group, and if it fails, one of these standby routers inherits the lead position and the Hot Standby group address. Hosts use the Hot Standby address as the address of their default gateway.

hub   1. Generally, a term used to describe a device or network that serves as the center of a star or hub-and-spoke topology. 2. In Ethernet and IEEE 802.3, an Ethernet multiport repeater.

hub-and-spoke topology   A topology that consists of one central network and a set of remote networks each with one connection to the central network and no direct connections to each other. Traffic between remote networks goes through the hub network.

I

IANA   Internet Assigned Numbers Authority. Organization operated by ICANN that manages IP address-space allocation, domain-name assignment, and autonomous system number assignment. IANA also maintains a database of assigned protocol identifiers used in the TCP/IP protocol stack.

ICANN   Internet Corporation for Assigned Names and Numbers. A nonprofit corporation with global participants dedicated to keeping the Internet secure, stable, and interoperable, tasked with delegating authorization for naming and numbering on the Internet.

ICMP   Internet Control Message Protocol. Network layer TCP/IP protocol that reports errors and provides other information relevant to IP packet processing. Documented in RFC 792.

IEEE   Institute of Electrical and Electronics Engineers. Professional organization whose activities include the development of communications and network standards. IEEE LAN standards are the predominant LAN standards today.

IEEE 802.1D   IEEE specification that describes an algorithm that prevents bridging loops by creating a spanning tree.

IEEE 802.1p   IEEE LAN protocol for supporting QoS on LANs. Specifies mechanisms in bridges to expedite the delivery of time-critical traffic and to limit the extent of high-bandwidth multicast traffic within a bridged LAN. IEEE 802.1p is now a standard part of IEEE 802.1D.

IEEE 802.1Q   IEEE LAN protocol for supporting VLANs across various media.

IEEE 802.2   IEEE LAN protocol that specifies an implementation of the LLC sublayer of the data link layer. See also *LLC*.

IEEE 802.3   IEEE LAN protocol that specifies an implementation of the physical layer and the MAC sublayer of the data link layer. IEEE 802.3 uses CSMA/CD access at a variety of speeds over a variety of physical media. IEEE 802.3 is similar to Ethernet.

IETF   Internet Engineering Task Force. Task force consisting of numerous working groups responsible for developing Internet and TCP/IP standards.

IGMP   Internet Group Management Protocol. Used by IP hosts to report their multicast group memberships to an adjacent multicast router. Defined in RFC 1112.

IGRP   Interior Gateway Routing Protocol. An interior routing protocol developed by Cisco to address the problems associated with routing in large, heterogeneous networks. Compare with *Enhanced Interior Gateway Routing Protocol*.

Institute of Electrical and Electronics Engineers   See *IEEE*.

Integrated Services Digital Network   See *ISDN*.

Integrated Services working group   See *ISWG*.

integrity   Keeping data unchanged and safe from tampering as it traverses the network.

Inter-Switch Link   See *ISL*.

interface   1. Connection between two systems or devices. 2. A port on a device.

Interior Gateway Routing Protocol   See *IGRP*.

Intermediate System-to-Intermediate System   See *IS-IS*.

International Organization for Standardization   See *ISO*.

Internet   Term used to refer to the largest global internetwork, connecting hundreds of thousands of networks worldwide using the TCP/IP protocol stack.

Internet Assigned Numbers Authority   See *IANA*.

Internet Control Message Protocol   See *ICMP*.

Internet Corporation for Assigned Names and Numbers   See *ICANN*.

Internet Engineering Task Force   See *IETF*.

Internet Group Management Protocol   See *IGMP*.

Internet Protocol   See *IP*.

Internet service provider   See *ISP*.

Internet Society   See *ISOC*.

Internet telephony   Generic term used to describe various approaches to running voice traffic over IP networks, in particular, the Internet. See also *VoIP*.

internetwork   Collection of networks interconnected by routers.

Internetwork Packet Exchange   See *IPX*.

internetworking   General term used to refer to the industry and technologies devoted to connecting networks together.

IOS   See *Cisco IOS*.

IP   Internet Protocol. Network layer protocol in the TCP/IP stack offering a connectionless internetwork service. IP provides features for addressing, differentiated services, forwarding packets, and fragmentation and reassembly. Defined in RFC 791.

IP address   A unique address assigned to an interface using TCP/IP. An IPv4 32-bit address is written as four octets separated by periods (dotted decimal format). Each address consists of a network number, an optional subnetwork number, and a host number. An IPv6 128-bit address is written in hexadecimal.

IP multicast   Routing technique that allows IP traffic to be propagated from one source to several destinations. Rather than sending one packet to each destination, one packet is sent to a multicast group identified by a single IP destination group address.

IPsec   IP Security Protocol. A set of open standards that provides data confidentiality, data integrity, and authentication between participating peers at the IP layer. VPNs use IPsec.

IPv4   Internet Protocol (IP), version 4.

IPv6   Internet Protocol (IP), version 6. Replacement for IPv4.

IPX   Internetwork Packet Exchange. Novell NetWare network layer (Layer 3) protocol used for transferring data between servers and workstations.

ISDN   Integrated Services Digital Network. Communication protocol, offered by telephone companies, that permits telephone networks to carry data, voice, and other source traffic.

IS-IS   Intermediate System-to-Intermediate System. OSI link-state hierarchical routing protocol based on DECnet Phase V routing.

ISL   Inter-Switch Link. Cisco-proprietary protocol that maintains VLAN information as traffic flows between switches and routers.

ISO   International Organization for Standardization. International organization that is responsible for a wide range of standards, including those relevant to networking. ISO developed the OSI reference model, a popular networking reference model. Because International Organization for Standardization has different acronyms in different languages (IOS in English, OIN in French for *Organisation Internationale de Normalisation*), its founders decided to give it a short, all-purpose name. They chose ISO, derived from the Greek *isos*, meaning equal.

ISOC   Internet Society. International non-profit organization, founded in 1992, that coordinates the evolution and use of the Internet.

ISP   Internet service provider. Company that provides Internet access to other companies and individuals.

ISWG   Integrated Services working group. Subset of the IETF dedicated to defining QoS mechanisms for the Internet and other TCP/IP-based networks.

J–K–L

jitter   Communication line distortion caused by the variation of a signal from its reference timing positions. See also *delay variation*.

keepalive message   Message sent by one network device to inform another network device that the virtual circuit between the two is still active.

Kerberos   An authentication system that provides user-to-host security for application layer protocols such as FTP and Telnet.

key   See *encryption key*.

L2TP   Layer 2 Tunneling Protocol. An IETF standard for tunneling private data over public networks.

LAN   Local-area network. High-speed, low-error data network covering a relatively small geographic area (up to a few thousand meters). LANs connect workstations, peripherals, terminals, and other devices in a single building or other geographically limited area.

late collision   An Ethernet collision that occurs after the first 64 bytes of a frame. Compare with *legal collision*. See also *collision* and *CSMA/CD*.

latency   1. A delay, a period between the initiation of something and the occurrence. 2. Delay between the time a device requests access to a network and the time it is granted permission to transmit. 3. Delay between the time a forwarding device receives a frame and the time that frame is forwarded out the destination port.

Layer 2 Tunneling Protocol   See *L2TP*.

Layer 3 switch   Switch that filters and forwards packets based on MAC addresses and network addresses. Also referred to as *multilayer switch*.

leased line Transmission line reserved by a communications carrier for the private use of a customer.

legal collision An Ethernet collision that occurs within the first 64 bytes of a frame. Compare with *late collision*. See also *collision* and *CSMA/CD*.

link Network communications channel consisting of a circuit or transmission path and all related equipment between a sender and a receiver.

link-state advertisement See *LSA*.

link-state routing algorithm Routing algorithm in which each router broadcasts or multicasts information regarding the cost of reaching its neighbors to all nodes in its area or areas. Compare with *distance vector routing algorithm*.

LLC Logical Link Control. Higher of the two data link layer sublayers defined by the IEEE. The LLC sublayer handles error control, flow control, framing, and the network layer (Layer 3) service interface. Includes both connectionless and connection-oriented services. Also known as IEEE 802.2.

LLC2 Logical Link Control, type 2. Connection-oriented LLC.

load balancing In routing, the capability of a router to distribute traffic over all its network ports that are the same distance from the destination address. Sometimes called *load sharing* to indicate that most protocols do not evenly balance traffic.

local-area network See *LAN*.

Logical Link Control See *LLC*.

LSA link-state advertisement. Multicast packet used by link-state protocols that contains information about neighbors and path costs. LSAs are used by the receiving routers to maintain their routing tables.

M

MAC Media Access Control. Lower of the two sublayers of the data link layer defined by the IEEE. The MAC sublayer handles access to shared media, such as whether token passing or contention will be used.

MAC address Standardized data link layer address that is required for every port or device that connects to a LAN. Other devices in the network use these addresses to locate specific ports in the network. MAC addresses are 6 bytes long and include a 3-byte vendor code that is controlled by the IEEE. Also referred to as a *hardware address*, *MAC layer address*, or *physical address*. Compare with *network address*.

MAN metropolitan-area network. A network that spans a metropolitan area. Generally, a MAN spans a larger geographic area than a LAN, but a smaller geographic area than a WAN.

manageability The ease with which a network can be managed and monitored, including the management of the network's performance, faults, configuration, security, and accounting capabilities.

Management Information Base See *MIB*.

maximum burst size See *MBS*.

maximum cell delay variation See *MCDV*.

maximum cell transfer delay See *MCTD*.

maximum transmission unit See *MTU*.

MBS maximum burst size. Parameter defined for ATM traffic management. MCR is defined for VBR transmissions.

MCDV maximum cell delay variation. In an ATM network, the maximum two-point

CDV objective across a link or node for the specified service category.

MCR   minimum cell rate. Parameter defined for ATM traffic management. MCR is defined for ABR transmissions.

MCTD   maximum cell transfer delay. In an ATM network, the sum of the MCDV and the fixed delay component across the link or node.

mean time between failure   See *MTBF*.

mean time to repair   See *MTTR*.

media   Plural of medium. The various physical environments through which transmission signals pass. Common network media include twisted-pair, coaxial, and fiber-optic cable; and the atmosphere (through which wireless microwave, laser, and infrared transmission occurs).

Media Access Control   See *MAC*.

mesh   Network topology in which devices are organized with many, often redundant, interconnections strategically placed between network nodes. See also *full mesh* and *partial mesh*.

message digest   Value returned by a hash function. Also referred to as *hash*.

metric   See *routing metric*.

metropolitan-area network   See *MAN*.

MIB   Management Information Base. Database of network management information that is used and maintained by a network management protocol such as SNMP. The value of a MIB object can be changed or retrieved using SNMP commands, usually through a network management system (NMS). MIB objects are organized in a tree structure that includes public (standard) and private (proprietary) branches.

minimum cell rate   See *MCR*.

MLP   See *MPPP*.

MMP   See *Multichassis MPPP*.

MPEG   Moving Picture Experts Group. Standard for compressing video.

MPLS   See *Multiprotocol Label Switching*.

MPPP   Multilink PPP. Method of splitting, recombining, and sequencing datagrams across multiple PPP circuits. Sometimes abbreviated as *MLP* or simply *MP*.

MTBF   mean time between failure. The average time that elapses between network or system failures.

MTTR   mean time to repair. The average amount of time it takes to fix a network or system when it fails.

MTU   maximum transmission unit. Maximum frame size, in bytes, that a particular interface or medium can handle.

multicast   Message that is sent to a subset of nodes on a network. Compare with *broadcast* and *unicast*.

multicast address   Single address that refers to multiple network nodes. Also referred to as *group address*. Compare with *broadcast address* and *unicast address*.

multicast group   Dynamically determined group of IP hosts identified by a single IP multicast address.

multicast routing protocol   Routing protocol used to route multicast packets. See also *DVMRP* and *PIM*.

multichassis MPPP   Extends MPPP support across multiple routers and remote-access servers. Multichassis MPPP enables multiple routers and access servers to operate as a single, large dialup pool, with a single network address and access number. Multichassis MPPP correctly handles packet fragmenting and reassembly when a user connection is split between two physical access devices. Sometimes abbreviated *MMP*. See also *MPPP*.

multihoming   Attaching a host or network to multiple physical network segments.

multilayer switch   Switch that filters and forwards packets based on MAC addresses and network addresses. Also referred to as *Layer 3 switch*.

Multilink PPP   See *MPPP*.

multimode fiber   Optical fiber with a relatively large core that supports more than one propagation mode. Typically used for communication over shorter distances, such as within a building or on a campus, with data rates of 10 Mbps to 10 Gbps. Compare with *single-mode fiber*.

multiplexing   Scheme that allows multiple logical signals to be transmitted simultaneously across a single physical channel. Compare with *demultiplexing*.

Multiprotocol Label Switching   Switching method that forwards IP traffic using a label. This label instructs routers in the network where to forward packets based on pre-established IP routing information.

N

NAT   Network Address Translation. Mechanism for reducing the need for globally unique IP addresses. NAT allows an organization with addresses that are not globally unique to connect to the Internet by translating those addresses into globally routable addresses.

NBMA   nonbroadcast multiaccess. Term describing a multiaccess network that does not inherently support broadcasting; for example, ATM.

NetBIOS   Network Basic Input/Output System. API used by applications on a LAN to request services from lower-level network processes. These services include session establishment and termination, and information transfer. NetBIOS is used by Windows operating systems primarily.

NetFlow   A Cisco optimization technique that identifies traffic flows and speeds the forwarding of traffic for a flow. When a flow is identified, the switching, security, QoS, and traffic-measurement services required for the flow are used to build an entry in a NetFlow cache. Subsequent packets in the flow are handled via a single streamlined task that references the cache. Also refers to NetFlow export records, which provide details of the traffic in a network.

NetWare   Distributed network-operating system developed by Novell. Provided transparent remote file access and numerous other distributed network services.

network address   Network layer address referring to a logical, rather than a physical, network device. Used by the network layer. Compare with *MAC address*.

Network Address Translation   See *NAT*.

Network File System   See *NFS*.

Network Information Center   See *NIC*.

network interface card   See *NIC*.

network layer   Layer 3 of the OSI reference model. This layer provides connectivity and path selection between two end systems. The network layer is the layer at which routing occurs.

network management system   See *NMS*.

network utilization   See *utilization*.

Network-to-Network Interface   See *NNI*.

Next Hop Resolution Protocol   See *NHRP*.

NFS   Network File System. A distributed file-system protocol suite developed by Sun Microsystems that allows remote file access across a network.

NHRP   Next Hop Resolution Protocol. Protocol used by routers to dynamically discover the MAC address of other routers and hosts connected to an NBMA network. These systems can then directly communicate without requiring traffic to use an intermediate hop, thus increasing performance in ATM, Frame Relay, and other environments.

NIC   1. network interface card. Board that provides network-communication capabilities for a computer system. 2. Network Information Center. Organization that historically served the Internet community by supplying addressing, naming, documentation, training, and other services.

NMS   network management system. System responsible for managing a network. An NMS is generally a powerful and well-equipped computer such as an engineering workstation. NMSs communicate with agents to help keep track of network statistics and resources.

NNI   Network-to-Network Interface. ATM standard that defines the interface between two ATM switches that are both located in a private network, or are both located in a public network.

nonbroadcast multiaccess   See *NBMA*.

O–P

OC   Optical Carrier. Series of physical protocols (OC-1, OC-2, OC-3, and so on) defined for SONET optical signal transmissions. OC signal levels put STS frames onto fiber-optic lines at a variety of speeds. The base rate is 51.84 Mbps (OC-1); each signal level thereafter operates at a speed divisible by that number (thus, OC-3 runs at 155.52 Mbps). See also *SONET* and *STS-1*.

offered load   The sum of all the data all network nodes have ready to send at a particular time.

Open Shortest Path First   See *OSPF*.

OSI reference model   Open System Interconnection reference model. Network architectural model that consists of seven layers, each of which specifies particular network functions such as addressing, flow control, error control, encapsulation, and reliable message transfer. The OSI reference model is used universally as a method for teaching and understanding network functionality. See *application layer*, *data link layer*, *network layer*, *physical layer*, *presentation layer*, *session layer*, and *transport layer*.

OSPF   Open Shortest Path First. Link-state, hierarchical interior routing algorithm proposed as a successor to RIP in the Internet community. OSPF features include least-cost routing, multipath routing, and load balancing. OSPF is an open, nonproprietary protocol.

packet   Logical grouping of information that includes a header containing control information and (usually) user data. Packets are most often used to refer to network layer units of data.

packets per second   See *pps*.

PAP   Password Authentication Protocol. Authentication protocol that allows PPP peers to authenticate one another. Unlike CHAP, PAP passes the password and host-name or username in clear text (unencrypted). Compare with *CHAP*.

partial mesh Term describing a network in which devices are organized in a mesh topology without requiring that every device have a direct connection to every other device. Compare with *full mesh*. See also *mesh*.

PBX private branch exchange. Digital or analog telephone switchboard located on a subscriber premises and used to connect private and public telephone networks.

PCR peak cell rate. Parameter for ATM traffic management. In CBR transmissions, a source can emit cells at the PCR at any time and for any duration and the negotiated QoS commitments should pertain.

phantom router See *virtual router*.

physical address See *MAC address*.

physical layer Layer 1 of the OSI reference model. The physical layer defines the electrical, mechanical, procedural, and functional specifications for activating, maintaining, and deactivating the physical link between end systems.

PIM Protocol Independent Multicast. Multicast routing architecture that allows the addition of IP multicast routing on existing IP networks. PIM does not require a specific unicast routing protocol and can be operated in two modes: dense mode and sparse mode. See also *dense-mode PIM* and *sparse-mode PIM*.

ping 1. ICMP echo message and its reply. Used in IP networks to test the reachability of a network device. 2. Generic term for an echo mechanism in any protocol stack.

plesiochronous transmission Term describing digital signals that are sourced from different clocks of comparable accuracy and stability.

Point-to-Point Protocol See *PPP*.

poison-reverse updates Routing updates that explicitly indicate that a network or subnet is unreachable, rather than implying that a network is unreachable by not including it in updates. Poison-reverse updates are sent to defeat routing loops.

port 1. Interface on an internetworking device (such as a router or switch). 2. In TCP/IP terminology, a transport layer process that sends and receives information from lower layers. Ports are numbered, and each numbered port is associated with a specific process.

PPP Point-to-Point Protocol. Protocol that provides router-to-router and host-to-network connections over synchronous and asynchronous circuits. PPP was designed to work with several network layer protocols, such as IP, IPv6, IPX, and AppleTalk.

pps packets per second. A measure of how quickly a switch or router can forward data.

precedence Outdated field in an IP header that indicated the priority of a packet. Replaced by the *DSCP* field. Precedence helped a router determine which packet to send when several packets were queued for transmission to the same output interface. See also *DSCP*.

presentation layer Layer 6 of the OSI reference model. This layer ensures that information sent by the application layer of one system is readable by the application layer of another.

priority queuing Cisco IOS routing feature in which frames in an interface output queue are prioritized based on various characteristics such as packet and interface type. Compare with *custom queuing*.

private branch exchange See *PBX*.

private key Digital code used to decrypt/encrypt information and provide digital signatures. This key should be kept secret by the owner; it has a corresponding public key.

propagation delay   Time required for data to travel over a network, from its source to its ultimate destination.

protocol analyzer   Hardware or software device offering various network troubleshooting features, including protocol-specific packet decodes, specific preprogrammed troubleshooting tests, and traffic generation.

Protocol Independent Multicast   See *PIM*.

proxy ARP   Proxy Address Resolution Protocol. Variation of the ARP protocol, in which an intermediate device (for example, a router) sends an ARP response on behalf of an end node to the requesting host. Defined in RFC 1027.

prune   In an IP multicast environment, the process wherein a router detects that there are no group members on one of its interfaces and stops sending a multicast stream out that interface.

public key   A digital code used to encrypt/decrypt information and verify digital signatures. This key can be made widely available; it has a corresponding private key.

pull   In client/server information-dissemination applications, requesting data from another computer or application. The web is based on pull technology in which a client uses a browser to request (pull) a web page. Compare with *push*.

push   In client/server information-dissemination applications, sending data to a client without the client requesting it. Increasingly, companies are using push technologies to deliver customized data to users without the users explicitly requesting it. An example is customized news and stock information that

is delivered on a daily basis. Compare with *pull*.

Q–R

QoS   quality of service. 1. Methodology for prioritizing traffic on an internetwork, usually to reduce delay for specific types of traffic such as VoIP. 2. Measure of performance for a transmission system that reflects its transmission quality and service availability.

queue   1. Generally, an ordered list of elements waiting to be processed. 2. In routing, a backlog of packets waiting to be forwarded over a router interface.

RADIUS   Remote Authentication Dial-In User Service. Protocol and database for authenticating users, tracking connection times, and authorizing services permitted to users. A remote-access server acts as a client of a RADIUS server.

RARP   Reverse Address Resolution Protocol. Protocol in the TCP/IP stack that provides a method for a diskless station to determine its IP address when its MAC address is known. Compare with *ARP*.

Real-Time Control Protocol   See *RTCP*.

Real-Time Transport Protocol   See *RTP*.

reassembly   The putting back together of an IP datagram at the destination after it has been fragmented either at the source or at an intermediate node. See also *fragmentation*.

recoverability   How quickly a network or computer system can recover from a problem.

redistribution   Allowing routing information discovered through one routing protocol to be distributed in the update messages of another routing protocol.

redundancy   The duplication of devices, services, or connections so that, if a failure occurs, the redundant devices, services, or connections can perform the work of those that failed.

reliability   The extent to which a network or computer system provides dependable, error-free service.

remote access   Analog and digital dial-in and dial-out technologies for reaching remote networks via remote-access servers.

Remote Authentication Dial-In User Service   See *RADIUS*.

Remote Monitoring   See *RMON*.

remote-access server   Communications server that connects remote nodes or LANs to an internetwork. Generally supports standard terminal services, such as Telnet, and remote-node, protocol-translation, and asynchronous-routing services.

remote-node services   A function of a remote-access server that allows PCs, Macs, and X Window terminals to connect to a remote network and access network services as if they were directly connected to the network.

rendezvous point   Router specified in sparse-mode PIM implementations to track membership in multicast groups and to forward messages to known multicast group addresses. See also *sparse-mode PIM*.

repeater   Physical layer device that regenerates and propagates electrical signals between two network segments.

repetitive pattern suppression   See *RPS*.

Request For Comments   See *RFC*.

resiliency   Capability of a network to withstand failures and still maintain network operation.

resource discovery   The processes and protocols that network users and applications employ to find network resources such as file, naming, and print servers.

Resource Reservation Protocol   See *RSVP*.

response time   The amount of time between a request for some network service and a response to the request.

Reverse Address Resolution Protocol   See *RARP*.

reverse-path forwarding   See *RPF*.

RFC   Request For Comments. Document series written by the IETF as the primary means for communicating information about the Internet and the TCP/IP protocols. RFCs are available online from numerous sources, including http://www.rfc-editor.org.

RIP   Routing Information Protocol. Interior distance vector routing protocol supplied with UNIX BSD systems and widely used in the early years of the Internet. Defined in RFC 1058 and RFC 2453.

RMON   Remote Monitoring. MIB agent specifications developed by the IETF that define functions for the remote monitoring of networked devices to facilitate statistics gathering, problem determination, and reporting.

round-trip time   See *RTT*.

route   Path through an internetwork.

route summarization   Consolidation of advertised addresses in routing protocols that causes a single summary route to be advertised instead of many individual routes.

router   Network layer device that uses one or more metrics to determine the optimal path along which network traffic should be forwarded. Routers forward packets from one network to another based on network layer information. Routers also perform network layer services on the network.

Routing Information Protocol   See *RIP*.

routing metric   Method by which a routing algorithm determines that one route is better than another. This information is stored in routing tables. Metrics include bandwidth, communication cost, delay, hop count, load, MTU, path cost, and reliability. Sometimes referred to simply as a *metric*. See also *cost*.

routing table   Table stored in a router or some other internetworking device that keeps track of routes to particular network destinations and, in some cases, metrics associated with those routes.

Routing Table Maintenance Protocol   See *RTMP*.

routing update   Message sent from a router to indicate network reachability and associated cost information. Routing updates are typically sent at regular intervals and after a change in network topology.

RPF   reverse-path forwarding. Multicasting technique in which a multicast datagram is forwarded out all but the receiving interface, if the receiving interface is the one used to forward unicast datagrams to the source of the multicast datagram.

RPS   repetitive pattern suppression. An option for WAN data circuits that replaces repeating strings of data by a single occurrence of the string and a code that indicates to the far end how many repetitions of the string were in the original data.

RSVP   Resource Reservation Protocol. A protocol that supports the reservation of resources across an IP network. Applications running on IP end systems can use RSVP to indicate to other nodes the

nature (bandwidth, jitter, maximum burst, and so on) of the packet streams they want to receive.

RTCP   Real-Time Control Protocol. Protocol that monitors the QoS of an RTP connection and conveys information about the ongoing session. See also *RTP*.

RTMP   Routing Table Maintenance Protocol. Distance vector routing protocol developed by Apple Computer for use with the AppleTalk protocol suite. RTMP was similar in behavior to RIP.

RTP   Real-Time Transport Protocol. IETF protocol that provides end-to-end network-transport functions for applications transmitting real-time data, such as audio, video, or simulation data, over multicast or unicast network services. RTP provides services such as payload type identification, sequence numbering, time-stamping, and data delivery.

RTT   round-trip time. Time required for a network communication to travel from the source to the destination and back. RTT includes the time required for the destination to process the message from the source and generate a reply.

runt frame   An Ethernet frame that is shorter than 64 bytes.

S

SAP   Service Advertising Protocol. IPX protocol that provided a means of informing network clients about available network resources and services via routers and servers.

scalability   Capacity of a network to keep pace with changes and growth.

SCR   sustainable cell rate. Parameter for ATM traffic management. For VBR connections, SCR determines the long-term average cell rate that can be transmitted. See also *VBR*.

SDH Synchronous Digital Hierarchy. European standard that defines a set of rate and format standards that are transmitted using optical signals over fiber. SDH is similar to SONET, with a basic SDH rate of 51.84 Mbps, designated as STS-1.

Secure Sockets Layer See *SSL*.

segment 1. A single network that is based on a particular Layer 2 protocol and is bounded by repeaters, bridges, or switches. 2. Term used in the TCP specification to describe a single transport layer unit of information.

Sequenced Packet Exchange See *SPX*.

server Node or software program that provides services to clients.

Service Advertising Protocol See *SAP*.

session layer Layer 5 of the OSI reference model. This layer establishes, manages, and terminates sessions between applications and manages data exchange between presentation layer entities.

shielded twisted-pair See *STP*.

shortest path first algorithm See *SPF*.

Simple Mail Transfer Protocol See *SMTP*.

Simple Network Management Protocol See *SNMP*.

simulation The process of using software and mathematical models to analyze the behavior of a system without requiring that an actual system be built.

single-mode fiber Fiber-optic cabling with a narrow core that allows light to enter only at a single angle. Such cabling has higher bandwidth than multimode fiber but requires a light source with a narrow spectral width (for example, a laser). See also *multimode fiber*.

SMTP Simple Mail Transfer Protocol. Internet protocol providing email services.

SNA Systems Network Architecture. Large, complex, feature-rich network architecture developed in the 1970s by IBM for communication between terminals and mainframes.

SNMP Simple Network Management Protocol. Network management protocol for TCP/IP networks. SNMP provides a means to monitor and control network devices, and to manage configurations, statistics collection, performance, and security.

SONET Synchronous Optical Network. High-speed synchronous network specification developed by Bellcore and designed to run on optical fiber. STS-1 is the basic building block of SONET. Approved as an international standard in 1988. See also *STS-1*.

spanning tree Loop-free subset of a network topology.

Spanning Tree Protocol Bridge protocol that uses the spanning-tree algorithm, enabling a learning bridge to dynamically work around loops in a network topology by creating a spanning tree. Bridges exchange BPDU messages with other bridges to detect loops, and then remove the loops by shutting down selected bridge interfaces.

spanning-tree algorithm Algorithm used by the Spanning Tree Protocol to create a spanning tree.

sparse-mode PIM One of two PIM operational modes. Sparse-mode PIM tries to constrain data distribution so that a minimal number of routers in a network receive irrelevant data. Packets are sent only if they are explicitly requested at the rendezvous point. In sparse mode, receivers are widely distributed, and the assumption is that downstream networks do not necessarily use the multicast datagrams that are sent to them. See also *dense-mode PIM*, *PIM*, and *rendezvous point*.

SPF   Shortest Path First algorithm. Routing algorithm that iterates on length of path to determine a shortest-path spanning tree. Commonly used in link-state routing algorithms. Sometimes called Dijkstra's algorithm.

split-horizon updates   Routing technique in which information about routes is prevented from exiting the router interface through which that information was received. Split-horizon updates are useful in preventing routing loops.

spoofing   1. Scheme used by routers to cause a host to treat an interface as if it were up and supporting a session. The router spoofs replies to keepalive messages from the host to convince the host that the session still exists. Spoofing is useful in routing environments such as DDR, in which a circuit-switched link is taken down when there is no traffic to be sent across it to save toll charges. See also *DDR*. 2. Action of a packet illegally claiming to be from an address from which it was not actually sent. Spoofing is designed to foil network security mechanisms such as filters and access lists.

SPX   Sequenced Packet Exchange. Reliable, connection-oriented protocol that supplements the datagram service provided by IPX in the NetWare protocol suite.

SQL   Structured Query Language. International standard language for defining and accessing relational databases.

SSL   Secure Sockets Layer. Encryption technology for the web used to provide secure transactions such as the transmission of credit card numbers for electronic commerce applications.

static route   Route that is explicitly configured and entered into a routing table.

store-and-forward switching   Frame-switching technique in which frames are completely processed before being forwarded out the appropriate port. This processing includes calculating the CRC and checking the destination address. In addition, frames must be temporarily stored until network resources (such as an unused link) are available to forward the frame. Compare with *cut-through switching*.

STP   shielded twisted-pair. Two- or four-pair wiring medium used in a variety of networks. STP cabling has a layer of shielded insulation to reduce noise and interference. Compare with *UTP*.

STS-1   Synchronous Transport Signal level 1. Basic building-block signal of SONET, operating at 51.84 Mbps. Faster SONET rates are defined as STS-*n*, where *n* is a multiple of 51.84 Mbps. See also *SONET*.

subinterface   A virtual interface on a single physical interface.

subnet   See *subnetwork*.

subnet address   Portion of an IP address that is specified as the subnetwork by the subnet mask.

subnet mask   32-bit address mask used in IP to indicate where the network portion of the address ends and the hosts portion starts.

subnetwork   In IP networks, a network sharing a particular subnet address. Subnetworks are networks that are arbitrarily segmented by a network administrator to provide a multilevel, hierarchical routing structure while shielding the subnetwork from the addressing complexity of attached networks.

sustainable cell rate   See *SCR*.

switch   1. Network device that filters, forwards, and floods frames based on the

MAC destination address of each frame. A switch operates at the data link layer of the OSI model. 2. A generic term for an electronic or mechanical device that connects devices or networks and relays data between devices or networks.

symmetric encryption   Encryption method that provides data confidentiality. When two end stations use symmetric encryption, they must agree on the algorithm to use and on the encryption key they will share. Compare with *asymmetric encryption*.

Synchronous Digital Hierarchy   See *SDH*.

Synchronous Optical Network   See *SONET*.

T

T1   Digital WAN facility provided by telephone companies in the United States. T1 transmits DS-1-formatted data at 1.544 Mbps. T1 lines can be leased for private use.

TACACS   Terminal Access Controller Access Control System. Authentication protocol that provides remote access authentication and related services, such as event logging. User passwords are administered in a central database rather than in individual routers, providing a scalable network-security solution.

tandem switching system   See *TSS*.

TCP   Transmission Control Protocol. Connection-oriented transport layer protocol that provides reliable full-duplex data transmission. TCP is part of the TCP/IP protocol stack.

TDM   1. time-division multiplexer. A device that implements time-division multiplexing. 2. time-division multiplexing. Technique in which information from multiple channels

can be allocated bandwidth on a single wire based on preassigned time slots.

TDR   time-domain reflectometer. Device capable of sending signals through a network medium to check cable continuity and other attributes. TDRs are used to find physical layer network problems.

Telnet   Standard terminal emulation protocol in the TCP/IP protocol stack. Telnet is used for remote terminal connection, enabling users to log in to remote systems and use resources as if they were connected to a local system. Telnet is defined in RFC 854.

Terminal Access Controller Access Control System   See *TACACS*.

throughput   Rate of information arriving at, and possibly passing through, a particular point in a network system.

time domain reflectometer   See *TDR*.

Time To Live   See *TTL*.

time-division multiplexer   See *TDM*.

time-division multiplexing   See *TDM*.

token   Frame that contains control information. Possession of the token allows a network device to transmit data onto the network.

top-down network design   A network-design methodology that calls for analyzing business and technical requirements and developing a logical design, including a topology and protocols, before selecting products and devices to implement the physical design.

topology   Logical arrangement of network nodes and media within a networking structure.

traceroute   Program available on many systems that traces the path a packet takes to a destination. It is mostly used to debug routing problems between hosts.

traffic shaping   Use of queues to limit surges that can congest a network. Data is buffered and then sent into the network in regulated amounts to ensure that the traffic will fit within the promised traffic envelope for the particular connection. Traffic shaping is used in ATM, Frame Relay, and other types of networks.

Transmission Control Protocol   See *TCP*.

transparent bridging   Bridging scheme often used in Ethernet and IEEE 802.3 networks in which bridges pass frames along one hop at a time based on tables associating end nodes with bridge ports. Transparent bridging is so named because the presence of bridges is transparent to network end nodes.

transport layer   Layer 4 of the OSI reference model. This layer is responsible for reliable network communication between end nodes. The transport layer provides mechanisms for the establishment, maintenance, and termination of virtual circuits; transport fault detection and recovery; and information flow control.

TTL   Time To Live. Field in an IP header that indicates how long a packet is considered valid.

TSS   tandem switching system. An intermediate switch that interconnects circuits from the switch of one telephone company central office to the switch of a second central office in the same exchange.

twisted pair   A commonly used transmission medium consisting of 22- to 26-gauge insulated copper wire. Can be either shielded (STP) or unshielded (UTP).

type of service   1. An outdated byte-sized field in an IP header that indicated precedence and type of service. Replaced by the *DSCP* field. See also *precedence* and *DSCP*. 2. Outdated 4-bit subfield within the type-of-service byte in an IP header that helped a router select a routing path when multiple paths were available. A source node could specify whether low delay, high throughput, high reliability, or low monetary cost is desired.

U

UBR   unspecified bit rate. QoS class for ATM networks. UBR allows any amount of data up to a specified maximum to be sent across the network, but there are no guarantees in terms of cell loss rate and delay. Compare with *ABR*, *CBR*, and *VBR*.

UDP   User Datagram Protocol. Connectionless transport layer protocol in the TCP/IP protocol stack. UDP is a simple protocol that exchanges datagrams without acknowledgments or guaranteed delivery, requiring that error processing and retransmission be handled by other protocols. UDP is defined in RFC 768.

UNI   User-Network Interface. ATM specification that defines an interoperability standard for the interface between ATM-based products (a router or an ATM switch) located in a private network and the ATM switches located within the public carrier networks.

unicast   Message that is sent to a single network node. Compare with *broadcast* and *multicast*.

unicast address   Address specifying a single network node. Compare with *broadcast address* and *multicast address*.

UNIX   Operating system developed in 1969 at Bell Laboratories. UNIX has gone through several iterations since its inception. These include UNIX 4.3 BSD (Berkeley Standard Distribution), developed at the University of California at Berkeley, and UNIX System V, Release 4.0, developed by AT&T.

unshielded twisted-pair   See *UTP*.

unspecified bit rate   See *UBR*.

UPC   usage parameter control. In ATM, the set of actions taken by the network to monitor and control traffic at the end-system access point.

usability   The ease with which network users can access a network and its services, including the ease of network addressing, naming, and resource discovery.

usage parameter control   See *UPC*.

user community   A set of network users that employ a particular application or set of applications and have similar network-design goals.

User Datagram Protocol   See *UDP*.

utilization   The percent of total available capacity in use on a network or circuit.

UTP   unshielded twisted-pair. Two or four-pair wire medium used in a variety of networks. Lacks shielding and is subject to electrical noise and interference. Compare with *STP*.

V

VAD   voice activity detection. A technology that compresses voice traffic by not sending packets in the absence of speech. Other types of traffic can use the extra bandwidth saved.

variable bit rate   See *VBR*.

variable-length subnet masking   See *VLSM*.

variance   1. In statistics, a measurement of how widely data disperses from the

mean. 2. In Cisco routers, a routing feature that allows IGRP and EIGRP to load balance traffic across multiple paths that do not have the same bandwidth, but whose bandwidth varies by some small amount that is configurable.

VBR   variable bit rate. QoS class for ATM networks. VBR is subdivided into a Real Time (RT) class and Non-Real Time (NRT) class. VBR (RT) is used for connections in which there is a fixed timing relationship between samples. VBR (NRT) is used for connections in which there is no fixed timing relationship between samples but that still need a guaranteed QoS. Compare with *ABR*, *CBR*, and *UBR*.

videoconferencing   Conducting a conference between two or more participants at different sites by using networking devices and protocols to transmit digital audio and video data. Generally each participant has a video camera, microphone, and equipment to transform analog signals into a digital bit stream for traversal across a LAN or WAN.

virtual circuit   Logical circuit created to ensure reliable communication between two network devices.

virtual LAN   See *VLAN*.

virtual private network   See *VPN*.

virtual private networking   See *VPN*.

virtual router   In HSRP, the third, non-physical router that is created when two or more physical routers share the same virtual IP address and virtual MAC address. See also *HSRP*.

VLAN   virtual LAN. Group of devices on one or more LANs that are configured (using management software) so that they can communicate as if they were attached to the same wire when they are located on several different LAN segments.

VLAN trunk   A single physical link that supports more than one VLAN.

VLAN Trunking Protocol   See *VTP*.

VLSM   variable-length subnet masking. Capability to specify a different subnet mask for the same network number on different subnets. VLSM can help optimize available address space.

voice activity detection   See *VAD*.

VoIP   Voice over IP. Protocols and products that enable the transmission of telephone calls over IP networks.

VPN   1. virtual private network. A network that implements virtual private networking. 2. virtual private networking. Set of processes and protocols that enables an organization to securely interconnect sites that are part of a private network via a public network, such as a service provider's network or the Internet.

VTP   VLAN Trunking Protocol. A Cisco switch-to-switch and switch-to-router VLAN management protocol that exchanges VLAN configuration changes as they are made to a network.

W

WAN   wide-area network. Data communications network that serves users across a broad geographic area and often uses transmission devices provided by common carriers.

WDM   wavelength-division multiplexing. A type of multiplexing developed for use on fiber-optic cables. WDM modulates each of several data streams onto a different part of the light spectrum.

web   Short for the World Wide Web. A large network of Internet servers that provides hypertext and other services to client applications, such as web browsers.

WFQ   weighted fair queuing. Congestion-management algorithm that identifies conversations (in the form of traffic flows), separates packets that belong to each conversation, and ensures that capacity is shared fairly between these individual conversations.

wide-area network   See *WAN*.

window   A protocol data structure that stores outgoing data and generally allows a sender to send a set of packets before an acknowledgment arrives.

windowing   Using windows as a flow-control mechanism when sending data.

wire speed   The theoretical maximum throughput of a network or circuit.

wiring closet   Specially designed room used for wiring a data or voice network. Wiring closets serve as a central junction point for the wiring and wiring equipment that is used for interconnecting devices.

World Wide Web   See *web*.

X

X.25   International standard that defines how a connection between a DTE and DCE is maintained for remote terminal access and computer communications in packet-switched networks.

xDSL   Group term that refers to the different varieties of digital subscriber line, such as ADSL and HDSL. See *DSL*, *ADSL*, and *HDSL*.

X Window System   Distributed, network-transparent, device-independent, multitasking windowing and graphics system originally developed by MIT for communication between X terminals and UNIX workstations.

Index

Numerics

A

T

cisco

ciscopress.com: Your Cisco Certification and Networking Learning Resource

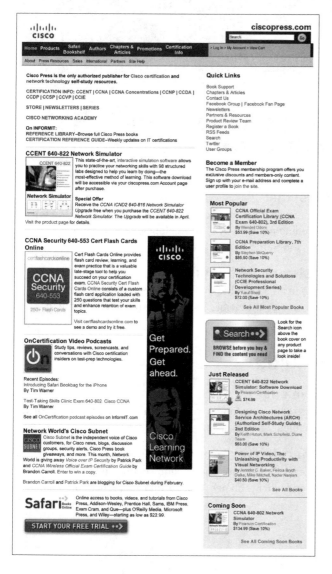

Subscribe to the monthly Cisco Press newsletter to be the first to learn about new releases and special promotions.

Visit **ciscopress.com/newsletters**.

While you are visiting, check out the offerings available at your finger tips.

–Free Podcasts from experts:
  - OnNetworking
  - OnCertification
  - OnSecurity

Podcasts

View them at **ciscopress.com/podcasts**.

–Read the latest author **articles** and **sample chapters** at ciscopress.com/articles.

–Bookmark the Certification Reference Guide available through our partner site at **informit.com/certguide**.

Connect with Cisco Press authors and editors via Facebook and Twitter, visit **informit.com/socialconnect**.

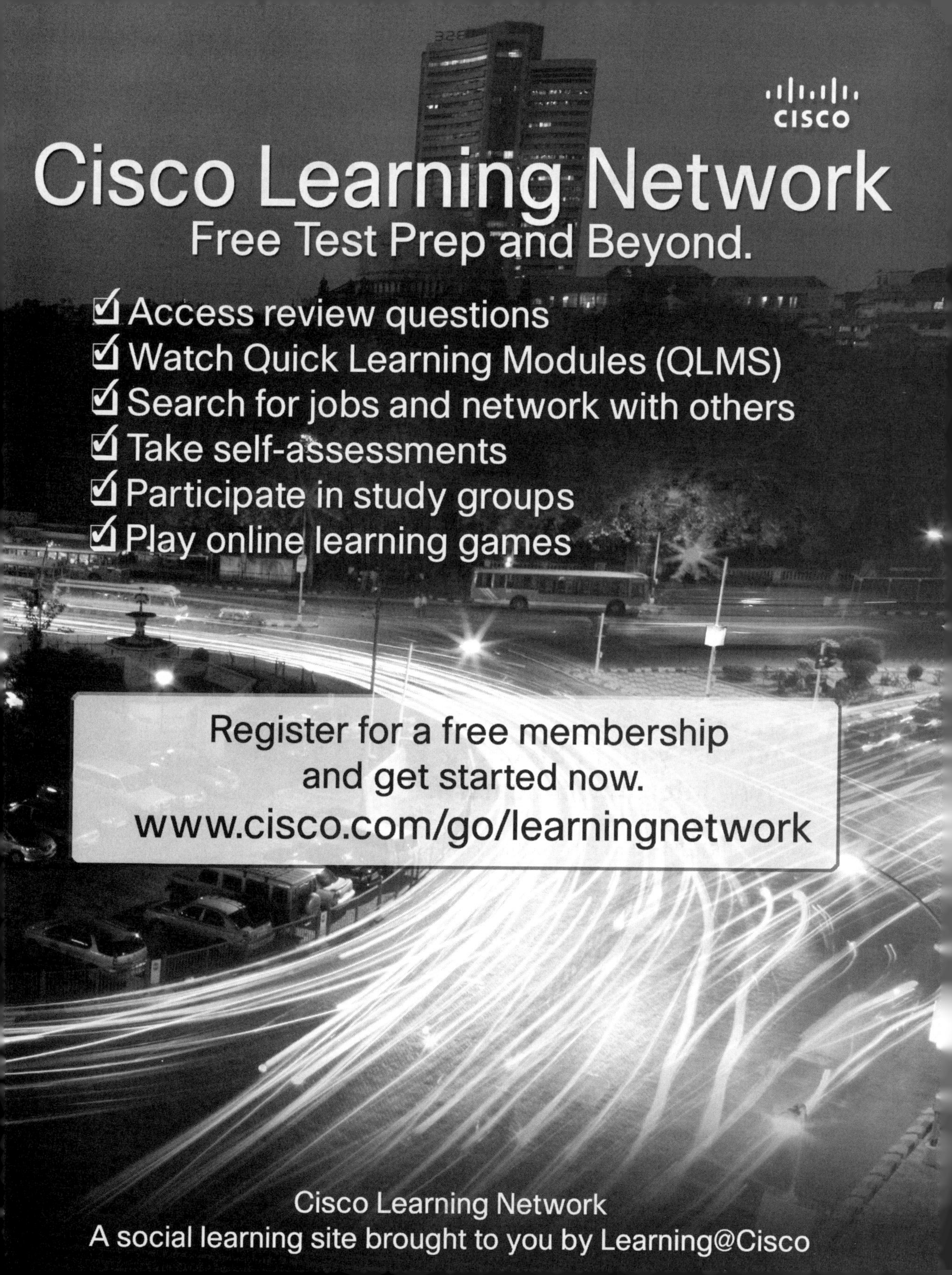

FREE Online Edition

Your purchase of **Top-Down Network Design** includes access to a free online edition for 45 days through the Safari Books Online subscription service. Nearly every Cisco Press book is available online through Safari Books Online, along with more than 5,000 other technical books and videos from publishers such as Addison-Wesley Professional, Exam Cram, IBM Press, O'Reilly, Prentice Hall, Que, and Sams.

SAFARI BOOKS ONLINE allows you to search for a specific answer, cut and paste code, download chapters, and stay current with emerging technologies.

Activate your FREE Online Edition at www.informit.com/safarifree

> **STEP 1:** Enter the coupon code: PPLWNCB.

> **STEP 2:** New Safari users, complete the brief registration form.
> Safari subscribers, just log in.

If you have difficulty registering on Safari or accessing the online edition, please e-mail customer-service@safaribooksonline.com

UNIVERSITY OF WOLVERHAMPTON
LEARNING & INFORMATION SERVICES